EU EXTERNAL RELATIONS AND THE POWER OF LAW

The breadth and depth of the scholarship of Marise Cremona is honoured in this collection of essays written by her colleagues and friends.

Taking Cremona's field-defining research as a point of reference, this collection of research articles examines the power of law in EU external relations. Echoing the expansive scope of Cremona's intellectual enquiries across the growing and diversifying field of external relations law, this volume offers new insights into the principles and procedures that underlie this area of law; the role and responsibilities of the EU as an international actor; and the strategies and instruments through which the Union pursues its external agenda.

Spanning the analysis of foundational concepts and more contemporary interventions in respect of the environment, human rights, foreign direct investment and even Brexit, what emerges from this collection is a richly conceptualised and clear examination of the multiple ways in which the power of law captures or eludes the EU's construction of a domain of external relations; a domain in which the EU interacts not only with its Member States but also other subjects of the international legal order.

EU External Relations and the Power of Law

Liber Amicorum in Honour of Marise Cremona

Edited by
Kenneth A Armstrong
Joanne Scott
and
Anne Thies

•HART•
OXFORD • LONDON • NEW YORK • NEW DELHI • SYDNEY

HART PUBLISHING

Bloomsbury Publishing Plc

Kemp House, Chawley Park, Cumnor Hill, Oxford, OX2 9PH, UK

1385 Broadway, New York, NY 10018, USA

29 Earlsfort Terrace, Dublin 2, Ireland

First published in Great Britain 2024

A catalogue record for this book is available from the British Library.

A catalogue record for this book is available from the Library of Congress.

ISBN: HB: 978-1-50994-095-0
ePDF: 978-1-50994-097-4
ePub: 978-1-50994-096-7

Typeset by Compuscript Ltd, Shannon

Acknowledgements

The editors would like to thank all the contributors to this volume who participated so willingly in a symposium held in honour of Professor Marise Cremona in Cambridge in May 2022. The editors also thank Marise for her participation in this event and for her engagement with the themes of this book. Our gratitude also extends to Professor Bruno de Witte who delivered an oral tribute to Marise at the event. We are grateful for the kind hospitality of Sidney Sussex College on a beautiful sunny Spring day and to the Centre for European Legal Studies (CELS) at the Faculty of Law, University of Cambridge for extending financial support to the symposium. We were delighted that Marise's husband, Adam Hodgkin, was also able to attend.

The editors are grateful to Tine Deschuytere, a PhD researcher at the European University Institute (EUI), who has helped in different ways in the preparation of this volume. She prepared the thematic bibliography of Marise's work which we drew on very heavily in our introduction and she ensured that all the chapters were in the correct style before submission to Hart Publishing. We are also grateful to the Academy of European Law at the EUI for making funds available to pay Tine for doing this work.

Finally, thanks are due to Sasha Jawed for her support in realising this project, as well as Tom Adams and Claire Banyard for their invaluable work in getting the manuscript ready for publication.

Contents

List of Contributors

Kenneth A Armstrong, Professor of European Law, University of Cambridge, and Fellow, Sidney Sussex College, Cambridge.

Gráinne de Búrca, Professor of Law, European University Institute, Fiesole (Italy).

Federico Casolari, Professor of European Union Law and Head of the Department of Legal Studies, University of Bologna (Italy).

Sir Alan Dashwood KC Henderson Chambers, Emeritus Professor of European Law, University of Cambridge and Emeritus Fellow, Sidney Sussex College, Cambridge.

Tine Deschuytere, PhD researcher, European University Institute (EUI), Fiesole (Italy).

Daniele Gallo, Professor of EU Law, Law Department, Luiss University (Italy).

Claire Kilpatrick, Part-Time Professor, European University Institute and Co-Director of Academy of European Law, Fiesole (Italy).

Panos Koutrakos, Professor of European Union Law and Jean Monnet Professor of European Union Law at City, University of London.

Päivi Leino-Sandberg, Professor of Transnational European Law, University of Helsinki (Finland).

Gracia Marín Durán, Professor of International Economic Law, Faculty of Laws, University College London.

Niamh Nic Shuibhne, Professor of European Union Law and Co-Director of Europa Institute, University of Edinburgh.

Sara Poli, Professor of EU Law, Department of Political Science, University of Pisa (Italy).

Joanne Scott, Professor of European Law, European University Institute and Co-Director of Academy of European Law, Fiesole (Italy).

Eleanor Spaventa, Professor of European Union Law at Bocconi Law School, and Director of the Bocconi Lab in European Studies (BLEST) Milan (Italy).

Anne Thies, Senior Lecturer in International and European Law, University of Glasgow.

Neil Walker, Regius Professor of Public Law and the Law of Nature and Nations, University of Edinburgh.

Ramses A. Wessel, Professor of European Law and Head of the European and Economic Law Department, University of Groningen (The Netherlands).

Abstracts

The Power of Routine and the Disruptive Politics of Brexit

Kenneth A. Armstrong

Inspired by, and building upon, Cremona's scholarship, Armstrong explores the relationship between law and politics in EU external relations taking 'Brexit' as his example. Drawing on a distinction proposed by van Middelaar, he explores the question of whether the disruptive politics of Brexit might exemplify the end of an era of 'rules-politics' in favour of a shift to a type of 'events-politics' which is characterised by greater political agility in the face of unexpected changes and challenges. His answer is that it does not. On the contrary, consistent with an historical institutional analysis, he argues that the process of UK withdrawal and the process of constructing a post-membership relationship were governed by *routines* in the form of path dependencies, standard operating procedures and norms or logics of appropriateness. Crucially, he argues that law plays a fundamental role in institutionalising routine, both in terms of the EU's substantive commitments, and in terms of its decision-making procedures. Cremona's elaboration of the structural principles of EU external relations is exemplary in this respect.

Armstrong tests his hypothesis derived from historical institutionalism through a careful analysis of different elements of UK exit and the formation of a post-exit partnership. This includes an examination of the role of the European Council and the conduct of Article 50 negotiations. He also shows how routine procedures in the form of the preliminary ruling mechanism served to give voice to the European Court of Justice which in turn relied on well established 'normative scripts and frames' from the sphere of EU external relations to ground its judgments. Path dependencies also shaped the negotiating position of both the EU and the UK in relation to the level playing field provisions in the Trade and Cooperation Agreement, albeit that the EU recorded greater success in projecting its internal rules and templates into the new agreement. Established EU procedures and EU (and international) norms also played a fundamental role in confronting instances of UK non-compliance in relation to the Irish Protocol.

At every step in the chapter, Armstrong brings to the fore not only the power of routine but also and concomitantly, the power of law. While he recognises the disruptive politics of Brexit and does not seek to downplay the role or force of politics, he does seek to rebalance the account by emphasising the role of routine as constituted and consolidated through law. Armstrong's account is analytical not normative but we find within it both instances of productive adaptability and excessive inflexibility within existing routine.

Resisting External Accountability: The European Union and Human Rights

Gráinne de Búrca and Claire Kilpatrick

In her analysis of EU trade policy, Cremona drew attention to the use of human rights clauses in EU trade agreements. More generally, she saw the relevance of the EU's core values – human rights, democracy and the rule of law – as foundational elements of EU external relations. In its expansion into policy domains beyond economic law issues of fundamental rights protection in the application and implementation of those policies raise more directly the responsibility and accountability of the EU for human rights protection.

The EU today has quite a strong and extensive body of human rights law, with numerous internal accountability institutions and mechanisms. However, despite the EU Treaty declaration that it is founded on respect for human rights, and despite assertions of openness to the UN and the international legal order, the EU to date has resisted external human rights accountability. This chapter argues that external accountability is a key dimension of modern human rights law. De Búrca and Kilpatrick argue that the EU's poor record in this respect – its decision to accede fully to just one international human rights treaty (the UN Convention on the Rights of Persons with Disabilities), and only partially to a second (the Istanbul Convention), while showing little interest in the wider body of international human rights treaties and their accountability mechanisms – is not justified by any compelling reasons, but instead undermines the EU's stature and credibility as an international actor.

EU Member States as States: Between EU and International Roles And Obligations

Federico Casolari and Ramses A. Wessel

In thinking about Marise Cremona's scholarship on the expansion of EU membership, in their contribution Casolari and Wessel map and analyse situations in which EU Member States act as States, either because State-functions have not been affected by EU membership, simply because they completely fall outside the scope of EU law, or because statehood is an essential asset in the context of EU law. In doing so, this contribution aims to shed light on the various identities States have in engaging with the Union.

The tension States may experience between being a State and a Member State at the same time is particularly visible in situations in which Member States' obligations under EU law collide with general obligations those States may have under international law. Not only in relation to the division of competences, but also in view of, for instance, the allocation of responsibilities, this question is gaining importance. Identities often overlap and are sometimes difficult to distinguish. To differentiate between the various identities, this chapter introduces the term 'EU States' to distinguish their identity from the one they have as 'Member States'.

The chapter demonstrates that Union membership has resulted in a DNA mutation of statehood, giving EU states a dual identity which mirrors, to some extent, the Janus-faced attitude of EU Treaties. As 'EU States', those States, on the one hand, are sovereign entities under international law, acting as the framers of the integration process; on the other hand, as Member States they act as subjects of an autonomous legal order, being first obliged to respect its 'basic constitutional charter'. The identity of EU members is fluid and dynamic as roles may overlap in specific situations and change over time. The argument presented in this chapter stresses the potentialities that the principle of sincere cooperation may express in reconciling the dual identity of EU States, contributing thus to shape a European space of shared and mutually dependent sovereignty.

Global EU Climate Action and the Principle of Common But Differentiated Responsibilities and Respective Capabilities

Gracia Marín Durán and Joanne Scott

Gracia Marín Durán and Joanne Scott examine two instances of global EU climate action which extend the carbon pricing under European Emissions Trading Scheme (ETS) to greenhouse gas emissions (GHG emissions) which are generated outside of the territory of EU Member States. The first is the EU Regulation establishing a carbon border tax adjustment mechanisms (CBAM) and the second is the EU Directive including maritime emissions within the scope of the ETS.

Marín Durán and Scott appraise these measures from the point of view of the principle of Common but Differentiated Responsibilities and Respective Capabilities that is enshrined in the United Nations Framework Agreement on Climate Change and the Paris Agreement. They argue that this principle is legally relevant in the context of EU global climate action and analyse when the principle should be taken into account by the EU, particularly in relation to extraterritorial GHG emissions that may sometimes fall within the primary jurisdiction of other States. In so doing, they rely on a distinction between first-order and second-order climate responsibilities that was put forward in Simon Caney's work.

The chapter argues that the EU has acted consistently with the CBDR-RC principle in relation to international shipping emissions. This is because the mode of apportioning such emissions between states has not been settled at the international level and the EU has acted to fill a 'system boundary gap'. Moreover, the EU's approach, which includes 50 per cent of emissions of voyages arriving and departing from EU ports, satisfies what Marín Durán and Scott characterise as the 'replication test'. If other countries were to emulate the EU's approach, no double-counting of GHG emissions would arise. However, Marín Durán and Scott caution that if the EU were to decide in the future to include a greater proportion of shipping emissions in its ETS, the principle of CBDR-RC would be relevant and may necessitate the differential treatment of emissions which fall within the first-order responsibility of States which have lower levels of responsibility for causing climate change and lower capabilities when it comes to addressing its causes and effects.

By contrast, Marín Durán and Scott argue that the EU has acted inconsistently with the principle of CBDR-RC in relation to CBAM. Here, the EU is exercising second-order climate responsibilities and ought, therefore, to take this principle into account. In view of this, the authors propose two adjustments to the design of this measure to bring it in to line with this principle. The first is an exemption for Least Developed Countries and Small Island Developing States in order to recognise their special status under Article 4.6 of the Paris Climate Change Agreement. The second is that the EU should ensure that CBAM-generated revenue be used to support decarbonisation efforts in other affected developing countries.

The Autonomy of EU Law In External Relations: an Elusive Principle

Panos Koutrakos

The chapter by Panos Koutrakos analyses recent case law addressing the principle of autonomy in the context of the relationship between investment arbitration and EU law. The chapter begins by identifying four themes underpinning the genesis and development of the principle: its judicial origin, the internal and external dimension of it, the principle's scope, and the principle's link to 'furthering the powers of the Court of Justice'. In the subsequent section, Koutrakos analyses recent case law in the field of investment arbitration and EU law, identifying two different approaches of the Court, depending on whether it is dealing with intra- or extra-EU relations. In its final section, the chapter analyses the different approaches to autonomy on 'legal and practical grounds' and reflects on their pitfalls at the current stage of development of the EU legal order ('maximalism versus pragmatism').

The chapter demonstrates that the principle of autonomy has been construed differently, depending on the legal context of the disputes. Koutrakos argues that the Court has been taking a more pragmatic approach where the relationship with third countries is concerned. Yet, the Court's approach to autonomy in intra-EU disputes has been 'uncompromising' and demonstrated a 'whiff of maximalism', which 'has not been justified in legal terms and is unwarranted in practical terms'.

Environmental Information and 'External Pressure': Assessing EU Compliance with its International Obligations Under the Aarhus Convention

Päivi Leino-Sandberg

Päivi Leino-Sandberg's chapter addresses the theme of transparency and participation in EU external relations. She argues that the EU legal framework, together with the Court's case law and the related practices of the EU institutions, raise serious concerns about the compatibility of EU law with the Aarhus Convention. Unusually, Leino-Sandberg's methodology is not based merely upon a distant reading of the law but also on direct engagement in the process of seeking access to documents. She has submitted numerous, largely unsuccessful, requests for access to the legal analyses or opinions prepared by the different EU institutions concerning the compatibility of EU law with the Aarhus Convention. More recently, she appealed a denial decision to the General Court, and the judgment was issued in March 2024. Her actions are mirrored also by Client Earth, the environmental NGO that has engaged in legal mobilisation in a bid to secure better protection for Aarhus rights within the EU. Leino-Sandberg's actions in this respect raise multiple legal questions, for example concerning the meaning of environmental information under the Aarhus Convention and the scope of the various exceptions laid down in the EU's access to documents regulation.

Leino-Sandberg argues that while the recent reform of the EU's Aarhus Regulation has brought progress as far as access to environmental justice is concerned, transparency and participation rights are far from being adequately protected in EU external relations, including in relation to the conclusion of trade agreements. She concludes that 'without doubt, the most important obstacle to transparency and participatory rights remains the institutions' steadfast refusal to properly apply the [legal] framework, a refusal that seems to be rooted in a peculiar understanding of the role of NGOs and researchers in democratic life'. She demonstrates that notwithstanding the CJEU's insistence that exceptions to access to documents should be narrowly construed and carefully reasoned, the EU institutions continue to rely heavily on the international relations exception even in circumstances in which this seems difficult to justify. Most disconcerting is the presentation of evidence that within the EU, participation in decision-making by NGOs has sometimes been characterised as a form of 'external interference' or 'external pressure'. In this and other respects, Leino-Sandberg's direct engagement with the process of seeking access to documents has offered new insights that cast doubt on the EU's commitment to informed participation in EU external relations.

What Does the Concept of 'Structural Principles' Add to EU Law?

Niamh Nic Shuibhne

Niamh Nic Shuibhne's chapter draws inspiration from Marise Cremona's field-defining work on 'structural principles'. Her aim in this chapter is to demonstrate how both the language and the functioning of 'structural principles' of EU law add significant value to the task of expressing, evaluating, and evolving the European Union's legal order. Above all, structural principles enable us, in Cremona's words, 'to understand better the role that law plays in this construction project'.

Following an overview of the structural principles of EU law as conceived by Cremona, the chapter explores how they add value to EU constitutional law by addressing two related questions. First, why is the categorising of certain principles of EU law as 'structural' principles worthwhile in the first place? Using some key examples, it is argued that categorising principles is not an abstract or semantic task, and the concept of structural principles sheds valuable light on some of the darker corners of EU constitutional law. Second, what does considering the concept of structural principles in the internal dimension of the EU's constitution add beyond the context of EU external relations? The analysis builds on Cremona's external relations focus in terms of advocating both a greater translation of legal ideas from EU external relations to its internal sphere, on the one hand and a wider reflection on the extent to which the two dimensions of EU constitutional law (should) cohere when they are looked at holistically. A key theme that emerges is that distinctions drawn between different types of structural principles that make sense in the context of EU external relations law become much more blurred in the EU's internal constitutional sphere.

Overall, the chapter argues that structural principles have both explanatory and normative value in EU law. They give us critical new tools to hold a deeper conversation about the constitutional evolution of the Union across different parts of the EU's legal order, both discretely and more universally. The tools that Marise Cremona has crafted have become even more apt, and thus even more significant, over time.

Enhancing European Technological Sovereignty: The Foreign Investment Screening Regulation and Beyond

Sara Poli and Daniele Gallo

Sara Poli and Danielle Gallo's chapter explores the theme of technological sovereignty, understood as referring to the EU's capacity to use and develop technologies to protect the integrity of the EU and its Members and the importance of Member States being self-sufficient in critical technologies and infrastructure. The premise of the chapter is that the EU is better placed than its individual Member State to address the challenge of achieving technological sovereignty and that the EU can use its competences in this respect without intruding unduly on Member States' sovereignty to protect national security and public order.

The chapter examines the use of Article 114 TFEU as a 'strategic' legal basis to protect key strategic assets. Highlighting the importance of the proposed 'EU Chip Act', the chapter explores the EU's regulation on foreign subsidies, the critical entities directive and the recently adopted EU measure on cybersecurity. Rich with contemporary examples, the chapter pays particular attention to legal questions that have been at the heart of Marise Cremona's work, including the issues of competence and legal basis.

The chapter also zooms in on the EU's Regulation for the screening of foreign direct investments (Regulation 2019/452). It argues that though the measure is of fundamental importance in the manner it elevates the notion of public good from the national to the European level, this transformation has occurred 'more or less *en souplesse* in acts of an apparently purely technical nature'. It assesses this complex legal instrument with a view to understanding whether the EU is endowed with sufficient powers in relation to foreign ownership of tech companies or critical infrastructure to protect the EU's technological sovereignty. They reach a nuanced conclusion in this respect. On the one hand, the authors recognise that national sovereignty over national security and public order make it impossible for the EU to have an intrusive and unified instrument governing foreign direct investment. On the other hand, they argue that by recognising FDI as a matter of common interest, the Regulation has the potential to strengthen European technological sovereignty. The subtle balance of power between the Member States on the one hand and the Member States and the Commission is crucial in this respect. 'Depending on how the FDI screening mechanism is applied in the future by the Commission, the Union may become an actor in transition toward technological sovereignty or merely a witness to fragmented efforts by individual Member States to preserve national technological sovereignty in Europe.'

Remedying Constitutional Heresies: The Charter, Damages and Jurisdiction in the Common Foreign And Security Policy

Eleanor Spaventa

Eleanor Spaventa's chapter analyses the intersection between the Common Foreign and Security Policy (CFSP) and EU fundamental rights. The focus is on judicial protection as an essential tool to ensure protection of any fundamental rights. On the one hand, the provisions of the EU Charter bind the EU institutions and so, in theory, guarantee a minimum of fundamental rights protection in all fields of EU action. On the other hand, the limited jurisdiction of the Court of Justice of the EU in relation to the CFSP poses challenges as to the justiciability of those rights. This issue has improved significantly post-Lisbon: restrictive measures against natural or legal persons are now fully reviewable. Nonetheless, the issue of justiciability of fundamental rights in relation to CFSP measures has become much more prominent – something that is reflected also in Marise Cremona's writing – and it translates in a more varied and nuanced case law as to the boundaries of the Court's jurisdiction.

Starting from the premise that exclusion of jurisdiction is a (constitutional) exception which needs to be interpreted narrowly, the Court has found that, in some instances, it can review acts which find their legal basis in a CFSP decision, even if they do not impose restrictive measures (either when a connection can be made with an EU provision over which the Court has jurisdiction or when there is an employment relationship with an entity established through a CFSP decision and the issue relates to staff management). Furthermore, the Court has also clarified that its jurisdiction in relation to restrictive measures is not limited to direct actions, but also extends to preliminary rulings and actions for damages.

As welcome as these developments may be, in her chapter, Spaventa proposes a range of solutions aimed at plugging jurisdictional gaps. It is claimed that the European Council, the Council and the High Representative have a positive duty to ensure that any CFSP act is fundamental rights compliant. For this reason, Spaventa argues that: (i) any CFSP instrument should include a national jurisdictional clause, clearly allocating responsibility to one or more jurisdictions for the purposes of judicial review, and (ii) an action for damages against the Council can be brought for failure to ensure the protection of fundamental rights when adopting a CFSP instrument.

EU Trade Policy and the Promotion of Gender Equality: Disseminating international law and mobilising internal stakeholders

Anne Thies

Anne Thies' chapter addresses a topic that has been somewhat neglected by legal scholars, namely the promotion of gender equality in EU trade-related instruments. Increasing awareness of the link between trade and gender has led to the inception of gender impact assessments and the inclusion of gender equality provisions in trade agreements. Given the EU's constitutional commitment to gender equality, including its obligation to promote gender equality in external action, it is not surprising that the EU has not been left behind in emphasising the use trade instruments to achieve greater gender equality. Thies observes that there is a procedural dimension to this commitment in that the EU has institutionalised gender impact assessments and seeks to take account of the gender dimension when negotiating free trade agreements. However, she also highlights the substantive dimension which flows from the inclusion of gender equality provisions in the text of the relevant agreements.

Thies' chapter offers a tour de force of recent developments, both in relation to the EU's stated aspirations and its actual practice. Her analysis explores not only the gender equality dimension of sustainable development chapters in EU FTAs but of other trade-related developments such as GSP+, public procurement and the emerging due diligence obligations of companies. Thies offers a critical overview of these developments. She raises important concerns about the enforcement of gender equality obligations, drawing interesting comparisons with environmental and climate commitments also included in EU FTAs. However, she also highlights the EU's recent efforts to mobilise EU stakeholders to play a fuller and more proactive role in the implementation and enforcement of the gender equality aspects of trade policy, including through the establishment of a variety of diverse complaints mechanisms such as the Single Entry Point under the EU's 'Access2Market' Platform. Thies argues that there is an opportunity for the EU to increase its credibility as 'good global actor' by further regulating EU internal actors that have the capacity to advance gender equality and the economic empowerment of women. Rooting such obligations within the sphere of the EU legal order would increase the enforceability of obligations related to the advancement of gender equality and women's economic empowerment, complementing the limited enforcement of international law obligations of the EU and its trading partners.

Europe in the Global Imaginary, the Globe in the European Imaginary: The Legacy of Sovereignty

Neil Walker

In his chapter, Neil Walker notes: 'we cannot simply dismiss the sovereignty legacy when investigating the EU, and we never could'. Instead, he invites us to consider two puzzles. The first concerns a world of external relations that remains dominated by states who engage with one another as sovereign entities. In its external relations, as an international organisation, the EU is an outlier in an area dominated by states. As Walker asks where does the EU 'fit into this overall system of mutual sovereigntist expectations, and of practice predicated upon these mutual expectations'? The second puzzle relates to the broader potential of sovereignty to frame issues of identity and self-identification. To the extent that the EU does not conform to a sovereigntist logic, how, if at all, might the global political configuration be (re)modelled in the European political imaginary?

In addressing these two puzzles (or these two sides of the one puzzle) Walker reflects first on the questions posed about Europe as it has been framed through the still globally-dominant lens of sovereignty, and so very much from the perspective of the global political imaginary. In the second place, the contribution reverses focus, now posing the question of how to frame the global level from a distinctly European-centred perspective. It does so by reference to what escapes the lens of sovereignty – to those elements of the European polity that are structured by the absence rather than the presence of sovereigntist considerations, and which combine to form a powerful alternative world view within the EU's own political imaginary.

Introduction

KENNETH A ARMSTRONG, JOANNE SCOTT
AND ANNE THIES

PROFESSOR MARISE CREMONA is an outstanding scholar, colleague and friend. She has been so appreciated within the community of European lawyers that a number of her closest collaborators decided to come together to produce a book in her honour. This includes colleagues from different institutions, including several from the European University Institute (EUI) in Florence where Marise was Professor of European Law from 2006 to 2017. During this period, she was Co-Director of the Academy of European Law at the EUI and also served as the Institute's President ad interim from 2012 to 2013. Before that Marise was Professor of European Commercial Law and Deputy Director at the Centre for Commercial Law Studies (CCLS) at Queen Mary, University of London.

Marise's scholarship covers a broad expanse within the field of European Union Law, with a particular but non-exclusive focus on EU external relations law. We include in this volume as an essential reference point, a thematic bibliography of Marise's principal works. As readers will see, the list is long and impressive. That body of work is also the essential inspiration for the themes and preoccupations of the chapters in this edited collection. In this Introduction, we seek to summarise and highlight the many and different ways in which the scholarship of Marise Cremona has defined and contributed to our understanding of the power of law in EU external relations.

As will become apparent, much of Marise's scholarship is concerned with substantive issues in EU external relations law, most notably EU trade policies adopted under the Common Commercial Policy. Here, Marise analyses various multilateral and bilateral approaches to trade liberalisation, as well as the inclusion of non-economic provisions and considerations in the regulation of international trade. Given the central position of EU trade law in the field of EU external relations, Marise's contributions have given her a significant position of influence in our collective understanding of the power of law in shaping European and international economic relations.

A different strand of scholarship where we again hear the voice of Marise Cremona is to be found in her research and writing on the expanding sphere of influence of EU law in the European 'neighbourhood'. Tracking the expansion of the EU through waves of membership enlargement, as well as the EU's management of its economic and non-economic relationships with European states, Marise has published several pieces exploring the inclusion of human rights, democracy and rule of law commitments in EU external policies or as external policies in their own right. The power of EU law emerges as a phenomenon beyond its own borders as the Union extends its reach as a global actor.

Much of Marise's work engages with 'constitutional' and foundational issues in EU external relations law. At one level, the analysis is undertaken in respect of the primary law of the treaties, the instruments through which EU external relations is pursued, and interpretations of these legal texts by the Court of Justice of the European Union (CJEU). In the context of the evolving landscape of EU external relations, this approach is reflected in several of the contributions in this collection. At another level, Marise's attention is drawn to deeper, 'structural' principles of a legal order that claims its own autonomy. Marise's scholarship on structural principles exemplifies the conceptual and analytical clarity of her work. Her publications cover competence-related issues and issues of legal basis (or the principle of conferral), the principle of subsidiarity, the duty of cooperation, inter-institutional balance, rule of law, coherence and autonomy and their effect on EU external relations policymaking structures. Together, this substantial body of work confirms Marise Cremona's status as one of the world's leading scholars on EU external relations law.

While rooted in foundational concepts and underlying legal principles, many of Marise's publications analyse and shed important light on the specific policy fields that her work interrogates: the Common Commercial Policy, the Common Foreign and Security Policy, Justice and Home Affairs, Economic and Monetary Union and issues of environmental governance. This body of scholarship also examines institutional aspects of EU external relations law, such as the role of the CJEU and international dispute settlement, the European External Action Service and the Lisbon Treaty reform process more generally. Beyond these specific policy areas – and beyond EU external relations – Marise has contributed to the broad field of European Legal Studies with a particular focus on EU internal market law; the challenges of enforcement; and the effects of new technologies within the landscape of EU law. From a methodological perspective, and together with colleagues at the EUI, she has published research exploring the role of the Historical Archives of the European Union which are housed in Florence in conducting research on EU law. Marise's publications also address a wide variety of topics outside of EU law. In particular, she has covered various aspects of UK trade and criminal law as well as WTO law.

A final aspect of her legal enquiry can be found in Marise's interest in the EU as an international legal actor. She examines the EU's legal personality for international acts adopted in the framework of EU external relations and how the EU is perceived as an international actor. Marise also examines the EU's role in promoting its values, principles and objectives through EU external action, including by drawing on the notion of coherence as a structural principle of EU law in this area.

What we cannot do justice to is Marise's role as a doctoral supervisor in the many fields of law in which she has researched and taught, Inspiring new generations of scholars is a legacy which cannot be measured in a list of publications. Nor can the friendships and collaborations forged over a long and distinguished academic career be fully represented in the contributions to this edited collection. Instead we have brought together a group of scholars who have engaged with Marise at different times and places across her career and who, in their own ways, have produced contributions in her honour.

The chapters contributed by Nic Shuibhne, Koutrakos and Spaventa focus on foundational concepts and jurisdictional issues in EU external relations. These essays highlight the potential of rights and principles to shape EU external relations law, with the role of the CJEU as an institutional actor to the fore. In the chapters of Armstrong, Casolari and Wessel, and Walker, it is 'states' – former or current 'Member States', or the legacy of state sovereignty – that provide the entry and focal point for broader reflections on the organisation of EU external relations, whether in practical terms, or in our conceptual imagination. A further group of essays looks to the external accountability – for human rights protection in the chapter by de Búrca and Kilpatrick – and internal implementation of the EU's international obligations and commitments – for environmental protection in the chapters by Marín Durán and Scott, and by Leino-Sandberg. As these essays remind us, the power of law in EU external relations may be the power of international law. A pair of chapters recall that the Union is a strategic actor and the instruments it deploys both internally – Poli and Gallo's exploration of the EU's foreign investment screening regulation – and externally – Thies' analysis of gender in EU trade instruments – offer the EU opportunities (whether or not they are realised in practice) for the pursuit of different strategic goals by the EU in its external relations.

The volume closes with an Epilogue by Professor Sir Alan Dashwood. Written by an eminent legal scholar and practitioner noted for his own clarity of thought and exposition, the Epilogue is a fitting tribute to an academic 'entrepreneur' whose ability to foresee trends and to bring people together in their legal analysis is such an important thread binding together not only her body of work but also the people who admire her so greatly. That is the power of Professor Marise Cremona.

Part I

The Power of Rights and Principles in EU Law

What does the Concept of 'Structural Principles' Add to EU Law?

NIAMH NIC SHUIBHNE*

1. INTRODUCTION

THIS CONTRIBUTION FOCUSES on Marise Cremona's edited volume, *Structural Principles in EU External Relations Law*,[1] and more specifically, on the concept and ideas presented in her Introduction to that book.[2] The aim is to show how both the language and the functioning of 'structural principles' of EU law add significant value to the task of expressing, evaluating, and evolving the European Union's legal order. Above all, structural principles enable us, in Marise's words, 'to understand better the role that law plays in this construction project'.[3]

In the spring of 2018, I was working on the principle of the autonomy of EU law and EU decision-making. The more that I read about it, the more I became curious about, but also perplexed by, 'what' autonomy actually was. Fundamentally, it did not seem to behave or have the same qualities as just 'any' principle of EU law. Marise read an early draft of that paper for me,[4] and she sent to me in return the (at that time) soon to be published text of her Introduction for the *Structural Principles* book. I was sitting on a bus when her email arrived yet even on a small mobile phone screen, I could not stop reading Marise's chapter. It exemplifies her work's characteristic signature of original ideas that then seem so obvious (but only after she points us to them), a seamless knitting together of bigger questions and careful legal detail, and a sharp and straightforward clarity of expression that somehow never loses any elegance or complexity.

Substantively, Marise introduced to EU law a concept that brings us into new constitutional places. In this chapter, I apply the 'structural principles' concept that Marise developed from examples in EU external relations law to EU constitutional law more generally in order to demonstrate the full span of its purpose and reach. In *Structural Principles*, Marise observed that '[a]ll the principles discussed here also operate in the context of internal action', but she then asked, '[d]o they operate

* School of Law, University of Edinburgh.

[1] M Cremona (ed), *Structural Principles in EU External Relations Law* (Oxford, Hart Publishing, 2018).

[2] M Cremona, 'Structural Principles and their Role in EU External Relations Law' in Cremona (ed) (n 1) 3.

[3] ibid 29.

[4] Later published as N Nic Shuibhne, 'What is the Autonomy of EU Law, and Why Does that Matter?' (2019) 88 *Nordic Journal of International Law* 9.

differently when the action is external and if so how?'.[5] The task for this contribution is to consider the converse of those questions: do structural principles operate differently when the action is *internal* and if so, how?

Following a brief overview of the structural principles of EU law as conceived by Marise (Section 2), I go on to explore how they add value to EU constitutional law by addressing two related questions. First, why is the categorising of certain principles of EU law as 'structural' principles worthwhile in the first place (Section 3)? I argue that categorising principles is not an abstract or semantic task. Far from an exercise in playing with an academic toybox, the concept of structural principles sheds valuable light on some of the darker corners of EU constitutional law. To illustrate that claim, the two areas that I highlight here are the making and assessment of primary EU law that is 'extra-Treaty'; and how grouping principles of EU law together brings out distinctive aspects of their behaviour and of their weight.

Second, what does considering the concept of structural principles in the internal dimension of the EU's constitution add beyond the original book's own context of EU external relations (Section 4)? This part of the chapter is not about challenging Marise's starting point. Instead, it is about building on it, in terms of advocating both a greater translation of legal ideas from EU external relations to its internal sphere, on the one hand;[6] and a wider reflection on the extent to which the two dimensions of EU constitutional law (should) cohere when they are looked at holistically, on the other. A key theme that emerges is that distinctions drawn between different types of structural principles that make sense in the context of EU external relations law become much more blurred in the EU's internal constitutional sphere. We can see that occurring in two ways: through examples of 'relational' principles becoming 'systemic' principles, and through examples of principles exhibiting both relational and systemic qualities simultaneously.

Overall, as summarised in Section 5, this chapter argues that structural principles have both explanatory and normative value in EU law. They give us critical new tools to hold a deeper conversation about the constitutional evolution of the Union across different parts of the EU's legal order, both discretely and more universally. As I also aim to show through the examples that I use in this chapter, most of which post-date the publication of *Structural Principles* itself, the tools that Marise has crafted have become even more apt, and thus even more significant, over time.

2. WHAT ARE THE STRUCTURAL PRINCIPLES OF EU (EXTERNAL RELATIONS) LAW?

This brief account of the Introduction to *Structural Principles* will not do justice to the richness of the ideas that Marise discusses there, but it provides a sketch of their key features, and one with which I hope she would agree! Returning to the starting

[5] Cremona, 'Structural Principles' (n 2) 16.

[6] For an example of how such translation can bring transformative ideas from one space to the other, see A Thies, 'The Search for Effectiveness and the Need for Loyalty in EU External Action' in Cremona (ed) (n 1) 263.

point of my first reading of that work, why did Marise's characterisation of autonomy as a *structural* principle of EU law resonate so powerfully? In essence, I think it was because the language of structural principles so compellingly illuminates the depth and extent of the work that autonomy performs within – and for – the EU legal order. Marise was arguing that some principles of EU law merit particular attention because they exhibit distinguishing qualities. From there, I proposed an argument that autonomy is in fact an 'existential' principle of EU law,[7] aiming to capture the sense that even within structural principles as a set, autonomy is a *particularly* powerful principle of EU law. Why? Not for the sake of playing around with adjectives, but because the unfolding character, functioning, and consequences of autonomy 'entail important implications for a better understanding of the EU Treaties as the Union constitution'.[8] At the time, structural principles performed, for my purposes, a mainly explanatory purpose. What I argue in this chapter is that structural principles do vital work in a normative sense too; something that has come into clearer focus as the Union's constitutional premises have been consolidated but also progressed through the EU's responses to recent challenges such as Brexit and rule of law regression.

In a general sense, though with specific reference to, and examples from, EU external relations on the whole, Marise defined 'structural' principles as those that are 'drawn from the Treaties and elaborated by the Court' in order, first, to *establish* and, second, to *protect* 'an institutional space within which policy may be formed, in which the different actors understand and work within their respective roles'.[9] In that sense, structural principles could be said both to create and to organise the conditions within which the institutional balance mandated by the Treaties can be realised.[10] But it is so much more than that too, for these principles are structural also 'in the sense of defining and being inherent *to the deep structure of the EU*'.[11] Marise did not suggest that her book provides an exhaustive list, something that is returned to again below. But she did indicate that the structural principles of EU external relations law must include sincere cooperation, conferral, institutional balance, mutual solidarity, subsidiarity, and autonomy. Moreover, '[s]ome of the principles that [Marise] identified as structural are usually included in lists of *general* principles: effectiveness, transparency, and proportionality and equality (which are ingredients of the rule of law). Others, however, are not, including conferral, sincere cooperation, autonomy and institutional balance'.[12] Marise also suggested that structural principles are 'not concerned with the *substantive content* of policy, but

[7] Nic Shuibhne (n 4).

[8] C Contartese, 'The Autonomy of the EU Legal Order in the ECJ's External Relations Case Law: From the "Essential" to the "Specific Characteristics" of the Union and Back Again' (2017) 54 *CML Rev* 1628, 1637.

[9] Cremona (n 2) 5.

[10] The principle of institutional balance 'requires that each of the institutions must exercise its powers with due regard for the powers of the other institutions' (Case C-133/06 *Parliament v Council* ECLI:EU:C:2008:257, [2008] ECR I-3189, para 57). That balance is provided for across several provisions of the TEU and TFEU, supported by the principle of conferral in Art 13(2) Consolidated version of the Treaty on European Union (TEU) [2016] OJ C202/13 ('Each institution shall act within the limits of the powers conferred on it in the Treaties, and in conformity with the procedures, conditions and objectives set out in them. The institutions shall practice mutual sincere cooperation').

[11] Cremona (n 2) 15 (emphasis added).

[12] ibid (emphasis added).

rather with *process* and the *relationships* between the actors in those processes, and their normative content reflects this'.[13] It is arguable, though, that structural principles do cross into substantive terrain: and perhaps even more so since *Structural Principles* was published. This point is picked up in more detail later in the chapter: fundamentally, I am curious to know if Marise would still delimit the substantive reach of structural principles in the same way now; or if their development since she conceived them might be accepted as informing the 'substantive content' of EU law too (see Section 3 below). However, it might also be the case that the substantive implications of structural principles are evident more in the internal than external dimension of EU law (see Section 4 below).

Marise further distinguished 'relational' structural principles, which 'govern the relationships between actors or legal subjects (not [relationships between] norms)';[14] and 'systemic' structural principles, which are 'concerned with the operation of the system as a whole, with building the EU's identity as a coherent, effective and autonomous actor in the world'.[15] For the relational category of structural principles, Marise identified 'four relational axes'[16] ie Member State-Member State (with special focus on the principle of mutual solidarity); Member State-Union Institutions (concerned mainly with the principles of conferral, sincere cooperation, and subsidiarity); Inter-Institutional Relations (illustrated through the principles of institutional balance and transparency); and Union Institutions–Individuals/Third Countries/International Organisations (addressing, in particular, autonomy and the rule of law). For structural principles grouped in the systemic category – comprising autonomy, coherence, and effectiveness – their systemic nature 'implies that these principles serve to guide and shape the other [ie relational] structural principles and their implementation'.[17] However, both the distinction between relational and systemic structural principles *per se* and the notably greater predominance of the former in terms of how the principles of EU law were categorised in *Structural Principles* can, I think, be explained by its central focus on EU external relations law (Section 4 below).

More generally, Marise emphasised that structural principles of EU law 'are legal norms; they have a legal function and breach of them may result in the illegality of the resulting measure'.[18] As principles, they are 'somehow fundamental, justifying and underpinning the specificity and detail of rules, both procedural and substantive'.[19] At the same time, though, '[s]ince principles are not designed to give a once-and-for-all answer to a concrete question (which does not prevent them from being decisive in a particular case), they are open to adjustment and re-interpretation over time and in changing circumstances'.[20] Thus, as already alluded to above, Marise's list

[13] ibid 12 (emphasis in original).

[14] ibid 17 (ie conferral, subsidiarity, institutional balance, sincere cooperation, solidarity, unity, transparency and rule of law).

[15] ibid 18.

[16] ibid.

[17] ibid 28.

[18] ibid 12.

[19] ibid 13.

[20] ibid 18.

of structural principles was intended to be neither exhaustive nor fixed. Relatedly, she emphasised that the 'nature' of structural principles is, like that of principles of EU law more generally, similarly 'flexible and capable of evolution'.[21] Fluidity is thus possible – and maybe even expected. What are the advantages – but also the risks – of building *structures* on inherently fluid principles? In that light, it is especially interesting to observe the migration of structural principles from one category to another: and more specifically, from relational to systemic. Given that systemic principles have a specific purpose – as noted just above, they 'serve to guide and shape the other [ie relational] structural principles and their implementation' – what are the conditions under which a relational principle might or should be upgraded to a systemic principle?

I argue that examples of precisely this transformation are taking place in the (internal) case law of the Court of Justice at the time of writing, and the main motivations would seem to be twofold: first, the need to jumpstart more effective Union responses to intensive, urgent challenges; underpinned by, second, a method of attributing real legal bite to the values on which the Union is founded. A first example concerns the principle of solidarity. As Marise reflected in *Structural Principles*, solidarity was largely perceived as a relational principle of EU law; invoked mainly to perform normative work when trying to determine, or to justify, how the Member States (should) relate to the Union and to each other to address transnational challenges having specific and often uneven national effects:[22] for example, when trying to determine, or to justify, where responsibility should lie in terms of the impact on national public finances that transnational freedom of movement and migration more generally can produce.[23] In more recent case law, however, solidarity has been invoked in a very striking and harder *legal* way. Thus, in the evolution of EU policies on both migration and energy, solidarity has been acquiring the features of a systemic structural principle.

For migration, the Court has determined that decisions adopted on the basis of Article 78(3) Treaty on the Functioning of the European Union (TFEU) 'for the purpose of helping the Hellenic Republic and the Italian Republic to better cope with an emergency situation characterised by a sudden influx of third-country nationals on their territory, must, in principle, be divided between all the other Member States, in accordance with the principle of solidarity and fair sharing of responsibility

[21] ibid 5.

[22] See generally E Küçük, 'Solidarity in EU Law: An Elusive Political Statement or a Legal Principle with Substance?' in A Biondi, E Dagilytė and E Küçük (eds), *Solidarity in EU Law. Legal Principle in the Making*, (Cheltenham, Edward Elgar Publishing, 2018); A Sangiovanni, 'Solidarity in the European Union' (2013) 33 *OJLS* 213.

[23] See eg D Kramer, 'Earning Social Citizenship in the European Union: Free Movement and Access to Social Assistance Benefits Reconstructed' (2016) 18 *CYELS* 270; P Neuvonen, *Equal Citizenship and its Limits in EU Law: We the Burden?*, Modern Studies in European Law (Oxford, Hart Publishing, 2016); A Somek, 'Solidarity Decomposed: Being and Time in European Citizenship' (2007) 32 *EL Rev* 787; D Thym, 'The Elusive Limits of Solidarity: Residence Rights of and Social Benefits for Economically Inactive Union Citizens' (2015) 52 *CML Rev* 17; F de Witte, *Justice in the EU: The Emergence of Transnational Solidarity*, Oxford Studies in European Law (Oxford, Oxford University Press, 2015).

between the Member States'.[24] The Court therefore found that 'it is not permissible, if the objective of solidarity inherent to [the contested decisions] and the binding nature of those acts is not to be undermined, for a Member State to be able to rely, moreover without raising for that purpose a legal basis provided for in the Treaties, on its unilateral assessment of the alleged lack of effectiveness, or even the purported malfunctioning, of the relocation mechanism established by those acts … in order to avoid any obligation to relocate people incumbent upon it'.[25] Solidarity retains its relational purpose in these statements, since it determines how the Member States must relate to both the Union and, more especially, to each other in the implementation of shared responsibility for EU migration policy. But through the finding that unilateralism is antithetic to a Union based on solidarity, something systemic was emerging too: captured most vividly by Advocate General Sharpston's depiction of solidarity as 'the lifeblood of the European project' per se.[26]

These nascent systemic traces were further progressed in the Court's subsequent consideration of solidarity in the field of EU energy policy. It confirmed in *Germany v Poland* that 'the spirit of solidarity between Member States, mentioned in [Article 194 TFEU], constitutes a specific expression, in the field of energy, of the principle of solidarity, which is itself one of the fundamental principles of EU law'.[27] It directly addressed the 'allegedly abstract nature of the principle of solidarity' – recalling the principles that it articulated for EU migration law, the Court underlined that 'there is nothing that would permit the inference that the principle of solidarity referred to in Article 194(1) TFEU cannot, as such, produce binding legal effects on the Member States and institutions of the European Union'.[28] It also recalled that 'the principle of solidarity entails rights and obligations both for the European Union and for the Member States, the European Union being bound by an obligation of solidarity towards the Member States and the Member States being bound by an obligation of solidarity between themselves' – illustrating solidarity's relational qualities – 'and with regard to the common interest of the European Union and the policies pursued

[24] Joined Cases C-715/17, C-718/17 and C-719/17 *Commission v Poland, Hungary and the Czech Republic (Temporary Mechanism for the Relocation of Applicants for International Protection)* ECLI:EU:C:2020:257, para 80. Art 78(3) Consolidated version of the Treaty on the Functioning of the European Union (TFEU) [2016] OJ C202/47 provides: 'In the event of one or more Member States being confronted by an emergency situation characterised by a sudden inflow of nationals of third countries, the Council, on a proposal from the Commission, may adopt provisional measures for the benefit of the Member State(s) concerned. It shall act after consulting the European Parliament'.

[25] Joined Cases C-715/17, C-718/17 and C-719/17 *Commission v Poland, Hungary and the Czech Republic (Temporary Mechanism for the Relocation of Applicants for International Protection)* ECLI:EU:C:2020:257, para 182. Offering a deeply passionate argument for the importance of solidarity to the very purpose of the Union, see also Opinion of Advocate General Sharpston in Joined Cases C-715/17, C-718/17 and C-719/17 *Commission v Poland, Hungary and the Czech Republic (Temporary Mechanism for the Relocation of Applicants for International Protection)* ECLI:EU:C:2019:917, especially paras 235–238 and 253–254 of the Opinion.

[26] Opinion of Advocate General Sharpston in Joined Cases C-715/17, C-718/17 and C-719/17 *Commission v Poland, Hungary and the Czech Republic (Temporary Mechanism for the Relocation of Applicants for International Protection)* ECLI:EU:C:2019:917, para 253.

[27] Case C-848/19 P *Germany v Poland* ECLI:EU:C:2021:598, para 38. See further A Boute, 'The principle of solidarity and the geopolitics of energy: *Poland v. Commission (OPAL pipeline)*' (2020) 57 *CML Rev* 889.

[28] Case C-848/19 P *Germany v Poland* ECLI:EU:C:2021:598, para 42.

by it', advancing the principle more systemically.[29] Thus, even if 'the variety of forms in which the principle of solidarity manifests itself makes it difficult for that principle to be applied in the same way and to the same extent in all areas of EU competence … there is no reason not to regard solidarity, in some of those areas of competence, as having *the capacity to operate as a "guiding principle"* for the actions of the European Union in those fields, in which cases this has an impact on its effects in law'.[30]

Reading contemporary case law on migration and energy together provides strong empirical support for Marise's hypothesis that a relational structural principle can change shape. It suggests, more specifically, that a relational structural principle can become a systemic structural principle. The hardening demands of solidarity as a principle that produces legal obligations chime with Marise's understanding of systemic structural principles as 'not simply concerned to define the static relations between actors, but … designed to guide their conduct, to ensure that the actors do in fact act'.[31] For legal researchers, it is difficult to 'prove' what the motivations might be when we detect a shift from the relational to the systemic. However, it is clear that when that shift does occur in the case law, the obligations that EU law imposes on the Member States extend and become (more) enforceable.

The case law summarised above also asks us to think about a principle exhibiting both relational and systemic qualities simultaneously. There are other examples of this hybridity too; notably the principle of conditionality, which is addressed in Section 3 below. In Section 4 below, I suggest that both the 'quantity' of systemic principles in the internal sphere of EU constitutional law as well as a principle's capacity to exhibit both relational and structural features at the same time are more evident since *Structural Principles* was published – in the sense of both the developments in the law since then and also as a consequence of translating structural principles beyond the context of EU external relations law. Before that discussion, however, the extent to which inclusion in Article 2 Treaty on European Union (TEU) supercharges the values and principles expressed there to claims as systemic principles, by definition, will first be considered as part of broader reflections on the value of categorising principles. Does such categorisation produce hierarchy among legal principles? And is the resulting 'deep structure of the EU' clearly identifiable in the Treaties, or not?

3. WHAT IS THE POINT OF CATEGORISING PRINCIPLES OF EU LAW?

Marise directly confronted the objection that trying to categorise principles of EU law could be dismissed as a pointless exercise, that the 'value of a classification of general principles is limited'.[32] Nonetheless, she defended the 'increase [in] our understanding' that classification brings. In her view, it sheds light on 'the contribution to policy-making of each different actor (Member States as well as the institutions)

[29] ibid para 49.
[30] Opinion of Advocate General Campos Sánchez-Bordona in Case C-848/19 P *Germany v Poland* ECLI:EU:C:2021:218, para 72 (emphasis added).
[31] Cremona (n 2) 18.
[32] ibid 15.

and the balance and constructive relationships between them; their accountability to individuals and third countries affected by their decisions and the transparency that underpins that accountability' – insights of particular importance for EU external relations, she argued, since 'the substantive content of that policy is left so undefined by EU Treaty law'.[33]

I strongly agree with the essence of that defence. As manifestations of primary law,[34] general principles of EU law are both positive shapers and negative constrainers of the actions taken by the EU institutions as well as by the Member States. They are, in other words, extremely powerful. And this means that their nature and functioning will always merit careful and appropriate attention. In this part of the chapter, therefore, three related sets of questions are discussed to illustrate the constitutional puzzles that categorising certain principles of EU law as structural principles provokes, addressing, first, whether this categorisation institutes a formal hierarchy among principles of EU law; second, the fact that some structural principles of EU law are not actually present, explicitly at least, in the EU Treaties – that they are, for present purposes and with reference to the EU context, 'extra-Treaty'; and third, the significance of assessing how principles behave collectively.

3.1. Does the Concept of Structural Principles Institute a Formal 'Hierarchy' of Principles?

In thinking further about the added value of categorisation as *structural* principles more specifically, a first question that we could ask is: what *kind* of primary law is constituted by the structural principles of EU law? In this respect, Marise resisted thinking about principles of EU law in terms of hierarchy since 'the nature of principles is not to be hierarchic; they accommodate each other and a principle may be given more weight in one case than another'.[35] That understanding reflects very well the more general idea that when two or more legal norms compete, all can be legally valid. In political terms, choices between valid but competing norms are constantly made. When these choices come to be reviewed within the framework of EU law, the objective is to carry out an assessment 'with a view to reconciling the requirements of the protection of those different rights and freedoms and a fair balance between them'.[36]

However, while Marise preferred a non-hierarchical understanding of structural principles, she was not, at the same time, 'preclud[ing] the possibility that the Court appears to *privilege* certain principles over others'.[37] Is the idea of a non-hierarchical yet privilege-accommodating primary law framework entirely tension-free? We saw in Section 2 above that Marise identified a special role for systemic structural principles

[33] ibid.

[34] See eg Case C-826/19 *Austrian Airlines* ECLI:EU:C:2021:318, para 41; Joined Cases C-402/07 and C-432/07 *Sturgeon and Others* ECLI:EU:C:2009:716, [2009] ECR I-10923, para 48; Joined Cases C-402/05 P and C-415/05 P *Kadi and Al Barakaat International Foundation v Council and Commission* ECLI:EU:C:2008:461, [2008] ECR I-6351, para 308.

[35] Cremona (n 2) 14.

[36] Case C-283/11 *Sky Österreich* ECLI:EU:C:2013:28, para 60.

[37] Cremona (n 2) 14 (emphasis added).

since 'the systemic nature of coherence, effectiveness and autonomy implies that these principles serve to guide and shape the other structural principles and their implementation'.[38] She also argued that systemic principles 'make it clear that structural principles are not simply concerned to define the static relations between actors, but are designed to guide their conduct, to ensure that the actors do in fact act'.[39] If the systemic nature of certain structural principles 'implies that these principles serve to guide and shape the other[s]' in this way, how is that not 'hierarchy'? And what, more substantively, is the difference between hierarchy and privilege in this context? I return to these questions below.

3.2. Structural Principles, the EU Treaties, and Primary EU law

While most of the principles addressed in *Structural Principles* now find expression in the Treaties, they did not appear there initially, and autonomy still does not. Moreover, if we expand the inquiry to internally facing EU law, principles such as primacy, direct effect, and mutual trust can be added to the list of structural principles that are not addressed directly in the Treaties, as returned to in Section 4 below. We are familiar with how principles can begin life in the case law of the Court of Justice and be added to the Treaties *later* – protection of fundamental rights being the most developed example, considering the trajectory from the earliest statements about it in the Court's case law;[40] to incrementally increasing references to the protection of fundamental rights as the result of successive Treaty amendments; to the binding nature of the Charter of Fundamental Rights achieved, finally, through the amendments added by Lisbon Treaty.[41] However, some structural principles of EU law are still not codified in the Treaties, yet they have the legal power to generate, in large part, the constitutional frame that sits around the whole Union enterprise.

In that light, the making of primary EU law is, perhaps surprisingly and leaving analyses of Treaty-making aside,[42] relatively under-explored. Looking at primary law-making more substantively than formally, Christophe Hillion's depiction of the 'quasi-primary law-making power' exercised by the European Council in the Brexit negotiations provides an important reminder that primary law can – still – evolve

[38] ibid 28.

[39] ibid 18.

[40] See especially Case 29/69 *Stauder* ECLI:EU:C:1969:57, [1969] ECR 419.

[41] See especially Art 6(1) Consolidated version of the Treaty on European Union (TEU) [2016] OJ C202/13: 'The Union recognises the rights, freedoms and principles set out in the Charter of Fundamental Rights of the European Union of 7 December 2000, as adapted at Strasbourg, on 12 December 2007, which shall have the same legal value as the Treaties. The provisions of the Charter shall not extend in any way the competences of the Union as defined in the Treaties. The rights, freedoms and principles in the Charter shall be interpreted in accordance with the general provisions in Title VII of the Charter governing its interpretation and application and with due regard to the explanations referred to in the Charter, that set out the sources of those provisions'.

[42] eg for the Lisbon Treaty D Ashiagbor, N Countouris and I Lianos (eds), *The European Union after the Treaty of Lisbon* (Cambridge, Cambridge University Press, 2012); P Craig, *The Lisbon Treaty: Law, Politics and Treaty Reform*, 1st edn (Oxford, Oxford University Press, 2013); M Dougan 'The Treaty of Lisbon 2007: Winning Minds, Not Hearts' (2008) 45 *CML Rev* 617.

without Treaty change and generate significant legal effects. To take a specific example, the European Council's 'Guidelines' for the Brexit negotiations[43] demonstrated that institutional behaviour can structure an entire process or field of activity even though there is a certain vagueness around its grounding authority or substantive content.[44]

I would argue that *Structural Principles* underlines, more generally, why *extra-Treaty primary EU law* deserves particularly close scrutiny. In her Introduction, Marise acknowledged 'the dominant role of the Court of Justice in identifying and interpreting principles' and that the 'flexibility' of such principles 'allows them to develop from small beginnings to powerful tools in the hands of the Court and to take on somewhat unpredictable forms on occasion'.[45] Returning to the example of fundamental rights, analyses of *Opinion 2/13* challenged the Court's protection of the 'essential characteristics' of EU law, which are not expressed or provided for as such in the Treaties, above its protection of fundamental rights, which *is* expressly mandated by several Treaty provisions and by the Charter.[46] Given the outcome in *Opinion 2/13*, could we therefore characterise the Court's conception of the 'essential characteristics' of EU law as an expression of the EU's extra-Treaty 'deep structure'?[47]

In *Structural Principles*, Marise considered *Opinion 2/13* with reference to relational principles, focusing on how the 'essential characteristics' of EU law 'have given rise to a structured network of principles, rules and mutually interdependent legal relations linking the EU and its Member States, and its Member States with each other'.[48] Since *Opinion 2/13* was delivered, we now find consistent and repeated references to:

> ... the fundamental premiss that each Member State shares with all the other Member States, and recognises that they share with it, the common values, contained in Article 2 TEU, on which the European Union is founded. That premiss is *based on* the specific and essential characteristics of EU law, *which stem from* the very nature of EU law and the autonomy it enjoys in relation to the laws of the Member States and to international law.

[43] European Council, 'Special Meeting of the European Council (Art.50) (29 April 2017) – Guidelines for Brexit Negotiations' (2017) EUCO XT 20004/17.

[44] See C Hillion, 'Withdrawal under Article 50 TEU: An Integration-Friendly Process' (2018) 55 *CML Rev* 29, 52. Raising similar questions about the input of the European Council in the context of EU budget conditionality, see also Editorial Comments, 'Compromising (on) the General Conditionality Mechanism and the Rule of Law' (2021) 58 *CML Rev* 267.

[45] Cremona (n 2) 15.

[46] Opinion 2/13 *Accession of the Union to the ECHR* ECLI:EU:C:2014:2454, para 168. For critique, see eg S Peers, 'The EU's Accession to the ECHR: The Dream Becomes a Nightmare' (2015) 16 *German Law Journal* 213, 221; P Eeckhout, 'Opinion 2/13 on EU Accession to the ECHR and Judicial Dialogue – Autonomy or Autarky?' (2015) *Jean Monnet Working Paper* 01/15, 16; D Kochenov, 'EU Law without the Rule of Law: Is the Veneration of Autonomy Worth It?' (2015) 34 *Yearbook of European Law* 74. It can be noted, however, that Article 1 of Protocol (No 8) relating to Article 6(2) of the TEU on the accession of the Union to the European Convention on the Protection of Human Rights and Fundamental Freedoms (Protocol 8) [2016] OJ C202/273, does require that '[t]he agreement relating to the accession of the Union to the [ECHR] provided for in Article 6(2) of the Treaty on European Union shall make provision for preserving the *specific characteristics of the Union and Union law*' (emphasis added).

[47] Cremona (n 2) 15.

[48] ibid 17–18, referring to Opinion 2/13 (*Accession of the Union to the ECHR*) ECLI:EU:C:2014:2454, paras 165–167.

> That premiss implies and justifies the existence of mutual trust between the Member States that those values will be recognised and, therefore, that the EU law that implements them will be respected.[49]

On the 'specific and essential characteristics of EU law', the Court further underlines that:

> … [the] autonomy of EU law with respect both to the law of the Member States and to international law is justified by the essential characteristics of the European Union and its law, relating in particular to the constitutional structure of the European Union and the very nature of that law. EU law is characterised by the fact that it stems from an independent source of law, namely the Treaties, by its primacy over the laws of the Member States, and by the direct effect of a whole series of provisions which are applicable to their nationals and to the Member States themselves. Those characteristics have given rise to a structured network of principles, rules and mutually interdependent legal relations binding the European Union and its Member States reciprocally as well as binding its Member States to each other.[50]

In common with the structural principles of EU law, we can highlight two things from these extracts. First, and building on the discussion of shapeshifting in Section 2 above, I would argue that, over time, the Court's statements have taken on systemic character too. Second, while there is some reference to Treaty-based elements through the significance attributed to the values in Article 2 TEU, there is much wider appeal in this case law to the structural principles that are extra-Treaty: to autonomy, mutual trust, primacy, and direct effect.

Can we determine whether the structural principles considered by the Court to constitute the 'specific and essential characteristics' of EU law impose an intention of hierarchy or one of privilege? I come back to this dilemma below. For now, if it can be agreed that the extracts above do provide an expression of the (Court's understanding of the) deep structure 'of the European Union and its law', further questions about the extra-Treaty elements of that understanding can be raised. For example, what does a principle being 'drawn from the Treaties and elaborated by the Court'[51] actually mean? In other words, how *much* Treaty do we need to constitute a structural principle? Relatedly, given the extent of constitutional control that the Court creates and/or retains by moulding the EU constitution around structural principles that are *not* in the Treaties, does this case law fall within or exceed the mandate established by Article 19(1) TEU, that the Court 'shall ensure that in the interpretation and application of the Treaties the law is observed'? And finally, how can EU primary law that is not expressed in the Treaties be changed through a process of political rather than judicial decision-making?[52]

[49] Case C-157/21 *Poland v Parliament and Council* ECLI:EU:C:2022:98, para 143 (emphasis added).

[50] Case C-621/18 *Wightman and Others* ECLI:EU:C:2018:999, para 45; referring to Case C-284/16 *Achmea* ECLI :EU:C:2018:158, para 33.

[51] Cremona (n 2) 5.

[52] This question expands on related debates about the over-constitutionalisation brought about by EU case law, in terms of the consequential constraining of political discretion with respect to the EU legislator: see eg PAJ Syrpis, 'The Relationship between Primary and Secondary Law in the EU' (2015) 52 *CML Rev* 461; G Davies, 'The European Union Legislature as an Agent of the European Court of Justice' (2016) 54 *Journal of Common Market Studies* 846.

If we take direct effect as an example: the words do not appear anywhere in either the TEU or TFEU. Yet in *Van Gend en Loos*, the Court rationalised direct effect as a principle of EU law by conducting an audit across 'the spirit, the general scheme and the wording' of the European Economic Community (EEC) Treaty's provisions.[53] Notwithstanding the increasingly interesting role played by the European Council in the task of constitutional framing, as flagged above, the Court undoubtedly enjoys the most powerful interpretative role and considerable interpretative discretion when determining whether 'new' principles of EU law can justifiably be constituted and described as such. *Van Gend en Loos* does provide a template, but the extent to which the Court has always adhered to it has been questioned with respect to the birth of some general principles of EU law: for example, the principle of non-discrimination on grounds of age.[54] For present purposes, the critical point is this: where principles come from and how robustly they are rationalised matters – even more if they are not expressed in, even if drawn from, the Treaties; and even more still, I would suggest, if they are (or become) structural principles of EU law – part of its specific and essential characteristics, and thus the principles that 'serve to guide and shape the others'.[55]

However, as also alluded to above, structural principles have become, over time, more clearly rooted in respect for the values and principles expressed in Article 2 TEU. In its 258 paragraphs, *Opinion 2/13* mentioned Article 2 TEU only once.[56] As already shown through the example of solidarity in Section 2 above, Article 2 TEU has since then been invoked to much greater effect and that shift in reasoning can perhaps overcome some of the criticisms of the 'selfish'[57] or 'fearful'[58] Court's first efforts. In *Opinion 2/13* itself, in other words, institutional and/or systemic self-interest were arguably more urgent than articulating what protecting the deep structure of the EU is actually *for*. Moreover, while the Court's presentation of that structure was used to resist EU accession to the ECHR in *Opinion 2/13*, the same structure has, over time, been drawn from to affirm, more positively, the consent-based nature of membership of the Union,[59] and the vital importance of sustaining compliance with the values on which the Union is founded throughout (and not just before) such membership.[60]

It is not, then, that some of the structural principles of EU law are extra-Treaty entirely; but instead, that they are only *partly* or *implicitly* located there: that some circumstance or event or need (or combination thereof) can activate elements already

[53] Case 26/62 *Van Gend en Loos v Administratie der Belastingen* ECLI:EU:C:1963:1, [1963] ECR 1.

[54] See especially Case C-144/04 *Mangold* ECLI:EU:C:2005:709, [2005] ECR I-9981, paras 74–75. Reflecting on protection against age discrimination as a general principle of EU law, see eg M Schmidt 'The Principle of Non-discrimination in Respect of Age: Dimensions of the ECJ's *Mangold* Judgment' (2006) 7 *German Law Journal* 505, 518–520.

[55] Cremona (n 2) 28.

[56] Opinion 2/13 *Accession of the Union to the ECHR* ECLI:EU:C:2014:2454, para 168.

[57] B de Witte, 'A Selfish Court? The Court of Justice and the Design of International Dispute Settlement beyond the European Union' in M Cremona and A Thies (eds), *The European Court of Justice and External Relations Law: Constitutional Challenges*, Modern Studies in European Law (Oxford, Hart Publishing, 2014) 33.

[58] E Spaventa, 'A Very Fearful Court? The Protection of Fundamental Rights in the EU after Opinion 2/13' (2015) 22 *Maastricht Journal of European and Comparative Law* 35.

[59] Case C-621/18 *Wightman and Others* ECLI:EU:C:2018:999.

[60] Case C-156/21 *Hungary v Parliament and Council* ECLI:EU:C:2022:97 and Case C-157/21 *Poland v Parliament and Council* ECLI:EU:C:2022:98.

scattered across the 'spirit, the general scheme and the wording' of the Treaties and confer on those elements the title and the salience of a principle of primary EU law – and maybe even one that belongs to EU law's specific and essential characteristics, inaugurating a systemic structural principle of EU law.[61] That process usually happens through the functioning of judicial review, for which, as Marise expressed it, there is 'little by way of *clear* guidance in the constituent Treaties'.[62] though there is guidance nonetheless when the Court needs to look for it.

However, recalling again the example about the European Council exercising 'quasi-primary law-making power'[63] in its framing and oversight of the Brexit negotiations, and also subsequently in the process of adopting the Conditionality Regulation,[64] Katy Sowery had earlier identified very similar concerns with respect to the 'informal mechanisms of primary law change' that she observed in the EU's response to the Eurozone crisis.[65] The very idea of primary EU law changing 'informally' raises really serious constitutional questions. To crystalise that concern, the concept of structural principles provides a vital analytical counterpoint – one that we can use to undertake a legal assessment of EU institutional conduct. Moreover, Marise's dual emphasis on the essential legal nature yet capacity for adaptation of the structural principles can be highlighted again here, since both qualities take on sharpened significance when the EU and its legal arsenal must confront urgent challenges.[66]

3.3. Insights from the Collective Behaviour of Principles of EU Law

A further feature of the added value of Marise's categorisation work stems from the fact that it asks us to think about 'solidarity' or 'autonomy' or 'sincere cooperation' not only as important principles of EU law on their own terms, but also in terms of *how principles behave when they are grouped together* in a certain way. That, in turn, brings us back to one of the most difficult questions that *Structural Principles* provokes: how do the principles that constitute 'the deep structure' of the EU legal order relate to the other principles of EU law if not in some form of hierarchy? In other words, when we group certain principles together rather than considering them only individually, because we agree that some but not all principles of EU law are

[61] Tracing the evolution and increasing importance of mutual trust, for example, see V Mitsilegas 'Trust' (2020) 21 *German Law Journal* 69; K Lenaerts '*La vie après l'avis*: Exploring the Principle of Mutual (Yet Not Blind) Trust' (2017) 54 *CML Rev* 805; N Cambien, 'Mutual Recognition and Mutual Trust in the Internal Market' (2017) 2 *European Papers* 93. Reflecting another aspect of the Brexit negotiations in terms of the possible emergence of another new (structural?) principle, see eg Editorial Comments, 'Is the "Indivisibility" of the Four Freedoms a Principle of EU Law?' (2019) 56 *CML Rev* 1189.

[62] Cremona (n 2) 11 (emphasis added).

[63] Hillion (n 44).

[64] Editorial Comments, 'Editorial Comments, 'Compromising (on) the General Conditionality Mechanism and the Rule of Law'. Regulation (EU, Euratom) 2020/2092 of the European Parliament and of the Council on a general regime of conditionality for the protection of the Union budget [2020] OJ L433I/1.

[65] K Sowery, 'The Nature and Scope of the Primary Law-Making Powers of the European Union: The Member States as the "Masters of the Treaties"?' (2018) 43 *EL Rev* 205, 218.

[66] See further B de Witte, 'EU Emergency Law and its Impact on the EU Legal Order' (2022) 59 *Common Market Law Review* 3; N Nic Shuibhne, 'Did Brexit Change EU Law?' (2021) 74 *Current Legal Problems* 195.

structural principles, it really does become more difficult to avoid seeing fault-lines of a hierarchical nature. Even accepting that these fault-lines are inherently flexible, fluid, and adaptable to change – and without having to rank principles in terms of relational hierarchy *vis-à-vis* each other in an individual sense – is it not fair to say that the structural principles of EU law *operate* hierarchically when we assess their functioning collectively and, moreover, that certain normative choices are made and reinforced because we categorise them as such as in the first place?

For example, looking again at how the case law expressing the specific and essential characteristics of the EU and of EU law has developed, it could be argued that the values and principles referred to in Article 2 TEU have instituted a form of hierarchy. Article 2 TEU was first invoked in quite a functional sense in case law on judicial independence and the rule of law. In *Portuguese Judges*, the Court blended the fact that the rule of law is mentioned in Article 2 and the statement in Article 19(1) TEU that 'Member States shall provide remedies sufficient to ensure effective legal protection in the fields covered by Union law' to conceive a Member State responsibility to ensure an independent national judiciary on the basis of the latter's role in the Union's judicial system.[67] Moreover, that responsibility applies even where a situation does not come within the scope of Article 47 of the Charter, ie even when a Member State is not 'implementing Union law' within the meaning of Article 51 of the Charter.[68] That idea is already an indication of hierarchy: the responsibility to ensure an independent judiciary takes precedence over express limitations on the scope of the Charter, justified by recourse to the fact that the rule of law is a value contained in Article 2 TEU. Since that case law step was taken, the significance of Article 2 TEU has only increased, noting the statements in the Court's assessment of the Conditionality Regulation, for example, that 'compliance by a Member State with the values contained in Article 2 TEU is *a condition for the enjoyment of all the rights* deriving from the application of the Treaties to that Member State' and that those values '*define the very identity* of the European Union as a common legal order'.[69] That sounds very structural indeed – and systemically structural, more particularly.

The context and the resonance of the case law summarised above connect very evidently to the seriousness of the rule of law regression that the Union continues to face not from outside but from within its own borders. But if Article 2 TEU is being used to convey a hierarchy of priorities within the structure of EU law, there are implications for the other values and principles in Article 2 – including democracy, equality, minority rights, and solidarity – that will have to be followed through too: the very idea of a 'deep structure' argues against selectivity here. A structural principle cannot be a structural principle only *sometimes*, in other words. There are some emerging signs that this is indeed the case, if we consider that, at the time of writing, the Commission has launched further infringement proceedings against Poland on the basis of Article 2 TEU: not in connection with the rule of law and Article 19(1)

[67] Case C-64/16 *Associação Sindical dos Juízes Portugueses* ECLI:EU:C:2018:117, para 37.

[68] eg Case C-824/18 *AB and Others (Appointment of judges to the Supreme Court – Actions)* ECLI:EU:C:2021:153, para 111; Case C-896/19 *Repubblika* ECLI:EU:C:2021:311, para 36.

[69] Case C-156/21 *Hungary v Parliament and Council* ECLI:EU:C:2022:97 and Case C-157/21 *Poland v Parliament and Council* ECLI:EU:C:2022:98, paras 126 and 144 respectively.

TEU as a specific expression of that value; but rather, in connection with democracy, with Article 10 TEU providing the 'specific expression' bridge.[70]

Nevertheless, the 'unwritten' deep structure elements continue to be highlighted too, alongside this intensifying emphasis on Article 2 TEU. For the Court still holds to the fact that sharing the common values contained in Article 2 TEU is 'based on the specific and essential characteristics of EU law, which stem from the very nature of EU law and the autonomy it enjoys'.[71] Taking that into account, how do the Article 2 values and the specific and essential characteristics intersect, and what happens if they conflict? As already noted above, for example, the conflict between autonomy, an essential but unwritten characteristic, and respect for fundamental rights, which is included in Art 2 TEU, was not particularly well handled in *Opinion 2/13*. And few would disagree that 'hierarchy' was conferred on autonomy in that context.

Thus, it may be that when we think about hierarchy and privilege with respect to principles in an *individual* sense, the notion of 'privilege' is indeed more apt. In any given case, where different principles might be relevant and where they can 'legitimately pull in different directions',[72] one or more principles will have to be 'privileged' over others in that specific case to resolve it. Importantly, that does not mean that the privileged principle(s) will then be hierarchically superior in all cases. As introduced above, the Court's 'fair balance' method can provide, from internal market law, the language that we need here: '[w]here several rights and fundamental freedoms protected by the European Union legal order are at issue, the assessment of the possible disproportionate nature of a provision of European Union law must be carried out with a view *to reconciling the requirements of the protection of those different rights and freedoms and a fair balance between them*'.[73] In that sense, privilege is more about relative *weight* than formal hierarchy; and it is more about weight in a specific set of circumstances than weight more generally. As Marise expressed it, principles 'may be held in tension with one another without being seen as contradictory or conflicting'.[74]

However, when we group general principles of EU law together more *collectively* because they exhibit the characteristics of structural principles, then I would argue that the privilege that we accord them by doing so is not only about weight – it is about hierarchy. Article 2 TEU provides helpful explanatory and normative perspective when it is added to the Court's reasoning. However, it neither constitutes nor contains the hierarchical element by itself. Rather, the very fact of selecting or ascribing to certain principles the mantle of structural principles, whether they are expressed in Article 2 TEU or not, is responsible for imbuing that hierarchy in the first place: to recall Marise's words, we categorise certain principles in this way because they 'guide and shape the others'. It is absolutely right to say that '[p]rinciples point to a particular direction of argument or line of reasoning'.[75] It seems, though, that once the concept

[70] European Commission, 'Rule of law: Commission Launches Infringement Procedure against POLAND for Violating EU Law with the New Law Establishing a Special Committee' (2023) Press Release IP/23/3134.
[71] ibid.
[72] Cremona (n 2) 14.
[73] Case C-283/11 *Sky Österreich* ECLI:EU:C:2013:28, para 60 (emphasis added).
[74] Cremona (n 2) 14.
[75] Cremona (n 2) 14.

of structural principles enters the frame, there is also more likely to be a particular *outcome* – a trumping of limits in some cases, as we saw in *Portuguese Judges*; a resistance to Union policy in others, as we saw in *Opinion 2/13*. The substantive dimension of structural principles in such cases bridges to the final question examined in this chapter: is it more necessarily more significant when we move the lens away from EU external relations law?

4. THE INTERNAL AND EXTERNAL DIMENSIONS OF THE EU'S CONSTITUTION

At the beginning of her Introduction to *Structural Principles*, Marise stated that a central purpose of the book was to consider 'whether [and] to what extent, law may operate differently in the external from the internal context'.[76] She suggested that for EU external relations, the Court of Justice is 'engaged in establishing and protecting an institutional space within which policy may be formed, in which the different actors understand and work within their respective roles' – contrasting these functions with the Court's more 'interventionist' and 'substantive policy choice' impact on policy fields such as the creation of the internal market.[77] Similarly, using the principle of unity as an example, Marise distinguished how structural principles acquire shape in the differing contexts of the Union's internal and external activities. She therefore suggested that '[s]tructural principles in the internal context may be concerned primarily with the structure that it is the Union's mission to build' (considering, for example, the 'unity of the market' or of the 'internal space within which freedom of movement may take place') – while unity in the external context, in contrast, 'insofar as the EU has a mission to construct … is to construct the EU itself as an effective external actor. Thus, for example, unity becomes a question of the unity of the international representation of the Union and its Member States'.[78] Reflecting on these words again and bringing into the picture the case law developments that occurred after *Structural Principles* was published, structural principles are clearly relevant to both the internal and external dimensions of the EU's constitution, yet they do seem to behave differently in each of those dimensions. Looking at how they are applied in the internal dimension more specifically, many more structural principles seem systemic rather than relational, or exhibit both relational and systemic qualities simultaneously.

At one level, it is simply a fact that certain principles of EU law have internal effect only or at least an external effect that is significantly more limited than the effect felt internally: most notably here, primacy, direct effect, and mutual trust.[79] But while there is obvious concern for how the Union relates to the Member States as well as to how the Member States relate to each other in the internal dimension of EU law, something else seems to be going on more often too: the 'mission to construct' is also

[76] Cremona (n 2) 3.

[77] ibid 5.

[78] ibid 16–17.

[79] The external effects of mutual trust are particularly limited, confined to date to third states with which the Union has a close and special relationship: see eg Case C-897/19 PPU *Ruska Federacija* ECLI:EU:C:2020:262.

more obviously systemic than relational, or at least, it is palpably systemic alongside being relational. *Opinion 2/13* stands in the borderland between securing the Union's internal robustness and enabling the external scrutiny of its actions, and the chapter in this volume by Gráinne de Búrca and Claire Kilpatrick demonstrates why the latter is necessary to make the former more, not less, secure. However, as developments with respect to both Brexit and the rule of law have now shown too, greater systemic vulnerability will inevitably result when challenges to the EU system come entirely from within. That is another reason why relational determinations tend to exhibit parallel systemic significance in the EU's internal constitutional world. If a policy focused externally, one agreed between the EU and a third country, should fail, then that external agreement fails. If a policy focused internally, between the EU and its Member States or between the Member States themselves, should fail, then doubts about the EU more existentially are not usually far behind.

Importantly, Marise never isolates the Union's internal and external domains either rigidly or artificially: quite the contrary, noting, for example, her statement that '[t]hese principles I have termed structural, since they help to define the structure of the EU as an international actor, both internally and externally'.[80] The qualities of structural principles articulated for the purposes of EU external relations law on their own terms are not unknown in internal policy fields either. For example, drawing from the 'mission to build' impetus of EU external relations noted above, Marise acknowledges that structural principles 'in the internal context may be concerned primarily with the structure that it is the Union's mission to build: that is, its construction of an Area of Freedom, Security and Justice (AFSJ), of an internal market, of an economic and monetary union (EMU) (Article 3 TEU)'.[81]

Additionally, actions connected to external relations can have internal as well as external implications: for Marise, 'principles operating to structure EU external policy-making they have a specific function. This is both internal and external in effect. Internal in the sense of structuring internal processes (how decisions are made). External in the sense that the legal particularities of the EU as an international actor, eg joint participation of EU and Member States in mixed agreements, or the status of international law within the EU legal system, find their source in these principles'.[82] Using Brexit as an example again, the extent to which processes developed for external relations were applied to the negotiation of the Withdrawal Agreement between the EU and the UK, which took place while the latter was still a Member State, was striking as regards the extent to which things went beyond the basic pointers to *some* of those processes in Article 50 TEU itself.[83]

The internal and external domains of EU law have specific contexts that do not always enable such direct or even particularly useful translation or migration between them.[84] But reflecting more consciously across them can spark, nevertheless, more

[80] Cremona (n 2) 29.
[81] ibid 3.
[82] ibid 15–16.
[83] See generally Hillion (n 44).
[84] As discussed by L Azoulai, 'Structural Principles in EU Law: Internal and External' in Cremona (ed) (n 1) 39.

rounded understandings of how principles can have different dimensional functions yet be linked through overarching conditions and objectives. For example, appeals to coherence and unity are more familiar in EU external relations law but they have emerged in case law on the internal dimension of the constitution too: notably in *Melloni*, where the Court required that the 'primacy, *unity* and effectiveness of EU law' should not be 'compromised' in the multi-layered system of EU fundamental rights protection.[85] Unity is not the same thing as uniformity or uniform application of EU law: it enables recognition of context. As a principle, it is more developed in EU external relations, but it has untapped potential for managing some of the complexities of the Union's internal legal dimension.

In that light, as emphasised at the outset of this chapter, the fact that structural principles of EU law might in other ways behave differently in the internal and the external dimensions of EU law is not a point of disagreement with the thesis of *Structural Principles*. It is not, in other words, about challenging the demonstrable role within or value to EU external relations law that Marise narrated (based, fundamentally, on how she differentiated the nature of the framing Treaty provisions for internal and external Union policies respectively[86]). Rather, it is about asking in the first instance, as undertaken in Section 3 above, what happens when we translate the concept of structural principles to EU internal law. And it is about asking, in the second place, whether structural principles can, notwithstanding accepted internal/external differences, enable greater coherence in both EU legal spheres. It is about asking, for example, how 'the Union is called upon to construct itself, to build its actorness and agency'[87] in internal policy fields just as much as in external ones. It is about reflecting more deeply on where 'we see law being used, through structural principles, to construct the Union as an autonomous [internal] actor'.[88]

In the opening page of her Introduction to *Structural Principles*, Marise observed that '[t]he nature of the Treaty provisions on EU external action, with a set of open-ended policy objectives and fewer policy-directed legal obligations on the Member States, has left much to the agenda-setting of the political institutions'.[89] As noted in Section 3 above, this insight essentially provides the key as to why the role of law, and thus also of the structural principles of EU law, is less substantive and more processual in EU external relations law. Applying a slightly adjusted version of the same idea to the EU's internal legal sphere brings another insight: that with respect to the deep structure of the EU's constitution, the relative silence of the Treaty about many of the 'specific and essential characteristics' of EU law has left much of the 'agenda-setting' to the Court. Similarly, we can translate another of Marise's comments to the internal context: 'insofar as the EU has a mission to construct, it is to construct the EU itself as an effective external actor'[90] becomes 'insofar as the *Court* has a mission to construct, it is to construct the EU itself as an effective actor *both* internally and externally'.

[85] Case C-399/11 *Melloni* ECLI:EU:C:2013:107, para 60.
[86] Cremona (n 2) 6–7.
[87] ibid 11.
[88] ibid.
[89] ibid 3.
[90] ibid 17.

Thus, even if, to a large extent, the same principles – apply in both the internal and external dimensions of EU law, their impact tends to land in different constitutional and institutional places. What *Structural Principles* underlines in that light is that new dynamics in internal EU law are not so new in external EU law. That is why it was interesting to see the political institutions get more involved in substantive, *legal* agenda-setting in response to recent internal challenges. Returning to the Brexit example, the European Council and later the terms of the Withdrawal Agreement itself highlighted not only the autonomy of EU law but also the autonomy of EU decision-making generally.[91] How we scrutinise and assess a key actor such as the European Council in this new mode of internal 'agenda-setting' deserves attention. And how Marise conceived structural principles for EU external relations law provides the reasoning that we need this this internal development since they '[establish] a framework expressed in (or implied from) the Treaties, protecting an institutional space within which policy may be formed, in which the different actors understand and work *within their respective roles*'.[92]

Finally, Marise's work on structural principles also raises important questions about 'the extent to which the EU as an international actor is legally bounded'.[93] Disconnects between the internal and external development of the structural principles of EU law are pointedly evident in this respect. For example, the Court's ruling in the *Kadi* case provoked the criticism that it seriously underplayed the obligations of the Union itself and of the Member States as the bearers of sovereign responsibility in the wider world.[94] But these questions concern a tension that has to be resolved within rather than in contest with the Court's self-understanding of the EU legal order as one constructed through structural principles. That approach would not reject the critical – the binding – importance of international law.[95] But it does provide some explanation for choices that agitate towards closedness rather than openness to the influence of international law within the EU legal order. In that light, the EU as an international actor must also be assessed with reference to its specific and essential characteristics, which is something that Marise and I have now had the opportunity to start to examine together by showing how principles flow both inwards from EU external relations and outwards to international agreements – even structural principles such as mutual trust and solidarity.[96]

[91] European Council, 'Special Meeting of the European Council (Art.50) (29 April 2017) – Guidelines for Brexit Negotiations' (2017) EUCO XT 20004/17, para 1: '[t]he Union will preserve its autonomy as regards its decision-making as well as the role of the Court of Justice of the European Union'.

[92] Cremona (n 2) 12 (emphasis added).

[93] ibid 26.

[94] Joined Cases C-402/05 P and C-415/05 P *Kadi and Al Barakaat International Foundation v Council and Commission* ECLI:EU:C:2008:461, [2008] ECR I-6351, which includes the statement at para 316 that 'the review by the Court of the validity of any [Union] measure in the light of fundamental rights must be considered to be the expression, in a community based on the rule of law, of a constitutional guarantee stemming from the [TFEU] as an autonomous legal system which is not to be prejudiced by an international agreement'. See further, G de Búrca, 'The European Court of Justice and the International Legal Order After *Kadi*' (2010) 51 *Harvard International Law Journal* 1.

[95] eg Case C-104/16 P *Council v Front Polisari* ECLI:EU:2016:973; Case C-266/16 *Western Sahara Campaign UK* ECLI:EU:C:2018:118.

[96] M Cremona and N Nic Shuibhne, 'Integration, Membership and the EU Neighbourhood' (2022) 59 *Common Market Law Review* 155.

The paradox that we wanted to highlight and interrogate in that work was this: if the structural principles are so emblematic of the EU legal order and its autonomy – put another way, if the specific and essential characteristics are *so* specific and *so* essential to the EU legal order; and if Article 2 TEU's common values 'define the very identity of the European Union as a common legal order' – how can it be that, in certain circumstances, those legal characteristics and values can be applied in external contexts beyond membership of the Union? In our joint paper, we trace how conditionality migrated inwards from accession to membership, and how mutual trust was used to underline the special relationship that the EU enjoys with certain third countries. We therefore went beyond establishing mutual trust and conditionality as structural principles on their own terms and used them to articulate and assess the legal dimensions of Union membership and the Union's legal behaviour in its neighbourhood in more depth. We do not rule out the significance of international law, but we do try to understand the relevant developments through both outward- *and* inward-facing drivers.

We probably must admit that, like the Court, we ended up right back in the gravitational pull of the principle of autonomy. What I would emphasise here, though, is that we uncovered both synergies and contradictions by pooling our usually more discrete internal and external constitutional perspectives: and most importantly, that the structural principles of EU law provided the analytical bridge between them.

5. CONCLUSION

Marise Cremona's conception of structural principles of EU law gently challenges us to think harder about the defining components of the EU's constitution – of its primary law; its external and internal dimensions; and the relative interpretative power of the Court of Justice in evolving all of this, which manifests a very particular aspect of the power of law more generally. Marise's introduction to the *Structural Principles* volume will provoke different readers in different ways, and for much longer than the reading of it: qualities of a truly original and significant contribution.

Here, I have focused on *why* categorisation of principles is worthwhile, highlighting questions about hierarchy and extra-Treaty primary law; and on *how* using structural principles as a bridge can deliver something greater than the internal and external parts of the EU's constitution can deliver on their own terms. Fundamentally, structural principles expose the work that legal principles do within that constitution, collectively as much as individually; how and why certain principles have different functions when compared to others; and what all of this means for our deepening understanding of the EU legal order.

In writing this chapter, I was especially struck by the resonance of Marise's taxonomy and ideas from 2018 with the extraordinary surge of constitutional developments that have taken place already since then. I have used examples drawn from Brexit, rule of law conditionality, and the legal hardening of solidarity to show that structural principles continue to change and therefore continue to matter. These recent developments underline, in turn, that Marise managed to capture with uncanny prescience intimations of something that has become even more important meanwhile. *Structural Principles* therefore launched an agenda that is very much still in progress and under construction, in both an academic or conceptual sense and for constitutional evolution in real terms. *Structural Principles* was, and remains, profoundly relevant and profoundly inspiring. And I really cannot think of higher and more meaningful accolades for a piece of academic work.

The Autonomy of EU Law in External Relations: An Elusive Principle

PANOS KOUTRAKOS

1. INTRODUCTION

WHILE NOT NEW, the principle of autonomy of EU law has assumed considerable significance in the last few years in the context of the relationship between EU and international investment law, in particular regarding the adjudication by arbitral tribunals and the enforcement of arbitral awards by courts of the Member States. A somewhat limited body of case-law by the European Court of Justice has had profound implications for Member States and investors alike and has attracted attention from both policy-makers and legal scholars.[1]

The objective of this chapter is not to provide an exhaustive analysis of the principle and its implications. Instead, by focusing on the recent case-law, it will make a three-fold argument: autonomy has not been construed in an one-dimensional manner, as its scope and implications depend on the legal context of the dispute in question; in intra-EU disputes the Court interprets autonomy in an uncompromising manner whereas its approach is more pragmatic when it comes to the relationship between the EU and third countries; there is a whiff of maximalism in the Court's approach to autonomy in intra-EU disputes which has not been justified in legal terms and is unwarranted in practical terms.

The analysis is structured as follows. First, it will identify four main themes that underpin the genesis and development of the principle. Second, it will zoom in and reflect on recent judicial developments that shape the principle in the context of the relationship between investment arbitration and EU law. Third, it will zoom out and analyse the different approaches to autonomy on legal and practical grounds and will reflect on their pitfalls at the current stage of development of the EU legal order.

[1] From the voluminous literature, see J Klabbers and P Koutrakos (eds), 'An Anatomy of Autonomy: Special Issue' (2019) 88 *Nordic Journal of International Law* 1–133 and M De Boeck, *EU Law and International Investment Arbitration: The Compatibility of ISDS in Bilateral Investment Treaties (BITs) and the Energy Charter Treaty (ECT) with the Autonomy of EU Law*, Nijhoff Studies in European Union Law (Leiden, Brill Nijhoff, 2022) 21.

2. THE ORIGINS AND DEVELOPMENT OF AUTONOMY

The origins and development of the principle of autonomy may be charted through the prism of four themes.

The first theme is about its judicial origin: the principle of autonomy of EU law is the outcome of judicial creation. There is no reference to it in primary law. Instead, the principle emerged in the early constitutional case-law of the Court of Justice which stressed the fundamentally distinct character of the then new legal order. It was the conception of the latter as 'a new legal order of international law for the benefit of which the states have limited their sovereign rights'[2] that led to what appears now to be the unavoidable conclusion that, '[b]y contrast with ordinary international treaties, the EEC Treaty has created its own legal system which, on the entry into force of the Treaty, became an integral part of the legal systems of the Member States and which their courts are bound to apply'.[3]

It was this extraordinary character of the Community's founding document, the unique legal features of its rules and their normative implications for the Member States that became the foundations of the autonomy of the Community, and later the Union, legal system. As the Court put it in *Costa* itself, '… the law stemming from the Treaty, an independent source of law, could not, because of its special and original nature, be overridden by domestic legal provisions, however framed, without being deprived of its character as Community law and without the legal basis of the Community itself being called into question'.[4]

The second theme has to do with the internal and external dimensions of the principle. It was the above notion of the Union legal order as a new and distinct part of international law that gave rise to the process of constitutionalisation which led gradually and inexorably to the constitutional maturity and complexity of the current EU legal order.[5] In this early context, autonomy had an internal dimension: it was intended to bolster the normative features of the nascent legal system in order to enable it to withstand challenges from national law. It was for this reason that the unique features of EU law were relied upon in order to enable the Court of Justice to assume a constitutional function and introduce the principles which shape the relationship between the EU legal order and the Member States and which also determine the legal status of individuals. In addition to supremacy and direct effect,[6] these principles include the liability of national authorities for a violation of EU law,[7] the

[2] Case 26/62 *Van Gend en Loos v Administratie der Belastingen* ECLI:EU:C:1963:1, [1963] ECR 1.

[3] Case 6/64 *Costa v E.N.E.L.* ECLI:EU:C:1964:66, [1964] ECR 585.

[4] ibid.

[5] On the 'new' aspects of the EU legal order, see S Weatherill, 'From Myth to Reality: The EU's "New Legal Order" and the Place of General Principles Within It' in S Vogenauer and S Weatherill (eds), *General Principles of Law: European and Comparative Perspectives* (Oxford, Hart Publishing, 2017).

[6] See A Dashwood, 'From *Van Duyn* to *Mangold* via *Marshall*: Reducing Direct Effect to Absurdity?' (2007) 9 *CYELS* 81.

[7] See M Dougan, 'The Vicissitudes of Life at the Coalface: Remedies and Procedures for Enforcing Union Law before the National Courts' in G de Búrca and P Craig (eds), *The Evolution of EU Law*, 2nd edn (Oxford, Oxford University Press, 2011).

gradual transformation of national courts into EU courts,[8] and the reliance upon general principles and fundamental human rights as a matter of EU law against both EU and national measures.

Over the years, the internal function of autonomy has met its objectives: the above principles have been accepted and applied by domestic courts as a matter of course and the EU and domestic legal orders interact successfully on the basis of a pragmatic understanding of their relationship.[9] Since the 1990s, however, an external dimension of the principle of autonomy has emerged clearly and, at times, forcefully. This is now about protecting the distinct characteristics of the mature EU legal order from interferences that originate beyond the Union.

This aspect of autonomy first appeared in *Opinion 1/91* where the Court of Justice held that the European Economic Area Agreement constituted 'a threat … to the autonomy of the Community legal order':[10] it would impinge on the exclusive jurisdiction of the Court of Justice (provided now under Article 344 Treaty on the Functioning of the European Union (TFEU)) to rule on the division of competence, and hence, the responsibility between the then European Economic Community (EEC) and its Member States in relation to the issues covered by the Agreement, and would interfere with the binding jurisdiction of the Court in relation to EU law issues adopted after the entry into force of the Agreement.

The internal and external functions of autonomy are not easy to distinguish, either in conceptual or in policy terms. The EU's judges render their judgment with an eye to national courts and, for instance in the *Kadi* cases,[11] in full awareness of the potential role that national judges might be called upon to assume if judicial review in Luxembourg were viewed as deficient. It is recalled that the *Kadi I* judgment was handed down at a time of considerable disquiet amongst international lawyers and policy-makers about the design and functioning of the UN sanctions system. The compliance of the latter with fundamental human rights was widely contested, so much so that, following the *Kadi* cases, a gradual adjustment took place at the UN in order to make the process of the adoption of smart sanctions and its review more transparent and fair.[12] Had the Court of Justice not acknowledged the issues of the clearly problematic UN system for the protection of fundamental human rights, the courts of the Member States might have stepped in and, by protecting human rights under domestic constitutional law, challenged the legality of the relevant UN measures. However, by doing so, and given the initial deference shown to the latter by the

[8] See A Arnull, 'Judicial Dialogue in the European Union' in J Dickson and P Eleftheriadis (eds), *Philosophical Foundations of European Union Law* (Oxford, Oxford University Press, 2012).

[9] See G de Búrca, 'The Evolution of EU Human Rights Law' in de Búrca and Craig (eds) (n 7).

[10] Opinion 1/91 *Draft Agreement relating to the creation of the European Economic Area* ECLI:EU:C:1991:490, [1991] ECR I-6079, para 35.

[11] Joined Cases C-402/05 P and C-415/05 P *Kadi and Al Barakaat International Foundation v Council and Commission* ECLI:EU:C:2008:461, [2008] ECR I-6351.

[12] See D Hovell, *The Power of Process: The Value of Due Process in Security Council Sanctions Decision-Making* (Oxford, Oxford University Press, 2016) and G Sullivan, *The Law of the List: UN Counterterrorism Sanctions and the Politics of Global Security Law*, Global Law Series (Cambridge, Cambridge University Press, 2020).

Court of First Instance, as it then was, domestic courts would also have cast doubt on the authority of the CJEU, as the *Bundesverfassungsgericht* had done in the 1970s and early 1980s following the *Solange I* judgment.[13]

Viewed from this angle, by protecting the EU legal order against international rules that threatened the Union's system of human rights protection, the Court put the protection of fundamental human rights at the very centre of the EU legal order (they were viewed as principles which 'form part of the very foundations of the Community legal order', a formulation repeated three times in the *Kadi I* judgment).[14] In doing so, it avoided yet another battleground where recalcitrant domestic courts which might take it upon themselves to protect domestic human rights law and, therefore, challenge the supremacy of EU law. In the multi-layered constitutional order of the EU, the intrinsic linkages between the internal and external function of autonomy condition the construction of the principle by the Court of Justice.

The third theme is about what underpins the principle: autonomy is about power. Over the years, the interpretation of the principle of autonomy has acquired a strong self-referential dimension – de Witte describes it as 'a subtext of selfishness'.[15] Whilst it accepts, in principle, that a treaty setting up a judicial body with jurisdiction binding on the institutions of the parties, including the EU's judiciary, may be compatible with the EU's primary rules,[16] the Court of Justice has been less than enthusiastic in its approach to such arrangements in practice. In *Mox Plant*, the initiation of a dispute between two EU Member States before an arbitral tribunal set up under the 1982 United Nations Convention on the Law of Sea (UNCLOS) was deemed to 'involve a manifest risk that the jurisdictional order laid down in the treaties and, consequently, the autonomy of the Community legal system may be adversely affected'.[17] In *Opinion 1/09*, the establishment of a European and Community Patents Court was viewed as contrary to the right of national courts to refer questions about EU patent law to the Court of Justice.[18] Most controversially, the Court held in *Opinion 2/13* that the draft agreement on the Union's accession to the European Convention of Human Rights (ECHR), negotiated between 2010 and 2013, was incompatible with the Union's primary law.[19]

Finally, the fourth theme is about the scope of the principle: there is considerable ambiguity, if not vagueness, inherent in what autonomy is actually about. In *Opinion 1/00*, for instance, the Court held that compliance with the principle would entail that 'the essential character of the powers of the Community and its institutions as

[13] BverfG 2 BvL 52/71 *Beschluß des Zweiten Senats vom 29. Mai 1974*, BVerfGE 37, 271.

[14] Joined Cases C-402/05 P and C-415/05 P *Kadi and Al Barakaat International Foundation v Council and Commission* ECLI:EU:C:2008:461, [2008] ECR I-6351, paras 282, 290, and 304.

[15] B de Witte, 'A Selfish Court: The Court of Justice and the Design of International Dispute Settlement Beyond the EU' in M Cremona and A Thies (eds), *The European Court of Justice and External Relations Law: Constitutional Challenges*, Modern Studies in European Law (Oxford, Hart Publishing, 2014) 39.

[16] Opinion 1/91 *Draft Agreement relating to the creation of the European Economic Area* ECLI:EU:C:1991:490, [1991] ECR I-6079, paras 39–40.

[17] Case C-459/03 *Commission v Ireland* ECLI:EU:C:2006:345, [2006] ECR I-4635, para 154.

[18] Opinion 1/09 *Creation of a Unified Patent Litigation System* ECLI:EU:C:2011:123, [2011] ECR I-1137.

[19] Opinion 2/13 *Accession of the Union to the ECHR* ECLI:EU:C:2014:2454.

conceived in the Treaty remain unaltered'.[20] This statement is open-ended and, given the judicial origins of the principle it purports to define, may only mean what the Court tells us it means on the basis of concrete cases about the compatibility with EU law of specific international treaties.

This theme of ambiguity is underlined by the *Achmea* judgment,[21] the line of reasoning of which is lacking in clarity. Whilst, for instance, the Court considers the violation of autonomy to be based on the violation of Articles 267 about the preliminary reference procedure and 344 TFEU,[22] the latter is not analysed in the judgment. Instead, autonomy is viewed through the lens of safeguarding the rights of domestic courts. This may be because Article 344 TFEU does not substantiate the broad reading of autonomy put forward in the judgment. After all, this provision refers to Member States only, and, therefore, does not cover actions brought by individuals.[23] This lack of clarity is compounded by the high level of abstraction in which the language of the judgment is couched. This makes it difficult to gauge the precise content of the principle of autonomy and its implications for the Union's broader investment policy. The abstract language of the judgment is all the more striking given the distinctly literal interpretation that characterises the recent case-law in other strands of EU external relations, such as treaty-making under Article 218 TFEU.[24] As such, it may whet the appetite for a wide construction of autonomy.

On the other hand, there are also elements in the judgment that may suggest a narrower understanding of what autonomy is about, confining the judgment to the specific context of the case.[25] After all, this was not just about any Bilateral Investment Treaty between Member States (intra-EU BIT), but one whose jurisdiction clause in relation to the arbitration tribunal established thereunder was unusually broad in its scope. It is in this context that the reference to the principle of mutual trust must be understood,[26] a point clarified in the later *Opinion 1/17*.[27]

The ambiguity that underpins the articulation of autonomy is not confined to the case-law on investment arbitration. A case in point is the judgment in *Mox Plant*[28] which has attracted considerable criticism, especially by international lawyers.[29]

[20] Opinion 1/00 *Agreement on the establishment of a European Common Aviation Area* ECLI:EU:C:2002:231, [2002] ECR I-3493, para 12.

[21] Case C-284/16 *Achmea* ECLI:EU:C:2018:158.

[22] Art 344 TFEU reads as follows: 'Member States undertake not to submit a dispute concerning the interpretation or application of the Treaties to any method of settlement other than those provided for therein'.

[23] This point was also made by the referring court (Case C-284/16 *Achmea* ECLI:EU:C:2018:158, paras 15–17), as well as Advocate General Wathelet (Opinion of Advocate General Wathelet in Case C-284/16 *Achmea* ECLI:EU:C:2017:699, paras 138–159).

[24] This theme is developed in P Koutrakos, 'Institutional Balance and Sincere Cooperation in Treaty-Making under EU Law' (2019) 68 *ICLQ* 1.

[25] See, for instance, A Dashwood, 'Article 26 ECT and Intra-EU Disputes – The Case against an Expansive Reading of Achmea' (2021) 46 *EL Rev* 415.

[26] Case C-284/16 *Achmea* ECLI:EU:C:2018:158, para 58.

[27] Opinion 1/17 *CETA* ECLI:EU:C:2019:341, paras 126–129.

[28] Case C-459/03 *Commission v Ireland* ECLI:EU:C:2006:345, [2006] ECR I-4635.

[29] Koskenniemi considered the judgment 'stunning' and 'squarely on the oldest, and most conservative trajectory of European thinking about the role of international law and its relations with national law': M Koskenniemi, 'International Law: Constitutionalism, Managerialism and the Ethos of Legal Education' (2007) 1 *European Journal of Legal Studies* 8.

Again, one would have to go past the unnecessarily convoluted reasoning of the judgment in order to consider its eminently sensible conclusion in the light of the specific legal and factual context of the case: given that the United Nations Convention on the Law of the Sea enabled its parties that were EU Member States to settle an UNCLOS dispute by having recourse to EU enforcement procedures,[30] the request by an EU Member State that the UNCLOS Arbitral Tribunal interpret and apply EU law would challenge the exclusive jurisdiction of the Court of Justice and, ultimately, the autonomy of the EU legal order. As the case pertained to the interpretation of Article 344 TFEU, the concept of autonomy underpinning the judgment in *Mox Plant* is not as broad as it might appear.[31]

What follows from the above is a rather narrow, Court-centred approach to the definition and implications of autonomy. A striking illustration of this theme was provided in *Opinion 2/13*: whilst ostensibly about the protection of human rights and the implementation of Article 6(2) TEU which requires that the Union accede to ECHR, the line of reasoning underpinning the Opinion had nothing to do in fact with the protection of fundamental human rights.[32] It was, instead, about the institutional and procedural arrangements negotiated carefully – and not without some input from the Court of Justice itself – in order to ensure that the interpretation of EU law would be a matter left for the Court of Justice. This approach led to the co-operation with the European Court of Human Rights (ECtHR) being treated suspiciously, even though the relationship between the two courts had been deeply symbiotic.[33]

It has not, however, always been thus. The earlier case-law provided some indications that the application of the principle was not all about enhancing the powers of the Court of Justice. In *Opinion 1/00*, for instance, it was pointed out that, in accordance with autonomy, 'the procedures for ensuring uniform interpretation of the rules of the [envisaged] Agreement and for resolving disputes will not have the effect of binding the Community and its institutions, in the exercise of their internal powers, to a particular interpretation of the rules of Community law referred to in that agreement …'.[34] This illustrates a rather restrained understanding of what autonomy would mean for the Union's judiciary: it is about whether international judicial bodies would be endowed with the power to interpret and apply EU rules in a manner that would be binding on the EU's institutions. This definition also includes domestic courts, in so far as they act as EU courts,[35] a point to which this analysis will return below.

[30] Art 282 United Nations Convention on the Law of the Sea (Montego Bay, 10 December 1982) (UNCLOS).

[31] See P Koutrakos, *EU International Relations Law*, 2nd edn (Oxford, Hart Publishing, 2015) 184–191.

[32] See, amongst others, B de Witte, 'The Relative Autonomy of the European Union's Fundamental Rights Regime' (2019) 88 *Nordic Journal of International Law* 65.

[33] See, for instance, M Cartabia and S Ninatti, 'Fundamental rights in the European Court of Justice and the European Court of Human Rights' in S Douglas-Scott and N Hatzis (eds), *Research Handbook on EU Law and Human Rights* (Cheltenham, Edward Elgar Publishing, 2017); S Greer, JH Gerards and R Slowe, *Human rights in the Council of Europe and the European Union: Achievements, Trends and Challenges*, Cambridge Studies in European Law and Policy (Cambridge, Cambridge University Press, 2018), in particular chs 4 and 5.

[34] Opinion 1/00 *Agreement on the establishment of a European Common Aviation Area* ECLI:EU:C:2002:231, [2002] ECR I-3493, para 13.

[35] Under Art 19(1) second subparagraph Consolidated version of the Treaty on European Union (TEU) [2016] OJ C202/13, 'Member States shall provide remedies sufficient to ensure effective legal protection in the fields covered by Union law'.

It follows from the above that not only is the scope of autonomy somewhat nebulous and its limits ill-defined, but its functions have also been intrinsically linked to furthering the powers of the Court of Justice. In other words, autonomy is, really, about power – what this power would cover, however, which actor would be endowed with it, and under which conditions is a matter left entirely for the Court of Justice to determine.

3. TWO DIMENSIONS OF AUTONOMY

Autonomy has not been construed in a one-dimensional manner. Instead, the scope and implications of the principle depend on the legal context within which a specific dispute arises.

3.1. Autonomy in Intra-EU Relations: A Most Orthodox Approach

As mentioned above, the judgment in *Achmea* provided ammunition for an expanding reading of the implications of autonomy in the context of intra-EU BITs while not without ruling out entirely a context-specific construction of the scope of the principle. This point is confirmed in Case C-109/20 *PL Holdings*.[36]

This reference from the Swedish Supreme Court arose from a dispute between a Luxembourg company (PL Holdings) and Poland due to the fact that the former was forced by the Polish Financial Supervision Authority to sell its shares in a Polish bank. PL Holdings initiated arbitration proceedings against Poland under Article 9 of the 1987 BIT between Belgium/Luxembourg and Poland. In proceedings for the annulment of the arbitral award, the Svea Court of Appeal had held that the arbitration clause of the intra-EU BIT was invalid in the light of the ECJ judgment in *Achmea*. However, it also held that a Member State and an investor from another Member State could still conclude an *ad hoc* arbitration agreement in respect of the same dispute, based on their common intention, as in a commercial arbitration. In fact, such an agreement had emerged in that case, as Poland had participated in the proceedings without entering a formal jurisdiction objection in accordance with domestic law. This was the question referred, on appeal, by the Supreme Court: in proceedings under an intra-EU BIT presumed to be invalid in the light of *Achmea*, may a Member State enter into an *ad hoc* agreement with an investor from another Member State by not objecting to the arbitration clause in due time?

The Grand Chamber held that the principle of autonomy may not be circumvented under those circumstances: domestic law may not enable a Member State, party to a dispute under an intra-EU BIT, to submit that dispute to an arbitral body with the same characteristics as that envisaged under the BIT by concluding an *ad hoc* arbitration agreement identical to that deemed illegal in the light of *Achmea*.

[36] Case C-109/20 *PL Holdings* ECLI:EU:C:2021:875.

This conclusion followed from the same principles that had been relied upon in *Achmea:* to remove a dispute that may pertain to the application and interpretation of EU law from the jurisdiction of domestic courts would deprive that law of the full effectiveness that the EU legal system may guarantee. Such an outcome would be contrary to the principle of mutual trust between the Member States, the preliminary reference procedure (Article 267 TFEU), the principle of sincere cooperation (Article 4(3) Treaty on the European Union (TEU)), and the autonomy of EU law (Article 344 TFEU). In effect, the parties to the dispute may not be allowed to remedy the invalidity of the arbitration clause in an intra-EU BIT by means of a contract with an investor from another Member State. In fact, the primacy of EU law and the duty of sincere cooperation require that Member States challenge the validity of the arbitration clause or the *ad hoc* arbitration agreement in any arbitration body before which a dispute is brought.

This judgment does not only confirm but also buttresses the significance of the *Achmea* principle so that it may not be circumvented by means of domestic law. It articulates clearly and in forceful terms both the duty of Member States to challenge the validity of an arbitration clause in an intra-EU BIT before any arbitration tribunal or domestic court,[37] and that of domestic courts of Member States to set aside an arbitration award made on the basis of an arbitration agreement that would violate the *Achmea* principle.[38]

On the one hand, it is worth noting the narrow legal context of the case: at the core of the preliminary reference was a domestic procedural device (not objecting to the arbitration clause in due time could be seen as entering into an *ad hoc* agreement with an investor from another Member State) that would be difficult to be seen as anything other than a means to bypass the *Achmea* principle and enable the Member State and the investor from another Member State to usurp, for all intents and purposes, jurisdiction from a domestic tribunal and confer it on an arbitral tribunal. Viewed from this angle, the judgment in *PL Holdings* is about the specific application of the *Achmea* principle in a narrow set of circumstances and it should come as no surprise that the Court refused to limit the temporal effects of its judgment.[39]

On the other hand, there are indications of a broader construction of what the *Achmea* principle is about: the duty of the Member States is attributed not just to the *Achmea* judgment but the principles of the primacy of EU law and of sincere cooperation.[40] It is noteworthy that the principle of primacy does not feature in the *Achmea* judgment itself expressly other than once and only in the context of a direct reference to *Opinion 2/13*.[41] The judgment also relies (twice)[42] on the Agreement on the Termination of intra-EU BITs that 23 EU Member States signed in 2020 and states that, from the date of the accession of the above States, the arbitration clauses of

[37] ibid paras 52 and 55.
[38] ibid para 55.
[39] ibid paras 58–69.
[40] ibid para 52.
[41] Case C-284/16 *Achmea* ECLI:EU:C:2018:158, para 33 with reference to paras 165–167.
[42] Case C-109/20 *PL Holdings* ECLI:EU:C:2021:875, para 46 of the judgment with reference to Article 4(1) of the Agreement and para 53 of the judgment with reference to Article 7(b) of the Agreement.

the BITs referred to therein could not serve as the basis for arbitration proceedings between an investor and those Member States.[43] This is noteworthy, given the distinct reluctance of arbitral tribunals to endorse the *Achmea* principle.[44] It is also worth-noting that, in her Opinion in *PL Holdings*, Advocate General Kokott had argued for a wide application of *Achmea* (the judgment itself does not refer to her Opinion in relation to this issue).[45] However, the terms in which the judgment is couched are remarkably broad, suggesting that *Achmea* would apply to any intra-EU BIT, irrespective of whether its arbitration clause referred to domestic law or not (that was the conclusion reached by the Paris Court of Appeal in *Slot Group v POL*).[46] This was confirmed in Case C-638/19 P *Commission v European Foods* where prior case-law on autonomy was set out in similarly broad terms.[47]

A subsequent Grand Chamber judgment confirmed this broad construction of autonomy. In fact, the judgment in Case C-741/19 *Komstroy* (which predated the one in *PL Holdings* by a few weeks)[48] marked a distinct expansion of the *Achmea* principle.

The facts of this reference from the *Cour d'appel de Paris* were convoluted. For the purposes of this chapter, suffice it to say that they involved a Ukrainian company claiming to be an investor in Moldova which brought an action against Moldova under Article 26(4)(b) Energy Charter Treaty (ECT) for what it considered to be serious breaches of undertakings made under the Charter. The case was brought before the referring court on appeal against the decision of the lower court to annul a 2013 arbitral award on the ground that the arbitral tribunal had been wrong to declare that it had had jurisdiction. The questions referred were entirely about the definition of the term 'investment' under Articles 1(6) and 26(1) ECT. While the answers to them are not relevant to this chapter, another point in the judgment is: the Court held that a dispute between a Member State and in investor of another Member State concerning an investment made by the latter in the first Member State may not be subject to arbitration proceedings under Article 26(2)(c) ECT. Given the significance of the judgment, the remaining section will analyse the following three questions: how did the Court justify its jurisdiction in this case, how did it explain its choice to answer a question that had not been asked, and how did it answer that question.

On the first question, the Court established its jurisdiction by reference to the conclusion of the ECT by the EU, the latter having competence in the area of foreign investment (exclusive as regards direct and shared as regards indirect investment). It also held that the dispute was in fact, governed by EU law: on the one hand, it is possible that the relevant ECT provisions containing the term 'investment' would be applied in an EU context (for instance in an action concerning a dispute between a third country investor and a Member State) in which case it was necessary 'to forestall

[43] Agreement for the termination of Bilateral Investment Treaties between the Member States of the European Union [2020] OJ L169/1.

[44] For an exception to this trend, see *Green Power K/S and Obton A/S v Spain* SCC Case No V 2016/135.

[45] Opinion of Advocate General Kokott in Case C-109/20 *PL Holdings* ECLI:EU:C:2021:321, paras 61–63.

[46] *Slot Group as v Republic of Poland* PCA Case No 2017-10, Judgment of the Paris Court of Appeal dated 19 April 2022.

[47] Case C-638/19 P *Commission v European Foods and Others* ECLI:EU:C:2022:50, paras 138–139.

[48] Case C-741/19 *Republic of Moldova v Komstroy LLC* ECLI:EU:C:2021:655.

future differences of interpretation';[49] on the other hand, the seat of the arbitral tribunal had been chosen by the parties to be on the territory of a Member State whose courts are under a duty to comply with EU law under Article 19 TEU,[50] while the Court itself is required to respond to the questions referred, given the principle of cooperation that governs the preliminary reference procedure.[51]

Second, the Court justified its reference to the applicability of Article 26 ECT to intra-EU disputes by pointing out that, in order to answer the question about the definition of investment under the ECT, it was 'necessary … to specify which disputes between one Contracting Party and an investor of another Contracting Party concerning an investment made by the latter in the area of the former may be brought before an arbitral tribunal pursuant to Article 26 ECT'.[52]

The approach to both the above issues is problematic. As far as the Court's jurisdiction is concerned, the judgment goes farther than previous case-law upon which it relies regarding the significance of uniform interpretation. For instance, the judgments in Case C-53/96 *Hermès*[53] and Joined Cases C-300/98 and C-392/98 *Dior and Others*[54] were about provisions of the Agreement on Trade-Related Aspects of Intellectual Property Rights (TRIPS) which, while applied to domestic intellectual property law, were also applicable to intellectual property governed by EU secondary legislation. On the other hand, the judgment in Case C-130/95 *Giloy*[55] was about domestic tax legislation reproducing a provision from the Community Customs Code. Both these contexts differed considerably from that in *Komstroy* where there was no specific EU substantive hook in which the interpretation of the relevant ECT provisions could be hang. As for the reference to the set of arbitration on the territory of a Member State, it by no means follows from the involvement of domestic courts and their duties under Article 19 TEU that all disputes brought before them would be subject to EU law. The relevant part of the judgment is as obscure in its assumptions as it is broad-brush about its implications. In any case, given the tight control that it exercises over the preliminary reference procedure and the remarkable flexibility it is prepared to exercise over how it responds to references from domestic courts, depending on the circumstances, the Court's reliance on its duty under Article 267 TFEU is disingenuous at best.

This point may also apply to the statement that to rule on which parties may rely on Article 26 ECT was 'necessary' in order to answer the substantive questions about investment. In Dashwood's pithy words, this 'is simply untrue'.[56] Let us not lose sight

[49] ibid para 29 and also para 31.

[50] ibid para 34.

[51] ibid para 35.

[52] ibid para 40.

[53] Case C-53/96 *Hermès International v FHT Marketing Choice* ECLI:EU:C:1998:292, [1998] ECR I-3603.

[54] Joined Cases C-300/98 and C-392/98 *Dior and Others* ECLI:EU:C:2000:688, [2000] ECR I-11307. See also J Heliskoski, 'The Jurisdiction of the European Court of Justice to Give Preliminary Rulings on the Interpretation of Mixed Agreements' (2000) 69 *Nordic Journal of International Law* 395, 404 et seq.

[55] Case C-130/95 *Giloy v Hauptzollamt Frankfurt am Main-Ost* ECLI:EU:C:1997:372, [1997] ECR I-4291.

[56] A Dashwood, '*Republic of Moldova v Komstroy LCC:* Arbitration under Article 26 ECT Outlawed in Intra-EU Disputes by Obiter Dictum' (2022) 47 *EL Rev* 127, 131. Commenting on the choice of addressing the Article 26 intra-EU arbitration issue, he writes the 'purported justifications offered by the Court of Justice are so threadbare as to appear almost contemptuous' (ibid).

of the context: in a dispute between an operator from a third country (Ukraine) and another third country (Moldova), the Court changed the question actually referred in order to answer another question, namely 'whether a dispute between a Member State and in investor of another Member State concerning an investment made by the latter in the first Member State may be subject to arbitration proceedings under Article 26(2)(c) ECT'.[57]

Finally, the negative answer that the Court gave to the above question was based firmly on a broad reading of the principle of autonomy as articulated in *Achmea*. In five paragraphs, the judgment construes autonomy by bringing together the legal elements that, over the years, have emerged as intrinsically linked to autonomy: Article 344 TFEU about the allocation of powers laid down in the Treaties and which may not be affected by an international agreement;[58] the autonomy of EU law in respect both to domestic law of EU Member States and international law and to the essential characteristics of EU law and the ensuing mutually interdependent legal relations between the EU and its Member States;[59] the EU constitutional framework and the judicial system that is necessary to ensure that the EU's specific characteristics and its autonomy are preserved and which is 'intended to ensure consistency and uniformity in the interpretation of EU law', mainly through the role of domestic courts and the ECJ under Article 19 TEU and the preliminary reference procedure[60] and the dialogue established under the latter, with the objective 'of securing the uniform interpretation for EU law, thereby ensuring its consistency, its full effect and its autonomy as well as, ultimately, the particular nature of the law established by the Treaties'.[61]

In this construction of autonomy, a couple of things are worth-noting. While the main authority on which the Court relies is the judgment in *Achmea*, it is also *Opinion 1/17 (CETA)* that we find referred to in the judgment, their different legal contexts notwithstanding. This is striking, given that, in the latter, handed down more than a year after the former, there is only one reference to *Achmea* in which the Court distinguishes between the legal contexts that gave rise to the two rulings (namely an intra-EU investment agreement and an agreement governing investment between the EU and a third country).[62] By relying on both authorities in this manner, the judgment in *Komstroy* appears to lay down deeper roots for the principle. It is also interesting that there should be no reference in *Komstroy* to the principle of mutual trust[63] which had been central to the line of reasoning in *Achmea*.[64]

[57] Case C-741/19 *Republic of Moldova v Komstroy LLC* ECLI:EU:C:2021:655, para 47.

[58] ibid para 42 with reference to Case C-284/16 *Achmea* ECLI:EU:C:2018:158, para 32.

[59] Case C-741/19 *Republic of Moldova v Komstroy LLC* ECLI:EU:C:2021:655, para 43 with reference to Case C-284/16 *Achmea* ECLI:EU:C:2018:158, para 33 and Opinion 1/17 *CETA* ECLI:EU:C:2019:341 para 109.

[60] Case C-741/19 *Republic of Moldova v Komstroy LLC* ECLI:EU:C:2021:655, para 45 with reference to Case C-284/16 *Achmea* ECLI:EU:C:2018:158, paras 35–36 and Opinion 1/17 *CETA* ECLI:EU:C:2019:341 para 111.

[61] Case C-741/19 *Republic of Moldova v Komstroy LLC* ECLI:EU:C:2021:655, para 46 with reference to Case C-284/16 *Achmea* ECLI:EU:C:2018:158, para 37.

[62] Opinion 1/17 *CETA* ECLI:EU:C:2019:341, paras 126–127.

[63] This is a point that Dashwood makes in Dashwood, '*Republic of Moldova v Komstroy LCC*' at 132.

[64] Case C-284/16 *Achmea* ECLI:EU:C:2018:158, paras 34 and 58.

Having articulated the foundations and implications of autonomy, the Court went on to apply the principle to arbitration proceedings brought by an investor from a Member State against another Member State. It held that such proceedings are incompatible with the principle on three interlinked grounds: an arbitral tribunal may be 'required to interpret, or even apply, EU law' (as its jurisdiction under Article 26(6) ECT covers the ECT and the latter is an act of the EU);[65] an arbitral tribunal may not refer questions about EU law to the Court of Justice (as it is not a court or tribunal of an EU Member State under Article 267 TFEU); arbitral awards under Article 26(8) ECT are final and binding on the parties to the dispute and any review that a court of a Member State where the seat of the arbitral tribunal is established under the arbitration rules governing the dispute can only be carried in so far as the domestic law of the Member State so permits (the French Code of Civil Procedure provision, for instance, only provides for limited review concerning, in particular, the jurisdiction of the arbitral tribunal).

Where does this take us? The features of the judgment identified so far, namely the eagerness to answer a question that was not asked and was not relevant to the dispute in the main proceedings, the reliance on authorities their different legal contexts notwithstanding, and the broad language in which the judgment is couched, all point towards the same direction: autonomy is construed broadly and does not tolerate the involvement of adjudication bodies other than the CJEU and domestic courts in cases where there is any risk of deviation from EU law in the context of either an intra-EU BIT or a treaty such as the ECT.[66] The ECtHR[67] is also to be added to this list, as may be any tribunal that does not meet the exacting drafting standards set by CETA.[68]

In the light of the above, there is a degree of maximalism in the *Komstroy* line of reasoning which, along with the broad-brush approach one has come to expect from the Court in this context, does not make autonomy any less ambiguous. For instance, why is the notion of an arbitral tribunal interpreting EU law outside the judicial system of the EU legal order so objectionable? Are there grounds of concerns about arbitral tribunals showing complete disregard for what EU law means? In his criticism of the judgment in *Komstroy*, Dashwood argues that '[t]o put it, perhaps overpolitely, the idea that the interpretation and application of the ECT itself by an ECT tribunal, even in an intra-EU dispute, would be capable of compromising the autonomy and the particular nature of EU law in any real sense strains credulity'.[69] And to what extent does the quest for 'the full effectiveness'[70] of EU law cease to be a commendable constitutional imperative and becomes a cloak to disguise an absolutist claim to authority?

[65] Case C-741/19 *Republic of Moldova v Komstroy LLC* ECLI:EU:C:2021:655, para 50.

[66] In *Komstroy*, the multilateral nature of ECT is deemed irrelevant: Article 26 ECT 'is intended, in reality, to govern bilateral relations between two of the Contracting Parties, in an analogous way' to the BIT that gave rise to *Achmea* (Case C-741/19 *Republic of Moldova v Komstroy LLC* ECLI:EU:C:2021:655, para 64). For criticism of this position, see Dashwood (n 56) above at 137–138.

[67] See Opinion 2/13 *Accession of the Union to the ECHR* ECLI:EU:C:2014:2454.

[68] Opinion 1/17 *CETA* ECLI:EU:C:2019:341.

[69] A Dashwood, '*Komstroy* and Opinion 1/20 – Curious and Curiouser' (2022) 59 *CML Rev* 51, 55.

[70] Case C-741/19 *Republic of Moldova v Komstroy LLC* ECLI:EU:C:2021:655, para 62.

3.2. Autonomy in Extra-EU Relations: A More Pragmatic Approach

In the context of a bilateral mixed agreement between the EU and its Member States and a third country, the Court of Justice applied a more pragmatic understanding of autonomy. The pragmatism that is illustrated in *Opinion 1/17* on the compatibility of the Investor-State Dispute Settlement mechanism established under the Comprehensive Economic and Trade Agreement (CETA) between the EU, its Member States and Canada may be approached from three different perspectives, namely principled, policy, and procedural.

First, principled pragmatism is about openness to the role of other international tribunals. The oft-repeated[71] but rarely followed principle that an agreement concluded by the EU may confer jurisdiction to interpret its provisions on a new court whose decisions may be binding on the EU is followed through: the Court opines that the jurisdiction of the EU and domestic courts to interpret international agreements concluded by the EU does not take precedence over either the jurisdiction of the courts of the Union's interlocutors or that of the international courts established under such agreements.[72] It is in this context that reference is made to the 'reciprocal nature of international agreements'.[73] This emphasis on the role of non-EU courts is also apparent in other parts of the Opinion, where it is considered 'consistent' with the nature of the CETA Tribunal beyond the EU legal system that there should be no mechanism for its interactions with the Court of Justice[74] or for review of its decisions by the latter.[75]

Second, there is policy pragmatism in *Opinion 1/17* that is illustrated by the firm acknowledgment of the powers of the Union's institutions. In recognising the powers of other, non-EU, courts to interpret agreements concluded by the EU, the Court refers expressly to 'the need to maintain the powers of the Union in international relations'.[76] This point of emphasis is noteworthy, especially given the ongoing effort of the EU to reform the traditional Investor-State Dispute Settlement System and replace it, ultimately, with a Multilateral Investment Court.[77] In light of the ongoing negotiations under the auspices of the United Nations Commission on International Trade Law (UNCITRAL),[78] the reference in the Opinion to 'the need to maintain the powers of the Union in international relations' is a reminder of the intense policy

[71] Opinion 1/91 *Draft Agreement relating to the creation of the European Economic Area* ECLI:EU:C:1991:490, [1991] ECR I-6079, paras 40 and 70; Opinion 1/09 *Creation of a Unified Patent Litigation System* ECLI:EU:C:2011:123, [2011] ECR I-1137, paras 74 and 76; Opinion 2/13 *Accession of the Union to the ECHR* ECLI:EU:C:2014:2454, paras 182–183.

[72] Opinion 1/17 *CETA* ECLI:EU:C:2019:341, para 116.

[73] ibid para 117.

[74] ibid para 134.

[75] ibid para 135.

[76] ibid para 117.

[77] See 'Concept Paper "Investment in TTIP and beyond – the path for reform Enhancing the right to regulate and moving from current ad hoc arbitration towards an Investment Court"' (*European Commission*, 5 May 2015), available at circabc.europa.eu/ui/group/7fc51410-46a1-4871-8979-20cce8df0896/library/84f1ee41-1c66-4bd2-adda-47f074336110/details.

[78] The negotiating directives are set out here: Council of the European Union, 'Negotiating directives for a Convention establishing a multilateral court for the settlement of investment disputes' (2018) 12981/17 ADD 1 DCL 1.

context within which the CETA Opinion was rendered: it would have been a truly brave choice for the Union's judiciary to make the Union's executive and legislature unravel their policy on this matter.

Third, there is also procedural pragmatism in *Opinion 1/17*. This is about the Court's approach to the procedural constraints that are imposed on the jurisdiction of the non-EU tribunal under the treaty concluded by the EU. The Court held that the principle of autonomy was complied with, as the jurisdiction of the CETA Tribunal would be confined to the provisions of CETA itself[79] and would be exercised in accordance not with EU law but with international law applicable to the parties. Viewed against the prior case-law on autonomy, the jurisdiction of the CETA Tribunal would be narrow: it would not extend to the interpretation and application of EU law, as had been the case in *Opinion 1/09*;[80] it would not trigger the principle of mutual trust, given that it would not pertain to relations between Member States, as had been the case in *Achmea*;[81] and it would not extend to the determination of responsibility as between the EU and/or a Member State in actions brought before the Tribunal,[82] hence meeting the requirement set out in *Opinion 2/13*.[83] This kind of procedural pragmatism needs to be viewed against the various provisions of the CETA Agreement which are emphatic in their objective to define the jurisdiction of the CETA Tribunal as narrowly as possible. In particular, these provisions read as if the drafters of CETA took utmost care to avoid any inferences that EU law, rather than CETA itself, would be interpreted in a binding manner by the CETA Tribunal. They were, therefore, in striking contrast to the broad scope of the jurisdiction clause in Article 8(6) of the Netherlands-Slovakia BIT in *Achmea*.

However, in addition to the narrow CETA context, there is another layer that emerges from a careful reading of *Opinion 1/17*. Pragmatism is not merely a question of treaty guarantees. There is also a leap of faith that characterises the Court's approach and that is absent in previous (and subsequent) case-law. A case in point is the approach to the power of the CETA Tribunal 'to consider … the domestic law of the disputing party as a matter of fact' under Article 8.31.2 CETA. This provision was viewed as consistent with the powers of the EU Courts, as it would not give rise to an interpretation of EU law by the Tribunal: whilst the examination by the latter 'may, on occasion, require that the domestic law of the respondent Party be taken into account', 'that examination cannot be classified as equivalent to an interpretation, by the CETA Tribunal, of that domestic law', as it would only be as a matter of fact in cases where the Tribunal would be bound to follow the interpretation of EU law given by the EU authorities, whilst, in any case, the latter would not be bound by the Tribunal's own interpretation.[84] This approach differs from the formalist scepticism

[79] Art 8.31 Comprehensive Economic and Trade Agreement (CETA) between Canada, of the one part, and the European Union and its Member States, of the other part [2017] OJ L11/23.
[80] Opinion 1/09 *Creation of a Unified Patent Litigation System* ECLI:EU:C:2011:123, [2011] ECR I-1137. The point was made in Opinion 1/17 *CETA* ECLI:EU:C:2019:341, in paras 123–125, as well as in para 133 regarding the Appellate Tribunal.
[81] Opinion 1/17 *CETA* ECLI:EU:C:2019:341, paras 126–129.
[82] Art. 8.21 CETA.
[83] Opinion 1/17 *CETA* ECLI:EU:C:2019:341, para 132.
[84] ibid para 131.

that permeated prior case-law. In *Opinion 2/13*, for instance, the Court had objected to the co-respondent mechanism because it would only be granted an opportunity to rule subject to an assessment by the ECtHR that there had been no CJEU case-law on the matter. This somewhat innocuous provision had been viewed by the Court of Justice as tantamount to conferring on the Strasbourg Court jurisdiction to interpret the CJEU's case-law.[85] Similar considerations apply to subsequent case-law too: in the context examined in *Komstroy*, the approach to EU law by arbitral tribunal under Article 26 ECT would not bind any EU authorities (in fact, it would only be binding in the context of the specific dispute).[86]

4. MAXIMALISM VERSUS PRAGMATISM

The above analysis of the post-*Achmea* case-law suggests that the Court's approach has not been one-dimensional: in intra-EU disputes, a most orthodox reading of autonomy has gradually prevailed and been imposed without consideration of the different legal context of the treaty pursuant to which arbitral tribunals exercise jurisdiction; in the case of an agreement concluded by the EU with a third country, a more pragmatic approach is visible.

There are four perspectives through which these approaches may be examined. The first is about the quest for full effectiveness and complete certainty which the case-law seeks to achieve in the context of intra-EU disputes. This normative claim, and the uncompromising terms in which it is couched, appear to ignore the elusive nature of the quest. The effectiveness of EU law is constantly negotiated within a legal order that is flexible enough to tolerate dissent. Consider, for instance, the principle of supremacy and the different ways in which different domestic courts of last instance understand it. The expression of the possibility of dissent in principle does not necessarily entail obstacles to the effectiveness of EU law in practice. And the occasional dissent in practice does not necessarily derail the functioning of the EU legal order.[87] Is there such evidence to suggest that tribunals beyond the system of EU law would be eager to trample on the authority of the CJEU to interpret EU law? Is there no scope for an approach that is more understanding of and conciliatory towards the different ways in which non-EU courts may deal with EU-related issues? The maximalist approach of the Court is noteworthy even in the context of the ECtHR, an international court which has shown comity towards the Court of Justice and to which the latter refers as a matter of course.[88] And while the Court's case-law examined in this chapter is all about autonomy as a matter of principle, rather than practice, one wonders why the more pragmatic streak that one finds in the constitutional case-law of the Court of Justice is viewed by the same Court as so

[85] Opinion 2/13 *Accession of the Union to the ECHR* ECLI:EU:C:2014:2454, paras 236–245.

[86] See Dashwood (n 56) 136.

[87] This issue has been inherent in the development of the EU legal order and has assumed new relevance in the light of the *Weiss* case-law of the *Bundesverfassungsgericht* and the Judgment in the name of the Republic of Poland of 7 October 2021 in K3/21 by the Constitutional Tribunal.

[88] See the analysis in de Witte (n 15).

clearly unsuitable when it comes to the role of other international courts and arbitral tribunals. In fact, such scepticism is all the more remarkable given the openness to international law that the Court has shown in other contexts (a case in point being its approach to customary international law).[89]

The second perspective is about the role of domestic courts. The orthodox version of autonomy we find in judgments such as *Achmea* and *Komstroy* not only brings domestic courts to the fore but it also makes their defence a *raison-d' être* for the Court's hostile approach to the jurisdiction of arbitral tribunals. In fact, this has been the case for some time. In *Opinion 1/09*, the Court concluded that the draft Agreement on the European and Community Patents Court, drawn up in the context of the European Patent Convention, was not consistent with the principle, as it would undermine the rights of domestic courts to refer questions about the interpretation of EU law to the Court of Justice.[90] The pivotal role of domestic courts for the EU's system of judicial review was also stressed in *Opinion 2/13*.[91] Their prominence in the context of autonomy aims to strengthen the powers with which they are endowed under EU law. However, this aspect of the role of domestic courts is intrinsically linked to the protection of the jurisdiction of the Court itself. After all, so intertwined is the function of domestic courts and the Court of Justice in the EU's judicial system that safeguarding the jurisdiction of the latter entails the protection of the former. The emphasis on the role of the domestic courts makes the principle of autonomy appear less self-referential than it is and aims to address the view that autonomy amounts to 'a rhetorical shield to help to protect the Court's own exclusive jurisdiction'.[92] Put differently, the more it focuses on domestic courts, the less autonomy may appear to be about the Court itself. There is, for instance, some delicious irony in the fact that the Court's concern in *Achmea* for protecting the power of the domestic court to refer would be expressed in response to a preliminary reference.

In this vein, there is a thread that brings together the perspective of domestic courts with the quest for absolute certainty that characterises the case-law on autonomy. The judgments examined in this chapter put emphasis on the limits of domestic law when it comes to adjudicating on arbitral tribunals but not nearly enough on what domestic courts may be required to do in practice as a matter of EU law when confronted with, for instance, a question of enforcing an arbitral award. Put differently, there is a somewhat paternalistic streak in how domestic courts are approached within the context of autonomy. The rhetoric is about their significance in the EU's judicial architecture, but, in fact, they are not entrusted with protecting autonomy themselves. This approach is in contrast with a more liberal view of the position of the domestic court: in his Opinion in *Achmea*, Advocate General Wathelet had relied upon the role of the latter in enforcing arbitral awards in order to point out how they

[89] See, for instance, E Denza, 'International Aviation and the EU Carbon Trading Scheme: Comment on the *Air Transport Association of America* Case' (2012) 37 *EL Rev* 314, 323.

[90] Opinion 1/09 *Creation of a Unified Patent Litigation System* ECLI:EU:C:2011:123, [2011] ECR I-1137, paras 80–89.

[91] Opinion 2/13 *Accession of the Union to the ECHR* ECLI:EU:C:2014:2454, paras 175–176.

[92] B de Witte, 'European Union Law: How Autonomous is its Legal Order?' 65 (2010) *Zeitschrift für öffentliches Recht* 141, 150.

could, in fact, protect autonomy.[93] Having pointed out that arbitral awards may only be enforced by domestic courts, he had argued that, in principle, the latter are largely granted leeway under international investment law to rely upon EU law and protect EU rules as a matter of public policy.[94] His approach, therefore, highlighted a different function for domestic courts in the context of autonomy: rather than in need of protection, they were, actually, themselves active guarantors of the principle.

The third perspective brings this analysis back to where it began, that is the internal-external dimension of autonomy. In her typology of structural principles, Cremona writes about autonomy and how 'it underpins the Court's approach to the rule of law in *Kadi* and to mutual trust in *Opinion 2/13*'.[95] In both *PL Holdings* and *Komstroy*, the Court refers to the judgment in *Associação Sindical dos Juízes Portugueses*[96] which first became the starting point and, then a point of reference for what is now a burgeoning body of case-law on the rule of law.[97] Viewed from this angle, the introduction of an uncompromising understanding of autonomy in intra-EU relations is directly linked to the increasingly prominent role that the Court is bound to assume in order to deal with recalcitrant domestic authorities whose understanding of rule law in the organisation and delivery of justice runs counter to EU values.

While the above perspective may appear justified from a normative point of view, the way in which the case-law on autonomy has approached it raises questions. In terms of consistency, why is the principle of mutual trust, so prominent in the case law on the rule of law, absent from the *Komstroy* judgment? Given the increasing body of case-law on the rule of law and the independence of domestic courts of Member States, is it tenable for the Court to deprive investors of the protection afforded by arbitral tribunals? And if this is tenable from a conceptual point of view, may it suggest some lack of pragmatism?

The point about pragmatism is also apposite to the wider discussion about the relationship between the Court of Justice and arbitral tribunals. Given the considerable ongoing intra-EU disputes before arbitral tribunals under the ECT, a maximalist approach to autonomy gives rise to increasing uncertainty about the enforcement of arbitral awards that complicates further the position of domestic courts. It also does little to ensure legal certainty regarding the protection of investors.

[93] Opinion of Advocate General Wathelet in Case C-284/16 *Achmea* ECLI:EU:C:2017:699, paras 229 et seq.

[94] As the Convention on the Settlement of Investment Disputes between States and Nationals of other States (ICSID Convention) (Washington, 18 March 1965) requires that domestic courts view an arbitral award as if it were a judgment by a domestic court of last instance, Advocate General Wathelet suggested that the Member States should avoid the choice of ICSID in their BITs (Opinion of Advocate General Wathelet in Case C-284/16 *Achmea* ECLI:EU:C:2017:699, para 253). He also pointed out that that point was irrelevant in *Achmea*, as the award had not been rendered pursuant to the ICSID Convention.

[95] M Cremona, 'Structural Principles and their Role in EU External Relations Law' in M Cremona (ed), *Structural Principles in EU External Relations Law* (Oxford, Hart Publishing, 2018) 28.

[96] Case C-64/16 *Associação Sindical dos Juízes Portugueses* ECLI:EU:C:2018:117.

[97] See the overview and analysis in L Pech and D Kochenov, 'Respect for the Rule of Law in the Case Law of the European Court of Justice: A Casebook Overview of Key Judgments since the Portuguese Judges Case' (2021–3) *Swedish Institute for European Policy Studies (SIEPS)*.

While autonomy owes its genesis and development to the ingenuity of the Court of Justice, its implications may not become fully apparent unless actors such as arbitral tribunals and domestic courts of the Member States and third countries take a consistent view of how to approach the relationship between EU and international investment law. It is ironic that, for the principle to become fully effective in the way intended by judgments such as *Komstroy*, the above courts and tribunals should adopt a more flexible stance than that adopted by the Court of Justice.

Remedying Constitutional Heresies: The Charter, Damages and Jurisdiction in the Common Foreign and Security Policy

ELEANOR SPAVENTA*

1. INTRODUCTION

IT IS A great honour to contribute to a volume celebrating the scholarship and career of Marise Cremona: needless to say, her studies have shaped greatly our understanding of the Common Foreign and Security Policy (CFSP), external relations and the dynamics of EU law more broadly. Indeed, my interest in the CFSP was also the result of a gentle push by Marise, when together with Bruno de Witte, she asked me to contribute to an edited collection on the constitutional fundamentals of EU Foreign Relations law.[1] But, perhaps even more importantly Marise has been for us all an example of how academic debates and interactions should occur. Her intellectual rigour has always gone hand in hand with a great kindness and respect towards all colleagues, junior and senior, never dismissing ideas or individuals, yet generously contributing to our own development. Marise has always been a pioneer in understanding and supporting female academics, especially at a time when female role models were few and far between, and helped many of us navigating the complex journey from PhD students to junior academics, a journey all the more complex once family responsibilities enter the equation.

Building on our shared interests, this contribution analyses the intersection between the CFSP and fundamental rights. In particular, my focus is on judicial protection as an essential tool to ensure protection of any fundamental right. If, on the one hand, the provisions of the EU Charter of Fundamental Rights (Charter) always bind the EU institutions – in theory guaranteeing a minimum of fundamental rights protection in all fields of EU action – then, on the other hand, the limited jurisdiction of the Court of Justice in relation to the CFSP poses challenges as to the actionability of those rights. True, this issue has improved significantly as a result of the changes introduced by the Lisbon Treaty. Restrictive measures against natural or legal persons are now fully reviewable, whereas before Lisbon, annulment proceedings

* I am very grateful to Michael Dougan, Christophe Hillion and Kenneth Armstrong for commenting on this chapter, and to the participants in the workshop for an excellent experience and a very stimulating discussion. The usual disclaimer applies.

[1] M Cremona and B de Witte (eds), *EU Foreign Relations law: Constitutional Fundamentals*, Essays in European Law 13 (Oxford, Hart Publishing, 2008).

could only be brought against implementing measures, if any, adopted in the (then) European Community legal system.[2] Yet, at the same time, concerns have not gone away. First of all, action in the domain of CFSP has not only increased dramatically over the past years, but also foreign policy has become more and more entangled with migration 'management',[3] hence potentially affecting individuals' fundamental rights on a much larger scale. Second, the rule of law crisis within the EU has rendered the constitutional fallacy of the limited jurisdiction of the Court of Justice over certain parts of the Treaties all the more evident. Third, the stance adopted by the Court of Justice in *Opinion 2/13*,[4] where it stated that it could not tolerate the European Court of Human Rights having full jurisdiction over the CFSP when the EU courts do not, has added a bar to EU accession to the European Convention on Human Rights (ECHR), a bar which is as much unnecessary as it is difficult to overcome.[5]

The issue of justiciability of fundamental rights in relation to CFSP measures has thus become much more prominent,[6] something that is reflected also in Marise Cremona's writing,[7] and it translated into a more varied and nuanced case law as to

[2] See eg Joined Cases C-402/05 P and C-415/05 P *Kadi and Al Barakaat International Foundation v Council and Commission* ECLI:EU:C:2008:461, [2008] ECR I-6351, and compare with Case C-355/04 P *Segi and Others v Council* ECLI:EU:C:2007:116, [2007] ECR I-1657 and Case C-354/04 P *Gestoras Pro Amnistía and Others v Council* ECLI:EU:C:2007:115, [2007] ECR I-1579 where the listing of 'terrorists' organisation was made through a 3rd pillar Common Position over which the Court did not have jurisdiction. And see generally S Poli, 'The Right to Effective Judicial Protection with Respect to Acts Imposing Restrictive Measures and its Transformative Force for the Common Foreign and Security Policy' (2022) 59 *CML Rev* 1045.

[3] See eg Operation *Irini* discussed below; even the positive response to the influx of refugees from Ukraine, with the activation of the temporary protection directive (Council Directive 2001/55/EC on minimum standards for giving temporary protection in the event of a mass influx of displaced persons and on measures promoting a balance of efforts between Member States in receiving such persons and bearing the consequences thereof [2001] OJ L212/13) is as much a choice of foreign policy as it is of migration management. Naturally the entanglement between migration and foreign policy brings also challenges about the correct legal basis, see eg C-263/14 *Parliament v Council* ECLI:EU:C:2016:435. On the centre of gravity test in relation to CFSP measures see eg L Lonardo, '*Commission v Council (Kazakhstan)*: The Subject-matter Question in EU External Relations Law, or the Asymmetry of Art. 40 TEU' (2020) 45 *EL Rev* 427; G De Baere and T Van den Sanden, 'Interinstitutional Gravity and Pirates of the Parliament on Stranger Tides: The Continued Constitutional Significance of the Choice of Legal Basis in post-Lisbon External Action' (2016) 12 *European Constitutional Law Review* 85.

[4] Opinion 2/13 *Accession of the Union to the ECHR* ECLI:EU:C:2014:2454; see eg B de Witte and S Imamovic, 'Opinion 2/13 on Accession to the ECHR: Defending the EU Legal Order against a Foreign Human Rights Court' (2015) 40 *EL Rev* 683; T Lock, 'The Future of the European Union's Accession to the European Convention on Human Rights after Opinion 2/13: Is it Still Possible and is it Still Desirable?' (2015) 11 *European Constitutional Law Review* 239; E Spaventa, 'A Very Fearful Court? The Protection of Fundamental Rights in the European Union after Opinion 2/13' (2014) 22 *Maastricht Journal of European and Comparative Law* 35; and for a reflection on the impact of the Court's more recent case law on its own objections in Opinion 2/13 see Editorial (JS), 'Is Opinion 2/13 obsolescent?' (2017) 42 *EL Rev* 449.

[5] See further de Búrca and Kilpatrick in this volume.

[6] There is now a significant body of literature on CFSP jurisdiction and justiciability, also as a result of the case law examined below in Section 2. See eg C Hillion and RA Wessel, '"The Good, the Bad and the Ugly": Three Levels of Judicial Control over the CFSP' in S Blockmans and P Koutrakos (eds), *Research Handbook on the EU's Common Foreign and Security Policy*, Research Handbooks in European Law (Cheltenham, Edward Elgar, 2018); C Hillion, 'The EU External Action as Mandate to Uphold the Rule of Law Outside and Inside the Union' (2023) 29 *Columbia journal of European Law* 228; P Koutrakos, 'Judicial Review in the EU's Common Foreign and Security Policy' (2018) 67 *ICLQ* 1; C Hillion, 'A Powerless Court? The European Court of Justice and the Common Foreign and Security Policy' in M Cremona and A Thies (eds), *The European Court of Justice and External Relations Law: Constitutional Challenges* (Oxford, Hart Publishing, 2014).

[7] See eg M Cremona, '"Effective Judicial Review Is of the Essence of the Rule of Law": Challenging Common Foreign and Security Policy Measures' (2017) 2 *European Papers* 671.

the boundaries of the Court's jurisdiction. Starting from the premise that exclusion of jurisdiction is a (constitutional) exception, which needs to be interpreted narrowly, the Court has found that, in some instances, it can review acts which find their legal basis in a CFSP decision, even if they do not impose restrictive measures. This is the case when either a connection can be made with an EU provision over which the Court has jurisdiction (such as the Financial Regulation or Article 218 Treaty on the Functioning of the European Union (TFEU))[8] or when there is an employment relationship with an entity established through a CFSP decision and the issue relates to staff management.[9] Furthermore, the Court has also clarified that its jurisdiction in relation to restrictive measures is not limited to direct actions, but also extends to preliminary rulings and actions for damages.[10] As welcome as this case law might be, it is only a small dent in the shelter of an entire policy field from judicial interference. The question, therefore, remains as to whether such shelter compromises the right to effective judicial protection, a right which is considered fundamental in order to guarantee the rule of law.

In this chapter, we are going to propose a range of solutions, which might well be cumulative, aimed at plugging the jurisdictional gap. To be clear, none of the proposed solutions is a substitute for constitutional reform, and yet this is where we are. We will start by analysing the case law of the Court in relation to its own jurisdiction in CFSP matters (Section 2). We will then consider cognate case law in relation to the EU institutions' duties to respect the Treaties and the Charter whenever they act (Section 3), and assess the potential implication of this case law for the area of CFSP (Section 4). We will then argue that the European Council, the Council and the High Representative have a positive duty to ensure that any CFSP act is fundamental rights compliant, which means also ensuring that there is no gap in judicial protection arising from action in the CFSP. For this reason, I argue that: (i) any CFSP instrument should include a national jurisdictional clause, clearly allocating responsibility to one or more jurisdictions for the purposes of judicial review, hence ensuring the rule of law, both in terms of access to judicial redress and legal certainty; and (ii) an action for damages against the Council can be brought for failure to ensure the protection of fundamental rights when adopting a CFSP instrument.[11] This solution might also assuage the fears expressed by the Court in *Opinion 2/13*, both because national courts are part of the EU judicial system and in certain instances might make preliminary references to the Court as to the correct interpretation of the Charter; and because it would expand the Court's jurisdiction in relation to the non-contractual liability of the EU. Furthermore, it also might make it easier (until accession but also after it) to determine when remedies have been exhausted for the purposes of an action in front of the ECtHR.

[8] Case C-439/13 P *Elitaliana v Eulex Kosovo* ECLI:EU:C:2015:753; Case C-658/11 *Parliament v Council* ECLI:EU:C:2014:2025.

[9] Case C-455/14 P *H v Council and Commission* ECLI:EU:C:2016:569; Case C-14/19 P *CSUE v KF* ECLI:EU:C:2020:492.

[10] Case C-72/15 *Rosneft* ECLI:EU:C:2017:236; Case C-134/19 P *Bank Refah Kargaran v Council* ECLI:EU:C:2020:793.

[11] This chapter was completed in September 2023, before AG Ćapeta's Opinion in Joined Cases C-19/22 and C-44/22 *KS and KD* ECLI:EU:C:2023:901; the AG also suggested that the solution rests with asserting the possibility of establishing the non-contractual liability of the EU for breach of fundamental rights in CFSP cases, regardless of whether the measure imposes restrictions. For a summary and some comments on the Opinion see E Spaventa, 'Escaping Jurisdictional Blackholes' *Verfassungblog* 15 December 2023, verfassungsblog.de/escaping-jurisdictional-blackholes/.

2. THE JURISDICTION OF THE COURT OF JUSTICE IN THE CFSP

Article 24(1) Treaty on European Union (TEU), and Article 275 TFEU, provide for the exclusion of the Court's jurisdiction over the CFSP, except in order to monitor the boundary between the CFSP and other Union policies;[12] and to review the legality of restrictive measures adopted against persons and legal entities.[13] The Treaty provides hence for a general rule – exclusion of jurisdiction in CFSP – and a limited exception, which preserves the specificity of the CFSP, despite the fact that after the Lisbon Treaty, the CFSP has also been brought within the constitutional structure of the Union.[14] Needless to say, and as pointed out in the case law, the very limited jurisdiction over the CFSP is in tension with the general rule enshrined in Article 19(1) TEU which provides that the Court must ensure that in the interpretation and application of the Treaties the law is observed.

This said, in recent years, the Court has had the chance to determine the scope of the limit to its jurisdiction in CFSP acts: there are three different strands of case law. The first one concerns the reviewability of the procedural aspects of international agreements adopted within the CFSP; the second strand concerns jurisdiction over staff cases of operational units/missions established through the CFSP; and the third one concerns the types of actions available in relation to restrictive measures. Overall, and as we shall see in more detail below, the Court has stressed how the limitation of its own jurisdiction is the exception, and as such must be interpreted narrowly; and, quite naturally, it has linked the issue of judicial oversight to the need to ensure the rule of law in the EU.[15]

2.1. Review of Procedures

In *Mauritius*,[16] the European Parliament complained, inter alia, that the Council had failed to inform it 'immediately and fully' at all stages of the negotiations of the EU-Mauritius agreements and therefore had breached the procedure provided

[12] On the boundaries between CFSP and other EU action, see eg M Cremona, 'Managing EU Cooperation Agreements, Council Discretion and Legal Basis: European Commission v Council of the European Union (C-180/20)' (2022) 47 *EL Rev* 273; L Lonardo, '*Commission v Council (Kazakhstan)*' (n 3). And see more generally M Cremona, 'The Position of the CFSP/CSDP in the EU's Constitutional Architecture' in Blockmans and Koutrakos (eds) (n 6).

[13] See generally Poli (n 2).

[14] See Cremona (n 12) 20.

[15] On the rule of law in external relations see Hillion (n 6).

[16] Case C-658/11 *Parliament v Council* ECLI:EU:C:2014:2025; see also C-263/14 *Parliament v Council* ECLI:EU:C:2016:435; see eg A Ott, 'The Legal Bases for International Agreements post-Lisbon: Of Pirates and the Philippines' (2014) 21 *Maastricht Journal of European and Comparative Law* 739; P Van Elsuwege, 'Securing the Institutional Balance in the Procedure for Concluding International Agreements: *European Parliament v. Council (Pirate Transfer Agreement with Mauritius)*' (2015) 52 *CML Rev* 1379; De Baere and Van den Sanden (n 3); C Eckes, 'Common Foreign and Security Policy: The Consequences of the Court's Extended Jurisdiction' (2016) 22 *European Law Journal* 492; on Art 218 Consolidated version of the Treaty on the Functioning of the European Union (TFEU) [2016] OJ C202/47 see eg J Heliskoski, 'The Procedural Law of International Agreements: A Thematic Journey through Article 218 TFEU' (2020) 57 *CML Rev* 79; AP van der Mei, 'EU External Relations and Internal Inter-Institutional Conflicts: The Battlefield of Article 218 TFEU' (2016) 23 *Maastricht Journal of European and Comparative Law* 1051.

for by Article 218(10) TFEU. The Council argued that since the agreement was based on a CFSP legal basis, the Court lacked jurisdiction *ex* Article 24(1) TEU/275 TFEU not only on the agreement but also over the procedural aspects regulated by Article 218 TFEU. The Court found that the exception to its own jurisdiction had to be interpreted narrowly and that, even though the agreement was based on Article 37 TEU (CFSP), Article 218 TFEU is of general application and does not fall within the CFSP. For this reason, the fact that the agreement pertained to the CFSP was immaterial to the jurisdiction of the Court to interpret Article 218 TFEU. In other words, the fact that the act pertained to the CFSP was not in itself sufficient to exclude the Court's jurisdiction over a general provision of the TFEU. Similarly, in *Elitaliana*,[17] the issue related to a tender for the supply of helicopters run by Eulex Kosovo. The applicant had not been successful in the tender and brought proceedings for annulment and compensation. The Court of Justice found that even though Eulex was a mission established by a CFSP act,[18] the exclusion of its jurisdiction in CFSP matters was the exception and therefore had to be interpreted narrowly. Since the case related to the interpretation of the Financial Regulation, an EU act, the Court had full jurisdiction.

2.2. Staff Cases

In *H v Council*,[19] the issue related to an employment dispute between a magistrate seconded from Italy to the EU Police Mission (EUPM) in Bosnia and Herzegovina, another mission established through a CFSP act.[20] In asserting its jurisdiction, the Court recalled the, by then, familiar principle of the narrow interpretation of the derogation from its jurisdiction; furthermore, it recalled that the EU (including the CFSP) is founded on the values of equality and rule of law and that '(t)he very existence of *effective judicial review* designed to ensure compliance with provisions of EU law is inherent in the existence of the rule of law'.[21] Whereas the contested decisions were set within the CFSP, EU staff seconded to EUPM remained subject to the Staff Regulations (and hence to the Court's jurisdiction), whilst those seconded by the Member States were not, even though both were subject to the same rules for the performance of their 'theatre level' duties. The Court thus held that the exclusion of its jurisdiction could not be so extensive as to justify the exclusion of jurisdiction in relation to staff management vis-à-vis staff seconded by the Member States, when it would have jurisdiction over the same issues in relation to EU staff.

[17] Case C-439/13 P *Elitaliana v Eulex Kosovo* ECLI:EU:C:2015:753.

[18] Council Joint Action 2008/124/CFSP on the European Union Rule of Law Mission in Kosovo, EULEX KOSOVO [2008] OJ L42/92, as modified, consolidated text 17 October 2022, latest amendment by Council Decision (CFSP) 2023/122 amending Joint Action 2008/124/CFSP on the European Union Rule of Law Mission in Kosovo [2023] OJ L16/32.

[19] Case C-455/14 P *H v Council and Commission* ECLI:EU:C:2016:569.

[20] Decision 2009/906/CFSP on the European Union Police Mission (EUPM) in Bosnia and Herzegovina (BiH) [2009] OJ L322/22, no longer in force.

[21] Case C-455/14 P *H v Council and Commission* ECLI:EU:C:2016:569, para 41 (emphasis added).

The Court went even further in the *SatCen* case,[22] another body set up under a CFSP decision;[23] here, the SatCen Staff regulations provided for an ad hoc Appeals Board for staff disputes against which rulings there was no appeal.[24] Restating the ruling in *H v Council and others*,[25] both the General Court and the Court of Justice found that the exclusion of their jurisdiction in relation to CFSP is a derogation from the general rule contained in Article 19(1) TEU, and that the principle of effective judicial protection enshrined in Article 47 Charter requires that such an exclusion be interpreted narrowly. Furthermore, in examining the repartition of jurisdiction between the Union and national courts *ex* Article 274 TFEU, both courts noted that in this case jurisdiction could be asserted (and should be asserted) because the Staff Regulations excluded the jurisdiction of national courts so that it fell upon the EU courts to ensure effective judicial review.

2.3. Restrictive Measures

In a different line of case law, the Court has interpreted the scope of its jurisdiction under Articles 24(1) TEU/275 TFEU to encompass preliminary rulings and actions for damages at least in those instances that concern restrictive measures. Thus, in *Rosneft*,[26] the Court needed to determine its own jurisdiction to deliver a preliminary ruling in relation to the CFSP decision establishing sanctions for Rosneft. The company had already brought a direct challenge, which was pending at the time of the preliminary ruling, in front of the General Court.[27] Yet, it had also attacked the national measures implementing the Decision, and related Regulation,[28] in front of the national court, which in order to determine the domestic dispute requested a ruling also on the validity of the CFSP decision. The Council and the intervening Member

[22] Case C-14/19 P *CSUE v KF* ECLI:EU:C:2020:492; and Case T-286/15 *KF v CSUE* ECLI:EU:T:2018:718 in front of the General Court (GC).

[23] Now, Council Decision 2014/401/CFSP on the European Union Satellite Centre and repealing Joint Action 2001/555/CFSP on the establishment of a European Union Satellite Centre [2014] OJ L188/73.

[24] Art 28 Decision 2009/747/CFSP concerning the Staff Regulations of the European Union Satellite Centre [2009] OJ L276/1.

[25] Case C-455/14 P *H v Council and Commission* ECLI:EU:C:2016:569.

[26] Case C-72/15 *Rosneft* ECLI:EU:C:2017:236.

[27] Case T-715/14 *NK Rosneft and Others v Council* ECLI:EU:T:2018:544, appealed Case C-732/18 P *Rosneft e.a. v Council* ECLI:EU:C:2020:727.

[28] Council Decision 2014/512/CFSP concerning restrictive measures in view of Russia's actions destabilising the situation in Ukraine [2014] OJ L229/13 as amended by Council Decision 2014/872/CFSP amending Decision 2014/512/CFSP concerning restrictive measures in view of Russia's actions destabilising the situation in Ukraine, and Decision 2014/659/CFSP amending Decision 2014/512/CFSP [2014] OJ L349/58; and Council Regulation (EU) No 833/2014 concerning restrictive measures in view of Russia's actions destabilising the situation in Ukraine [2014] OJ L229/1 as amended by Council Regulation (EU) No 1290/2014 amending Regulation (EU) No 833/2014 concerning restrictive measures in view of Russia's actions destabilising the situation in Ukraine, and amending Regulation (EU) No 960/2014 amending Regulation (EU) No 833/2014 [2014] OJ L349/20.

States argued that Articles 24(1) TEU and 275 TFEU, which expressly refer to actions brought in accordance with the conditions laid down in Article 263(4) TFEU, had to be interpreted to the effect that jurisdiction under Article 234 TFEU was excluded. The Court disagreed: it found that the reference in Article 275 TFEU to Article 263(4) TFEU was aimed at determining which type of decisions could be challenged, and not the procedure used for such a challenge. Since the implementation of sanctions is the responsibility of the Member States, the possibility to request a preliminary ruling is essential to ensure effective judicial protection, especially if also the national rule is under attack. To strengthen its reasoning the Court once again referred to the rule of law as a value enshrined in Articles 2 and 21 TEU, and to Article 47 Charter on effective remedies, which also justified a strict interpretation of the derogations contained in Article 24(1) TEU and 275 TFEU. As a result, the preliminary ruling procedure is admissible also in relation to acts adopted in the context of the CFSP, provided that the Court has jurisdiction *ratione materiae* (ie that the act prescribes restrictive measures).

In *Bank Refah Kargaran*,[29] the Court extended this reasoning also to the action for non-contractual liability of the EU *ex* Article 340 TFEU. Since the exclusion of jurisdiction of the Court is a derogation from Article 19(1) TEU it has to be interpreted strictly. Furthermore, actions for damages are part of the effective legal remedies referred to in Article 47 Charter and whereas, such action is always available in relation to Regulations implementing a CFSP decision, that might not be sufficient since some restrictive measures, such as a travel ban, might be contained only in the CFSP act. For this reason, the action for damages is available to persons and entities who are subjected to restrictive measures for the harm caused by those measures.

It is worth noting that, whereas the Court has extended the type of action available to individuals beyond judicial review in direct actions, to embrace also indirect review in preliminary rulings and actions for damages, it has established a direct link with its jurisdiction under the Treaties, so that those actions are only possible in relation to restrictive measures and Article 40 TEU. In other words, this case law, perhaps somehow differently from the *SatCen* and *H v Council* line of case law (which however is circumscribed to staff management issues), fully respects the jurisdictional boundaries set out in the Treaties by simply offering a purposive interpretation of Articles 24(1) TEU and 275 TFEU to maximise the effectiveness of legal remedies. For this reason, it is of no help in those instances in which CFSP action might affect fundamental rights, but without imposing restrictive measures on individuals. So the question remains – how to ensure that the rule of law, and the right to an effective remedy, are fully respected when the EU acts in the sphere of the CFSP? For those who might dismiss this as a mere academic exercise, an example might serve to illustrate

[29] Case C-134/19 P *Bank Refah Kargaran v Council* ECLI:EU:C:2020:793. Of no direct relevance here, but still worth recalling because of its importance is Case C-872/19 P *Venezuela v Council (Affectation d'un État tiers)* ECLI:EU:C:2021:507 where the Court accepted that Venezuela could bring Art 263(4) TFEU proceedings to challenge sanctions against entities established within its territory.

this point: there are many military missions adopted under the Common Security and Defence Policy (CSDP), such as Operations *Irini* and *Atalanta*,[30] and many civilian missions of the EU, such as the Border Assistance Mission in Libya (EUBAM Libya) or in Palestine, adopted under the CFSP,[31] which might have a direct or indirect bearing on individuals. In relation to those operations – undoubtedly sensitive from a fundamental rights perspective – there is a problem when an act potentially breaching the Charter is attributable exclusively to the EU rather than to Member States' officials (whether military or civilian).

Take for instance Operation *Irini*,[32] an EU military crisis management operation to enforce the arms embargo against Libya; assist and develop the operations of the Libyan coastal guard; and combat human smuggling. The political control and strategic direction of the operation rests with the Political and Security Committee (PSC), composed of the Member States' ambassadors in Brussels and chaired by representatives from the European External Action Service, under the responsibility of the Council and the High Representative. On the other hand, the military direction is vested upon the EU Operation Commander, under the monitoring of the EU Military Committee, and ultimately under the responsibility of the Council. There is no reference in the Decision establishing Operation *Irini* to fundamental rights but for a passing reference to international human rights law (not the Charter) in relation to operations concerning people smuggling, and references to data protection. In relation to the processing of the latter, the Decision specifies that it has to be carried out in accordance with the law of the flag state of the carrier on which the Crime Information Cell is hosted; in relation to staff of Union agencies represented in the Crime Information Cell, information shall be processed in accordance with the legal framework applicable to the respective agencies. Therefore, at least in relation to data protection, the *territorial scope* of the protection is determined by the flag of the vessel with a specific regime for staff of union agencies. The question then is whether a violation of fundamental rights, which occurs through personnel stationed on the vessel, treated as territory of the flag for the purposes of data protection, could be attracted within the latter's constitutional sphere; or rather whether, absent national

[30] Council Decision (CFSP) 2020/472 on a European Union military operation in the Mediterranean (EUNAVFOR MED IRINI) [2020] OJ L101/ 4 as amended, consolidated version following Council Decision (CFSP) 2023/653 amending Decision (CFSP) 2020/472 on the European Union military operation in the Mediterranean (EUNAVFOR MED IRINI) [2023] OJ L81/27; Council Decision (CFSP) 2022/2441 amending Joint Action 2008/851/CFSP on a European Union military operation to contribute to the deterrence, prevention and repression of acts of piracy and armed robbery off the Somali coast [2022] OJ L319/80.

[31] Council Decision 2013/233/CFSP on the European Union Integrated Border Management Assistance Mission in Libya (EUBAM Libya) [2013] OJ L138/15 as amended, consolidated version 1 July 2021; Council Decision 2013/354/CFSP on the European Union Police Mission for the Palestinian Territories (EUPOL COPPS) [2013] OJ L185/12 as amended.

[32] Council Decision (CFSP) 2020/472 on a European Union military operation in the Mediterranean (EUNAVFOR MED IRINI) [2020] OJ L101/ 4 as amended, consolidated version following Council Decision (CFSP) 2023/653 amending Decision (CFSP) 2020/472 on the European Union military operation in the Mediterranean (EUNAVFOR MED IRINI) [2023] OJ L81/27. For a thorough analysis of Operation *Sophia*, the precursor to Operation *Irini*, see J De Coninck, 'Effective Remedies for Human Rights Violations in EU CSDP Military Missions: Smoke and Mirrors in Human Rights Adjudication?' (2023) 24 *German Law Journal* 342.

personnel discretion, the fact that the conduct is attributable to the EU entails the exclusion of any domestic protection (always bearing in mind that there would not be, as things stand, protection at EU level). The question is far from being merely academic – whereas in certain circumstances the potentially offending conduct might be 'mixed' – so that there is also an act of the Member State that can be attacked in front of the national court – that might not be the case in all circumstances. Take for instance the case of Libya, which is not a safe port for the purposes of human rights law. Theoretically, no person who has reached the EU territory, including its waters, can be deported to Libya under, as the case might be, constitutional law, EU asylum and fundamental rights law, European Convention of Human Rights law, or international law.[33] For obvious reasons this also means that push backs, ie actively preventing asylum seekers from reaching the EU territory, as well as pull backs, actively alerting the Libyan coastal guard to the existence of migrants' boats with a view to ensuring that those boats are pulled back to land, might be unlawful under domestic, EU, ECHR and international law.[34] Whereas in case of mixed offending conduct, with action by the authorities of a Member State acting on intelligence provided by the *Irini* Operation, domestic constitutional protection would (or should) apply,[35] when the responsibility lies exclusively with the forces and/or the operation commander of the EU, established within the CFSP (including the CSDP), a jurisdictional vacuum might arise, so that the national courts might not be able to assert jurisdiction and, unless there is a restrictive measure, the Court of Justice does not have jurisdiction *ex* Art 24(1) TEU and 275 TFEU.

In what follows, we examine the possible solutions to remedy this gap. In order to do so, we will briefly recall some case law in relation to the Charter obligations of the EU institutions, to argue, first, that the European Council, the Council and the High Representatives have a duty to include a jurisdictional clause in any act adopted under the CFSP so as to ensure effective judicial protection under Article 47 Charter; and, second, that failure to do so might trigger the non-contractual liability of the EU.

3. THE EU INSTITUTIONS' OBLIGATIONS UNDER ARTICLE 51 CHARTER

In order to thoroughly analyse potential residual protection for non-restrictive measures falling within the CFSP, it is necessary to take a leap in our analysis and consider

[33] See eg International Convention on Maritime Search and Rescue (Hamburg, 27 April 1979); unfortunately, the theory and the practice might be increasingly diverging, see eg I Goldner Lang and B Nagy, 'External Border Control Techniques in the EU as a Challenge to the Principle of Non-Refoulement' (2021) 17 *European Constitutional Law Review* 442.

[34] See eg N Markard, 'The Right to Leave by Sea: Legal Limits on EU Migration Control by Third Countries' (2016) 27 *EJIL* 591.

[35] To the author's knowledge activities under Operation *Irini*, per se, have not been challenged in front of the Italian courts, albeit there have been two unsuccessful attempts to request access to documents to determine whether the Italian coastal guard, alerted by Operation *Irini* planes as to the presence of a dingy in distress, was responsible for the damages incurred by the claimants as a result of the Libyan authorities taking charge of the boat; TAR Lazio Roma, Sez. III, Sent., (data ud. 22/03/2023) 18/04/2023, n. 6694; TAR Lazio Roma, Sez. III, Sent., (data ud. 22/03/2023) 03/04/2023, n. 5607.

the case law on the (legal) responsibilities of the institutions in other areas of EU law. In particular, what interests us is whether the obligation vested upon the EU's institutions to respect the Charter might be of use in plugging the effective remedies' gap in relation to those CFSP acts which do not entail restrictive measures as per Articles 24(1) TEU and 275 TFEU.[36] In this case law, and as detailed below, the Court clarified that the EU institutions are always bound by the Charter, no matter in which field they are acting, and that failure to respect this obligation, and failure to supervise the discharge of this obligation by the Commission, might incur the non-contractual liability of the EU.

In *Segi* and *Gestoras Pro Amnistia*,[37] one of the first cases on the listing of 'terrorist' organisations before the changes brought about by the Lisbon Treaty, the claimants were listed as terrorist groups in a Joint Action adopted under the then third pillar (Justice and Home Affairs), an act over which the Court did not have jurisdiction. In its rulings the Court made clear that the institutions' fundamental rights obligations are not conditional upon the Court having jurisdiction and, indeed, faced with an exclusion of its own jurisdiction, the Court referred to the duties of Member States, and especially their courts and tribunals, to interpret national procedural law so as to ensure the possibility of challenging a decision or national measure relating to the drawing up of an act of the EU. In *Ledra Advertising*,[38] the Court went further: it might be recalled that the issue related to the Commission's responsibilities in relation to acts adopted within the context of the European Stability Mechanism (ESM),[39] so when acting altogether outside the scope of the EU Treaties. The Court clarified that whenever the Commission acts, even outside the framework of the Treaties, it is bound by the Charter; furthermore, this obligation to respect the Charter translates in a legal obligation to be vigilant and refrain from acting when its conduct might give rise to such a breach.[40] Failure to comply with this obligation might give rise to the non-contractual liability of the EU (and the Commission), over which naturally the Court has jurisdiction.

[36] See Article 51(1) Charter of Fundamental Rights of the European Union (Charter) [2016] OJ L202/389: 'The provisions of this Charter are addressed to the institutions, bodies, offices and agencies of the Union with due regard for the principle of subsidiarity'.

[37] Case C-355/04 P *Segi and Others v Council* ECLI:EU:C:2007:116, [2007] ECR I-1657 and Case C-354/04 P *Gestoras Pro Amnistía and Others v Council* ECLI:EU:C:2007:115, [2007] ECR I-1579, especially paras 51 and 56; and see E Spaventa 'Remembrance of Principles Lost: on Fundamental Rights, the Third Pillar and the Scope of Union Law' (2006) 25 *Yearbook of European Law* 153. Indeed, the importance of fundamental rights as constitutional fundamentals of the EU has been made clear over and over, see eg Joined Cases C-402/05 P and C-415/05 P *Kadi and Al Barakaat International Foundation v Council and Commission* ECLI:EU:C:2008:461, [2008] ECR I-6351.

[38] Joined Cases C-8/15 P to C-10/15 P *Ledra Advertising v Commission and ECB* ECLI:EU:C:2016:70, noted by R Repasi, 'Judicial Protection Against Austerity Measures in the Euro Area: *Ledra* and *Mallis*' (2017) 54 *CML Rev* 1123; P Dermine, 'The End of Impunity? The Legal Duties of "Borrowed" EU Institutions under the European Stability Mechanism Framework' (2017) 13 *European Constitutional Law Review* 369; and see A Poulou, 'Financial Assistance Conditionality and Human Rights Protection: What is the Role of the EU Charter of Fundamental Rights?' (2017) 54 *CML Rev* 991.

[39] Treaty Establishing the European Stability Mechanism (Brussels, 2 February 2012).

[40] See also Case C-285/14 *Florescu and Others* ECLI:EU:C:2017:448.

The Court elaborated further on the supervisory duties of the Commission, and the consequences of failure to discharge such a duty, in *Chrysostomides*.[41] Here a group of claimants brought an action for damages against, inter alia, the Euro Group for its role (in the form of two statements) in relation to decisions concerning the emergency liquidity assistance to Cyprus. The preliminary issue for consideration was whether the Euro Group could be considered an institution, as non-contractual liability of the EU is limited to the latter, the EU's servants and the ECB. The General Court had found that the concept of institution should be interpreted differently in relation to direct actions (Article 263 TFEU) and non-contractual liability *ex* Article 340 TFEU.[42] Whereas pursuant to the ruling in *Mallis*,[43] the Euro Group would not be considered an institution in the context of a direct action for judicial review,[44] it should be so considered for the purposes of non-contractual liability. The different personal scope of the two provisions was justified, in the General Court's opinion, because the action for non-contractual liability 'was established as an independent form of *judicial remedy*, having its own particular place in the system of means of redress and subject to conditions for its use formulated in the light of its specific purpose'.[45] In the same way as the material scope of the two provisions differ, since Article 263 TFEU only allows challenges to acts intended to produce legal effects, whereas that is not the case in relation to Article 340 TFEU, the concept of 'institution' across the two provisions also differs: Article 340 TFEU is the basis for an action which is compensatory in nature and complements direct actions provided for in Article 263 TFEU. In this respect whether within the latter provisions the concept of 'institutions' must be limited to those that can adopt acts having legal effects, in the former what matters is whether the institution was established by the Treaties and is intending to contribute to the Union's objectives, which was the case for the Euro Group. The General Court reinforced its reasoning by stating that

> (a)ny contrary solution would clash with the principle of the Union based on the *rule of law*, in so far as it would allow the establishment, within the legal system of the European Union itself, of entities whose acts and conduct could not result in the European Union incurring liability.[46]

On appeal, the Court of Justice overruled the General Court on this point. It found that the Euro Group could not be considered an institution of the EU, and therefore could not be the subject of an action pursuant to Article 340 TFEU. However, addressing concerns about the rule of law and effective legal remedies, the

[41] Joined Cases C-597/18 P, C-598/18 P, C-603/18 P and C-604/18 P *Council v K. Chrysostomides & Co. and Others* ECLI:EU:C:2020:1028, noted by A Karatzia and M Markakis, 'Financial Assistance Conditionality and Effective Judicial Protection: *Chrysostomides*' (2022) 59 *CML Rev* 501.

[42] Case T-680/13 *Chrysostomides, K. & Co. and Others v Council and Others* ECLI:EU:T:2018:486.

[43] Joined Cases C-105/15 P to C-109/15 P *Mallis and Malli v Commission and ECB* ECLI:EU:C:2016:702.

[44] The Court has however found that an act of the Committee of the Permanent Representatives of the Governments of the Member States to the European Union (COREPER) is not necessarily sheltered from judicial review under Art 263 TFEU; rather, because the EU is based on the rule of law, an act of COREPER which is intended to produce legal effects can be reviewed; see Joined Cases C-626/15 and C-659/16 *Commission v Council (Antarctic MPAs)* ECLI:EU:C:2018:925.

[45] Case T-680/13 *Chrysostomides, K. & Co. and Others v Council and Others* ECLI:EU:T:2018:486, para 109 (emphasis added).

[46] ibid para 114 (emphasis added).

Court held that the applicants could attack (as they had done) the legal acts which flowed from the political agreement reached in the Euro Group. And that, in any event, the Commission, in its role as Guardian of the Treaties, has a duty to ensure that the statements/agreements in the Euro Group comply with EU law (including the Charter). Failure to discharge that supervisory duty, the Court held, might give rise to the non-contractual liability of the EU if the other conditions for liability are satisfied.

The case law recalled above is important for our purposes since it might point to a way to bridge the gap in protection arising from the exclusion of jurisdiction of the Court in relation to CFSP acts which do not entail restrictive measures: the EU institutions are always bound by the Charter, regardless of the actionability of claims in front of the Court, and (some) EU institutions also have supervisory duties which can be the subject of claims for non-contractual liability of the EU *ex* Art 340 TFEU, over which the Court has jurisdiction. Furthermore, rule of law considerations loom large in both this strand of case law, and in the case law examined above on jurisdiction over CFSP related measures. Indeed, the rule of law is the thread that connects both the assertion of jurisdiction over the behaviour of EU institutions acting outside the scope of the EU Treaties (ESM cases) and the assertion of jurisdiction over some CFSP derived acts not entailing restrictive measures.

It is necessary to assess, then, whether this common thread, the rule of law, also translates in legally significant principles that can be of use in establishing some remedial action for breaches of fundamental rights occurred by virtue of the adoption of a CFSP act.

4. THE DUTY TO RESPECT THE CHARTER AND THE SUPERVISORY DUTY TO ENSURE THAT THE CHARTER IS RESPECTED

Article 51(1) Charter clearly states that EU institutions, bodies, offices and agencies are bound by the Charter, and the Court has interpreted this as an absolute obligation, so that it applies regardless of whether the EU institution is acting within or outside the scope of EU law. This means that whereas the Charter is limited in its application in relation to acts of the Member States, it is not limited in relation to acts of the EU; there is no exclusion to its scope of application and, therefore, EU institutions are bound by the Charter when they act in the field of the CFSP.[47] In this respect, the issue of jurisdiction of the Court is immaterial to the legal obligations of the EU institutions, so that when the European Council is identifying the strategic interests and objectives of the EU; when the High Representative is formulating a proposal or implementing a decision;[48] and when the Council is adopting an act, they are always bound by Articles 2 and 21 TEU (especially for our purposes the

[47] To this effect see also C Hillion, 'Decentralised Integration? Fundamental Rights Protection in the EU Common Foreign and Security Policy' (2016) 1 *European Papers* 55.

[48] The High Representative is not an Institution for the purposes of Art 13(1) Consolidated version of the Treaty on European Union (TEU) [2016] OJ C202/13 and arguably when acting within the CFSP is not acting as part of the Commission. Nonetheless, it would fall within the concept of 'bodies, offices or agencies', see 'Explanations relating to the Charter of Fundamental Rights' [2007] OJ C303/17, at C 303/32: 'The expression 'bodies, offices and agencies' is commonly used in the Treaties to refer to all the authorities set up by the Treaties or by secondary legislation'.

rule of law and protection of fundamental rights) which, as held by the Court in *H v Council*, apply also to the CFSP by virtue of Article 23 TEU.[49] Furthermore, all institutions are also bound by the specific provisions contained in the Charter, as per the Court's ruling in *Ledra Advertising*, including Article 47 Charter. The latter is applicable both in itself, and because of its functional link with the rule of law,[50] and this is fully demonstrated by the fact that, when it has jurisdiction, the Court does apply the Charter to decisions adopted within the context of the CFSP.[51] To this end, great care should be taken in separating the issue of legal obligations imposed upon the institutions from the justiciability of those obligations in front of the EU courts. The fact that a right might not be (easily) enforced does not detract from its existence, since in the case of the CFSP the lack of enforceability is not due to an ontological quality of the provision,[52] but to a constitutional oddity in the European Union legal system. And, to be clear, this constitutional oddity does not relate to the fact that certain policy choices might pertain to the political discretion of the decision maker, and that this might be particularly true in relation to foreign policy choices whether operated at national level or at EU level. Rather, the oddity relates to subtracting an entire area from judicial reach, regardless of the actual nature of the decision; and, without any investigation as to whether a certain policy choice has exceeded even the broadest political discretion. This choice, as discussed in Neil Walker's chapter, might well have been the result of the reluctance of Member States to concede sovereignty in relation to one of the 'core' State's functions, and might have been constitutionally coherent when that very sovereignty ultimately rested with the Member States. However, once part of the sovereignty is relinquished at EU level, such as is the case for conduct attributable only to the EU in relation to operations in the Mediterranean and elsewhere, then the exclusion of the Court's jurisdiction is not only a constitutional oddity, it becomes a constitutional heresy in a Union which, as per Article 2 TEU, is founded on 'the values of respect for human dignity, freedom, democracy, equality, the rule of law and respect for human rights'.[53] This said, the applicability of the Charter to the CFSP has certain logical consequences.

[49] See also *Rosneft* discussed above in Section 2.

[50] See the case law on sanctions starting from the ruling in *Kadi I*, as well as the case law recalled above.

[51] See case law analysed in Section 2 above, as well as case law on sanctions; see also Hillion (n 47).

[52] There is extensive literature in relation to enforceable vis-à-vis non-enforceable fundamental rights which, to a certain extent, has also informed the debate in EU law on the difference between 'principles' and 'rights' in the Charter; see eg T Lock, 'Rights and Principles in the EU Charter of Fundamental Rights' (2019) 56 *CML Rev* 1201.

[53] In this respect see *Markovic and Others v Italy* (2007) 44 EHRR 52: 'Nevertheless, it would not be consistent with the rule of law in a democratic society or with the basic principle underlying Article 6 § 1 – namely that civil claims must be capable of being submitted to a judge for adjudication – if, for example, a State could, without restraint or control by the Convention enforcement bodies, remove from the jurisdiction of the courts a whole range of civil claims or confer immunities from civil liability on large groups or categories of persons' (para 97). It is worth stressing again that, even though and as also stated by the ECtHR, it might in some cases be difficult to clearly separate the issue of procedural jurisdiction from that of substantive assessment as to existence/infringement of the right, such distinction does exist. Hence, there is a world of difference between an *a priori* exclusion of jurisdiction and the recognition by a Court that a right has not been breached because a certain conduct falls within the discretion of the decision maker. For a very critical appraisal of the ECtHR position in relation to political discretion see Dissenting Opinion of Judge Zagrebelsky, Joined by Judges Zupančič, Jungwiert, Tsatsa-Nikolovska, Ugrekhelidze, Kovler and Davíd Thór Björgvinsson, in the *Markovic* case (p 49 and following).

First of all, when the Member States give effect to, or implement, an obligation arising from the CFSP, then State authorities are also bound by the Charter as a matter of EU law. Article 51 of the Charter does not distinguish between different areas of EU law, generally referring to when the Member States 'implement EU law', so that implementation of CFSP decisions must still fall within the scope of 'implementation' for the purposes of the Article 51 of the Charter. It would then be open to a national court to enquire with the Court of Justice as to the proper interpretation of the Charter in relation to a national measure implementing a CFSP act.[54] The fact that this request might entail an indirect review of the CFSP act is immaterial as demonstrated by the ruling in *Kadi*. There, the Court refused to share the General Court's view that it should refrain from carrying out judicial review of an EU measure because the latter was implementing a Security Council Resolution. In other words, the fact that judicial review of a provision over which the Court has jurisdiction might de facto entail a sort of indirect review of a provision over which the Court does not have jurisdiction is immaterial. Hence, if the Charter applies because the domestic act is implementing EU law, then there is no reason why the Court should not have jurisdiction on a preliminary ruling to determine the scope of application of Charter's rights.[55] To be clear, this would not extend the jurisdiction of the Court over the CFSP as the interpretation would be on the scope of the relevant provision of the Charter in relation to acts of the Member State implementing EU law.

Second, when the institutions are adopting an act within the field of the CFSP, they are under a duty to consider whether that act complies with the Charter (*Ledra, Chrysostomides*). This means not only ensuring that single provisions might not infringe fundamental rights, but also, and I would argue more importantly, ensuring that the act, as a whole, affords effective legal remedies so as to be compatible with Article 47 Charter. Since a secondary act cannot modify the Treaties, and hence cannot confer jurisdiction where the Treaty excludes it, then in order to ensure the existence of effective legal remedies such jurisdiction must be identified as pertaining to national courts.[56] This suggestion, which at first sight might seem very ambitious, is far from unprecedented; after all, as mentioned above, the decision establishing Operation *Irini* does contain jurisdictional clauses in relation to data protection. It is submitted then that such jurisdictional clauses should be extended to all fundamental rights also in relation to operations which are under direct EU command and do not require national implementation, such as for instance a direct communication with the Libyan coastal guard to effect pull backs from EU waters to Libyan waters with a view to bringing back refugees on Libyan soil (thus potentially engaging Articles 4, 18 and 19 Charter).[57] In practice, this would mean that the competent domestic courts

[54] See also C-400/10 PPU *McB*. ECLI:EU:C:2010:582, [2010] ECR I-8965.

[55] The Court has found that whereas for the purposes of judicial review under Art 263 TFEU an act must have binding legal effects, that is not the case in relation to review through preliminary rulings, see eg Case C-911/19 *FBF* ECLI:EU:C:2021:599.

[56] We shall not enter in the discussion as to whether jurisdiction would be 'bestowed' or simply identified as pertaining to national courts.

[57] On the use of informal practices of the EU to avoid accountability see generally C Molinari, 'The EU and its Perilous Journey through the Migration Crisis: Informalisation of the EU Return Policy and Rule of Law Concerns' (2019) 44 *EL Rev* 824.

have jurisdiction over CFSP acts when the European Courts have none; and that they would be able to adjudicate on the validity of such acts vis-à-vis the EU constitutional legal system, and specifically vis-à-vis the Charter. Nor should we consider the constitutional principles of the EU, and specifically the principle of supremacy and the hermeneutic monopoly of the Court also in relation to declaration of nullity of EU acts (*Foto-Frost* principle) to be an obstacle to such an interpretation. As argued by Advocate General Kokott in her View in *Opinion 2/13*, not only does the *Foto-Frost* principle not apply, but the national courts have a positive obligation to ensure that CFSP acts are compatible with higher ranking EU law,[58] including the Charter.

Third, as we have seen above, when the institution is acting outside the scope of EU law, failure to ensure respect for fundamental rights might trigger the non-contractual liability of the EU, even if the Court does not have jurisdiction over the main act (such as is the case over the memoranda of understanding adopted within the ESM in *Ledra Advertising*). Here, pursuant to the case law, we should distinguish the non-contractual liability arising from the adoption of the act, over which the Court would not have jurisdiction; and the non-contractual liability arising from a failure to discharge the supervisory duty bestowed upon the Commission by the Treaties.[59] We recalled above the case of *Bank Refah Kargaran*, where the Bank that had been subjected to sanctions brought an action for the non-contractual liability of the EU in relation to the CFSP decision. In accepting jurisdiction, the Court of justice was careful in circumscribing it: it held that the EU courts 'have jurisdiction to rule on an action for damages *in so far as* it seeks to obtain compensation for the harm allegedly caused by *restrictive measures* taken against natural or legal persons pursuant to CFSP Decisions'[60] This qualification seems, therefore, to exclude jurisdiction for the non-contractual liability for CFSP acts which do not entail restrictive measures, such as for instance the engagement with the Libyan coastal guard in order to effect push/pull backs. However, the question is open as to whether the Court would accept jurisdiction for an action against the European Council/Council/High Representative in relation to their failure to ensure the protection of Charter rights, and in particular Article 47 on effective judicial remedies, in adopting a given CFSP act. Much in the same way as in *Mauritius*, the proximity between the procedural requirements in Article 218 TFEU and the agreement adopted under the CFSP did not exclude the jurisdiction of the Court, the proximity between the CFSP and the institutional responsibilities under the Charter should not exclude jurisdiction over Article 340 TFEU. This said, the fact that the non-contractual liability would arise because of the institutional failure to ensure that the Charter is respected, rather than by the operation of the act itself, might make establishing the causal link between damage and illegal conduct extremely difficult. Similarly, it could be argued that if and when

[58] See View of Advocate General Kokott in Opinion 2/13 *Accession of the Union to the ECHR* ECLI:EU:C:2014:2475, especially at para 100. See also Koutrakos (n 6). For a more nuanced view, but still stressing national courts' role in protecting fundamental rights in the sphere of CFSP, see Hillion (n 47).

[59] This said, unfortunately actions for the non-contractual liability of the EU seldom succeed; see the statistics provided for in R Mańko, 'Action for Damages against the EU' (European Parliamentary Research Service, 7 December 2018), www.europarl.europa.eu/thinktank/en/document/EPRS_BRI(2018)630333.

[60] Case C-134/19 P *Bank Refah Kargaran v Council* ECLI:EU:C:2020:793, para 44 (emphasis added).

the Council exercises its supervisory functions over the missions, it also has a duty to make sure that there is no breach of the Charter, and failure to ensure that might trigger the non-contractual liability of the EU (with the same caveat that it might be very difficult to prove causation between illegal conduct and damage).[61]

Finally, in the cases recalled above the Court has also imposed a more general supervisory obligation on the Commission, in its role as guardian of the Treaties. However, as it is well known, the Commission does not have a formal role in relation to the CFSP,[62] and can neither bring enforcement proceedings or direct proceedings but for an action to police the competence boundaries of the CFSP. For this reason, it is unlikely that the High Representative could incur non-contractual liability as a Vice President of the Commission, since in her role within the CFSP she is not conferred with general supervisory powers, and indeed the Treaty separates as much as possible the High Representative's role within the CFSP from her role within the Commission.

5. CONCLUSIONS

The EU has developed into a more mature constitutional system, and the inclusion of the CFSP in its structure is a sign of this maturity. Yet, the increase in the activity in CFSP together with the fact that there is no longer a structural distinction between CFSP and the other fields of EU action, has resulted in a deeper accountability gap. On the one hand, political responsibility for the choices made in the CFSP might be confused and confusing, making it incredibly difficult to determine where responsibility for given choices lie – just think about the complex web of formal and informal agreements in relation to the 'securitisation' of the EU borders. On the other hand, not only does the Court of Justice not have full jurisdiction over the CFSP, but national courts might presume that the EU constitutional principles (supremacy, *Foto-Frost*) which in other fields prevent them from asserting full and unfettered jurisdiction, apply also to the field of the CFSP. Needless to say that, from a fundamental rights perspective, this double accountability gap is both dangerous and unacceptable: it cannot be the purpose of the EU to shelter executive action from democratic and judicial review. Furthermore, the judicial gap constitutes at present an (insurmountable) barrier to accession to the ECHR, hence contributing to lowering the standards of fundamental rights protection in the EU.

This said, I argue in this contribution that not all is lost: first of all, and as argued in the scholarship and by Advocate General Kokott,[63] we should never forget that the EU judicial system is composed not only of the European Court of Justice, but

[61] For a different perspective, analysing the issue of potential actions for non-contractual liability not taking into account the jurisdictional problems (ie actions against based on the CFSP decision) see De Coninck (n 32).

[62] See e.g. Wessel (n 6).

[63] See also Koutrakos (n 6). For a more nuanced view, but still stressing national courts' role in protecting fundamental rights in the sphere of CFSP, see Hillion (n 47); View of Advocate General Kokott in Opinion 2/13 *Accession of the Union to the ECHR* ECLI:EU:C:2014:2475, especially at para 100.

also of the domestic courts, and it is through them that we can start remedying the gap in protection in the CFSP. Yet, in order for this to be possible and effective, their jurisdiction has to be made clear in any CFSP act, much as is the case now in relation to data protection within Operation *Irini*. For this reason, I argued that Article 47 Charter imposes on the institutions a duty to include a jurisdictional clause in any act adopted within the CFSP (and CSDP), and failure to discharge that duty might engage the non-contractual liability of the EU. Furthermore, when the Member States implement or give effect to a CFSP act they are, in principle, bound by the Charter: this means that it is open to national courts to refer the matter of interpretation of Charter rights to the Court of Justice, further strengthening not only the protection of individuals but also the EU constitutional system. This approach might also serve the purpose of unblocking the impasse created by *Opinion 2/13* in relation to accession: after all, it would ensure that through the insertion of jurisdictional clauses CFSP acts are always subject to judicial review at national level as a matter of EU law. In this respect, national courts would act as EU courts, so that the preoccupation of the Court of Justice that the European Court of Human Rights would have jurisdiction over acts which are not subject to judicial control in the EU legal system would be overcome, also by virtue of the possibility for national courts to refer, in certain instances, preliminary questions as to the interpretation of the Charter. Finally, introducing jurisdictional clauses as a matter of course in all CFSP acts, would also make it easier for the ECtHR to determine when remedies have been exhausted.

Part II

States, Sovereignty and the Power of Law Beyond Borders

The Power of Routine and the Disruptive Politics of Brexit

KENNETH A ARMSTRONG

1. INTRODUCTION

WHATEVER ELSE IT may be, the European Union (EU) is an international organisation. For scholars of international relations, the status of an entity as an international organisation typically gives rise to a set of issues concerning the emergence of international organisations in the international order, and differing understandings as to their autonomy from, and influence over, the states which create them. A thread that connects these concerns is the idea that routinised decision-making reduces the transaction costs of international cooperation – a justification for the creation of international organisations – and once created, the routines of decision-making provide contexts for strategic intergovernmental bargaining (realists) or for preference formation (constructivists).[1] In making sense of why international organisations matter, it is often routines that matter.

In this contribution, I look beyond the realm of how international organisations shape the internal relations of the states that create them to the external relations of the EU as an international organisation. The argument is that the power of routine can influence how an international organisation conducts its external relations. The idea of 'routine' draws inspiration from institutionalist theories of decision-making.[2] Three themes of that literature inform how the idea of 'routine' is deployed in this analysis. The first are the effects of path-dependencies and policy 'lock-ins' which constrain the range of options apparently available to decision-makers. The second theme highlights standard operating procedures, routinised decision-making processes, boiler plate language and templates used to organise and formalise how decisions are made and instrumentalised. The final theme concerns how routines embed and diffuse norms and logics of what is, or is not, appropriate organisational

[1] MN Barnett and M Finnemore, 'The Politics, Power, and Pathologies of International Organizations' (1999) 53 *International Organization* 699.

[2] PA Hall and RCR Taylor, 'Political Science and the Three New Institutionalisms*' (1996) 44 *Political Studies* 936; JG March and JP Olsen, 'The New Institutionalism: Organizational Factors in Political Life' (1983) 78 *The American Political Science Review* 734; BG Peters, *Institutional Theory in Political Science: The 'New Institutionalism'* (London, Pinter, 1999); MA Pollack, 'The New Institutionalism and EC Governance: The Promise and Limits of Institutional Analysis' (1996) 9 *Governance* 429.

behaviour. Understanding how routines shape politics is the basis for conceptualising how an international organisation like the EU conducts not just its managements of relations between its Member States but also its own external relations.

In developing this argument, the analysis confronts a counterclaim that it is these sorts of routines and rules-based politics that are a source of weakness rather than power not least when it comes to the policy agendas that constitute external relations. Van Middelaar draws a distinction between what he terms 'rules-politics' and 'events-politics'.[3] In his analysis, 'rules-politics' is associated with an era, and a style, of governance, suitable for depoliticised market-making, or what Majone would term the European 'regulatory state'.[4] Consistent with neofunctionalist theories of integration, for van Middelaar the 'rules-politics' mode of governance – the 'Community Method' – seeks to shift political 'dramas' to the 'backstage'. By contrast, the dramas and crises that are a feature of contemporary European integration – and which are as likely to be externally generated as internally – are 'frontstage' and highly politicised, placing greater demands on EU institutions to supply novel, bespoke, agile responses. Van Middelaar's assessment of the state of the Union is nothing less than a call for a more strategic and more political Union as a global actor. To that end, he sees a need for the Union to cast off the straitjacket of its regulatory past. Explicitly he states:

> Historically, treaties and established rules were the Union's greatest achievements, but they do not offer an adequate or effective basis for joint action in all unforeseen circumstances.

For van Middelaar, the crucial question as to which type of politics is required for which type of problem is '[D]oes the matter at hand fit with existing rules and frameworks or is it completely unexpected, entirely contingent, or extremely sensitive?'. While recognising that problems rarely fit into simple categories, the point of drawing his distinction at all is to support van Middelaar's point that the EU needs different working methods – and different sources of institutional legitimacy – for the conduct of decision-making in the post-Maastricht era. If right, it has profound implications for EU external relations. It would also appear to push back strongly against the power of routine, and even the power of law.

The UK's withdrawal from the EU following the 2016 EU membership referendum ought to be a clear example of 'events-politics'. No Member State had ever left the Union. The mechanism that had been created by the Lisbon Treaty for the withdrawal of a Member State – Article 50 Treaty on European Union (TEU) – was untested. Brexit was the product, and driver, of a disruptive politics and a critique of 'business-as-usual' and contemporary political orthodoxies. That Brexit was a front of stage European 'drama' could not be in doubt.[5] Yet, the argument presented here is that when confronted with the disruptive politics of Brexit, the EU sought to manage and direct that politics through the power of routine.

[3] L van Middelaar, *Alarums and Excursions: Improvising Politics on the European Stage* (Newcastle upon Tyne, Agenda Publishing, 2019).

[4] G Majone, 'The Rise of the Regulatory State in Europe' (1994) 17 *West European Politics* 77.

[5] P Craig, 'Brexit: A Drama in Six Acts' (2016) 41 *EL Rev* 447; P Craig, 'Brexit a Drama: The Endgame – Part I' (2020) 45 *EL Rev* 163; P Craig, 'Brexit a Drama, the Endgame – Part II: Trade, Sovereignty and Control' (2021) 46 *EL Rev* 129.

In Section 2, the institutionalist foundations of the power of routine are elaborated. In so doing, it is recognised that the 'power' of routine is the bureaucratic power of an organisation. But the EU is also a highly legalised bureaucracy that includes a sophisticated judicial architecture.[6] Indeed, for van Middelaar, a depoliticised 'rules-politics' is achieved by, and through, law. If that is right, and if rule-politics is a weakness rather than a strength of the EU as an international organisation, it would seem to follow that the power of law ought also to be diminished where 'events-politics' is in the ascendency. Accordingly, in Section 3 the analysis reflects further on how the power of routine relates to the power of law and how that relationship is configured in the drama of Brexit.

Section 4 analyses the power of routine in relation to the process by which the UK withdrew from the EU. This may appear as an unusual example of EU 'external' relations given that it concerns one of the EU's own Member States. Yet as will become clear, from the moment the UK notified the EU of its intention to withdraw, the UK occupied an ambivalent position. On the one hand, it remained bound by, and subject to EU law. On the other hand, the negotiations concerning its departure treated it as if it were already a 'third' state. In Section 5 we have a clearer example of EU external relations as the Union and the UK sought to negotiate their post-membership relationship. Once more, we find the EU seeking to exert influence and to manage the disruptive politics of Brexit through strategies to export its own distinctive internal style of governance to its future external relations with the UK.

2. THE POWER OF ROUTINE

The institutionalist themes that inspire the conceptualisation of the power of routine were intimated in the Introduction. In this section, these themes are elaborated to provide the conceptual foundations for the substantive analyses of Brexit in Sections 4 and 5. When applied to Brexit, institutionalism and the claim that institutions matter in political life[7] could be limited to the analysis of the behaviour of EU institutions as actors. There is certainly ample scope to explore issues, for example, of institutional leadership not least between the European Council and the European Commission.[8] Nonetheless, an institutionalist approach can do more than this by expanding the ways in which we understand how institutions shape politics.

The first institutionalist preoccupation is with the path dependency of political choices. Consistent with historical institutionalism,[9] this temporal dimension locates decision-making in time and tends to explain decisions as bounded by policy

[6] KW Abbott, R Keohane, A Moravcsik, AM Slaughter and D Snidal, 'The Concept of Legalization' (2000) 54 *International Organization* 401.

[7] March and Olsen, 'The New Institutionalism'.

[8] See especially LA Schuette, 'Forging Unity: European Commission Leadership in the Brexit Negotiations' (2021) 59 *Journal of Common Market Studies* 1142.

[9] S Bulmer, '*Politics in Time* Meets the Politics of Time: Historical Institutionalism and the EU Timescape' (2009) 16 *Journal of European Public Policy* 307; and see P Pierson, 'The Path to European Integration: A Historical Institutionalist Analysis' (1996) 29 *Comparative Political Studies* 123.

lock-ins and the legacies of past decisions. Opportunities for change present at critical junctures which take decision-makers down new paths which form alternative path-dependencies. In this way, the power of routine is – to echo van Middelaar's own words – about fitting problems within rules and frameworks, ways of thinking and doing. Cutting against the novelty, rupture and improvisation of events-politics, the political event is re-temporalised within established policy paradigms, frames and modes of decision-making.

The second institutionalist theme give us a proceduralist orientation to the power of routine. It foregrounds the ways in which bureaucracies work within, or create, standard operating procedures for routinised decision-making. It is the point of international organisations that endure across time that they make the processes of international cooperation and decision-making more consistent, less likely to result in irresolution and more predictable by their routine production. As well as this proceduralist orientation there is an associated instrumentalist aspect in the deployment of boiler-plate language, templates and forms of wording, as well as particular forms of instruments through which the organisation communicates and orders its relations both internally and externally.

The third and final institutionalist theme has a more sociological orientation in its exploration of the role that institutions play in shaping behaviour according to institutional norms and logics. While rationalist approaches to politics often imply the operation of a logic of consequences in which behaviour depends on the intended or expected effects of strategic choices, norms or logics of appropriateness suggest that institutions shape politics by reference to what actors perceive to be the correct or expected thing to do in particular sets of circumstances. This is not quite the same as first order questions of whether a specific problem can be located in a particular set of rules; it is concerned with second-order questions that expand beyond the moment or the event to grapple with both phenomenological issues – what sort of problem or event is this – and identity issues – what does it mean for the organisation to respond to this problem or event not just in terms of geopolitical strategy but also geopolitical identity?

It is important to recognise that institutionalist literature does not make the claim that these organisational routines are necessarily efficient or produce optimal results. Indeed, there is common cause between van Middelaar's depiction of 'rules-politics' and concerns that routines persist through time in ways that could result in sub-optimal decision-making. Nothing in the analysis presented here fundamentally takes issue with that insight. And indeed, there will be examples where it will be asserted that in its dealings with the UK, the EU may have locked itself into processes and solutions that could be considered to have limited rather than increased the size of the landing zone for optimal outcomes. Instead, there are two points to make.

The first is that it may simply be unrealistic to expect international organisations to behave differently. As a shared service for political cooperation and decision-making, routinised decision-making is hardwired into how such organisation behave. Politicisation of EU decision-making in response to crises and novel challenges remains embedded in the routines and styles of institutionalised decision-making. The second point pushes further. When confronted with a disruptive politics that calls into question the mission and relevance of an international organisation, the deployment of routines is both a means of managing that external political environment and a means of asserting the power and relevance of the organisation. It may even be a way of expressing counter-narratives: organised multilateralism rather than disorganised unilateralism; politics within law rather than politics without law; collective unity rather than sovereign isolation. These are loaded and contestable ways of framing the UK's withdrawal from the EU. But as will be argued in Sections 4 and 5, the power of routine operates not only at an organisational and instrumental level but also at an ideational and existential level.

3. THE POWER OF ROUTINE AND THE POWER OF LAW

The power of routine is a bureaucratic power of institutions in their dealings with interlocuters. In an international organisation like the European Union, the powers of its institutions are expressed in law and exercised through legal instruments. Commitments and values which those institutions are expected to uphold and to which routines give effect are also located in EU law. A sophisticated judicial architecture interprets that law and ensures that EU institutions act according to law. The power of routine and the power of law are structurally coupled in a highly legalised international organisation like the EU.

This legalisation, judicialisation and, indeed, constitutionalisation, of EU decision-making produces the depoliticisation of which van Middelaar and others complain.[10] An agile and responsive 'events-politics' that looks to bespoke rather than routine responses, would also seem to require delegalisation or a significantly looser coupling of the relationship between law and politics, and between the power of law and the modalities of EU governance. The counterclaim that routines are simply the pervasive form of institutional response even to novel and unprecedented events would conversely suggest a more prominent role for law.

As a contribution to a collection of essays about the power of law in EU external relations, the analysis presented in the following sections does, indeed, give space to the explanatory power of law. But rather than seeing law and politics as a zero-sum game, and in order to draw attention to the bureaucratic power of institutional routines, the emphasis is placed on the connections, disconnections and misconnections between these routines and law. Crucially, and consistently with scholarship on 'transformations' in European integration and the changing relationship between law and evolving patterns of governance,[11] this coupling between the power of routine and the power of law is fashioned in multiple ways across different decision-making

[10] See eg D Grimm, 'The Democratic Costs of Constitutionalisation: The European Case' (2015) 21 *European Law Journal* 460; G Davies, 'The European Union Legislature as an Agent of the European Court of Justice' (2016) 54 *Journal of Common Market Studies* 846.

[11] M Dawson, *New Governance and the Transformation of European Law: Coordinating EU Social Law and Policy*, Cambridge Studies in European Law and Policy (Cambridge, Cambridge University Press, 2011); DM Trubek and L Trubek, 'New Governance and Legal Regulation: Complementarity, Rivalry and Transformation' (2007) 13 *Columbia Journal of European Law* 539; JHH Weiler, 'The Transformation of Europe' (1991) 100 *Yale Law Journal* 2403; G de Búrca and J Scott, *Law and New Governance in the EU and the US*, Essays in European Law (Oxford, Hart Publishing, 2006).

contexts.[12] For the purposes of this contribution, these encounters between the power of routine and the power of law are explored in two different contexts as the EU sought to manage and direct the disruptive politics of Brexit.

The first set of orientations connects with Marise Cremona's scholarship on the legal foundations of EU external relations and, in particular, the Union's external competence and the 'structural principles' governing its exercise.[13] The analysis is focused around the primary law of the treaties in creating both a mechanism for a Member State to withdraw from the Union, and a legal competence for the EU to negotiate a withdrawal agreement. Introduced by the Lisbon Treaty and untested at the time of its deployment to manage the UK's departure from the EU, Article 50 TEU could fairly be considered to be an example of the power of law without the power of routine. Nonetheless, attention is drawn to the ways in which the novel circumstances of Brexit provoked institutional responses from the EU that adopted or adapted the routines of EU decision-making, not least routines associated with EU external action and the negotiation of EU international agreements. The effects of path dependencies, standard operating procedures and norms of appropriateness will be explored. In this way, the disruptive politics of Brexit were confronted not just with the power and normative pull of EU primary law but also with the institutional routines that sought to make sense of how to use this mechanism in an unprecedented situation.

The second group of issues examined in Section 5 resonate more strongly with Cremona's work on EU membership, the effects of EU law within the European 'neighbourhood' (and beyond), as well as the Union's influence as a global actor.[14] Whereas that scholarship has underlined the reach of EU law beyond its borders, the context of EU contraction – of the rejection of EU membership and its legal disciplines – through the withdrawal of a Member State intuitively suggests a diminished power and influence of EU law in the post-membership context. In other words, even if we find that the power of routine and the power of law exert a strong influence in the withdrawal process itself, the post-membership context ought to create more space for the influence of disruptive politics and less space for the influence of EU routines and EU law. The analysis tests this assumption by reference to the struggles between the EU and the UK over the appropriate model for their future relationship, and more particularly, during the negotiation of 'level playing field' obligations within their Trade and Cooperation Agreement. On the one hand, the Union sought

[12] KA Armstrong, 'The Character of EU Law and Governance: From "Community Method" to New Modes of Governance' (2011) 64 *Current Legal Problems* 179.

[13] M Cremona, 'EU External Relations: Unity and Conferral of Powers' in L Azoulai (ed), *The Question of Competence in the European Union* (Oxford, Oxford University Press, 2014); M Cremona, 'Structural Principles and their Role in EU External Relations Law' (2016) 69 *Current legal problems* 35; M Cremona, 'External Relations of the European Union: The Constitutional Framework for International Action' in P Craig and G de Búrca (eds), *The Evolution of EU Law*, 3rd edn (Oxford, Oxford University Press, 2021).

[14] M Cremona (ed), *The Enlargement of the European Union*, The Collected Courses of the Academy of European Law XII/1 (Oxford, Oxford University Press, 2003); M Cremona, 'The Union as a Global Actor: Roles, Models and Identity' (2004) 41 *CML Rev* 553, M Cremona, 'The European Union and Regional Trade Agreements' in C Herrman and JP Terhechte (eds), *European Yearbook of International Economic Law 2010* (Berlin, Springer, 2010): M Cremona and N Nic Shuibhne, 'Integration, Membership, and The EU Neighbourhood' (2022) *CML Rev* 155; M Cremona and J Scott (eds), *EU Law beyond EU Borders: The Extraterritorial Reach of EU Law*, The Collected Courses of the Academy of European Law XXVII/1 (Oxford, Oxford University Press, 2019).

to export the routines and instruments of its internal regulatory practices to its post-membership relationship with the UK. On the other hand, it was to the routines of other EU free trade agreements and the looser discipline of international trade law that the UK looked for its template for a post-membership economic relationship with the EU. Meanwhile, joint acceptance of the need for a set of arrangements to protect the integrity of the EU single market across the frontier with Northern Ireland dramatised not just the potential for EU law to extend beyond EU borders but also the reach of the EU's enforcement machinery when confronted with a disruptive politics of unilateralism and political freelancing.

It is through the more detailed analysis presented in the subsequent sections that the effects of the power of routine on the disruptive politics of Brexit will be assessed. In so doing, the analysis readily acknowledges that decision-making throughout the Brexit process was saturated with politics. But even in these moments of drama and conflict, the claim made here is that it was through the bureaucratic power of routine – often embedded within, and expressed through, the power of law – that the EU as an international organisation responded to Brexit.

4. THE UK'S WITHDRAWAL FROM THE EUROPEAN UNION

In the three subsections that follow, the legal framework of Article 50 TEU and its encounter with the disruptive politics of Brexit is examined relative to the routines embedded within: (1) bureaucratic leadership – the role of the European Council – (2) the negotiation of international agreements – the EU-UK Withdrawal Agreement – and (3) adjudication – the preliminary ruling on the right to revoke a notified intention to leave the EU. Before doing so, it is worth dwelling a moment on Article 50 TEU itself as the legal centrepiece of the withdrawal process. That Article 50 TEU became synonymous with the Brexit process was path-dependent and the product of a norm of appropriateness that meant that the UK maintained a fidelity to EU law even as it imitated a process to end its application to the UK.

The path-dependency of Article 50 TEU is to make the obvious point that the UK's departure from the EU post-dated the entry into force of the Lisbon Treaty which introduced this withdrawal mechanism into the TEU. The Lisbon Treaty was itself the path-dependent result of the earlier failure of the Constitutional Treaty and its convention process which had deliberated and agreed a treaty-based withdrawal mechanism. The Lisbon Treaty repurposed the relevant provisions of the Constitutional Treaty to create Article 50 TEU. Had the UK or any other state sought to leave the Union prior to Lisbon, it would have been far less clear how that would have happened.[15] True, Article 50 TEU formalises in EU law the right of a state under international law to withdraw from a treaty and in that way the default rules of instruments such as the Vienna Convention on the Law of Treaties might have provided guidance. More significantly, however, Article 50 TEU goes further in seeking an 'orderly' withdrawal by means of the negotiation of an agreement to settle the

[15] On which see JV Louis, 'Le droit de retrait de l'Union européenne' (2006) 42 *Cahiers de droit européen* 293.

terms of exit. Lisbon 'constitutionalised' the withdrawal mechanism not merely as a textual recognition of a right to withdraw, it also brought the subsequent negotiations within the normative power and pull of EU law.[16]

Significantly, and despite the disruptive politics of Brexit sometimes encouraging the UK Government to look to either domestic law – the repeal of the European Communities Act 1972 – or public international law – the Vienna Convention on the Law of Treaties – as alternative means to bring Brexit about, there was never any serious movement to leave the EU by alternative means. Even the risk (or strategy) of a 'no deal' Brexit would have been the result of the operation of law in which the treaties would cease to apply two years after the notification of intention to leave (Article 50(3) TEU). It is striking, therefore, that Article 50 TEU was regarded by all sides as the appropriate and only legal framework through which to manage the UK's exit from the Union. All of which brought the negotiations within the legal discipline and institutional routines of EU decision-making.[17]

With this assertion of the power of EU law in mind, in the subsections below, the analysis drills down into the ways in which the disruptive politics of Brexit was managed through routines (or the adaptation of routines) of EU decision-making.

4.1. The European Council

Article 22 TEU assigns to the European Council the task of identifying the strategic interests and objectives of the Union in its external relations. A striking feature of Article 50 TEU is also its repeated references to the European Council. It is to this body that the withdrawing state notifies its intention to leave the Union.[18] It is the European Council that provides guidelines for the conduct of the negotiations between the Union and the withdrawing state.[19] Any extension of the time period for the conduct of those negotiations is a matter for the European Council in agreement with the departing state. Article 50 TEU even clarifies that the departing state will not be represented in the European Council when it considers matters relating to that state's withdrawal from the EU.

This central position of the European Council is in many ways indicative of a broader trend in post-Maastricht European integration that has been described as the 'new intergovernmentalism'.[20] That trend moves in a similar direction to van Middelaar's

[16] See eg C Hillion, 'Accession and Withdrawal in the Law of the European Union' in A Arnull and D Chalmers (eds), *The Oxford Handbook of European Union Law* (Oxford, Oxford University Press, 2015).

[17] KA Armstrong, '(Br)Exit From the European Union – Control, Autonomy, and the Evolution of EU Law' in Craig and de Búrca (eds), *The Evolution of EU Law*.

[18] See European Council, 'United Kingdom Notification under Article 50 TEU' (2017) XT 20001/17.

[19] European Council, 'Special Meeting of the European Council (Art.50) (29 April 2017) – Guidelines for Brexit Negotiations' (2017) EUCO XT 20004/17.

[20] CJ Bickerton, D Hodson and U Puetter, 'The New Intergovernmentalism: European Integration in the Post-Maastricht Era' (2015) 53 *Journal of Common Market Studies* 703; U Puetter, *The European Council and the Council: New Intergovernmentalism and Institutional Change* (Oxford, Oxford University Press, 2014); F Schimmelfennig, 'What's the News in "New Intergovernmentalism"? A Critique of Bickerton, Hodson and Puetter' (2015) 53 *Journal of Common Market Studies* 723.

call for a more agile and more politicised Union when faced with unprecedented events. Yet the claims of new intergovernmentalism are deeper than a mere foregrounding of an ascendent European Council. The fundamental point is actually about the emergence of routine and often institutionalised forms of policy coordination underpinned by consensual norms of decision-making. What is striking about the European Council is precisely the fact that, so routine became the earlier informal summits of European leaders they took on institutional form.[21] The strategic role of the European Council in EU external relations and within the Article 50 withdrawal mechanism is a potent representation of the effect of the power of routine in EU decision-making.

We need to be clear, however, about the role played by the European Council in the Article 50 process. As will become apparent in the following subsection, the substantive negotiations followed the institutional routines associated with the negotiation of international agreements under Article 218 TFEU in which the European Council plays no part. Instead, the European Council performed the specific functions allocated to it under Article 50 TEU, while also seeking to maintain its consensual mode of decision-making.

Rightly, we should recognise that the European Council did have to adapt its standard operating procedures in its response to Brexit. The need for adaptation is envisaged in Article 50 TEU:

> … the member of the European Council or of the Council representing the withdrawing Member State shall not participate in the discussions of the European Council or Council or in decisions concerning it.

An 'EU27 European Council' formation (pre-triggering of Article 50) and a 'European Council (Art.50)' formation (post-triggering) became routine institutional formations to manage the business of Brexit. In this way, the European Council modulated its operations between the normal and scheduled meetings of all the principals of the Member States and as a new routine in which the UK Prime Minister would leave meetings. Between the UK's notification of its intention to leave the EU and its eventual withdrawal, 13 meetings (including special sessions) of the European Council in its Article 50 formation were held.

Perhaps more than anything else, the European Council (Art 50) format symbolised the unity of the EU27; a unity whose power the Union sought to maintain and exploit in its negotiations with the UK. Indeed, attempts by the UK to circumvent the European Commission and to appeal directly to European leaders were habitually blocked. It was one thing for the European Commission to seek instructions or guidance from its political principals in the European Council but another for the UK to try and bypass the European Commission and go straight to the European Council or indeed to individual premiers. By insisting on the routines of its decision-making including the logic of appropriateness governing the division of responsibilities between the European Council and the European Commission, the Union sought to manage a difficult relationship between the EU27 and a state that remained a Member State, but which was also in the process of leaving the EU.

[21] S Bulmer and W Wessels, *European Council: Decision-making in European Politics* (London, Macmillan, 1987).

4.2. The Article 50 Negotiations

Article 50 TEU tells us that the Union shall negotiate an agreement with the withdrawing state following the procedure laid down in Article 218(3) Treaty on the Functioning of the European Union (TFEU). A withdrawal agreement is then concluded on behalf of the Union by the Council (acting by a qualified majority) with the consent of the European Parliament (EP). In this way, Union law adapts the routine procedures for the negotiation of international agreements with third countries to the novel circumstances of a state leaving the EU. Although the negotiations would be unprecedented on both sides, the Union had its experience of negotiating international agreements – and the institutional routines that have developed over time – as a template from which to organise its dealings with the UK.

The most immediate institutional manifestation of standard operating procedures was the appointment of the European Commission as the Union's negotiator. While the highly political nature of these negotiations was reflected in the appointment by the European Commission President of Michel Barnier as the chief negotiator, the appointment of Sabine Weyand as his deputy sent a signal that the Union would rely on the experience and expertise of its trade negotiators in its dealing with the UK. A further clear example of the power of routine was the process put in place to keep the European Parliament abreast of the negotiations in the knowledge that its consent would ultimately be required further downstream. Drawing on the experiences of past international agreements, routine contacts were held not just with Guy Verhofstadt who acted as the Parliament's liaison with the Commission's negotiating team, but also through meetings of the presidents of the political groupings. From past experiences of leveraging its formal powers to give consent to international agreements, the EP sought to replicate a role for itself as a 'quasi-negotiator'.[22]

The UK was in a different position when it came to negotiating with the EU. For one thing, and in a path-dependent manner, the UK had ceded most of its trade negotiating experience to the EU during the course of its EU membership. This was unfamiliar terrain for UK officials. Three chief negotiators were appointed by successive UK Prime Ministers. Meanwhile the disruptive politics of Brexit made it difficult for the UK to define and maintain a position on what it wanted from these negotiations. If the EU27 repeatedly reinforced the unity of the EU, then the politics of Brexit were steadfastly divisive domestically and in ways that inhibited the UK in its negotiations with the EU.[23]

So far, the general tenor of the argument has been that the Union relied on the power of routine successfully to pursue and implement its negotiating objectives with the UK. However, there is a counter argument that inflexibility and formalism in the following of routines were ultimately damaging to the negotiation of the UK's withdrawal. Indeed, institutionalist analysis itself highlights that institutions and

[22] E Bressanelli, N Chelotti and W Lehmann, 'Negotiating Brexit: The European Parliament between Participation and Influence' (2019) 41 *Journal of European Integration* 347.

[23] For more detailed analysis see E Jones, 'The Negotiations' in F Fabbrini (ed), *The Law & Politics of Brexit: Volume II: The Withdrawal Agreement* (Oxford, Oxford University Press, 2020).

routines may persist even when they become inefficient. An example of this could be the EU's insistence that the proper approach to its negotiations with the UK was to sequence discussion around the UK's exit from the Union and the formation of a post-membership relationship.

The EU made it clear that it would not be willing to conduct parallel negotiations on the Withdrawal Agreement and any agreement embodying a future economic relationship with the UK. The Union insisted that its competence to negotiate a future trade arrangement was that applicable to the Union's relations with non-Member States and it was only once the UK ceased to be a Member State that formal negotiations could commence. This was also reflected in Article 50 TEU itself insofar as the negotiations on the Withdrawal Agreement should take into account the 'framework' of their future relationship. For the EU this meant that only a non-binding Political Declaration setting out heads of areas for future cooperation could be agreed. Moreover, the time period for the conduct of the Article 50 TEU negotiations did not appear conducive to parallel strands of negotiations. No doubt the 'stick' of the pressure of time and the 'carrot' of a trade agreement to follow were believed to be a means of exerting influence and pressure on the UK. This approach to the sequencing of negotiations – based on an interpretation of the legal competence of the Union construed in light of norms of appropriateness about how an orderly withdrawal and a new relationship should be forged – may have had unforeseen consequences when confronted with the disruptive politics of Brexit.

First, in the absence of a total package, there would inevitably be a gap between the entry into force of a withdrawal agreement and the start of a new legal relationship. A transition period would be needed.[24] But rather than this transition period acting as a continuous bridge to its future relationship with the EU, the UK utilised it merely as a means of avoiding a 'cliff edge' Brexit. Instead, the UK insisted that the transition period would not be extended, and used the pressure of a short transition to limit the EU's ambitions for what it might negotiate with the EU for its post-membership relationship.

Second, if the issue of how to avoid a hard border on the island of Ireland was not settled in the context of the overall future relationship, the Withdrawal Agreement would need to establish structures and processes that could be applied in the absence of a wider settlement. Of the many discontents with the agreement negotiated by the EU with Prime Minister May, it was the idea of an Irish 'backstop' that became a focal point for the political pressures that ultimately saw her removal as Prime Minister. But – as we shall later see – even the installation of a new UK Prime Minister and a renegotiated Protocol on Ireland/Northern Ireland failed to resolve a central point of tension in the EU-UK negotiations.

Third, in taking literally the wording of Article 50, a willingness only to agree a non-binding Political Declaration setting out the 'framework' of their future relationship was consequential in two ways. Fears of a 'blind Brexit' prevented opposition parties in the UK from having confidence in where the Brexit process would take the UK and limited consensus formation. And for the UK Government, the absence

[24] KA Armstrong, 'The Transition' in Fabbrini (ed) (n 23).

of anything tying their hands allowed a new government under Boris Johnson to pursue a very different approach to negotiating the post-membership relationship with the EU. In other words, through its insistence on its routines, the EU created path dependencies that perhaps produced outcomes that were suboptimal from the EU's perspective.

4.3. The Silence of the Treaties and the Voice of the Court

For EU lawyers, the power of law is often treated as synonymous with the power of the Court of Justice of the EU. As the contributions to this volume make clear, when it comes to the external governance of the Union, the role of the Court may often be less substantive particularly when external relations manifest themselves in the high politics of foreign policy. Nonetheless, as Marise Cremona reminds us, in its articulation of 'structural principles' of EU law, the power of law and the power of the Court can still be felt in organising the institutional space in which external relations are conducted.[25]

When we examine Article 50 TEU, there is no express role identified for the Court of Justice. A role for the Court can be inferred in respect of any withdrawal agreement negotiated following the procedure laid down in Article 218 TFEU given the specific jurisdiction of the Court under Article 218(11) TFEU to give an Opinion on the compatibility of an agreement with the treaties. Otherwise, it would not be immediately apparent how the power of law – either the jurisdiction of the Court or the influence of structural principles – might be exerted. Thus, when commentators asked whether a Member State could revoke its withdrawal notification, the lack of any express wording in Article 50 TEU to answer the question taken together with the absence of an express jurisdiction of the Court in respect of Article 50 TEU might suggest that any answer would be political rather than legal.

Yet, through a well-established institutional routine – the preliminary ruling mechanism in Article 267 TFEU – the power of EU law could make its influence felt. It is through its responses to questions of interpretation raised by national courts that the Court of Justice has been able to establish and institutionalise fundamental features of the EU legal order; features which impose a discipline on politics both procedurally and substantively. It was from such a reference by a Scottish court in *Wightman* that the Court of Justice was able to rule that, notwithstanding the absence of any express wording in Article 50 TEU, a Member State could unilaterally revoke its notice of intention to withdraw unless and until the treaties ceased to apply to that state.[26]

The Court of Justice gave its ruling despite arguments from both the United Kingdom and the European Commission that the reference was inadmissible on the grounds of being hypothetical and/or an attempt to obtain an advisory opinion of the Court outside of the specific avenues for seeking such an opinion laid down in the Treaties. These arguments and the Court's response to them – emphasising that

[25] M Cremona (ed), *Structural Principles in EU External Relations Law* (Oxford, Hart Publishing, 2018).
[26] Case C-621/18 *Wightman and Others* ECLI:EU:C:2018:999.

the Court will routinely answer questions referred by national courts unless there are well-established grounds for not doing so – can be seen as examples of the power of routine outside of the types of bureaucratic routines discussed elsewhere in this chapter. Indeed, the judgment of the Court utilises precisely the same boilerplate language it always uses when issues as to the admissibility of a reference from a national court are raised. Albeit structured as a set of institutional gatekeeping rules, they conform to a logic of the appropriateness of domestic court engagement with the Court of Justice and a willingness to consider questions of law notwithstanding the often highly political context in which such questions are raised. The argument presented by the UK Government against the admissibility of the reference in *Wightman* – that it would bring the Court into an arena of politics which other comparable 'supreme' courts may refuse to enter – was, therefore, rejected in favour of the maintenance of a channel of communication between domestic courts and the Court.

All of which still left open the question of how the Court would come to its conclusion on the revocability of a withdrawal notification. After all, the Court did have choices. It could have decided that revocation was possible but not unilaterally without the unanimous consent of the European Council (by analogy with its powers in respect of any extension of the time period for conducting withdrawal negotiations). That it decided that revocation was a 'sovereign choice' to be exercised unilaterally is buttressed by a range of textual and contextual arguments including application of structural and constitutional principles concerning the appropriate way to interpret Article 50 TEU.[27] The Court's decision was undoubtedly a novel answer to an unprecedented question, but its institutional response – procedurally and substantively – was embedded in familiar legal language and concepts.

5. DEFINING THE POST-MEMBERSHIP RELATIONSHIP

As Cremona's scholarship attests, and as the chapters in this volume make clear, the Union's external relations competence is much more than the exercise of the EU's well-established trade policy competence. What makes contemporary EU external relations such a vital field of European Legal Studies is its variety. But economic relationships with non-Member States still matter. They have particular relevance and importance in the European neighbourhood at a time when EU enlargement as a means of spreading the power and influence of EU law has faltered.[28] Moreover, as van Middelaar points out, the geopolitics of regional trade agreements such as the EU-Ukraine Deep and Comprehensive Free Trade Agreement – and other similar 'association agreements' with Georgia and Moldova – epitomise the strategic context in which the Union seeks to assert its external influence. All of which might suggest that the better test of the argument made here is to be found in the politics surrounding the UK's post-membership economic relationship with the EU.

[27] P Eeckhout and E Frantziou, 'Brexit and Article 50 TEU: A Constitutionalist Reading' (2017) 54 *CML Rev* 695.

[28] Cremona, 'The European Union and Regional Trade Agreements' (n 14).

No one can be in any doubt that, going into their negotiations, the EU and the UK had quite different approaches, expectations and interests. Nothing in the claims made here denies this central fact. The negotiations that produced the EU-UK Trade and Cooperation Agreement (TCA) – all undertaken in a very compressed time frame at the insistence of the UK – clearly required the parties to do something unprecedented in terms of downgrading the terms of their economic relationship. Moreover, in contrast to the highly structured process for accession to the EU and its extension of the reach and power of EU law over the acceding Member State, de-membership seemingly opens up a plethora of possible futures shaped by self-interest and geopolitical positioning.

All that said, the power of routine is not absent from the construction of the UK's post-membership economic relationship with the EU. In the first subsection that follows, the power of routine manifested itself in conflicts over which model of economic cooperation was appropriate for a former EU Member State. Strikingly, it is the absence of law and the presence of a 'political' declaration concerning the framework of a future relationship that helped open the space for the disruptive politics of Brexit to influence the direction of travel of those negotiations. However, in the second subsection the power of routine and the power of law appear more tightly coupled in the attempts by the EU to keep the UK within the normative orbit of the Union through 'level playing field' obligations. As the analysis demonstrates, the EU's attempt to specify these obligations in terms of the exportation of its own internal regulatory norms and practices was resisted by the UK with varying degrees of success. The third subsection focuses upon the Protocol on Ireland/Northern Ireland. Despite forming part of the Withdrawal Agreement negotiations, the reason for including it here is that it is a more specific example of a highly politicised agreement that came into operation once the UK was outside of the EU and governing trade in goods in respect of Northern Ireland. Intended to implement the commitment of all sides to avoid a hard border on the island of Ireland, the Protocol also epitomises the disruptive politics of Brexit both domestically and in the UK's relations with the EU. In fully acknowledging that the problem which the Protocol seeks to resolve has demanded agility and improvisation by the Union, it is its response to efforts by the UK to change the Protocol unilaterally that allows us to test whether the power of routine and the power of law are able to manage and mediate the disruptive politics of Brexit.

5.1. The Political Declaration on the Future Relationship

As discussed previously, following its own logic of appropriateness about the sequencing of the negotiations, formal talks on what would become the TCA were not launched until the UK had withdrawn from the EU. The broad terms of what might be negotiated had been set out in the Political Declaration that was agreed simultaneously with the Withdrawal Agreement. However, that Political Declaration did not lock the UK in to any firm commitments. If the EU saw the Declaration as setting out a direction of travel towards an ambitious association agreement with the UK – covering multiple areas of economic and political cooperation – then the UK tended to view it as a wish list from which it was free to depart. Somewhat in a reversal of their power position during the earlier Article 50 negotiations, it was the UK that used the pressure of time to dilute the EU's ambitions by giving negotiators a mere 11 months within which to negotiate, conclude and bring into force what would become the TCA. In this way, the absence of a legally binding Political Declaration prevented the EU securing policy lock-ins and instead the UK seized the opportunity to engage in unilateralism – its refusal to allow any extension of the transition period – to downgrade expectations and 'Get Brexit Done'. The disruptive power of Brexit politics succeeded in shaping the context for negotiations on the post-membership economic relationship. Nonetheless, into this relative legal vacuum came a debate about what was or was not an appropriate model or template for a future economic relationship.

The EU's position was well trailed during the withdrawal process. In a series of presentations, the European Commission set out a set of stylised choices about what could or could not form the basis of a negotiation. Indeed, there is, perhaps, no more visible symbol of the power of path dependency in the EU's external relations with non-Member States than an infamous infographic presented by EU chief negotiator Michel Barnier to the European Council (meeting as an Art 50 formation) on 15 December 2017.[29] Consistent with its stance that the UK would not be allowed to 'cherry-pick' a future relationship with the EU, the possible outcome of negotiations was presented as a series of 'if-then' choices cascading from EU membership through to a European Economic Area-style agreement, to a more sectoral Swiss-form of relationship, and from a Deep and Comprehensive Ukraine stye partnership to a type of customs union as exemplified by the EU's relationship with Turkey. Ultimately the result might simply be a Canadian or South Korean form of Free Trade Agreement (FTA).

For its part, as the Article 50 process was being initiated, the UK Government initially rejected the idea that any of these models were relevant; the novelty of Brexit required an improvised and bespoke solution. However, with a change in government, the position shifted, and the UK instead focused on obtaining a trade agreement with the EU like the EU-Canada trade agreement (CETA).

If the absence of legally defined commitments to a particular model of future cooperation was leveraged by the UK to limit EU ambitions for its future relationship with the UK, then the more concrete and highly contested negotiations around 'level playing field' obligations provided an opportunity for the EU to seek to export the Union's internal regulatory policies and practices to its future economic relationship with the UK. It is to these obligations that the analysis now turns.

5.2. The Level Playing Field Obligations – Extending EU Law Beyond EU Borders

In its approach to the negotiations of a new economic relationship with the UK, the EU insisted that access to the Union market had to be on the basis of fair conditions of competition. Fearing that the UK would use its regulatory autonomy to achieve

[29] 'Slide Presented by Michel Barnier, European Commission Chief Negotiator, to the heads of State and Government at the European Council (Article 50) on 15 December 2017' (*European Commission*, 19 December 2017) TF50 (2017) 21, commission.europa.eu/system/files/2017-12/slide_presented_by_barnier_at_euco_15-12-2017.pdf.

competitive advantage, the Political Declaration included robust commitments to a level playing field in competition and subsidy control, taxation, social and environmental standards. For the UK, however, the logic of Brexit was not to reproduce the balance of rights and obligations experienced during membership but to change them. Indeed, the UK looked to the routines of other EU FTAs – their structure, content and boilerplate legal texts – to resist attempts by the EU to impose a more stringent legal discipline through the level playing field obligations. The negotiations around the level playing field obligations dramatise a tension between a UK intent on recasting its relationship with the EU and asserting its autonomy on the international stage, and an EU fearful of regulatory competition from the UK and keen to keep the UK within its normative sphere of influence.

Scholarship on EU economic relations with non-Member States has highlighted the manner in which historic path dependencies in those relations shape the possibilities of negotiations to extend and deepen economic relations.[30] De-membership and the downgrading of economic relations would seem to rupture or break logics of incremental economic path dependency. Yet, as Cremona observed, the external actorness of the EU manifests itself in efforts to export internal EU ways of doing things to its external environment.[31] In other words, the very routines of regulatory practices which the UK sought to reject by leaving the EU would be the thing that the EU would seek to export to its post-membership relationship with the UK.

Scholarship on EU rules beyond EU borders points to this potential for exportation of the routines, models, templates and norms familiar to internal EU governance.[32] Importantly, the resulting EU external relationship may end up being characterised less by the high-level classification of a relationship implied by the Barnier infographic and more by how internal patterns of rules-based governance in different sectors manifest themselves externally.[33] It is with this in mind that we can evaluate how the conflicts between the EU and the UK played out in their struggles during the more detailed negotiations over the level playing field obligations.

The difference in the positions of the two sides was manifested by the publication of their respective draft texts. The UK's minimalist 'cut and paste' approach – using the templates and language of EU trade agreements like CETA and other international economic instruments – contrasted sharply with the maximalist position of the Union in which core aspects of its internal governance across competition, state aid, tax, environmental and social standards were brought into the EU's text of the level playing field obligations. Importantly, the depth and design of these obligations was highly asymmetric. This very 'uneven' level playing field reproduced the asymmetries of the Union's own internal governance and the extent to which responsibilities over

[30] J Gilson, 'The Strategic Partnership Agreement between the EU and Japan: The Pitfalls of Path Dependency?' (2016) 38 *Journal of European Integration* 791.

[31] Cremona, 'The Union as a Global Actor' (n 14).

[32] Cremona and Scott (eds) (n 14); S Lavenex and F Schimmelfennig, 'EU Rules beyond EU Borders: Theorizing External Governance in European Politics' (2009) 16 *Journal of European Public Policy* 791.

[33] S Lavenex, D Lehmkuhl and N Wichmann, 'Modes of External Governance: A Cross-National and Cross-Sectoral Comparison' (2009) 16 *Journal of European Public Policy* 813; Lavenex and Schimmelfennig (n 32).

competition and state aid were delegated to Union institutions in ways that are different from its responsibilities in the tax, environment and social spheres. For the Union, the path-dependencies and routines of its internal governance were the appropriate starting point for what it would seek to achieve in its negotiations with the UK.

A significant disagreement was over the control of subsidies to businesses. The UK's position was that for the future it would observe the World Trade Organisation Subsidy and Countervailing Measures (SCM) Agreement and would consult on whether to go further in domestic law to legislate for a UK subsidy control regime.[34] Its draft text defined subsidies in terms of the SCM and stated that both the UK and EU would reaffirm their rights and obligations under international agreements including the SCM. Objections to subsidies made by the other party would be the subject of consultations but with no dispute resolution mechanism attached.

The EU started from a very different position. Mirroring the approach taken in the Protocol on Ireland/Norther Ireland under which the UK agreed to comply with EU state aid rules listed in an Annex to the Protocol, the EU's draft agreement anticipated that the UK would give effect to acts and provisions of EU law listed in an Annex (including amended or replaced provisions). The EU sought to project key internal instruments into its external relations with the UK. Albeit that the European Commission would not enforce EU state aid rules directly against the UK, the EU insisted instead that the UK create an operationally independent authority with powers equivalent to that of the Commission and whose decisions would have the same legal effects. Given that the substantive requirements to be enforced would be instruments of EU law, the EU also sought to ensure that UK courts tasked with reviewing decisions of a domestic authority would have the ability to seek authoritative interpretations of those instruments from the Court of Justice of the EU.

The TCA compromise is delicately balanced. First, the UK won the linguistic battle in that the Agreement refers to 'subsidies' not 'state aid'. Second, and more significantly, the substantive provisions are neither as thin as the UK wanted in terms of reaffirming the SCM Agreement nor as far reaching as the EU sought in demanding continued compliance with specific EU rules. Instead, the Agreement itself is the direct source of detailed substantive definitions of what constitutes a subsidy, certain prohibitions and any exceptions. But in a path-dependent way, the substance of these rules mirror EU state aid rules.

The compromised reached on competition policy is almost exactly the reverse of what happened with subsidy control. Whereas the EU had proposed that the TCA itself contain substantive rules governing competition policy – consistent with EU prohibitions on anti-competitive agreements, abuses and concentrations of market power – these were stripped out leaving each party to maintain an effective competition law addressing these types of anti-competitive behaviour. Each party is to entrust competition law enforcement to operationally independent bodies. One explanation for the EU's willingness to accept that it could not directly export its internal

[34] The UK's plan can be found here: 'Government Sets out plans for New Approach to Subsidy Control' (*UK Government*, 9 September 2020), www.gov.uk/government/news/government-sets-out-plans-for-new-approach-to-subsidy-control. The Subsidy Control Act 2022 gained Royal Assent at the end of April 2022.

competition policy regime to its new relationship with the UK might be its assumption of a more pervasive path dependency. That is to say that competition policy itself could be said to encode the norms and logics of what constitutes a proper competition regime reproduced and diffused by an epistemic community of competition lawyers and officials inside and outside the EU. The EU may have felt that the UK would remain aligned with these norms and remain part of that community.[35] What is also clear is that both the EU (and its Member States) and the UK competition authorities will autonomously apply their own competition law regimes even to the same transactions and activities. The issue will be whether businesses perceive a difference in what they will do in the future to comply with UK law compared to their expectations of what Union law demands.

In their approach to taxation matters, the EU and UK began from a similar starting point, namely international standards on good governance in taxation matters including Organisation for Economic Co-operation and Development (OECD) standards against Base Erosion and Profit Shifting (BEPS). So, to the extent that there are substantive norms in play they are those applicable to both the EU and the UK through international bodies like the OECD; this is not an area where EU internal governing is being projected into the Union's relationship with the UK. What is particularly noteworthy, however, is the EU's insistence in including non-regression provisions. In its early draft, the EU had included a clause requiring the EU and the UK not to weaken or reduce levels of protection against tax avoidance below 'common high standards applicable in the Union and the United Kingdom at the end of the transition period'. The TCA does include a non-regression clause in tax matters but its focus is on limiting the ability of either party to defect from specific common international standards agreed in the OECD at the end of the transition period And while the EU had envisaged that the Partnership Council established under the TCA would have a power to modify common standards to include additional areas or higher standards, this was not accepted and was not included in the final text. What this illustrates then, is that in an area where the Union has less of a role and other international bodies have influence, there is less of a power of routine to be deployed to exert external influence. Any policy lock ins are external to the EU and apply both to it and the UK.

The issue of 'non-regression' – committing both sides not to reduce levels of protection below current levels – is dramatised in respect of social protection and environmental standards. On social and labour standards, the UK's approach was simply to cut and paste from the 'Trade and Labour' chapter of the EU's trade agreement with Canada. Under that agreement both Canada and the EU recognise the inappropriateness of reducing labour standards in order to promote trade and investment, with both parties committing not to waive or derogate from its labour standards.

The EU wanted something more demanding in its negotiations with the UK. First, the EU sought to more clearly define the benchmark of rules against which to assess non-regression. It defined this as the 'common standards applicable within the Union

[35] Nonetheless, in July 2021 the UK Government announced a consultation on *Reforming Competition and Consumer Policy* focusing on its new post-membership autonomy to do things differently: Department for Business, Energy and Industrial Strategy, 'Reforming Competition and Consumer Policy – Government Response to Consultation' (2022) CP656.

and the United Kingdom at the end of the transition period'. Second, there was an exhortation to increase levels of protection through their respective law and labour practices. Third – and most controversially – where the EU and UK increased their levels of protection, the new level would become the benchmark for non-regression and not the position at the end of the transition period.

The TCA recognises the regulatory autonomy of both parties to set their own levels of labour and social protection. However, both the EU and the UK have committed to neither weaken nor reduce – *in a manner affecting trade or investment* – their levels of protection as they existed at the end of the transition period. If standards are raised, there is no ratchet clause to heighten the benchmark level of standards to reflect such changes.

Lastly, in terms of environmental standards, and consistent with its approach to labour laws, the UK's pitch was simply to replicate the 'Trade and Environment' chapter of CETA in its draft EU-UK Agreement. Again, the EU sought something more expansive including express inclusion of rules relating to climate change (including targets) which was not included in the UK's draft agreement. What was agreed by way of non-regression mirrors the approach agreed on labour standards. Level of environmental and climate protection (including targets) as well as their effective enforcement are to be maintained at their level as at the end of the transition period.

Across the different aspects of the level playing field obligations, we can see the influence of path dependencies in defining the negotiating position of the Union but also the UK in its use of boilerplate language and templates from other EU FTAs and international economic instruments. The uneven nature of the commitments across the areas of subsidy control, competition and tax policies, labour and environmental standards reflects underlying qualities of EU internal governance (or reliance on international norms where EU powers are less developed). The EU sought to project these internal routines and templates into its external relations with the UK. Attempts by the UK to rely on a path dependency based on EU FTAs were effectively resisted by the EU even if it did not fully realise the maximalist version of its original preferences. The disruptive politics of Brexit was mediated and managed by the power of internal policy routine and the power (and reach) of EU law even beyond EU borders.

5.3. The Protocol on Ireland/Northern Ireland and the 'Windsor Framework'

There can be no clearer illustration of the disruptive politics of Brexit than the negotiations, attempted solutions and disputes over the effects of Brexit on the position of Northern Ireland as a constitutional and economic part of the UK which shares a land border with Ireland and the EU.[36] It is a unique feature of Brexit and certainly not one where there was an obvious template, routine or model that could simply be applied. That a solution had to be improvised cannot be in any real doubt and

[36] See eg K Hayward, 'Why it is Impossible for Brexit Britain to "Take Back Control" in Northern Ireland' (2020) 8 *Territory, Politics, Governance* 273; D Phinnemore, 'Northern Ireland: A "Place Between" in UK–EU Relations?' (2020) 25 *European Foreign Affairs Review* 631.

the types of solution that have been proposed or agreed are undoubtedly products of the disruptive politics of Brexit under successive UK governments.[37] Under Prime Minister May's leadership, a 'backstop' arrangement was proposed that would see the UK as a whole maintain alignment with EU rules on the movement of goods (with the kind of 'level playing field requirements' discussed above) if other solutions – including an agreement on an EU-UK future relationship – could not be found. Fearing that this backstop was less a safety net and more a trampoline into a relationship of dynamic alignment with the EU, this version of the Withdrawal Agreement failed, leading to the resignation of Prime Minister May.

Her replacement, Boris Johnson, pledged to renegotiate the Protocol. What emerged was an arrangement specific to Northern Ireland that would keep it in dynamic alignment with the EU while Great Britain would be free to pursue regulatory divergence with the EU, consistent with the UK government's rejection of any pre-commitment to a model of post-membership regulatory alignment with the EU.[38] Avoiding a hard border on the island of Ireland would, nonetheless, create a regulatory border in the Irish Sea for goods moving between Great Britain and Northern Ireland by introducing controls and checks intended to protect the EU's internal market where goods moved into that market via Northern Ireland. Following the 2019 General Election, the UK Government had a sufficient majority to push through this version of the Withdrawal Agreement, with the Protocol coming into effect at the end of the transition period on 31 December 2020.

Structures and mechanisms are created in the Protocol for joint working to manage any issues emerging in its implementation. Nonetheless, the UK's continuing ambivalence or antipathy to the Protocol produced a number of examples of unilateral actions by the UK which the EU considered to be inconsistent with the UK's obligations under the Withdrawal Agreement of which the Protocol is an integral part. It is these instances of the continuing disruptive politics of Brexit and the role of routine in their management with which we are concerned.

If the power of routine and its relationship to the power of law are to have explanatory value in conceptualising the EU's responses to examples of UK unilateralism, then a useful and instructive entry point is how the European Commission deployed its Article 258 TFEU enforcement prerogatives in its efforts to secure UK compliance with its commitments under the Withdrawal Agreement and under the Protocol. Two examples are illustrative of this phenomenon.

The first example came in response to legislation proposed by the UK Government in the form of the United Kingdom Internal Market Bill. While principally concerned with managing new regulatory divergences within the UK post-EU membership, it also had to reconcile its construction of a new legal architecture for free movement within the UK with its specific obligations on the movement of goods to and from Northern Ireland under the Protocol. Caught between two internal markets and two

[37] F Fabbrini (ed), *The Law & Politics of Brexit: The Protocol on Ireland/Northern Ireland* (Oxford, Oxford University Press, 2022).

[38] KA Armstrong, 'Regulatory Autonomy after EU Membership: Alignment, Divergence and the Discipline of Law' (2020) 45 *EL Rev* 207.

Unions,[39] the effect of the Protocol would be to carve out certain exceptions for the movement of goods. However, in the United Kingdom Internal Market Bill, the UK Government sought to empower UK ministers to adopt secondary acts that would be inconsistent with the UK's obligations in respect of Northern Ireland, and to require UK courts to treat such acts as not incompatible with UK commitments notwithstanding the terms of the Withdrawal Agreement (including the obligations on UK courts to give direct effect to the Agreement – see Article 4 of the Agreement).

The European Commission responded by sending a letter of formal notice to the UK; the first step in the Article 258 TFEU process that indicates the EU's willingness to bring a matter within the ambit of a legalised compliance mechanism. This was possible notwithstanding that the UK had left the EU, and notwithstanding that the Bill was still at a legislative stage and, as such, no substantive violation of the terms of the Protocol had occurred. As the UK was still in the transition period, both the European Commission and the Court of Justice retained their enforcement functions. As for the infringement complained of, in its letter of formal notice, the European Commission alleged a breach of the 'good faith' obligation contained in Article 5 of the Withdrawal Agreement. This clause reproduces the core elements of the 'sincere cooperation' obligation contained in Article 4(3) TEU inasmuch as neither party shall impede the attainment of the objectives of the Agreement and each shall act to ensure fulfilment of its objectives. While of application to securing compliance with any substantive EU law made applicable to the UK under the Agreement, the good faith obligation also applied to the Agreement itself to ensure its proper implementation. In this way, the Commission's response brought together the routine operation of its internal enforcement powers – including drawing on contemporary examples of their use to tackle rule of law backsliding in Poland – with obligations derived from the familiar 'relational' structural principle of sincere cooperation, to demand that the UK desist from its unilateral defection from commitments under the Agreement and the Protocol. The UK withdrew the offending provisions of its proposed legislation.

When the UK took further unilateral measures in respect of the movement of goods and pets between Great Britain and Northern Ireland, the European Commission had to consider its response. One response was to bring infringement proceedings as provided for expressly under the Protocol (Article 12) for the substantive breaches of the Protocol read together with the obligations contained in Article 5 of the Withdrawal Agreement. However, as well as issuing a letter of formal notice to the UK, it also sent what it described as a 'political letter' to the UK Government in which it also alleged a breach of Article 5 of the Withdrawal Agreement. What is noteworthy is that the breach alleged in this second letter included the requirement that the EU and the UK shall 'in full mutual respect and good faith, assist each other in carrying out tasks which flow from this Agreement'.

It should be recalled that the Joint Committee established under the Agreement is the focal point for decision-making and political problem-solving. Decisions are taken jointly rather than unilaterally. It is this institutional logic which is given particular

[39] S Weatherill, 'The Protocol on Ireland/Northern Ireland: Protecting the EU's Internal Market at the Expense of the UK's' (2020) 45 *EL Rev* 222.

legal expression in Article 5 and the point of the Commission's letters was to seek to commit the UK to the routines of consultation and negotiation through the joint institutions under the Agreement. But there is another point to the 'political' letter which highlights a recognition that attempts to export core structural principles of EU constitutional law to the Union's post-membership relationship with the UK might be resisted and regarded as inappropriate. After all, Brexit is intended to be a rupture and disruption in legal relations. Perhaps mindful of this and the UK's own desire to recast its relationship with the EU in terms of obligations under international law, the European Commission noted that the good faith obligation in Article 5 is also an expression of Article 26 of the Vienna Convention on the Law of Treaties and which requires performance of a treaty by the parties to it in good faith. In this way, the desire to institutionalise a routine of joint working under the Agreement is yoked to the power of law through international law at a meta-normative level. Accordingly, the description of this letter as 'political' is erroneous; it is an expression of the power of international law in EU external relations.

Nothing in the preceding analysis should be interpreted as a claim that law can, or should, displace politics; how could it in the context of Brexit? Political solutions to these post-membership skirmishes would be needed. With a further change of government in the UK and a new UK Prime Minister, Rishi Sunak, impetus was injected into finding acceptable means of implementing the Protocol with reduced checks and controls on the movement of goods. At the end of February 2023, the EU and the UK announced a political agreement in principle on changes to the implementation of the Protocol. This, 'Windsor Framework' would bring outstanding infringement procedures against the UK to an end. Whereas forces within the ruling Conservative Party and within unionist politics in Northern Ireland had called for an end to the Protocol, by contrast, for the EU the new framework would be implemented within the ambit of the Withdrawal Agreement and the Protocol;[40] changing the nomenclature did not alter the fact that both sides had agreed to make amendments to the Protocol using the amending power in Article 164 of the Withdrawal Agreement. For the European Commission, '[A]ll new arrangements fall within this pre-established framework'. Once again, the EU's response to the disruptive politics of Brexit is to be found in the power of routine.[41]

6. CONCLUSIONS

At first glance, the highly-charged politics that produced Brexit, and which prevailed throughout the UK's withdrawal from the EU, ought to be a strong candidate to test the claim that the EU should pivot from a type of 'rules-politics' – more typically

[40] See Decision No 1/2023 of the Joint Committee established by the Agreement on the withdrawal of the United Kingdom of Great Britain and Northern Ireland from the European Union and the European Atomic Energy Community laying down arrangements relating to the Windsor Framework [2023] OJ L102/61.

[41] In order to restore devolved government in Northern Ireland, the UK Government announced further changes to the implementation of the Windsor Framework: HM Government, *Safeguarding the Union*, Command Paper 1021 (January 2024).

associated with the 'de-politicised' world of regulatory policymaking – to a more agile, improvised and responsive 'events-politics'. Certainly, academic commentary on Brexit often limited itself to providing a gloss on the many political events and dramas that the UK's withdrawal from the EU produced. As such, it has often been difficult to find conceptual and analytical frameworks capable of looking beyond both the novelty and immediacy of Brexit as either a momentous political event or series of events.

The argument advanced here is that time and again the EU sought to manage the disruptive politics of Brexit through the deployment of the power of routine. Drawing upon core themes of institutionalist analysis – the structuring effects of path-dependent decision-making; the application of standard operating procedures and templates; and the influence of norms and logics of appropriateness embedded within organisational settings – it becomes apparent that the UK's withdrawal from the EU exhibits features we can characterise as derived from the power of routine. Notwithstanding that Brexit is a novel example of EU external relations, in the examples presented here, we can see the ways in which routines of decision-making have been applied or adapted to the Union's dealings with the UK. This power of routine manifests itself, and is embedded within, the law of EU treaties and international agreements, the substantive internal regulatory law and practices of the Union, and its adjudicative and legal enforcement mechanisms.

Perhaps, we ought to be unsurprised about this power of routine and the power of law given that the EU is an international organisation that persists through time and whose function is to facilitate and coordinate decision-making by its institutions and Member States. When confronted with novel and unprecedented events and a heightened politicisation of decision-making, the EU sought to resend to – and also to deflect – the disruptive politics of Brexit through routines that express its ways of working. But, nothing in the argument presented here should be taken to be an unquestioning defence of the EU's handling of its relationship with the UK and its management of the disruptive politics of Brexit. Path-dependent decision-making is as capable of reproducing pathologies of decision-making as it is of solving problems. The EU's approach to the sequencing of its negotiations with the UK is, perhaps, a case in point. Moreover, unstable equilibria may persist despite efforts to create stable institutions, routines and mechanisms for managing challenges. The Protocol on Ireland/Northern Ireland is a useful illustration of this.

Nonetheless, the point remains that the institutionalisation of routines of decision-making provides not just an explanation for the creation of international organisations like the EU but also how that organisation then behaves. When the politics of disruption is directed against an organisation and the routines of its institutions, it may be expected that the targets of that disruption will double down on their ways of doing things both defensively and as a projection of organisational self-confidence. What is particularly striking about the example of the UK's withdrawal from the EU is that the power of routine and the power of EU law are coupled not only in the management of the internal relations of Member States but also the EU's external relations with a former Member State.

EU Member States as States: Between EU and International Roles and Obligations

FEDERICO CASOLARI AND RAMSES A WESSEL*

1. INTRODUCTION

THE NEW LEGAL order of the European Union, the characteristics of which were famously clarified by the Court of Justice in its early case law,[1] changed the identity of the States that created the Union or later acceded to it. While, obviously, the Union was created by sovereign States using their – inherent – treaty-making power, their subsequent membership of that Union limited the way in which they could practice their sovereignty. Internally, principles such as primacy and direct effect set clear limits to the exercise of national (constitutional) rules and prerogatives. Externally, rules and principles on the attribution of competences or on sincere cooperation affected the way in which States could exercise their sovereignty in dealing with third States and other international organisations. All of this led to a situation in which the EU States became *Member* States first, leading to limitations on the exercise of their statehood both internally and in their external relations. While the European integration process has not meant the end of the States – despite the many comparisons with federative structures[2] – it is clear that it had an impact on the EU's constitutional framework and changed the scope of the exercise of statehood for the EU Member States.[3]

This contribution, however, is not about what EU Member States lost, but rather about what they kept in terms of statehood. While the topic is central to the study of EU law and is the background of most studies on EU external relations law, it does

* Federico Casolari is Professor of European Union Law, and Head at the Department of Legal Studies, *Alma Mater Studiorum* – Università di Bologna; Ramses Wessel is Professor of European Law, and Vice Dean at the Faculty of Law of the University of Groningen. The authors wish to thank Prof. Graham Butler (University of Southern Denmark) for his valuable suggestions.

[1] Case 26/62 *Van Gend & Loos* ECLI:EU:C:1963:1, [1963] ECR 1.

[2] See on the status of the EU and for further references C Eckes and RA Wessel, 'The European Union: An International Perspective' in T Tridimas and R Schütze (eds), *Oxford Principles of European Union Law – Volume 1: The European Union Legal Order* (Oxford, Oxford University Press, 2018) 74–102.

[3] See L Potvin-Solis (ed), *Le statut d'État membre de l'Union européenne* (Brussels, Bruyland, 2018).

not seem to have been addressed as such.[4] The same holds true for international law scholarship, which has largely ignored the emergence of this new and complex actor as well as the status of EU Member States in, for instance, mixed agreements.[5] In the present contribution, we aim to map and analyse situations in which EU Member States act as States, either because State-functions have not been affected, simply because they completely fall outside the scope of EU law, or because statehood is an essential asset in the context of EU law. In doing so, this contribution aims to shed light on the various identities States have in engaging with the Union. We believe that distinguishing these identities not only helps to understand how EU membership has affected the statehood of the members of the EU, but also to reveal that different situations and settings require these members to wear different hats. As we will see, in many situations the functioning of the EU legal order not only depends on the states as 'Member States', but also as 'States'.

The notion of different identities is not typical for EU Member States, but is one that is visible in international organisations more generally. Earlier research has shown that the identity of 'Member State' is just one of the possible positions States can have in relation to international organisations.[6] And even the qualification as 'Member State' hides several different identities. The different positions/roles and the connected identities States may have as creators of international organisations, members of international organisations, former members of international organisations, legal partners of international organisations or possible accountable back-ups for international organisations are even more complex in the context of the European Union. There, the tension States may experience between being a State and a Member State at the same time is particularly visible in situations in which Member States' obligations under EU law collide with general obligations those States may have under international law.[7] This question, is gaining importance not only in relation to the division of competences, but also in view of, for instance, the allocation of responsibilities.[8] In that context, the question is often whether (Member) State conduct can be

[4] A related theme can be found in E Spaventa, 'Constitutional Creativity or Constitutional Deception? Acts of the Member States Acting Collectively and Jurisdiction of the Court of Justice' (2021) 58 *CML Rev* 1697; as well as much earlier in G Bebr, 'Acts of Representatives of the Governments of the Member States' (1966) 14 *Sociaal-Economische Wetgeving* 529, 530. In relation to international dispute settlement the issue has been addressed in A Thies, 'EU Member States and International Arbitration: What's Left?' in M Cremona, A Thies and RA Wessel (eds), *The European Union and International Dispute Settlement* (Oxford, Hart Publishing, 2017) 133–157.

[5] See N Levrat and Y Kaspiarovich, 'Are EU Member States still States according to International Law?' (2019) *GSI Working Paper Prof. PhDc LAW* 2019/02, 4.

[6] *cf* IF Dekker and RA Wessel, 'Identities of States in International Organizations' (2015) 12 *International Organizations Law Review* 293.

[7] With regard to international agreements, see N Levrat, Y Kaspiarovich, C Kaddous and RA Wessel, 'Introduction: Torn between Two Lovers: The Application of both EU and International Law to the Participation of the EU and its Member States in International Agreements' in N Levrat, Y Kaspiarovich, C Kaddous and RA Wessel (eds), *The EU and Its Member States' Joint Participation in International Agreements*, Modern Studies in European Law (Oxford, Hart Publishing, 2022).

[8] See for instance A Delgado Casteleiro, *The International Responsibility of the European Union: From Competence to Normative Control*, Cambridge Studies in European Law and Policy (Cambridge, Cambridge University Press, 2018); and more recently A Delgado Casteleiro and C Contartese, 'International Responsibility of the EU and/or its Member States in International Agreements: From Joint Participation to "Participation"' in Levrat et al (n 7).

assessed independently of the decision taken by the European Union empowering the (Member) State to act.[9] The main question thus seems to be 'where the State ends and the Member State begins'; and this has consequences for the output, which is either a decision of the European Union or an international (legal or political) agreement concluded between States. To differentiate between the various identities, this chapter introduces the term 'EU States' to distinguish their identity from the one they have as 'Member States'.[10] Yet, it will also become clear that the various identities are not always clearly distinguishable and sometimes overlap, leading to a hybridisation of related instruments. As we will see, this may involve the applicability of the principle of sincere cooperation, a principle that may even be helpful to reconcile the different identities of the States participating in the European integration process.

The way in which EU States take collective decisions varies. Spaventa already found five types of what she termed 'hybrid collective acts of the Member States', all with a different degree of proximity to the EU legal system: political, institutional, functional, contextual, and legal.[11] That study, *inter alia*, found that 'The more intertwined the action of the Member States collectively and the EU, the more complex the constitutional challenge, especially in relation to democratic, parliamentary, and judicial scrutiny'.[12]

The present chapter, however, goes beyond the types of decisions and is more interested in the link between the different settings and the various identities of EU (Member) States. Section 2 will first of all consider the position of Member States in forging and changing the way in which they participate to the Union. In particular topics concerning the revision of EU Treaties, the strengthening of the cooperation and the decision to leave the Union will be explored. Section 3 will analyse the identities of Member States in implementing EU policies in the context of its legal framework. Section 4, finally, will address situations that apparently fall outside the scope of EU law and highlights where State sovereignty has not, or has only partially, been affected by EU law. A summary of most relevant outcomes is contained in Section 5.

2. EU MEMBER STATES AS STATES ESTABLISHING, SHAPING OR LEAVING THE UNION

In considering the different identities Member States may inhabit in shaping the EU constitutional framework, it is particularly apt to begin with the role they may take as 'Masters of the Treaties'. If it is undisputed that the creation of both the European Communities and the European Union was the result of a sovereign decision assumed by some European States according to their constitutional requirements, something

[9] More generally on this question: P Palchetti, 'Litigating Member State Responsibility: The Monetary Gold Principle and the Protection of Absent Organizations' (2015) 12 *International Organizations Law Review* 468–483.

[10] Compare Spaventa (n 4) 1701: 'There is a natural confusion about the very notion of Member States acting collectively: the wording seems to suggest a necessary link with the European Union (the Member States) and yet the action might pertain simply to the international/domestic constitutional dimension'.

[11] Spaventa (n 4).

[12] ibid at 1704.

which normally occurs when States decide to create new international organisations, the question related to the status Member States may exercise in changing what has been defined by the Court of Justice of the European Union as the 'constitutional legal framework' of the supranational legal order is less straightforward.[13]

There is no doubting that the revision of EU Treaties represents an expression of the primary role played by States in shaping the Union.[14] This is clearly visible in the so-called 'ordinary' revision procedure, enshrined in Article 48(2) Treaty on European Union (TEU) and Article 48(3) TEU: the launch of an intergovernmental conference and the adoption of a revision treaty to be ratified by EU States in conformity with their constitutional requirements clearly reveal that the ultimate responsibility for changing the EU Treaties solely rests with the EU States. At first sight, a different reasoning could be made with regard to the 'simplified' revision procedure of the Part Three of the Treaty on the Functioning of the European Union (TFEU) on 'Union Policies and Internal Actions', which implies a decision of the European Council to be taken unanimously. One could indeed maintain that in this case the revision is subject to the decision-making power of an EU institution. However, a closer inspection shows – also in this circumstance – the presence of intergovernmental elements in the procedure.[15] First, as already stated, the decision must be taken unanimously; second, it must be approved by Member States according to their constitutional requirements. These two procedural requirements make thus possible a comparison between the Decision adopted by the European Council and a treaty concluded in simplified form by the EU States. The intrinsic intergovernmental nature of the revision process is also visible – even if less clearly – in the *passerelle* clauses mentioned in Article 48(7) TEU, which also require a unanimous decision by the European Council and the approval by national parliaments.

Of course, the fact that EU Treaties provide for specific procedures to be followed in order to change them, represents per se a limitation to the EU States' action, strengthening the autonomy of the EU legal order.[16] This has been clarified by the Court of Justice in *Defrenne I*, where the Court maintained that 'the Treaty can only be modified by means of the amendment procedure carried out in accordance with Article 236 [today Article 48 TEU]'.[17] More recently, the Court has been asked to define its level of scrutiny on the legitimacy of the European Council's decisions adopted to revise Part Three of the TFEU. While recognising its jurisdiction on the matter, the Court has stated that 'it is for the Court to verify, first, that the procedural rules laid down in Article 48(6) TEU were followed and, secondly, that the amendments decided upon

[13] Opinion 2/13 *Accession of the Union to the ECHR* ECLI:EU:C:2014:2454, para 158.

[14] See M Dony, 'Le statut d'Etat membre et la participation à la fonction normative européenne' in Potvin-Solis (n 3) 281 ff 283. *cf* also the celebrated *Lissabon Urteil*, where the German Constitutional Court has made it clear that: 'Die Mitgliedstaaten bleiben die Herren der Verträge … Die souveräne Staatsgewalt bleibt nach den Regeln über die Zuständigkeitsverteilung und -abgrenzung gewahrt. Die neuen primärrechtlichen Regelungen über Vertragsänderungen stehen dem nicht entgegen'. BverfG 2 BvE 2/08 *Urteil des Zweiten Senats vom 30. Juni 2009* ECLI:DE:BverfG:2009:es20090630.2bve000208, paras 298–299.

[15] B de Witte, 'Treaty Revision Procedures after Lisbon' in A Biondi et al (eds), *EU Law after Lisbon* (Oxford, Oxford University Press, 2012), 3, 11.

[16] K Lenaerts, 'The Autonomy of European Union Law' (2019) 1 *I Post di Aisdue* 1, 7.

[17] Case 43/75 *Defrenne v SABENA* ECLI:EU:C:1976:56, [1976] ECR 455, para 58.

concern only Part Three of the FEU Treaty, which implies that they do not entail any amendment of provisions of another part of the Treaties on which the European Union is founded, and that they do not increase the competences of the Union'.[18]

In both rulings, the rationale of the limitations to the EU States' power to revise EU Treaties is clearly visible. It traces back to the notion of 'Community/Union of law' forged by the Court in its previous case law,[19] that is, the need to introduce a constitutional guarantee in the supranational legal order implying the respect of the rule of law by Member States and EU institutions.

This said, is it possible to identify further (implied) limitations to Member States' revision powers? A possible answer to this question could be based on the elements that, according to the Court of Justice, contribute to determining the constitutional legal framework of the Union, that is: (a) the constitutional structure of the Union as it is reflected in the principle of conferral and in the institutional legal framework; (b) the inherent characteristics of the Union, pertaining to the nature of its law, which are mainly illustrated by the principles of primacy and the direct effect; and (c) the sharing with Member States of fundamental values, representing in turn 'the fundamental premise' upon which the entire EU constitutional framework is based.[20]

In this respect it is worth mentioning the first Opinion of the Court on the Draft Agreement relating to the creation of the European Economic Area, *Opinion 1/91*, where the Court clearly stated that an amendment to EU Treaties carried out according to Article 48 TEU 'could not cure' the incompatibility of EU law – meaning its inherent nature – with possible agreements undermining the mandate of the Court.[21]

Again, in the Opinion on the Draft Agreement for the creation of a unified patent litigation system, *Opinion 1/09*, the Court, after recalling that the establishment of the Tribunal was likely to attribute to an international jurisdiction the competence to interpret and apply EU law, thus depriving courts of the Member States and the Court itself of their powers vis-à-vis EU law, concluded that this solution could 'alter the essential character of the powers which the Treaties confer on the institutions of the European Union and on the Member States and which are indispensable to the *preservation of the very nature of European Union law*'.[22]

In *Kadi*, while stressing that the jurisdictional mandate of the Court forms 'part of the very foundations of the Community [now Union]',[23] the Court also affirmed the mandatory nature of the principles of freedom, democracy, respect of fundamental rights as 'a foundation of the Union'.[24]

In the light of that, one might ask the question of whether the value-based framework upon which the Union and its institutional structure are based could

[18] Case C-370/12 *Pringle* ECLI:EU:C:2012:756, para 36.

[19] Case 294/83 *Les Verts v Parliament* ECLI:EU:C:1986:166, [1986] ECR 1339.

[20] Opinion 2/13 *Accession of the Union to the ECHR* ECLI:EU:C:2014:2454, paras 164 ff.

[21] Opinion 1/91 *Draft Agreement relating to the creation of the European Economic Area* ECLI:EU:C:1991:490, [1991] ECR I-6079, para 72.

[22] Opinion 1/09 *Creation of a Unified Patent Litigation System* ECLI:EU:C:2011:123, [2011] ECR I-1137, para 89; emphasis added.

[23] Joined Cases C-402/05 P and C-415/05 P *Kadi and Al Barakaat International Foundation v Council and Commission* ECLI:EU:C:2008:461, [2008] ECR I-6351, para 290.

[24] ibid para 303.

actually be revised by the EU States,[25] that framework defining, as recently emphasised by the Court of Justice in the two parallel decisions on the legality of the Budgetary Conditionality Regulation, 'the very identity of the European Union as a common legal order'.[26] The answer cannot easily be given, but there are indications that there could be limits to what can be changed without basically creating something else. This is further confirmed by the negative duties of loyalty imposed upon the EU States *qua* Member States under Article 4(3) TEU. As it is well known, those duties require Member States to refrain from acting when their action is likely to 'jeopardise the attainment of the Union's objectives'. Since the promotion of EU's values represents a paramount objective of its action (together with the promotion of peace and the well-being of its peoples), it follows that any action put in place by Member States to change the EU primary law in contrast with the fundamental values could be considered in violation of the duty of loyalty towards the Union.

It goes without saying that such a conclusion remains valid in so far as the revision of EU primary law does not produce a limitation of EU competences – a circumstance that is allowed under Article 48(1) TEU. In this case, areas where Member States regain their prerogatives are no longer subject to EU law.[27]

Having said this, the possibility that Member States collectively decide to adopt *extra ordinem* measures – acting in their quality of sovereign EU States – with a view to change the existing EU constitutional legal framework cannot be completely excluded.[28] Even though this possibility represents an extreme (an rather unlikely) scenario that risks jeopardising the proper functioning, if not the existence, of the EU legal order,[29] it essentially expresses the role of EU States as ultimate arbiters of the EU destiny. The examples of the New Settlement for the United Kingdom within the European Union and of the EU-Turkey Statement clearly show the disruptive essence of such an attitude. As Cannizzaro rightly explains, in both cases the unanimous consent of EU States expressed without triggering Article 48 TEU's mechanisms has led to the elaboration of solutions inconsistent with the EU constitutional framework, thus marking 'the [possible] return to a Europe of sovereign States and the definite disappearance of the notion of a European public interest, of which we are in desperate need'.[30]

[25] R Bieber, 'Les limites matérielles et formelles à la révision des traités établissant la Communauté européenne' (1993) 367 *Revue du marché commun et de l'Union européenne* 343; R Passchier and M Stremler, 'Unconstitutional Constitutional Amendments in European Union Law: Considering the Existence of Substantive Constraints on Treaty Revision' (2016) 5 *Cambridge Journal of International and Comparative Law* 337; A Rosas and L Armati, *EU Constitutional Law: An Introduction*, 3rd edn (Oxford, Hart Publishing, 2018) 45.

[26] Case C-156/21 *Hungary v Parliament and Council* ECLI:EU:C:2022:97, para 127; Case C-157/21 *Poland v Parliament and Council* ECLI:EU:C:2022:98, para 145.

[27] M Klamert, 'Article 48 TEU' in M Kellerbauer, M Klamert, J Tomkin (eds), *The EU Treaties and the Charter of Fundamental Rights: A Commentary* (Oxford, Oxford University Press, 2019) 309.

[28] B de Witte, 'Rules of Change in International Law: How Special Is the European Community?' (1994) 25 *Netherlands Yearbook of International Law* 299; F Casolari, *L'incorporazione del diritto internazionale nell'ordinamento dell'Unione europea* (Milan, Giuffrè Editore, 2008) 141–142; Rosas and Armati (n 25) 32.

[29] A Davì, *Comunità europee e sanzioni economiche internazionali* (Napoli, Jovene, 1993) 383–384.

[30] E Cannizzaro, 'Disintegration Through Law?' (2016) 1 *European Papers* 3, 6. See also below Section 3.1.

Apart from the EU Treaties' revision, some Declarations annexed to the Treaties are also clearly to be seen as instruments used by the EU States to shape the EU legal order. Indeed, much more than mere political interpretations of EU primary law, those Declarations allow EU States to further shape the legal framework within which they will play as Member States. One clear example of such an attitude is Declaration No. 38, in which the EU States already agree on which of them will have a permanent Advocate General, further specifying thus the content of Article 252 TFEU.[31] Another clear example is represented by Declaration No. 37 on Article 222 TFEU, basically allowing a Member State to make its own choice of means to comply with the solidarity obligations enshrined in Article 222 in the event of a terrorist attack or of natural and man-made disasters.[32]

The contribution of Member States in shaping the EU legal order may also be carried out without unanimous decisions.

In this respect, the so-called 'Euro Group' forms an interesting example as not all Member States participate. Yet, Article 136 TFEU reveals that decisions are taken by the Council and that 'only members of the Council representing Member States whose currency is the euro shall take part in the vote'. On the basis of this we do not seem to be dealing with EU States, but with a select group of Member States. This is confirmed by Article 1 of the Protocol (No 14) on the Euro Group.[33] Nevertheless, the identity of the members of the Euro Group is less clear than one could expect on the basis of these primary law provisions. Recently, the Court has established that 'the Euro Group does not have any competence of its own in the EU legal order'[34] and even that is an informal gathering of – in our terminology – EU States.

The related European Stability Mechanism (ESM) is established by those same Member States (Article 136(3) TFEU). Yet, this was done in the form of the Treaty establishing the European Stability Mechanism, to create the ESM as an international

[31] Declaration No. 38 on Article 252 of the Consolidated Version of the Treaty on the Functioning of the European Union (TFEU) regarding the number of Advocates-General in the Court of Justice [2016] OJ C202/350: 'The Conference declares that if, in accordance with Article 252, first paragraph, of the Treaty on the Functioning of the European Union, the Court of Justice requests that the number of Advocates-General be increased by three (eleven instead of eight), the Council will, acting unanimously, agree on such an increase. In that case, the Conference agrees that Poland will, as is already the case for Germany, France, Italy, Spain and the United Kingdom, have a permanent Advocate-General and no longer take part in the rotation system, while the existing rotation system will involve the rotation of five Advocates-General instead of three'.

[32] The Declaration states as follows: 'Without prejudice to the measures adopted by the Union to comply with its solidarity obligation towards a Member State which is the object of a terrorist attack or the victim of natural or man-made disaster, none of the provisions of Article 222 is intended to affect the right of another Member State to choose the most appropriate means to comply with its own solidarity obligation towards that Member State'. See M Gestri, 'EU Disaster Law', in A de Guttry et al (eds), *International Disaster Response Law* (The Hague, TMC Asser Press, 2012) 105, 108. See also below Section 3.1.

[33] Article 1 Protocol (No 14) on the Euro Group to the TFEU [2016] OJ C202/283 reads: 'The Ministers of the Member States whose currency is the euro shall meet informally. Such meetings shall take place, when necessary, to discuss questions related to the specific responsibilities they share with regard to the single currency. The [European] Commission shall take part in the meetings. The European Central Bank [(ECB)] shall be invited to take part in such meetings, which shall be prepared by the representatives of the Ministers with responsibility for finance of the Member States whose currency is the euro and of the Commission'.

[34] Joined Cases C-597/18 P, C-598/18 P, C-603/18 P and C-604/18 P *Council v K Chrysostomides & Co and Others* ECLI:EU:C:2020:1028.

body outside the EU framework.[35] Hinarejos pointed out that 'these international instruments have nevertheless significant links to the EU legal system; this is because of their allocation of tasks to EU institutions … and because of the general duty placed on Member States not to breach EU law, even when acting within the sphere of international law'.[36] The same was true for earlier similar agreements concluded between certain EU States, such as the Schengen framework or the Prüm Convention, in the area of justice and home affairs, and the Social Policy Agreement.[37] In fact, as the Court held in *Pringle* in relation to the establishment of the ESM, there was no possibility of doing this within the Union framework, so the Member States had to use their identity as States to set up a system that would allow to the Union to solve a crisis.[38] Hence, again a clear example of the fact the 'EU States' actually have a role to fulfil to allow the Union to reach its objectives.

We already know this construction from the financing of development aid. In the classic cases *Bangladesh Aid*[39] and *European Development Fund*,[40] the Court was confronted with structures that were created outside the EU framework and 'EU States' meeting within the Council and it held that the latter could use procedural steps drawing on the rules applicable to Union expenditure and could also associate Union institutions with the procedure thus set up. This would allow the Union institutions to participate in an intergovernmental fund established outside the legal framework of the EU Treaties.[41] The reasons to bring in the EU States on these types of situations may differ per case, but include 'the need for multi-speed or differentiated integration',[42] a lack of Union competences, or the 'high degree of flexibility and control'.[43]

Significantly enough, both the diplomatic and judicial practice concerning those intergovernmental instruments clearly reveals the need to make sure that the effectiveness of EU law is in any case preserved. Particularly illustrative of such a need is the text of Article 2 of the so-called 'Fiscal Compact',[44] which reads as follows:

> 1. This Treaty shall be applied and interpreted by the Contracting Parties in conformity with the Treaties on which the European Union is founded, in particular Article 4(3) of the Treaty on European Union, and with European Union law, including procedural law whenever the adoption of secondary legislation is required.

[35] A Hinarejos, 'Intergovernmentalism in the Wake of the Euro-Area Crisis' in R Schütze (ed), *Globalisation and Governance International Problems: European Solutions* (Cambridge, Cambridge University Press, 2018) 380. Hinarejos also mentions a few related agreements.

[36] ibid 380; B de Witte, 'Using International Law in the Euro Crisis: Causes and Consequences' (2013) *ARENA Working Paper* No. 4, 4 et seq.

[37] de Witte (n 15).

[38] Case C-370/12 *Pringle* ECLI:EU:C:2012:756.

[39] Joined Cases C-181/91 and C-248/91 *Parliament v Council and Commission* ECLI:EU:C:1993:271, [1993] ECR I-3685. See L Pantaleo, 'The Reviewability of Acts Adopted by the Member States Meeting within the Council: *Parliament v Council and Commission (Bangladesh Aid)*' in G Butler and RA Wessel (eds), *EU External Relations Law: The Cases in Context* (Oxford, Hart Publishing, 2022).

[40] Case C-316/91 *Parliament v Council* ECLI:EU:C:1994:76, [1994] ECR I-625. See S Bartelt, 'Legality of the European Development Fund and the European Parliament's Prerogatives: *Parliament v Council (European Development Fund)*' in Butler and Wessel (n 39).

[41] Bartelt (n 40) 267.

[42] Hinarejos (n 35) 383.

[43] ibid.

[44] Treaty on Stability, Coordination and Governance in the Economic and Monetary Union (Brussels, 2 March 2012).

2. This Treaty shall apply insofar as it is compatible with the Treaties on which the European Union is founded and with European Union law. It shall not encroach upon the competence of the Union to act in the area of the economic union.

From that Article the idea emerges that the Treaty shall in any case be applied in strict conjunction with EU law, the latter taking precedence over the former, also thanks to the duty of loyalty enshrined in Article 4(3).[45] It thus confirmed that the principle of sincere cooperation is called upon to play a relevant role in trying to reconcile the different identities of the States participating in the European process of integration.

A similar reading is also visible in the case law of the Court of Justice. Here again one can cite the *Pringle* judgment, where the Court stressed the circumstance that 'Member States may not disregard their duty to comply with European Union law when exercising their competences',[46] something we will consider again when analysing the situation where Member States claim to exercise their sovereign prerogatives.[47]

Further considering the different identities Member States may express in shaping the EU constitutional framework, one cannot ignore the peculiar situation of Member States leaving the Union. On the one hand, it is undisputed that the decision to leave the Union is the expression of a sovereign prerogative of Member States, pertaining thus to their identity as subjects of international law.[48] On the other hand, however, even if the EU institutions, as well as the other Member States, are required to consider the peculiar situation of the State concerned as a 'withdrawing Member State',[49] the latter is still subject to the full respect of EU law until the end of the process illustrated in Article 50 TEU.[50] This 'in-between' situation, where the State has started the disentanglement process, but is still required to act as a full member, may obviously lead to schizophrenic attitudes. Quite significantly, exiting from the Union could not be sufficient to overcome all the obstacles and difficulties related to such an awkward situation. Suffice it here to mention the actual condition of the United Kingdom. While that state is obliged to fully respect the legal commitments assumed in the light of the Withdrawal Agreement, including the adherence to the principle of sincere cooperation and the abstention from any act which could jeopardise the implementation of EU law,[51] the Trade and Cooperation Agreement marks the irrelevance of EU law for the future relations between the UK, the Union, and its Member States.[52] Pursuant to its Article 4, indeed, EU law has to be considered as

[45] L Azoulai, 'Appartenir à l'Union: Liens institutionnels et liens de confiance dans les relations entre les États membres' in F Berrod (ed), *Europe(s), Droit(s) européen(s), Une passion d'universitaire*, Liber amicorum *en l'honneur du professeur Vlad Constantinesco* (Brussels, Bruyland, 2015) 30.

[46] Case C-370/12 *Pringle* ECLI:EU:C:2012:756, para 69.

[47] See below Section 4.1.

[48] Case C-621/18 *Wightman and Others* ECLI:EU:C:2018:999, para 50.

[49] *cf* Recital 10 European Council Decision (EU) 2019/584 taken in agreement with the United Kingdom of 11 April 2019 extending the period under Article 50(3) TEU [2019] OJ L101/1.

[50] Case C-327/18 *R O* ECLI:EU:2018:733, para 45.

[51] See Art 5 Agreement on the withdrawal of the United Kingdom of Great Britain and Northern Ireland from the European Union and the European Atomic Energy Community (EU-UK Withdrawal Agreement) [2019] OJ C384I/1.

[52] J Larik and RA Wessel, 'The EU-UK Post-Brexit Trade Agreement: Forging Partnership or Managing Rivalry?' in A Łazowski and A Cygan (eds), *Research Handbook on Legal Aspects of Brexit* (Cheltenham, Edward Elgar, 2022) 122.

'domestic law' of one Party, thus being prevented from influencing the way in which the TCA shall be interpreted by the other Party.[53]

3. EU STATES ACTING IN THE CONTEXT OF THE EUROPEAN UNION

3.1. Decisions in the Framework of the Councils and Hybrid Acts

The classic solution for EU States to coordinate their acts in the absence of Union competences is to simply use the Council or the European Council as a forum for their 'intergovernmental' decision-making. This could be seen as a mere pragmatic use of a conference venue where they would be anyway and, in legal terms, they could equally meet in any local Brussels bar. Yet, practice reveals that in many cases the only reason that States meet is because they are also Member States. The practice of adopting acts in the framework of the Council(s) has been possible from the outset and was first developed under the European Coal and Steel Community (ECSC) Treaty 'in those instances in which the Community lacks power to act'.[54]

In fact, in a number of cases, the Treaties actually call upon EU States to take decisions this way, which indeed again puts their sovereign statehood into perspective. Situations like these may require a 'common accord of the governments of the Member States' and include the appointment of the Judges and Advocates-General of the Court of Justice[55] and the Judges of the General Court (Articles 19(2) TEU, 253 and 254 TFEU), the determination of the seat of the institutions of the Union (Article 341 TFEU),[56] and the amendment of the Treaties on the basis of Article 48(4) TEU (mentioned above). In view of the fact that in these situations collective action by the EU States is necessary for the EU to function, the statement by the General Court in the *Sharpston* case that it is 'immaterial' whether the EU States act within

[53] Trade and Cooperation Agreement between the European Union and the European Atomic Energy Community, of the one part, and the United Kingdom of Great Britain and Northern Ireland, of the other part (Trade and Cooperation Agreement/TCA) [2021] OJ L149/10. Significantly, the provision is named 'Public international law', making thus clear the prevailing role exercised by international law in the implementation and interpretation of the TCA. F Casolari, 'I principi del diritto dell'Unione europea negli accordi commerciali: una visione di insieme' in G Adinolfi (ed), *Gli accordi preferenziali di nuova generazione dell'Unione europea* (Turin, G Giappichelli Editore, 2021) 73, 101.

[54] Bebr (n 4); see also Pantaleo (n 39).

[55] On the interpretation of the provisions regulating the appointments of AGs, see the cases that were initiated by former AG Sharpston, eg Case T-180/20 *Sharpston v Council and Conférence des Représentants des Gouvernements des États members* ECLI:EU:T:2020:473, and Case C-424/20 P(R) *Council of the European Union v Eleanor Sharpston* ECLI:EU:C:2020:705, para 17, where the Vice-President of the Court of Justice has stressed the circumstance that the Member States – as Masters of the Treaties – have reserved to themselves the adoption of certain sensitive acts, such as those related to the appointment of Advocates-General. For a critical view on this point *cf* DV Kochenov and G Butler, 'Independence of the Court of Justice of the European Union: Unchecked Member States Power after the Sharpston Affair' (2022) 27 *European Law Journal* 262.

[56] Interestingly enough, the procedure for the earlier specialised Courts was different. Rather than through a 'common accord', the Judges of those Courts were appointed by the Council, acting unanimously. See G Butler, 'An Interim Post-Mortem: Specialised Courts in the EU Judicial Architecture after the Civil Service Tribunal' (2020) 17 *International Organizations Law Review* 586, 599.

the framework of the Treaties or 'other legal sources, such as international law' may have come as a surprise.[57]

Other situations, in which the Union needs the Member States to reach certain objectives, include Article 222 TFEU, the already mentioned 'solidarity clause', which provides that 'The Union and its Member States shall act jointly in a spirit of solidarity if a Member State is the object of a terrorist attack or the victim of a natural or man-made disaster'. One could argue that the reference to 'Member States' does not hide the fact that they would act as 'States' on the basis of national sovereign competences that have not been transferred to the Union.[58] While one could say that the same holds true for the collective defence obligation in Article 42(7) TEU,[59] or in fact for many other obligations in the area of the Common Security and Defence Policy,[60] it is important to underline that, in general, in the area of the Common Foreign and Security Policy the States act as *Member* States in the Council in support of what is essentially a Union policy.[61] This is also reflected in the fact that no mixed agreements have been concluded in the area of CFSP/CSDP.

In other cases, decisions are taken in the framework of the (European) Council with a view to coordinate issues for political reasons, or simply to make the EU work effectively. Situations may concern political solutions, such as the 'Decision of the Heads of State or Government of the 28 Member States of the European Union, meeting within the European Council' on the EU-Ukraine Association Agreement after the negative Dutch referendum on that agreement.[62]

Furthermore, the well-known EU-Turkey 'Statement' of 18 March 2016 in the framework of the migration crisis serves as a clear example of shifting from Member States to States.[63] The question was – and to a certain extent still is – whether this Statement was in fact an international agreement, that should not have been adopted by the 'Members of the European Council' and issued through a Press Release on the website, but which should have followed the official procedures of Article 218 TFEU. Many have criticised the way the Union side-stepped regular procedures[64] by

[57] Case C-684/20 P *Sharpston v Council and Conférence des Représants des Gouvernements des États members* ECLI:EU:C:2021:486, para 44.

[58] See more extensively on the solidarity clause Gestri (n 32) and S Villani, *The Concept of Solidarity within EU Disaster Response Law: A Legal Assessment* (Bologna, Bononia University Press, 2021). Villani also stresses the sovereignty of States in relation to taking care of the victims of natural disasters and other emergencies occurring on its territory (at 34).

[59] Art 42(7) Consolidated version of the Treaty on European Union (TEU) [2016] OJ C202/13: 'If a Member State is the victim of armed aggression on its territory, the other Member States shall have towards it an obligation of aid and assistance by all the means in their power…'.

[60] Such as 'Member States shall make civilian and military capabilities available to the Union for the implementation of the common security and defence policy, to contribute to the objectives defined by the Council'. (Art 42(3) TEU).

[61] Among many other references in the Treaties, see Art 24(2) TEU: '*the Union* shall conduct, define and implement a common foreign and security policy …' (emphasis added).

[62] European Council, 'European Council Meeting of 15 December 2016: Conclusions' (2016) EUCO 34/16, paras 22–25.

[63] 'EU-Turkey Statement' (*Council of the EU*, 18 March 2016) Press Release 144/16, www.consilium.europa.eu/en/press/press-releases/2016/03/18/eu-turkey-statement/pdf.

[64] P García Andrade, 'EU External Competences in the Field of Migration: How to Act Externally When Thinking Internally' (2018) 55 *CML Rev* 157; M Gatti, 'The EU-Turkey Statement: A Treaty That Violates Democracy' (*EJIL Talk*, 2016), www.ejiltalk.org/the-eu-turkey-statement-a-treaty-that-violates-democracy-part-1-of-2/.

concluding an informal 'Deal' which clearly used committing language: eg 'Turkey and the European Union reconfirmed their commitment', 'Turkey and the EU also agreed', etc.[65] The General Court of the EU held that it had no jurisdiction as, in its view, the 'deal' was concluded by the EU States and not by the EU; and the CJEU dismissed the appeal as 'manifestly inadmissible'.[66] This is unfortunate, as it leaves a number of questions unanswered, for instance whether the EU States (in the framework of the European Council) are free to conclude international arrangements that are not only circumventing procedural guarantees, but which are also in the realm of existing EU competences.[67] Indeed, it has been held that in this situation 'the detriment to the EU legal order would be that the EU Treaties and their effective means of democratic and judicial control would be undermined…'.[68]

Yet, apart from politics, there may also be clear legal reasons to adopt a 'Decision of the Representatives of the Governments of the Member States, meeting within the Council', as exemplified by the 2002 Decision on the financial consequences of the expiry of the ECSC Treaty and on the research fund for coal and steel.[69] This Decision was in fact necessary to allow the European Commission to manage the ECSC assets and liabilities after expiry of the ECSC Treaty. Many other examples can be found, ranging from setting up a Fund for the financing of the Convention on the future of the European Union,[70] to authorising the Union Presidency to negotiate, on behalf of

[65] *cf* Spaventa (n 4); and earlier T Spijkerboer, 'Minimalist Reflections on Europe, Refugees and Law' (2016) 1 *European Papers* 533; G Fernández Arribas, 'The EU-Turkey Agreement: A Controversial Attempt at Patching up a Major Problem' (2016) 1 *European Papers* 1097; J Poon, 'EU-Turkey Deal: Violation of, or Consistency with, International Law?' (2016) 1 *European Papers* 1195; Cannizzaro (n 30); E Cannizzaro, 'Denialism as the Supreme Expression of Realism – A Quick Comment on *NF v. European Council*' (2017) 2 *European Papers* 251; S Peers, 'The Draft EU/Turkey Deal on Migration and Refugees: Is It Legal?' (*EU Law Analysis*, 2016), www.eulawanalysis.blogspot.com/2016/03/the-draft-euturkey-deal-on-migration.html.

[66] Case T-192/16 *NF v European Council* ECLI:EU:T:2017:128. See M Gatti, 'Attribution of Authorship of 'EU' Legal Acts: *NF and Others v European Council*' in Butler and Wessel (n 39) 861.

[67] N Idriz, 'Taking the EU-Turkey Deal to Court?' (*Verfassungsblog*, 2017), www.verfassungsblog.de/taking-the-eu-turkey-deal-to-court/.

[68] G Butler, 'Pre-Ratification Judicial Review of International Agreements to Be Concluded by the European Union' in M Derlén and J Lindholm (eds), *The Court of Justice of the European Union: Multidisciplinary Perspectives*, Swedish Studies in European Law (Oxford, Hart Publishing, 2018) 53, 73; Spijkerboer (n 65). See more extensively on the question of side-stepping procedures in the conclusion of international agreements RA Wessel, 'Normative Transformations in EU External Relations: The Phenomenon of "Soft" International Agreements' (2021) 44 *West European Politics* 72; F Casolari, 'The unbearable "lightness" of soft law: on the European Union's recourse to informal instruments in the fight against irregular immigration' in F Ippolito et al (eds), *Bilateral Relations in the Mediterranean. Prospects for Migration Issues* (Cheltenham, Edward Elgar, 2020) 215.

[69] Decision of the Representatives of the Governments of the Member States, meeting within the Council, of 27 February 2002 on the financial consequences of the expiry of the ECSC Treaty and on the research fund for coal and steel – Statements [2002] OJ L79/42. See also T Buchta, 'Sometimes Less is More – A Critical View on AG Bobek's Opinion on the Seats of EU Agencies' (*European Law Blog*, 14 October 2021), www.europeanlawblog.eu/2021/10/14/sometimes-less-is-more-a-critical-view-on-ag-bobeks-opinion-on-the-seats-of-eu-agencies/.

[70] Decision 2002/997/EU of the Representatives of the Governments of the Member States, meeting within the Council of 20 December 2002 amending the Decision of the Representatives of the Governments of the Member States, meeting within the Council, of 21 February 2002 setting up a Fund for the financing of the Convention on the future of the European Union and laying down the financial rules for its management [2002] OJ L349/34.

the EU States, the provisions of a legally binding agreement,[71] or the elections of the European Parliament by direct suffrage.[72]

In addition, the method is used in relation to the conclusion of mixed agreements, often also to decide on provisional application (see also further below).[73] In the so-called 'hybrid acts' case,[74] the Court had to assess the legality of acts in the form of a decision by the Council and the EU States' representatives in a Council meeting to agree on the signing and provisional application of a mixed agreement. In this case, 'Member States and States' were combined in one single act to decide on the provisional application of an international agreement. The Commission argued that this hybrid act 'contaminates' the supranational procedures under the EU Treaty, especially the treaty-making procedure (Article 218 TFEU) and institutional balance (Article 13(2) TEU). While the Court agreed that – to use the terminology of this chapter – EU States cannot force EU Member States to violate EU procedures (including the voting rules), the practice may have continued, but now on the basis of informal agreements between the EU States.[75]

A similar situation arose in relation to the conclusion by the EU of the Istanbul Convention in accordance with Article 218(6) TFEU, in the absence of a common accord of all the EU States giving their consent to being bound by the Convention. Again, the reason for a common accord was clear: it makes sure that the Union can safely conclude an agreement, knowing that EU States will follow. In *Opinion 1/19*, the Court held that 'the Treaties do not prohibit the Council of the European Union …, from waiting … for the "common accord" of the Member States to be bound by that convention in the fields falling within their competences. However, the Treaties do prohibit the Council from adding a further step to the conclusion procedure laid down in that article by making the adoption of the decision concluding that convention contingent on the prior establishment of such a "common accord"'.[76] Hence, the Council may wait for EU States to agree, but this cannot be used to side-step the

[71] Decision 2011/712/EU of the Representatives of the Governments of the Member States, meeting within the Council of 10 June 2011 authorising the Presidency of the Council to negotiate, on behalf of the Member States, the provisions of a legally binding agreement on forests in Europe that fall within the competences of the Member States [2011] OJ L285/1.

[72] Decision 76/787 ECSC/EEC/Euratom, Decision of the representatives of the Member States meeting in the Council relating to the Act concerning the election of the representatives of the Assembly by direct universal suffrage [1976] OJ L278/1, modified by Council Decision 2002/772/EC of 25 June and 23 September 2002 amending the Act concerning the election of the representatives of the European Parliament by direct universal suffrage, annexed to decision 76/787 ECSC/EEC/Euratom [2002] OJ L283/1. This Decision was subject to judicial review in Case C-145/04 *Spain v United Kingdom* ECLI:EU:C:2006:543, [2006] ECR I-7917. See also Spaventa (n 4).

[73] See, for instance, Decision 2000/771/EC of the representatives of the Governments of the Member States, meeting within the Council, of 18 September 2000 on the provisional application of the Internal Agreement between the Representatives of the Governments of the Member States, meeting within the Council, on measures to be taken and procedures to be followed for the implementation of the ACP-EC Partnership Agreement [2000] OJ L317/375.

[74] Case 28/12 *Commission v Council* ECLI:EU:C:2015:282.

[75] See A Ott, 'The "Contamination" of EU Law by Informalization? International Arrangements in EU Migration Law' (*Verfassungsblog*, 2020), www.verfassungsblog.de/the-contamination-of-eu-law-by-informalization/.

[76] Opinion 1/19 *Istanbul Convention* ECLI:EU:C:2021:198, para 338.

existing procedure in Article 218 TFEU, which simply allows the Union to conclude an agreement on the basis of QMV. Again, the message seems to be that the Member States as States cannot stand in the way of living up to treaty procedures.

A missed opportunity to shed more light on the nature of decisions taken by the EU States is represented by the recent ruling delivered by the Court of Justice in some cases concerning, *inter alia*, the location of the new seat of the European Medicines Agency (EMA). Following the reasoning of AG Bobek,[77] the Court concluded that the decision taken by the Heads of State or Government of Member States on the new seat of the EMA 'is to be regarded as a measure adopted by the Member States alone [i.e. the EU States]',[78] thus falling outside the Court's jurisdiction according to Article 263 TFEU. More significantly, the Court has made it clear that 'the contested decision, which has been taken by the Member States in an area in which the Treaties do not provide for their action is deprived of any binding legal effects under EU law'.[79] In order to become relevant for EU legal order, such an act should thus be ratified by the EU legislature.[80]

While we can follow the logic of this argumentation, the examples in the present chapter underline that despite not being part of EU law proper, many decisions by the EU States are necessary for EU law to function. Irrespective of the fact that a 'common accord' may not be required by the Treaties,[81] and despite the Court's claim that these decisions have no 'binding legal effects under EU law', they do have a clear function in the EU legal order and also clearly have legal effects. In the words of Buchta, 'these decisions facilitate the proper implementation of EU law, and consequently without implementing the decisions, the proper application of EU law might be hindered'.[82] The latter is clearly supported by the fact that decisions of the Representatives of the Member States meeting within the Council are part of the Union's acquis that becomes binding on new Member States. All of this underlines our previous claim that the functioning of the EU legal order not only depends on acts by its Member States under EU law, but also on acts by EU States that are related to the EU's rules and procedures.

3.2. The Conclusion of International Agreements

On the basis of Article 216(1) TFEU, the Union has a competence to conclude international agreements. Paragraph 2 adds that these agreements are not only binding on the Union, but also on its Member States. As the Member States are not (necessarily)

[77] Opinions of Advocate General Bobek in Joined Cases C-59/18 *Italy v Council* and C-182/18 *Comune di Milano v Council* ECLI:EU:C:2021:812; in Joined Cases C-106/19 *Italy v Council and Parliament* and C-232/19 *Comune di Milano v Parliament and Council* ECLI:EU:C:2021:816; and in Case C-743/19 *Parliament v Council* ECLI:EU:C:2021:812. The AG refers back to Judgment of 30 June 1993 in Joined Cases C-181/91 and C-248/91 *Parliament v Council and Commission* ECLI:EU:C:1993:271, [1993] ECR I-3685, para 12.

[78] Joined Cases C-59/18 and C-182/18 *Italy v Council* ECLI:EU:C:2022:567, para 109.

[79] ibid para 110.

[80] ibid para 111.

[81] Art 341 Consolidated version of the Treaty on the Functioning of the European Union (TFEU) [2016] OJ C202/47 provides that: 'The seat of the institutions of the Union shall be determined by common accord of the governments of the Member States.' but does not mention the seat of Agencies. Based on a historical analysis of Art 341 TFEU, one could argue that the AG's interpretation may have been too strict. See also Buchta (n 69).

[82] Buchta (n 69).

contractual parties to these agreements, this leads to the well-known situation in which States are bound by international agreements, irrespective of the *pacta tertiis nec nocent nec prosunt* rule, that forms part of international treaty law.[83] In these situations, the EU States are thus bound to these agreements as Member States. Their commitments are not based on international law (and one may even argue, are not in line with international law) but on EU law and any question of accountability or responsibility needs to follow that route.

This situation is different in the case of mixed agreements, to which, it could be argued, the EU Member States are parties 'as States'. Mixed agreements are typically signed and concluded by the EU and its Member States jointly and all of them seem to be a 'party' in their own right and bound directly under public international law. At the same time, questions have arisen in relation to the identities of the Member States in this context.[84] First of all, one could argue that, despite the fact that the agreement is signed and concluded by the EU States and that national constitutional procedures have been followed to reach this result, on the side of the EU these agreements cannot simply be entered into by any (European) State, but just by EU Member States. In the case of bilateral mixed agreements in particular the Member States and the EU are presented as a 'team'. This is often underlined by the preamble, where it provides that the agreement is concluded between the third country, on the one part, and the European Union and its Member States, on the other part, jointly referred to as 'the Parties'.[85] Significantly, several mixed agreements include a clause defining the term 'Parties' as 'the Union or its Member States, or the Union and its Member States, in accordance with their respective competences, on the one hand, and [the third country], on the other'.[86] Furthermore, just as in the case of EU-only agreements, mixed agreements (again primarily bilateral ones) often have territorial application clauses defined in terms of the territory of EU Member States.[87]

While Advocate General Sharpston noted that Member States are parties to these agreements as sovereign States, 'not as a mere appendage of the European Union',[88]

[83] The rule is affirmed in Art 34 Vienna Convention on the Law of Treaties (Vienna, 23 May 1969).

[84] *cf* RA Wessel, 'Consequences of Brexit for International Agreements Concluded by the EU and its Member States' (2018) 55 *CML Rev* 101. Some of the arguments in this text are derived from this publication.

[85] See eg Comprehensive Economic and Trade Agreement (CETA) between Canada, of the one part, and the European Union and its Member States, of the other part [2017] OJ L11/23.

[86] Examples include Art 55 Partnership on Relations and Cooperation between the European Union and its Member States, of the one part, and New Zealand, of the other part [2016] OJ L304/1; Art 34 Strategic Partnership Agreement between the European Union and its Member States, of the one part, and Canada, of the other part [2016] OJ L329/45 and Art 482 Association Agreement between the European Union and its Member States, of the one part, and Ukraine, of the other part [2014] OJ L161/3.

[87] eg Art 126 Agreement on the European Economic Area [1994] OJ L1/3.

[88] Opinion of Advocate General Sharpston in Opinion 2/15 *Free Trade Agreement between the European Union and the Republic of Singapore* ECLI:EU:C:2016:992, para 77. This conclusion is relevant when difficulties arise in the ratification process of mixed agreements. According to AG Sharpston, indeed, 'the need for unity and rapidity of EU external action and the difficulties which might arise if the European Union and the Member States have to participate jointly in the conclusion and implementation of an international agreement cannot affect the question who has competence to conclude it' (para 566). See also G Kübek, 'The Non-Ratification Scenario: Legal and Practical Responses to Mixed Treaty Rejection by Member States' (2018) 23 *European Foreign Affairs Review* 21; G Van der Loo and RA Wessel, 'The Non-Ratification of Mixed Agreements: Legal Consequences and Solutions' (2017) 54 *CML Rev* 735.

this is not the whole story. As an 'integral part of EU law' – in the words of the EU Court[89] – these agreements are closely connected to other EU legislation and policies. Moreover, many mixed agreements are concluded without a strict indication of what falls under EU competences and what is still in the hands of the Member States. In fact, many Council decisions only refer to the participation of Member States in the agreement alongside the Union,[90] or explain in general terms that the agreement is only concluded insofar as the agreement's provisions fall under Union competences.[91] To distil the division of competences from the Council decision adopting the Agreement remains difficult. The Council decisions on signature and provisional application State that the listed provisions shall only provisionally apply 'to the extent that they cover matters falling within the Union's competence'.[92] Several Council decisions even explicitly state that 'the provisional application of parts of the Agreement does not prejudge the allocation of competences between the Union and its Member States in accordance with the Treaties'.[93] Thus, provisional application does not provide a clear indication of the provisions falling under Union or Member State competences. The same holds true for so-called 'Declarations of competence' that may be attached to an international agreement to give third parties an indication of the responsible parties on the side of the EU. Both the dynamic character of the division of competences and the sometimes not very concrete wording do not allow for too much reliance on these declarations in defining the exact delimitation.[94] In short, participation of EU States in mixed agreements underlines their EU membership rather than their status as sovereign States. On the EU-side mixed agreements seem to be concluded by the States both *as EU States* and *as*

[89] *cf* RA Wessel, 'International Agreements as an Integral Part of EU Law: *Haegeman*' in Butler and Wessel (n 39) 35.

[90] For example, the Council Decision 2010/48/EC concerning the conclusion, by the European Community, of the United Nations Convention on the Rights of Persons with Disabilities [2010] OJ L23/35. It states that 'both the Community and its Member States have competence in the fields covered by the UN Convention. The Community and the Member States should therefore become Contracting Parties to it, so that together they can fulfil the obligations laid down by the UN Convention and exercise the rights invested in them, in situations of mixed competence in a coherent manner'.

[91] See eg Council Decision 94/800/EC concerning the conclusion on behalf of the European Community, as regards matters within its competence, of the agreements reached in the Uruguay round multilateral negotiations (1986–1994) [1994] OJ L336/1 which states that these agreements 'are hereby approved on behalf of the European Community with regard to that portion of them which falls within the competence of the European Community'. For a more recent example, see Council Decision 2008/801/EC on the conclusion, on behalf of the European Community, of the United Nations Convention against Corruption [2008] OJ L287/1.

[92] ibid.

[93] See eg Council Decision 2016/2232/EU on the signing, on behalf of the Union, and provisional application of the Political Dialogue and Cooperation Agreement between the European Union and its Member States, of the one part, and the Republic of Cuba, of the other part [2016] OJ L337I/1. A similar formulation can also be found in Council Decision 2017/38/EU on the provisional application of the Comprehensive Economic and Trade Agreement (CETA) between Canada, of the one part, and the European Union and its Member States, of the other part [2017] OJ L11/1080. The Council and Member States also adopted numerous Statements and Declarations to the Council minutes in which they emphasise that the provisional application of the agreement in several areas such as transport and moral rights does not prejudge the allocation of competences between the EU and the Member States.

[94] See also A Delgado Casteleiro, 'EU Declarations of Competence to Multilateral Agreements: A Useful Reference Base?' (2012) 17 *European Foreign Affairs Review* 491.

Member States functioning within the institutional and substantive setting that governs the status and implementation of international agreements in the EU and domestic legal orders. And, in some agreements 'the Member States of the European Union' are indeed referred to as such.[95]

To overcome this complexity, and perhaps schizophrenia, it has been suggested that the EU and its Member States be viewed as 'one' party in the context of mixed agreements.[96] As we have seen, the way in which the agreements are presented support this idea. It would also overcome the problem that under international treaty law it is difficult to deal with composite entities, ever since the so called 'federal clause' did not prove to be an option for the International law Commission when codifying the law of treaties.[97] The famous Article 36*bis* that appeared in an International Law Commission's draft on the law of treaties between States and international organisations or between international organisations[98] would have made the position of Member States somewhat clearer by acknowledging their dual status.[99] In their recent study, Schaefer and Odermatt analysed the various ways in which the combination of the EU and its Member States is presented in international agreements: 'The term "EU Party" has even found its way into the text of so-called bilateral mixed agreements. These are mixed agreements which, despite the number of parties, are considered bilateral in structure, creating a relationship between the EU and its Member States, on the one hand, and the third State(s), on the other. While the prefixes vary from "*EC* Party" in the pre-Lisbon era to the "*EU* Party" since 2009 and "*Union* Party" in the Strategic Partnership Agreement (SPA) with Japan, these descriptions all use an international treaty law concept: the "Party"'.[100] In the view of the authors, the term 'EU Party' could be defined as 'the EU or its Member States or the EU and its Member

[95] See more extensively K Fernekeß, S Palevičienė and M Thadikkaran, 'The Future of the United Kingdom in Europe – Exit Scenarios and their Implications on Trade Relations' (2013) *Graduate Institute Trade and Investment Law Clinic Papers* 49.

[96] S Schaefer and J Odermatt, 'Nomen est Omen? The Relevance of "EU Party" in International Law' in Levrat et al (n 7).

[97] See more extensively Levrat and Kaspiarovich (n 5), as well as the 'Report of the Commission to the General Assembly: Document A/5209 – Report of the International Law Commission covering the work of its fourteenth session, 24 April–29 June 1962' (1962) 2 United Nations Yearbook of the International Law Commission 157; and D Turp and F Roch '1969 Vienna Convention: Article 6 Capacity of States to Conclude Treaties' in O Corten and P Klein (eds), *The Vienna Conventions on the Law of Treaties: A Commentary* (Oxford, Oxford University Press, 2011) 107.

[98] Draft Article 36*bis* read as follows: 'Obligations and rights arise for States members of an international organization from the provisions of a treaty to which that organization is a party when the parties to the treaty intend those provisions to be the means of establishing such obligations and according such rights and have defined their conditions and effects in the treaty or have otherwise agreed thereon, and if: (a) the States members of the organization, by virtue of the constituent instrument of that organization or otherwise, have unanimously agreed to be bound by the said provisions of the treaty; and (b) the assent of the States members of the organization to be bound by the relevant provisions of the treaty has been duly'. *cf* 'Report of the International Law Commission on the Work of its thirty-fourth Session: Draft Articles on the Law of Treaties between States and International Organizations of between International Organizations' (1982) 2(2) United Nations Yearbook of the International Law Commission 17.

[99] See extensively on this topic C Brölmann, *The Institutional Veil in Public International Law: International Organisations and the Law of Treaties*, Hart Monographs in Transnational and International Law (Oxford, Hart Publishing, 2007).

[100] Schaefer and Odermatt (n 96).

States' according to their respective competences and would thus help overcome the distinction between States and Member States that is (or should be) irrelevant for third parties.

Also importantly, schizophrenic approaches towards mixity are limited thanks to a terrific recourse, in the relevant case law of the European Court of Justice, to the duty of loyalty. As rightly stressed in the literature, the principle of sincere cooperation is mainly understood by the Court in contexts involving mixed agreements as a sort of master key, imposing abstention duties upon the Member States in order to ensure the effectiveness and unity of the external representation of the Union.[101] Even though such a trend has the merit to strengthen the external stance of the Union, it is undeniable that it risks shaping limitless duties of loyalty upon the Member States[102] – something which is inconsistent with their international subjectivity as well as with the mutual nature of the principle of sincere cooperation.

3.3. The Representation of the EU and its Member States in Multilateral Fora

A perhaps obvious situation occurs in relation to the membership of international organisations. In most cases, EU States are members in their own right, and have sometimes joined international organisations alongside the EU.[103] At the same time, the 'identity' of the participating States is not always clear. Even when they all are full sovereign members of an international organisation, the EU States occasionally act as EU Member States. First of all, they have clear obligations under the EU Treaties. Thus, Article 211 TFEU provides that 'Within their respective spheres of competence, the Union and the Member States shall cooperate with third countries and with the competent international organisations'. The first part of this sentence hints at the idea that the Member States here act as States; and the obligations flowing from their membership of international organisations sometimes return as EU law obligations.[104] And the sovereign participation of EU States in even the most

[101] M Cremona, 'Case C-246/07, *Commission v. Sweden (PFOS)*, Judgment of the Court of Justice (Grand Chamber) of 20 April 2010' (2011) 48 *CML Rev* 1639, 1654; F Casolari, 'The Principle of Loyal Cooperation: A "Master Key" for EU External Representation?' in S Besson and N Levrat (eds), *The European Union and International Law* (Genève, Schulthess, 2015) 91.

[102] A Delgado Casteleiro and J Larik, 'The Duty to Remain Silent: Limitless Loyalty in EU External Relations?' (2011) 36 *EL Rev* 524. *cf* F Casolari, 'Like a Bridge over Troubled Water: The 2/15 Opinion through the Lens of EU Loyalty' in I Bosse-Platière and C Rapoport (eds), *The Conclusion and Implementation of EU Free Trade Agreements: Constitutional Challenges* (Cheltenham, Edward Elgar, 2019) 85.

[103] See for a comprehensive overview RA Wessel and J Odermatt (eds), *Research Handbook on the European Union and International Organisations* (Cheltenham, Edward Elgar, 2019).

[104] In relation to development cooperation, for instance, a number of provisions have been included explicitly to strengthen commitments of both the Union and its Member States in that area. Thus, Art 208(2) TFEU provides the following: 'The Union and the Member States shall comply with the commitments and take account of the objectives they have approved in the context of the United Nations and other competent international organisations'. Art 210(1) TFEU adds to that an obligation of coordination, which means concretely that the EU and Member States must take account of the Millennium Development Goals (MDGs) and their planned post-2015 follow-up ('Sustainable Development Goals' or SDGs), drawn up in the context of the United Nations.

important international organisations is sometimes restrained by EU law (loyalty) obligations.[105]

In other situations, the Court has nevertheless argued that the Member State status should not stand in the way of EU States exercising their sovereign rights under international law. In the *Antarctica* case, the Court held that 'In the specific context of the system of Antarctic agreements, exercise by the European Union of the external competence at issue in the present cases that excludes the Member States would be incompatible with international law'.[106] In this case, as the Court held, international law arguments call for a shared competence to be exercised in a shared manner. Cases like these underline the continuing tension between the Union and its (or at least some of its) Member States in situations of external representation. At the same time, it remains clear that identities of States shift and that, despite the 'Member State first' rule, ultimately this should not affect statehood to the extent that it would cause serious conflicts under international law.[107]

A specific situation occurs when the Union's increased (or perhaps even exclusive) competences in a certain area have not led to it being a member of relevant international organisations. Examples have become scarce,[108] because a lack of formal membership is sometimes balanced by increased participation policies.[109] Yet, even with just an observer status, the Union will have to rely on its Member States – or sometimes just one[110] – in important and EU-law relevant international organisations such as the Council of Europe, the International Labour Organisation, the Arctic Council, the International Maritime Organisation, the International Atomic Energy Agency or the Organisation for International Carriage by Rail (OTIF). In areas in which the Union has an exclusive competence, but lacks the membership of the connected international organisation, it will have to rely on its Member States. At the same time, one could argue that, no longer being able to exercise their own competence, those States merely act as agents – or, as rightly pointed out by Marise

[105] See the clear obligations in Art 34(2) TEU: 'Member States which are also members of the United Nations Security Council will concert and keep the other Member States and the High Representative fully informed. Member States which are members of the Security Council will, in the execution of their functions, defend the positions and the interests of the Union, without prejudice to their responsibilities under the provisions of the United Nations Charter.'; as well as the general rule in Art 34 TEU that Member States shall uphold the Union's positions 'in international organisations and at international conferences where not all the Member States participate'. *cf* also the Opinion of Advocate General Maduro in Case C-402/05 P *Kadi and Al Barakaat International Foundation v Council and Commission* ECLI:EU:C:2008:11, [2008] ECR I-6351, para 32, where he argues that the duty of loyal cooperation 'requires Member States to exercise their powers and responsibilities in an international organisation such as the United Nations in a manner that is compatible with the conditions set by the primary rules and the general principles of [EU] law'.

[106] Joined Cases C-626/15 and C-659/16 *Commission v Council (Antarctic MPAs)* ECLI:EU:C:2018:925, para 128.

[107] To some extent, a similar solution seems to be imposed by the mutual nature of the duty of loyalty, which also implies loyalty obligations upon the Union towards the Member States.

[108] Even in the area of fisheries, the EU now seems to be represented in almost all regional fisheries management organisations (RFMOs). See P Heckler, 'Regional Fisheries Management Organisations: Defining the EU and Member State Roles' in Odermatt and Wessel (n 103).

[109] RA Wessel and J Odermatt, 'The European Union's Engagement with other International Institutions Emerging Questions of EU and International Law' in Odermatt and Wessel (n 103).

[110] An example being the Convention on the Conservation and Management of Pollock Resources in the Central Bering Sea (CCBSP) (Washington, 16 June 1994), where the EU does not have any formal status and must use the proxy of Poland to address the organisation. See Heckler (n 108).

Cremona,[111] as trustees – of the Union. In the context of the present chapter, we would say: EU States as Member States.

These situations reveal that the question of who is in charge (the EU, the Member States or the EU States) not only depends on internal EU rules, but also on the membership rules of the international body. Recently, the Court clarified the external representation of the Union in the so-called *IMO* case.[112] As summarised by Verellen:

> The case is interesting for at least two reasons. Firstly, it further clarifies the role of the Commission and the Member States in the EU's external representation in international organisations of which the EU is not a member. In particular, the Court confirms that the Commission has an exclusive competence to represent the EU externally only in so far as the relevant international legal rules allow the EU to act. If this is not the case – for example, when membership of an international organisation is open only to states and not to other international organisations – Member States are free to decide who is to defend the interests of the EU on the international stage. This can be the Commission, but it can also be a Member State, or even several Member States – each in the name of and on behalf of the EU Member States, but in the interest of the EU.[113]

Here we see that the international law context (the membership rules of an international organisation) clearly impacts the application of the EU law rules on who can represent the EU externally. The case also shows how difficult it is to apply the internal EU rules on competence division (and the EU's claim for exclusive competence based on the abovementioned *ERTA* case) to international situations.[114] Irrespective of the fact that Member States might have lost a competence in a certain area, the mere fact that they – and not the EU – are a member of an international organisation, has an effect on the application of the representation rules.

Here again the duty of loyalty towards the Union may contribute to clarifying the picture. In the *Commission v Greece* case, also dealing with the participation of Member States in the activity of the International Maritime Organisation,[115] the Court of Justice has made it clear first that '[t]he mere fact that the Community is not a member of an international organisation in no way authorises a Member State, acting individually in the context of its participation in an international organisation, to assume obligations likely to affect Community rules promulgated for the attainment of the objectives of the Treaty'.[116] After having stressed the (loyalty) abstention duties imposed upon the Member States, the Court has further defined their role in similar scenarios, by affirming that 'the fact that the Community is not a member

[111] M Cremona, 'Member States Agreement as Union Law' in E Cannizzaro, P Palchetti and RA Wessel (eds), *International Law as Law of the European Union*, Studies in EU External Relations 5 (Leiden, Martinus Nijhoff Publishing, 2012) 291, 306, maintaining that in such cases Member States 'participate in the agreement not only as sovereign States but also as Member States of (and under the authorisation of) the Union. Here … we can … draw an analogy with mixed agreements, where the Member States participate in their own right but also with commitments as Union Member States'.

[112] Case C-161/20 *Commission v Council (Organisation maritime international)* ECLI:EU:C:2022:260.

[113] T Verellen, 'Exercising EU External Competence in International Organisations of which the EU is not a Member: *European Commission v Council of the European Union ('IMO')* (C-161/20)' (2023) 48 *EL Rev* 362, 363.

[114] ibid.

[115] Case C-45/07 *Commission v Greece* ECLI:EU:C: 2009:81, [2009] ECR I-701.

[116] ibid para 30.

of an international organisation does not prevent its external competence from being in fact exercised, in particular through the Member States acting jointly in the Community's interest'.[117]

4. EU MEMBER STATES AS STATES UNDER INTERNATIONAL LAW

4.1. Member States' Retained Powers

Another scenario which deserves to be mentioned is related to areas where Member States still retain sovereign prerogatives pursuant to – or outside of – EU law. In such cases, one should conclude that Member States are still able to act as EU States pursuing their own objectives and interests. On closer inspection, however, the margin of manoeuvre they enjoy seems to become more and more limited considering (again!) their duty of loyalty towards the Union.

Reference is made here to a well-consolidated jurisprudence of the Court tracing back to the 1960s,[118] stressing the role that the duty of loyalty of Member States may play in preventing that the exercise of Member State prerogatives (or retained powers) undermines the fulfilment of EU objectives. There are numerous areas where such an approach – the 'framing of powers doctrine', as it has been called by Advocate General (AG) Pikamäe in his Opinion in the *Slovenia v Croatia* case[119] – have been affirmed: loss and acquisition of nationality,[120] maintenance of public order and safeguarding of internal security,[121] social security,[122] organisation of education systems,[123] organisation of justice,[124] and direct taxation.[125] From this perspective, the strengthening of the duty of loyalty of the Member States – especially the abstention duties flowing from the loyalty clause enshrined in Article 4(3) TEU – contributed to blurring the divide among EU and Member State prerogatives, leading in turn to a more flexible understanding of the principle of conferral.[126] The core question upon which the framing of

[117] ibid para 31.

[118] Case 30/59 *De Gezamenlijke Steenkolenmijnen in Limburg* ECLI:EU:C:1961:2, [1961] ECR 48.

[119] Opinion of Advocate General Pikamäe in Case C-457/18 *Slovenia v Croatia* ECLI:EU:C:2019:1067, para 138. On that doctrine, see L Azoulai, 'The "Retained Powers" Formula in the Case Law of the European Court of Justice: EU Law as Total Law?' (2011) 4 *European Journal of Legal Studies* 192. *cf* also B de Witte, 'Exclusive Member States Competences – Is There Such a Thing?' in S Garben and I Govaere (eds), *The Division of Competences between the EU and the Member States: Reflections on the Past, the Present and the Future*, Modern Studies in European Law (Oxford, Hart Publishing, 2017); L Boucon, 'EU Law and Retained Powers of Member States' in L Azoulai (ed), *The Question of Competence in the European Union* (Oxford, Oxford University Press, 2014).

[120] Case C-369/90 *Micheletti and Others v Delegación del Gobierno en Cantabria* ECLI:EU:C:1992:295, [1992] ECR I-4239, para 10.

[121] Case C-265/95 *Commission v France* ECLI:EU:C:1997:595, [1997] ECR I-6959, paras 33–35.

[122] Case C-647/13 *Melchior* ECLI:EU:C:2015:54, para 21.

[123] Joined Cases C-11/06 and C-12/06 *Morgan and Bucher* ECLI:EU:C:2007:626, [2007] ECR I-9161, para 24.

[124] Case C-619/18 *Commission v Poland (Independence of the Supreme Court)* ECLI:EU:C:2019:531, para 52.

[125] Case C-279/93 *Finanzamt Köln-Altstadt v Schumacker* ECLI:EU:C:1995:31, [1995] ECR I-225, paras 21–24.

[126] E Neframi, 'Principe de coopération loyale et principe d'attribution dans le cadre de la mise en œuvre du droit de l'Union' (2016) 52 *Cahiers de droit européen* 221.

powers doctrine is based is that of a relevant intertwinement between the exercise of Member States' powers/prerogatives and the effectiveness of EU law. The more such an intertwinement is evident and sound, the more the Court feels comfortable in invoking the duty of loyalty that Member States should have in regard to the Union.

The consequences of the EU's influence on Member States' prerogatives exercised on the international scene are clearly visible in the *Kadi* saga, where the Court of Justice has *de facto* downsized the autonomy of Member States in the fight against international terrorism by submitting their action to the legal constraints flowing from the EU constitutional framework (namely the constitutional obligations concerning the protection of fundamental values). But also relevant is the strategic autonomy approach recently adopted by EU political institutions, which is mainly understood as a political framework for the adoption of supranational legal tools aiming at securing EU interests in the physical and cyber space.[127] As some of the initiatives elaborated under that umbrella clearly reveal (eg: the tool to counter the use of economic coercion by third countries[128]), its potential impact on a Member State's powers is far from being irrelevant.

4.2. Member States-only Agreements

Obviously, Member States have remained 'States' and in areas in which they are still competent to do so, they have continued to conclude international agreements, either with third States or among themselves (*inter se*).[129] The EU Treaties even expressly mention the competence of Member States to enter into international agreements with third countries;[130] and this competence may also be included in EU secondary legislation.[131] While, *prima facie*, these agreements are not part of the Union's legal

[127] See Editorial Comments, 'Keeping Europeanism at bay? Strategic autonomy as a constitutional problem' (2022) 59 *CML Rev* 313; and contributions to the Special Issue (Volume 27) on strategic autonomy of the *European Foreign Affairs Review* published in April 2022.

[128] European Commission, 'Proposal for a Regulation of the European Parliament and of the Council on the protection of the Union and its Member States from economic coercion by third countries' (2021) COM(2021) 775 final.

[129] *cf* B De Witte, 'Old-fashioned Flexibility: International Agreements between Member States of the European Union' in G De Búrca and J Scott (eds), *Constitutional Change in the EU: From Uniformity to Flexibility?* (Oxford, Hart Publishing, 2000) 31–58.

[130] See eg Art 34(2) TEU; Arts 165(3), 166(3), 167(3), and 168(3) 191(4), 209(2), 212(3), 219(4), 214(4) TFEU.

[131] Examples include the air service agreements, which, after a judgment by the Court, suddenly proved to be covered by the Union's exclusive competences, but need time to be replaced; see Regulation (EC) No 847/2004 of the European Parliament and of the Council on the negotiation and implementation of air service agreements between Member States and third countries [2004] OJ L157/7. Similar situations arose in relation to the bilateral investment treaties (BITs): see Regulation (EU) No 1219/2012 of the European Parliament and of the Council establishing transitional arrangements for bilateral investment agreements between Member States and third countries [2012] OJ L351/40; and with respect to European private law see Regulation (EC) No 662/2009 of the European Parliament and of the Council establishing a procedure for the negotiation and conclusion of agreements between Member States and third countries on particular matters concerning the law applicable to contractual and non-contractual obligations [2009] OJ L200/25; and Regulation (EC) No 593/2008 of the European Parliament and of the Council on the law applicable to contractual obligations (Rome I) [2008] OJ L177/6 and Regulation (EC) No 864/2007 of the European Parliament on the law applicable to non-contractual obligations (Rome II) [2007] OJ L199/40.

order,[132] there may be clear links with EU law and in the case of *inter se* agreements Article 273 TFEU even grants jurisdiction to the Court. In external relations, the links with EU law are particularly clear when Member States are *authorised* by the EU to conclude international agreements, for instance, as already seen, in areas in which the EU retains specific competences, but for practical reasons it is not able to exercise them. Allan Rosas listed four main reasons why some international agreements do not count the EU among their contracting parties:[133] (1) many agreements were concluded by Member States before they became EU members or before an EU competence in a particular area became clearly established; (2) the agreement may concern a matter that is still outside an EU competence; (3) the EU Commission or the Council may prefer, for political or other non-legal reasons, not to conclude an agreement despite the existence of a Union competence to do so and, in the case of a multilateral convention, despite the existence in the agreement of a clause enabling an integration organisation like the EU to become a contracting party; and (4) a multilateral agreement may be closed to EU adherence by limiting the right to adhere to 'States'. To complicate things, agreements can be concluded before and after EU membership and can, in both cases, be concluded with third countries or between Member States *inter se*.

The case of the agreements concluded between EU Member States for settling disputes deserves a specific mention. Indeed, while the loyalty duty enshrined in Article 344 TFEU prevents Member States from submitting a dispute concerning the interpretation or application of the EU Treaties to disputes settlement mechanisms other than those mentioned in the Treaties,[134] EU States are still free to decide how to solve disputes falling outside the scope of EU law.[135] This does not mean, however, that the States may completely ignore their Union membership when similar disputes arise. As was made clear by the Court of Justice in *Slovenia v Croatia*, the obligations arising from the loyalty clause (Article 4(3) TEU) impose upon the concerned States a duty 'to strive sincerely to bring about a definitive solution consistent with

[132] Indeed, it is generally held that the general rules and principles of EU law are not applicable to these agreements. See A Rosas, 'The Status in EU Law of International Agreements Concluded by EU Member States' (2011) 34 *Fordham International Law Journal* 1304, 1314. *cf* also Case C-533/08 *TNT Express Nederland* ECLI:EU:C:2010:50, [2010] ECR I-4107. The Court 'does not, in principle, have jurisdiction to interpret, in preliminary ruling proceedings, international agreements concluded between Member States and non-member countries'.

[133] Rosas (n 132). See also R Schütze, 'EC law and International Agreements of the Member States – An Ambivalent Relationship' (2006) 9 *CYELS* 387; J Klabbers, *Treaty Conflict and the European Union* (Cambridge, Cambridge University Press, 2009); JW Van Rossem, 'Interaction between EU Law and International Law in the Light of *Intertanko* and *Kadi*: The Dilemma of Norms Binding the Member States but not the Community' (2009) 40 *Netherlands Yearbook of International Law* 183.

[134] Opinion of Advocate General Maduro in Case C-459/03 *Commission v Ireland* ECLI:EU:C:2006:42, [2006] ECR I-4635, para 55.

[135] As clearly illustrated in the *Jurisdictional Immunities of the State* case (ICJ, 2012) EU States may invoke the jurisdiction of an international tribunal (*in casu*, the International Court of Justice) on the basis of an *ad hoc* treaty law provisions for the peaceful settlement of disputes. But EU States may also rely on Art 273 TFEU to submit to the EU Court of Justice disputes relating to the subject matter of EU Treaties. *cf* Case C-648/15 *Austria v Germany* ECLI:EU:C:2017:664, where the Court was asked to solve a dispute between the two EU States in the taxation domain.

international law'.[136] Such an obligation may be read in the light of the circumstance stressed by AG Bot in *Hungary v Slovakia*: any crisis or paralysis in the diplomatic relations among Member States which is likely to jeopardise their 'good-neighbourly relations' risks undermining the EU integration process. In such a case, EU States are required to also act as Member States, and must refrain themselves from further disrupting the functioning of the Union.[137]

In sum, it becomes more and more difficult to deny that EU States-only agreements may have an effect on EU law. After all, '[a]fter 50 years of existence, the EU has engendered a dense legal order. On occasion, its legislative activity reaches beyond the EU's legal space and incidentally affects relations between third parties and EU members'.[138] It is also wise to remember that in *International Fruit*,[139] the Court had no difficulties in accepting a binding effect of the GATT 1947 on the Community, despite the fact that it was not a party to that agreement. On a different note, in *Intertanko*, the Court recognised, in the light of the principle of sincere cooperation, a duty to take account of an agreement concluded by all the Member States with third States in interpreting EU law.[140] Moreover, as already mentioned, some Council decisions authorise Member States to conclude international agreements 'in the interest of the Union',[141] and EU States-only agreements may be concluded with a view to strengthening the fulfilment of some EU objectives.

5. CONCLUDING REMARKS

As described in Luigi Pirandello's last novel, *One, No One and One Hundred Thousand*, the identities that EU States have acquired in light of their participation in the European integration process do not entirely correspond to the identity they (probably) believe they possess. Obviously, the EU Member States have not ceased to be States, both from a national constitutional and an international law perspective. What this chapter demonstrates, however, is that their Union membership has resulted in a DNA mutation of their statehood, giving them a dual identity which mirrors, to some extent, the Janus-faced attitude of EU Treaties. As 'EU States', those States, on the one hand, are sovereign entities under international law, acting as the framers of the integration process; on the other hand, as Member States they act as subjects of an autonomous legal order, being first obliged to respect its 'basic

[136] Case C-457/18 *Slovenia v Croatia* ECLI:EU:C:2020:65, para 109. See F Casolari, '*Inter se* Agreements between Member States, and the Outer Limits of the Court's Jurisdiction in Infringement Proceedings: *Slovenia v Croatia*' in Butler and Wessel (n 39) 981.

[137] Case C-364/10 *Hungary v Slovakia* ECLI:EU:C:2012:124, paras 58–59.

[138] M Ličková, 'European Exceptionalism in International Law' (2008) 19 *European Journal of International Law* 463, 466.

[139] Joined Cases 21–24/72 *International Fruit Company NV and Others v Produktschap voor Groenten en Fruit* ECLI:EU:C:1972:115, [1972] ECR 1219, paras 14–18. A Petti and J Scott, 'International Agreements in the EU Legal Order: *International Fruit*' in Butler and Wessel (n 39) 21.

[140] Case C-308/06 *Intertanko and Others* ECLI:EU:C:2008:312, [2008] ECR I-4057, para 53. See also F Casolari, 'Giving Indirect Effect to International Law within the EU Legal Order: The Doctrine of Consistent Interpretation', in Cannizzaro et al (n 111) 395.

[141] *cf* above Section 2 and Rosas (n 132) 1333.

constitutional charter'.[142] The identity of EU members is fluid and dynamic as roles may overlap in specific situations and change over time. Even though this could lead to idiosyncrasies and schizophrenic approaches undermining the integration process, this chapter has stressed the potentialities that the principle of sincere cooperation may express in reconciling the dual identity of EU States, contributing thus to shape a European space of shared and mutually dependent sovereignty.

Finally, as this book is devoted to the works of Marise Cremona, both authors wish to underline the impact of her work on their own thinking and writing. Marise, thank you so much for not only setting the stage of EU external relations law, but also for filling it with ever-new original ideas. It has been a true pleasure to work with you throughout all these years.

[142] Case 294/83 *Les Verts v Parliament* ECLI:EU:C:1986:166, [1986] ECR 1339, para 23.

*Europe in the Global Imaginary, the Globe in the European Imaginary: The Legacy of Sovereignty**

NEIL WALKER

1. SOVEREIGNTY AND BEYOND

When I first came to the study of the European Union (EU) 30 years ago from the perspective of state-based constitutional law and theory, I could not help but notice how little the concept of 'sovereignty' – so central in what was then very much my home terrain – figured in EU legal doctrine or its commentary. It would sometimes come to the surface in the analysis of relations between the EU and its Member States – the EU's 'internal external' relations so to speak – though, even here, it tended to be located in the background of more readily adaptable concepts of constitutional authority and (increasingly) constitutional 'identity',[1] or of legally-operative conflict principles such as 'supremacy' or 'primacy'.[2] Sovereignty was an even scarcer currency in the study of Europe's (proper) external relations, where the key focus instead was on the relationship between internal and external powers – both their content and their proper exercise – and on the novel ways in which, first, the European 'Community', and latterly the European 'Union', might be conceived of as an 'international' actor.[3] In this, notably, there was, and remains, a

* It has been a real honour to have been asked to contribute to a collection in appreciation of my old friend and colleague Marise Cremona, not least because my own expertise lies in matters quite distant from her own. I am only an occasional traveller to the remote lands of EU external relations, but on these visits my best guide, writing with unmatched clarity and insight, has always been Marise herself.

[1] See Article 4(2) Consolidated version of the Treaty on European Union (TEU) [2016] OJ C202/13, as introduced by the Treaty of Lisbon, ('The Union shall respect the equality of Member States … as well as their national identities, inherent in their fundamental structures, political and constitutional, inclusive of regional and local self-government …); for commentary, see eg D Fromage and B de Witte, 'National Constitutional Identity Ten Years on: State of Play and Future Perspectives' (2021) 27 *European Public Law* 411.

[2] A significant exception being the reference to the Member States 'limiting their sovereign rights' in the seminal *Costa* judgment; Case 6/64 *Costa v E.N.E.L.* ECLI:EU:C:1964:66, [1964] ECR 585.

[3] For a typically lucid overview of the developing lines of doctrine and scholarship over different phases of supranational authority, see M Cremona, 'External Relations of the European Union: The Constitutional Framework for International Action' in P Craig and G de Búrca (eds), *The Evolution of EU Law*, 3rd edn (Oxford, Oxford University Press, 2021).

clear contrast with the related discipline of International Relations (IR), where sovereignty persists as a key concept in at least some schools of thought.[4]

It is easy to see why the idea of sovereignty had, and has, such limited traction. EU legal scholars, like the drafters of the Treaties, saw themselves as crafting a language for a type of entity – something less than a state but more than a standard international organisation[5] – that had not previously been known to a world in which the state and its sovereignty was the master theme of politics and law. As to whether, and to what extent, this new entity might somehow transcend the logic of a sovereignty-centred approach, views differed, as we shall shortly see. But where legal scholars were in baseline agreement was that the legal meaning of Europe's new supranational entity could not simply be *reduced* to that of a self-contained, state-like, unitary, sovereign authority. Polity and sovereignty could no longer be viewed as isomorphic in their singularity of form. Instead, the multi-level, composite structure of the EU meant that the question of where sovereignty might lie – if it continued to lie anywhere at all – could not yield a self-evident answer. The creative function of European law was instead to construct the kind of normative architecture that would capture and guide what was newly complex and distinctive about this unprecedented entity. At least from some standpoints, this was the hard, interesting and sometimes urgent stuff; more than reminders and reiterations of the importance of state-centric sovereignty claims, that was the focus of attention.

Yet we cannot simply dismiss the sovereignty legacy when investigating the EU, and we never could. If anything, that holds all the more strongly in accounting for the EU's external relations than it does its internal structure, for two reasons. First, and most obviously, it is in the international arena that it is clearest and most consequential that the EU remains one of a type, and so something of an outlier. Today, in an age when states as discrete territorial units are still the dominant polity form, one key feature of that dominance resides in how states continue to view and treat themselves and their fellow states as both internally and externally sovereign; the two attributes understood to be symbiotically related. That is, they treat themselves as holding paramount authority within the territory of the polity, this both facilitating and, in turn, being reinforced by their possession of exclusive title – without interference or override from any outside authority – to act on behalf of the polity externally.[6] As this understanding of sovereignty spread – however unevenly – over the modern age, so a self-reinforcing, inter-state, pattern of mutual acknowledgment of the mutual exclusivity of sovereign authority developed as the template (always incompletely and

[4] The many examples include S Krasner, *Sovereignty: Organized Hypocrisy* (Princeton, Princeton University Press, 1999); TE Aalberts, *Constructing Sovereignty between Politics and Law*, New International Relations (London, Routledge, 2012).

[5] Or in the more famous and equally 'in-between' terms suggested by W Wallace, 'Less Than a Federation, More Than a Regime: The Community as a Political System,' in H Wallace, W Wallace, and C Webb (eds), *Policy Making in the European Community* (New York, John Wiley, 1983) 406.

[6] The related 'external sovereignty' attributes of exclusivity of title to represent the polity and freedom from external interference correspond to two of Krasner's senses of sovereignty, namely international legal sovereignty and Westphalian sovereignty; His set of four is completed by 'interdependence sovereignty' (referring to the de facto ability of public authorities to regulate the flow of people, goods, capital, information etc, across their borders) and 'domestic sovereignty', which refers to sovereignty's complementary internal dimension – the possession of paramount authority within the polity. See Krasner (n 4) ch 1.

imperfectly realised, and for long bent to the imperatives of empire)[7] of a general global system.[8] It is in looking outwards, in short, that the EU and, indeed, the Member States, are most exposed to the 'old' logic of sovereign power; a conclusion which is more readily drawn in the more empirically-minded discipline of IR. For where does the non-state but multi-state, non-national but supranational EU, both located within, and surrounded by, a world of (national or multinational) states, fit into this overall system of mutual sovereigntist expectations, and of practice predicated upon these mutual expectations?

The second and complementary reason why sovereignty figures more strongly in the external dimension is more subtle, and also one that takes us revealingly beyond sovereignty itself. In other work, I have sought to conceive of the continuing relevance of sovereignty today by discussing the notion of a 'sovereignty frame'. Closely related to what others have labelled a social or political imaginary,[9] the sovereignty frame speaks to 'an everyday, often taken-for-granted structure of thought through which the legal and political world as a whole is apprehended and shaped.'[10] This frame clearly has a structural component, enabled through the very systemic pattern of sovereignty, with its inherent latency, or tendency to reproduction. But it also has a reinforcing cultural component, though so deep rooted as to be as often tacitly realised as explicitly invoked. What this combination amounts to, in a nutshell, is a very broad anchoring idea – one that, if we look to the long history of the emergence of sovereignty in modern political life, combines structural qualities of finality, supremacy and comprehensiveness with other more culturally active and reflexive qualities of abstract or corporate unity and collective self-creation; qualities recognisably emergent in the move from the person-centred dynastic sovereign of mediaeval vintage to more inclusive notions of national – and ultimately, popular – sovereignty.[11]

It is the breadth and reflexivity of sovereignty that makes it so resiliently and so broadly relevant to our discussion. When we ask how Europe is modelled in the global political imaginary,[12] we are inhabiting the most general territory of the self-identification and other-identification of collective socio-political entities. Sovereignty offers one answer to that question, but also, and just as importantly, prompts us that, whatever its answer, the collective self-identification question itself cannot be avoided. It alerts us to the fact that even in the most complex and fine-grained legal inquiries and disputes over the standing, competences and obligations of the EU, the most basic question of the nature of its self-understanding and self-identification is implicit.

[7] On the imperial background of the EU's own Member States and how this shaped the process of European integration, see SR Larsen, 'European Public Law after Empires' (2022) 1 *European Law Open* 6.

[8] On the UN-led expansion of the state system in the post-colonial phase – an expansion that is also, and paradoxically, associated with the kind of thickening of international organisations that would also come to threaten the centrality of state sovereignty, see eg M Shaw, *The Theory of the Global State: Globality as an Unfinished Revolution*, Cambridge Studies in International Relations 73 (Cambridge, Cambridge University Press, 2000); HP Glenn, *The Cosmopolitan State*, Oxford Constitutional Theory (Oxford, Oxford University Press, 2013).

[9] See eg C Taylor, *Modern Social Imaginaries* (Durham NC, Duke University Press, 2003).

[10] N Walker, 'The Sovereignty Surplus' (2020) 18 *International Journal of Constitutional Law* 370, 381.

[11] ibid 381–385.

[12] MB Steger, *The Rise of the Global Imaginary: Political Ideologies from the French Revolution to the Global War on Terror* (Oxford, Oxford University Press, 2008).

And so the particular relevance of sovereignty should be seen as but one side of a coin. It offers its own answer to the reflexive identity question, but, when the coin is flipped over, a different answer to the same question requires to be carved out. It asks, to the extent that the EU does not conform to a sovereigntist logic, how, if at all, might the global political configuration be (re)modelled in the European political imaginary?

The aim of the present contribution is to address these two puzzles; or rather these two sides of the one puzzle. In the first place, it poses the question about Europe as it has been framed through the still globally-dominant lens of sovereignty, and so very much from the perspective of the global political imaginary. In the second place, the contribution reverses focus to pose the question of how to frame the global level from a distinctly European-centred perspective. It does so by reference to what escapes the lens of sovereignty; to those elements of the European polity that are structured by the absence rather than the presence of sovereigntist considerations, and which combine to form a powerful alternative world view within the EU's own political imaginary.

2. A WORLD FIT FOR STATES

The short, and entirely predictable, answer to our first question is that Europe does *not* fit very neatly into the global sovereigntist frame. The sovereigntist frame does indeed continue to influence both how the world of states views and treats the EU, and, in more limited measure, how the EU views and treats the world of states. But that influence – that awkward fit – distorts as much as it enlightens, creates as many problems as it resolves, and raises as many new questions as it answers old ones. Let us briefly consider why and how the global sovereigntist frame creates tensions in the EU's external relations, doing so from the point of view both of 'internal external' Member State political actors and institutions with regard to EU-level institutions, and of 'external external' third party actors and institutions.

Viewed from the 'internal external' perspective, the EU conforms to the logic of sovereignty in one important respect. For, in the words of Neil MacCormick, the EU retains 'a kind of compendious legal external sovereignty towards the rest of the world'.[13] Sovereignty, then, is retained to the extent that 'no state or other entity outside the Union has any greater power over Member States individually or jointly than before'[14] the EU existed, just as the internal re-arrangement of the authority to engage in external relations has led to no overall diminution of that authority. In other words, the overall quantum of sovereignty possessed by polities operating within the territory of the EU, and so available to be drawn upon in the conduct of external relations, is maintained from the pre-EU era.

Yet, alongside that element of continuity, arguably, there are two significant changes. The quantum of sovereignty may be the same, but, the new redistribution of governmental powers between EU and state levels could also indicate a reallocation of that quantum of sovereignty both in its 'internal external' dimension and in

[13] N MacCormick, *Questioning Sovereignty: Law, State and Nation in the European Commonwealth* (Oxford, Oxford University Press, 1999) 133.

[14] ibid 132.

its 'external external' dimension. On the one hand, the internal arrangement and distribution of that sovereignty may be different, and controversially so. On the other hand, the allocation of external sovereign title on the basis of the new internal distribution may also have altered.

What of the (re)arrangement of internal sovereignty? First, from a traditional state-sovereigntist perspective, some deny that there has been any significant change beyond the reassertion of an old unitary authority in a more variegated landscape. They view the Member States as still the ultimate sources and seats of authority and so as the sole domestic sovereign title-holders. A second perspective, by contrast, sees sovereign authority as having already shifted – or as in the gradual, and perhaps inexorable process of shifting – to the supranational level, yet destined to retain or regain its indivisible, either-or character at this new and higher level. A third view sees the sovereignty atom as split or divided between the two levels – state and supranational – matching and, indeed, consequential upon the internal split of legal competences between state and supranational that we find in the EU Treaty framework. And fourth, there are others still who, while also accepting that the internal sovereigntist atom has been split in this way, view such splitting as inimical to the monopolistic and indivisible logic of sovereignty and so as ushering in a fully post-sovereign and so sovereignty-transcending era.[15] In other words, as a matter of internal distribution, EU sovereignty can be seen as *aggregative* (of Member States), or as increasingly or fully *consolidated* (at the supranational level), or as *compound* (divided between the state and the EU level) or as *redundant* (no longer meaningfully understood as sovereignty at all).

How we proceed to characterise the EU's external-external authority in sovereigntist terms will differ depending on which of these internal-external perspectives we take. On the state-centred, aggregative view, the external authority of the EU as a distinct supranational level and site can only be indirect and upwardly delegated; simply a matter of convenient (and reversible) pooling of the national sources. On the consolidated view, by contrast, the EU level is, or is destined to become, the sole and direct sovereign authority, with the external authority of the Member States merely a residual or (downwardly) delegated affair. On the compound view, the division of external sovereign authority between states and supranational mirrors the new internal distribution of sovereign authority, which in turn reflects the distribution of powers specified within the EU's own competence catalogue. And on the redundant view, the distribution of external legal title amongst the range of polities internal to the EU, however we understand that distribution, is no longer underscored and informed by a sense of internal authority that is at all coherent in sovereigntist terms.

Each position has influential adherents and supports a significant macropolitical world-view (or range of world-views), and each can draw much from the complex picture and shifting sands of institutional design and doctrine, as well as emergent

[15] Such as MacCormick himself. For detailed discussion of these positions, see N Walker 'Late Sovereignty in the European Union' in N Walker (ed), *Sovereignty in Transition* (Oxford, Hart Publishing, 2003). See more recently, N Walker, 'Legal and Constitutional Theory of The European Union' in Craig and de Búrca (eds) (n 3); JP Beetz, 'Safeguarding, Shifting, Splitting or Sharing? Conflicting Conceptions of Popular Sovereignty in the EU-Polity' (2019) 41 *Journal of European Integration* 937.

or re-emergent tendencies in the broader theatre of European politics, to back their position. At the one (aggregative) extreme, a 'communitarian nationalist' position sits most comfortably.[16] That approach continues to be pursued politically, as seen most spectacularly in the unprecedented departure of one Member State, the United Kingdom, from the EU following a national referendum in 2016, and in the growth of overtly Eurosceptic attitudes and strategies of strongly nationalist regimes in Hungary, Poland and elsewhere. And it is also pursued legally through national apex courts interpreting the *vires* of the EU in a restrictive manner[17] and reading Treaty provisions cognisant of state constitutional structures, most prominently the 'national identity' clause, in an expansively pro-national fashion. This nationalist Euroscepticism is in some measure fuelled by the fear of its opposite, namely the relocation and consolidation of sovereignty at the European level.[18] Yet that kind of uncompromising Euro-federalism seldom finds explicit voice today, and sounds more as a long-term suggestion, or as the possible final destination of the neo-functional incrementalism that has long provided such an influential narrative of supranational development.[19] Between these extremes, we find a range of (compound) partial accommodations or (redundant) disaccommodations of sovereignty that are more explicitly focused on what is new in the European configuration and so is incapable of undistorted reduction to the old logic of sovereignty.[20]

But what *practical* difference does the choice of this or that reconceptualisation of internal and external sovereignty in the EU context make to the understanding of the actual division and allocation of its competences towards the external world? On one view, it is of little significance at the point of delivery, as this is determined by the detailed distribution of powers to this or that governmental level, regardless of where the deep seat(s) of sovereignty lies or is deemed to lie. This is a point likely to be particularly emphasised by those who tend towards a 'compound' or a 'redundancy' position. Yet if we take a step back, the very construction and ongoing negotiation of that detailed distribution of powers in the EU Treaties and in their judicial interpretation expresses a compromise between different senses of the proper balance between the national and the supranational, which, in turn, may reflect different deep imaginaries of the nature of sovereign power. In a nutshell, European integration has been and remains less advanced in areas such as security, migration and finance; all fields of 'high politics' (traditionally claimed to form the viable core of sovereign statehood), than it is in the 'low politics' of, for example, trade and the environment. The various understandings and accommodation of this distinction speaks again to the different 'sovereign' world-views of nationalists, 'Euro-federalists' and others. This same distinction, and the shifting understanding and accommodation around this

[16] See eg Beetz (n 15).

[17] Perhaps most notably, in the emphatic rejection of the paramount authority of the CJEU by the Polish Constitutional Tribunal in October 2021; see Judgment in the name of the Republic of Poland of 7 October 2021 in K3/21 by the Constitutional Tribunal.

[18] See eg Fromage and de Witte (n 1).

[19] See eg A Stone Sweet and W Sandholtz, 'Neofunctionalism and Supranational Governance' (*Social Science Research Network*, 6 April 2010), papers.ssrn.com/sol3/papers.cfm?abstract_id=1585123.

[20] For fuller discussion, see N Walker, 'Sovereignty in the European Union' in M Diamantidis and M Rosenfeld (eds), *Research Handbook on The Law And Politics Of Sovereignty* (Cheltenham, Edward Elgar, forthcoming).

distinction, carries through strongly – indeed, even more emphatically – to the external arena, and to the question both of the extent of EU-level external competence, and the capacity of the EU's institutions to exercise that competence absent the unanimous consent of Member States.

The complex compromise and ongoing institutional unsettlement around the question of the EU's external action in the 2007 Treaty of Lisbon is testimony to this. On the one hand, the old 'Three Pillar' structure which, since the Treaty of Maastricht of 1992, had set Second Pillar Common Foreign and Security Policy (together with Third Pillar Justice and Home Affairs) apart from the First Pillar economic and social policy mainstream, is abandoned as part of a larger trend towards institutional unity. Perhaps most eloquently symbolic of that trend, the EU is given a single legal personality that anchors it standing as an international actor in its own right.[21] On the other hand, this notional merging notwithstanding, quite different and more restrictive types of competence and institutional methodologies are retained for the high politics of common foreign and security policy as compared to the low politics of those strands of external action considered to be an extension of key areas of internal functional competence.[22]

The range of different possible understandings of the EU in sovereigntist (or post-sovereigntist) terms also affects the expectations and actions of those viewing the EU from the outside. Indeed, just because they are not party to the EU's negotiated settlement of the matter, it does so more profoundly. At the level of basic title to engage in international legal and political relations, the key actors with whom the EU is involved in its external relations are themselves states, though many other international organisations, including the United Nations (UN) and the World Trade Organization (WTO) also play an important subsidiary role here. For most practical purposes, the external world will view and treat the EU as a *compound* entity, and so with close reference to how the EU-internal division of competences maps on to the international legal personality of the Member States and the EU respectively. What matters here would again seem to be the particular foreground question of formal legal competence of the institutions of the EU or of other informal modes of expression and recognition of its role *in situ*, rather than the application of a conflicted and controversial general background logic of sovereignty. Yet the background logic of sovereignty continues to cast a long shadow. In part, this has to do with the substantive and institutional complexity and uncertainty associated with the division of competences. Also, and relatedly, it has to do with different background expectations and preferences as regards the kind of polity the EU should be or should become in sovereigntist terms – differences which echo those we find within the EU.

As regards the question of complexity and uncertainty, substantive complexity is particularly apparent in the case of 'mixed agreements', namely, those of the EU's international agreements that cover subject matters in respect of which both the EU and the Member States have competence. Mixed agreements can give rise to legal dispute where the European Commission claims the EU has exclusive competence;

[21] Art 47 TEU.

[22] See eg G de Baere, 'EU External Action' in C Barnard and S Peers (eds), *European Union Law* (Oxford, Oxford University Press, 2014); Cremona (n 3) 472–479.

or to legal uncertainty, because neither the agreement nor the EU Decisions on ratification or accession clearly resolve which party (the EU or the Member States in their own right) is exercising competence over what part of the agreement. What is more, and adding institutional complexity, for mixed agreements to take effect, the Member States as well as the EU must sign and conclude/ratify them. The process of ratification in the 27 Member States is an entirely domestic affair, and follows the national procedures for ratification of international agreements. If one or more of the Member States does not ratify the agreement, the agreement will not enter into force.

The complex institutional effects of mixed competence can also be seen in respect of the EU's representation in international organisations. The Treaty of Lisbon, as part of its broader re-organisation of external action, sought to address the gap in provision as regards the EU's external representation by creating a new integrated European External Action Service under the executive remit of the High Representative of the Union for Foreign Affairs and Security Policy (ie a European 'Minister for Foreign Affairs');[23] a post which itself combined the previous roles of High Representative of the Common Foreign and Security Policy ('high' politics) and the Commissioner for External Relations ('low' politics). Yet while this increases the EU's representative capacity in external relations, it also highlights unresolved questions about the appropriateness of such representation. Where the EU has exclusive competence, as in common commercial policy or fisheries, there it has correspondingly full membership of international organisations dealing with such matters – such as the World Trade Organization or various Regional Fisheries Bodies, though this does not necessarily exclude parallel Member State membership.[24] Where the EU has shared competence with the Member States, the picture becomes much more uneven and uncertain. The EU often has 'observer' or 'enhanced observer' status, but it may also be formally excluded and must then rely on those of its Member States who are members for purposes of representation and communication, as in the case of the UN Security Council or the International Monetary Fund. And while the exclusion or partial exclusion of the EU may sometimes be due to its own limited capacity, in most cases restrictions are instead on account of the sovereigntist logic of the international organisations themselves. In some cases the EU is simply not permitted to join, due to the state-centred constitutive charter of the organisation, or due to concerns of third parties about EU 'over-representation', and their consequent unwillingness to accept EU involvement.[25]

[23] As it would have been explicitly labelled under the abandoned European Constitution of 2004. Indeed, one not insignificant reason for the failure of the European Constitution was the hostility of those who opposed its liberal use of a 'state-like' language of textual self-description – of which 'Minister of Foreign Affairs' was a striking example; see eg N Walker, 'Not the European Constitution' (2008) 15 *Maastricht Journal of European and Comparative Law* 135.

[24] As in the case of the World Trade Organization (WTO). Indeed, the EU itself has only been a self-standing member of the WTO since 1995.

[25] See eg J Wouters, J Odermatt and T Ramopoulos, 'The EU in the World of International Organisations: Diplomatic Aspirations, Legal Hurdles and Political Realities' (2013) *Leuven Centre for Global Governance Studies Working Paper* No 121; see also J Wouters and AL Chané, 'Brussels Meets Westphalia: The European Union and the United Nations' (2016) *Leuven Centre for Global Governance Studies Working Paper* No 144.

These institutional complexities point to the more detailed ways in which background preferences and expectations of states that are related to their sovereignty imaginaries also affect the international relations of the EU. The EU's mixed agreements and layered representation in international organisations already complicate the playing field for the EU's international interlocutors. In turn, these complications may help crystallise a wariness or opposition towards the EU's in-between status. It is difficult to generalise about attitudes – elite or popular – towards the EU's geopolitical standing from the outside. Yet there is significant evidence to suggest that, even allowing for the anti-cosmopolitan bias associated with the resurgence of national populist rhetoric and practice in recent years – some of the most prominent examples being themselves EU Member States[26] – it is increasingly seen as a single institutional actor on the world stage. In economic terms, certainly, it is viewed as a 'superpower', albeit one that is often criticised for its lack of consistent leadership across and between various major policy domains such as agriculture, environment, trade and human rights.[27] What this points to is a sense of a polity that is deemed to have many of the voice privileges and much of the influence attached to external sovereignty.[28] Yet it is also a polity which is seen to lack the internal coherence and 'joined-up' transparency towards and accountability to the world normally associated with such a generous allocation of external sovereignty. This deficiency is due both to the vertical division of authority between Member States and the European institutions, and – reflecting and reinforcing the absence of strong centralised executive power across that vertical division – the functionally segmented, and so also horizontally divided, nature of the policy profile at the EU institutional level. In other words, the one-size-fits-all logic of sovereignty may be seen as allowing an anomalous, 'in-between' polity such as the EU certain dubious advantages in the sovereignty game.[29]

3. REIMAGINING THE WORLD

For all that the EU has been made to fit – however awkwardly – into the sovereigntist frame of international relations, there are important features of its own practice that are clearly not reducible to, or even apparently compatible with, a sovereigntist framework. What is more, and crucially, these features do not simply mark the EU out as an anomaly. Rather, they can also be seen, at least in some measure, as filling the 'sovereignty-shaped hole' in its self-identification through a concerted attempt to reimagine and refashion the global legal and political configuration as a whole in a somewhat different way.

[26] In particular, Hungary and Poland. See eg EK Jenne, 'Populism, Nationalism and Revisionist Foreign Policy' (2021) 97 *International Affairs* 323.

[27] See in particular S Lucarelli, 'Seen from the Outside: The State of the Art on the External Image of the EU' (2014) 36 *Journal of European Integration* 1.

[28] Indeed, the 'superpower' tag rather suggests a level of unilateral power – a 'hyperpower' – that arguably *exceeds* that associated with sovereignty, which is premised upon at least a formal sense of reciprocity and equality. My thanks to Kenneth Armstrong for this point.

[29] On the idea of sovereignty games, see R Adler-Nissen and T Gammeltoft-Hansen (eds), *Sovereignty Games: Instrumentalizing State Sovereignty in Europe and Beyond*, Palgrave Studies in Governance, Security and Development (Basingstoke, Palgrave Macmillan, 2008).

One commentator has neatly summed up the ways in which EU foreign policy departs from the state-sovereigntist norm as follows:

> … while foreign policy has conventionally been understood as policy autonomously formulated and developed by state actors in pursuit of national interests, implemented by them in the external affairs of the state, and resting mainly on specific rather than diffuse forms of reciprocity, the EU's governance model of foreign policy presupposes and promotes the intensification of interdependence and institution-building, and rests on the establishment of diffuse rather than specific forms of reciprocity.[30]

What is being referred to here has been packaged under various different labels. A particularly popular designation at various points in recent decades has been that of 'normative power Europe',[31] which in turn drew upon François Duchêne's earlier notion of a European 'civilian power' and Joseph Nye's broader concept of 'soft power'.[32] The normative power idea turns on a preference for achieving influence through the expression, pursuit and dissemination of certain core, and arguably universally resonant ideas, standards and values underpinning integration – in particular peace, liberty, democracy, the supranational rule of law, human rights, social solidarity, anti-discrimination and sustainable development – over a model of 'hard power' based upon the capacity for military threat or coercion and economic sanctions. The sharpness of the contrast between soft and hard, normative and coercive, however, is both a strength and weakness of this approach. For what it gains in bold definition and self-identification of the EU's global role and *raison d'être* it loses in terms of a tendency to caricature, and so to reduce the EU to the inverse of a certain understanding, itself reductionist, of state sovereign power.

The 'governance' model of foreign policy, for all that it too is subject to overexposure, is preferred by the author of the above quote, and is here pursued as more promising in speaking to a more accurately expansive and fluid range of factors and as implying no prior judgment as to the inherent attractiveness or superiority of the EU approach. It is an approach that is marked by a (relative) preference for 'milieu' or environmental goals over classical 'possession'[33] or 'national-interest' goals; for collective and multilateral, rather than unilateral, forms of action; and for the establishment of stably institutionalised systems of transnational regulation in various issue arenas over discrete interventions. And while it would be another (if lesser) version of the 'realist'[34] caricature to see the opposite set of attributions and predispositions (ie a narrow preference for protecting national assets such as territory,

[30] G de Búrca, 'EU External Relations: The Governance Mode of Foreign Policy' in B Van Vooren, S Blockmans and J Wouters (eds), *The EU's Role in Global Governance: The Legal Dimension* (Oxford, Oxford University Press, 2013).

[31] See eg I Manners, 'Normative Power Europe a Contradiction in Terms?' (2002) 40 *Journal of Common Market Studies* 235; I Manners, 'The Normative Ethics of the European Union' (2008) 84 *International Affairs* 45.

[32] J Nye, 'Soft Power' (1990) 80 *Foreign Policy* 153.

[33] Drawing on the terminology of A Wolfers, *Discord and Collaboration: Essays in International Politics* (Baltimore, John Hopkins University Press, 1965) ch 5.

[34] In the international relations sense of 'realism' as a function of the predominance of narrow state interests in international action and co-operation. See H Bull, 'Civilian Power Europe: A Contradiction in Terms' (1982) 21 *Journal of Common Market Studies* 149; R Kagan, *Of Paradise and Power: America and Europe in the New World Order* (New York, Knopf Publishers, 2003).

natural resources and trade advantages; for taking unilateral initiatives; and for a more 'transactional'[35] approach to international pacts) as somehow paradigmatic of the contemporary sovereign state, there is no doubt that the very absence of many of these traits has had a structuring effect on the EU's development of its governance model.

First, while the EU has its own interests as an economic and security community to defend, these interests are markedly less tied to the defence of material possessions than in the case of sovereign states, including the EU's own sovereign Member States; and the jeopardy of these interests is not tied to a sense of an existential threat to the basic unit of political community, as, once again, it would be in the case of sovereign states, including the EU's own Member States. Second, the EU is itself the product of a collectively negotiated, multilateral arrangement. As such, it lacks both the sense of the irreducible particularity and sharp distinctiveness of its interests that are associated with sovereign singularity. And, for all its gradually increased defence capability,[36] it also lacks the security infrastructure associated with the defence of the interests of sovereign statehood that provide a key basis and insurance for unilateral action. Law may be the EU's 'weapon of choice' in global relations, but its virtue is also one of necessity.[37] Third, the EU, lacking its own well-defined framework of 'high politics', is less inclined to see its external relations as involving arms-length strategic diplomacy with other holders of high political interests, and so less likely to see its embedding within long-term institutional frameworks as a constraint upon a vital margin of manoeuvre.

The governance model of external relations outlined here is one that has evolved gradually over the life of supranational Europe but which was also present in embryo from the outset.[38] 'External relations', as we have already noted, has long been associated with the 'low politics' of the pre-Union European Community (EC). The focus was on trade, development aid and a number of other discrete areas of policy in which the effective pursuit of internal competence required common policy towards the rest of the world. External policy, in short, and in keeping with classical neo-functional thinking, was largely seen as an extension and completion of internal policy, and so apt to be placed on the same systematic, rule-based footing. At the same time, to the limited extent that the EU was initially engaged in high politics of defence and international security, this was arranged on a purely informal basis under the auspices of European Political Cooperation (from 1970 onwards). Here, too, however, there was a gradual move to formalisation and the reduction of relations to stable, rule-based institutional framework, first under the Single European Act, then with the development of the Second Pillar of Common Foreign and Security Policy at the 1992

[35] See JHH Weiler, 'The Geology of International Law – Governance, Democracy and Legitimacy' (2004) 64 *Zeitschrift für ausländisches öffentliches Recht und Völkerrecht* 547.

[36] Now located within the framework of the Common Security and Defence Policy, introduced as part of the Common Foreign and Security Policy by the Treaty of Lisbon. See Arts 42–46 TEU. See eg P Koutrakos, 'The European Union in the Global Security Architecture' in Van Vooren, Blockmans and Wouters (eds) (n 30).

[37] See M Leonard, *Why Europe Will Run the 21st Century* (London, Fourth Estate, 2005) 36; see also J Larik, 'Entrenching Global Governance: The EU's Constitutional Objectives Caught between a Sanguine World View and a Daunting Reality' in Van Vooren, Blockmans and Wouters (eds) (n 30).

[38] Here I draw significantly on de Búrca (n 30) especially 43–46.

Treaty of Maastricht, and, most recently, as we have seen, with the partial attempt to integrate all external relations – high and low – under the one legal and institutional umbrella in the Treaty of Lisbon.

Other developments have reinforced the tendency towards rule-based multilateralism. The decision to admit a large bloc of Central and Eastern European states in the early 1990s was accompanied by a slow-burn strategy of conditionality. Successful completion of the admission process was dependent upon gradual and systematic endorsement of a programme of normative adjustment and compliance combining the low politics of assumption of the internal policy standards of the EU and the high political requirements of a functioning democracy, respect for the rule of law and human rights etc.[39] This strategy of embrace within a thick framework of institutional and normative interdependence can also be seen at work in the ever–expanding European Neighbourhood Strategy – launched in 2003[40] – as well as in the EU's inter-regional strategy where it forges relations with other regional groupings world-wide.

It is in these and other developments under the broad umbrella of governance that we can see the EU not merely asserting its own distinct identity in a predominantly sovereignty-framed structure of international relations, but in so doing, as also seeking to fashion or encourage an alternative template of international relations. Both aspects of this approach, as we shall see, are worth stressing: the ambition to recraft relations globally, but also the self-conscious self-placing of the EU at, or near, the centre of this process.[41] The approach can be broken down into three elements: namely the *content* of the policies and values pursued by the EU; the *method* or style of approach used; and the *form* of political organisation preferred and sponsored. Importantly, there is a close link between the three dimensions, and this link is in some measure revealing of that reflexive dimension of its collective self-imagining and self-projection with which we are especially concerned.

First, there is the question of *content*. Above we drew a distinction between possession and milieu goals, and sought to emphasise the extent to which the EU becomes involved in the pursuit of the latter. There is a significant sense in which, in response to economic, security and other increasing forms of global interdependence, the globe has gradually come to be viewed in some circles of international politics as approximating to a single community of risk. Confronting this global horizon, the EU has become increasingly involved in scaling up the provision of public goods such

[39] As in the famous Copenhagen criteria, later formalised as conditions of EU membership in Art 49 TEU.

[40] See Commission of the European Communities, 'European Neighbourhood Policy: Strategy Paper' (2004) COM(2004) 373 final. The policy was reviewed and revised in 2015, see 'Review of the European Neighbourhood Policy (ENP)' (*European Commission*), neighbourhood-enlargement.ec.europa.eu/review-european-neighbourhood-policy-enp_en. See also the European Security Strategy of the same period; 'A Secure Europe in a Better World: European Security Strategy' (*Council of the European Union*, 12 December 2003), www.consilium.europa.eu/ueDocs/cms_Data/docs/pressData/en/reports/78367.pdf. See more generally M Cremona, 'The European Neighbourhood Policy: Partnership, Security and the Rule of Law' in A Mayhew and N Copsey (eds), *European Neighbourhood Policy and Ukraine* (Brighton, Sussex European Institute, 2005).

[41] See eg Reflection Group on the Future of the EU 2030, 'Project Europe 2030: Challenges and Opportunities' (*Publications Office of the European Union*, 2010), www.consilium.europa.eu/media/30776/qc3210249enc.pdf.

as environmental protection, public health, global peace and human rights protection from the national to the intermediate supranational level.[42]

This concern with the global legal and political environment of public goods has become an increasingly pronounced theme within the EU's own formal legal mandate, with a concerted attempt within the Treaty of Lisbon both to develop a broader set of principles, values and goals of external action for the first time, and to treat these as continuous with the internal principles, values and goals.[43] Yet in this respect, the EU is by no means an outlier. It joins as well as encourages a broader trend in the recent constitutional law of states towards the specification of internationally oriented 'milieu' objectives to guide a country's foreign policy.[44]

In the pursuit of these claimed global objectives from a regional perspective, the EU is assisted by cultural and material factors. Culturally, to the considerable extent that its external goals and values are continuous with those that have already been agreed and negotiated internally by state parties that are also – and independently – committed to the same global public goods (and independently implicated in the various transnational institutions involved in their pursuit), the EU benefits from an internal consensus, and sense of policy convergence, that goes beyond its formal legal commitments.[45] Materially, the global reach of the EU as an economic player means that across a wide range of globally interdependent policy areas – from climate change and environmental pollution to financial services regulation; from maritime to air transport policy – it is able to use its leverage as the most valuable consumer market in the world to influence the extra-EU pursuit of internally prescribed common regulatory standards over and above those ordained by the formal legal commitments and standing policy preferences of the external parties involved.[46]

[42] See eg I Kaul (ed), *Global Public Goods*, The International Library of Critical Writings in Economics 321 (Cheltenham, Edward Elgar, 2016).

[43] The keystone provision of the TEU is Art (3)5: 'In its relations with the wider world, the Union shall uphold and promote its values and interests and contribute to the protection of its citizens. It shall contribute to peace, security, the sustainable development of the Earth, solidarity and mutual respect among peoples, free and fair trade, eradication of poverty and the protection of human rights, in particular the rights of the child, as well as to the strict observance and the development of international law, including respect for the principles of the United Nations Charter'. Taking this cue, the Unions external action goals are then fleshed out in detail in Art 21 TEU.

[44] See eg Larik (n 37) 12–14.

[45] See eg A Moravcsik, 'Europe is Still a Superpower' (*Foreign Policy*, 13 April 2017), www.foreignpolicy.com/2017/04/13/europe-is-still-a-superpower/.

[46] See in particular J Scott, 'Extraterritoriality and Territorial Extension in EU Law' (2013) 62 *American Journal of Comparative Law* 87, Scott develops the notion of 'territorial extension' (as opposed to clear 'extraterritoriality' – where the application of a measure is triggered by something other than a territorial connection with the regulating state) to refer to these 'in-between' cases where the application of a measure *is* triggered by an internal territorial connection, but in applying the measure the regulator is enabled, and indeed required, as a matter of law, to take into account conduct or circumstances abroad. The technique of territorial extension allows the use of economic power – (eg, the power to license activity within the EU, or to offer contracts to external parties,) as a type of unilateral leverage in pursuit of the spreading of common standards – a strategy described by Scott as one of 'contingent unilateralism'. See also J Weinzierl, 'Territoriality beyond the State: The EU's Territorial Claims and the Search for Their Legitimacy' (2021) 22 *German Law Journal* 650. For an extended study of the political economy underpinning the EU's regulatory leverage, see A Bradford, *The Brussels Effect: How the European Union Rules the World* (Oxford, Oxford University Press, 2020). For a broader, and philosophically acute, treatment of the ways in which notions of territorial jurisdiction in law can be flexibly extended beyond fixed geographical borders and other boundaries, see H Lindahl, *Fault Lines of Globalization* (Oxford, Oxford University Press, 2013) especially ch 2.

But while the EU may sometimes rely on the 'Brussels effect'[47] of its economic muscle to take 'contingently unilateral'[48] initiatives, its preferred *modus operandi*, as we have already noted, is to act collectively and on the basis of long-term institutional commitments. We see this in its Enlargement and Neighbourhood policies, and its broad preference for multilateral treaties and stable forms of rule-based and institutionally conducted engagement. We see it, too, in its own largely supportive relationships with other international organisations which share many of its own multilateralist, consensus-driven, rule-based governance attributes, from the United Nations to the Kyoto Protocol on climate change to the International Criminal Court.[49]

Content often shades into *method* too. That is to say, the method of governance preferred and pursued or sponsored is itself viewed as an expression of political value and substantive purpose. The emphasis on the international promotion of democracy and the rule of law,[50] for example, or support for more specific forms of international cooperation or adjudication (as in the case of the International Criminal Court), speak both to the presumed effectiveness of these modalities of governance in achieving ends, and to the affirmation of these modalities as themselves containers and reflections of core political values.

The circle of self-referentiality grows tighter if we take account of the tendency towards institutional isomorphism in the EU's approach. For there is a propensity to favour what is familiar, and in particular to draw upon internal forms and models of governance when engaged in external institutional building and support. This kind of approach can sometimes crystallise as explicit self-promotion. Here the EU effectively offers *itself*, and its own very *form* and processes of transnational economic and political 'enmeshment', as paradigmatic.[51]

This is most apparent in the EU's inter-regional policy, and in particular with its various frameworks of co-operation with such as the Andean Community, ASEAN, Central America, the Euro-Med region, the Balkans, Mercosur, the African, Caribbean and Pacific (ACP) countries and the African Union. Here the aims of the EU include support for the very idea of regional integration, the encouragement of robust forms of integration that track the EU's own model of economic building-blocks, and the development of frameworks of inter-regional co-operation which themselves replicate the EU's internal co-operative structures under an 'equal partner association' model.[52] Yet we can also see the projection of the EU's self-image in other and more subtle, but perhaps potentially more far-reaching ways. This is true not only in the way in which it seeks to interact with and influence other international organisations, but even in its interactions with states, in particular with large regional states such as the United States, Russia, China, Brazil and India. As Anne-Marie Slaughter

[47] Bradford (n 46).
[48] See Scott (n 46).
[49] See eg de Búrca (n 30) 53–56.
[50] Art 21(1) TEU.
[51] See R Kleinfeld and K Nicolaïdis, 'Can a Post-Colonial Power Export the Rule of Law? Elements of a General Framework' in G Palombella and N Walker (eds), *Relocating the Rule of Law* (Oxford, Hart Publishing, 2008); see further N Walker, 'The EU and the Rule of Law: Necessity's Mixed Virtue' in Palombella and Walker (eds).
[52] See further de Búrca (n 30) 42–45.

describes the development of 'intergovernmental networks'[53] between specialist government departments in functionally segmented areas as a growing feature of a 'new world order', she points to a trend in which the EU is significantly complicit. For what she is referring to is a process in which polities (including state polities), in no small part due to the influence that functionally-focused and differentiated non-state polities – of which the EU is the most prominent instance – are increasingly subject to a process of internal disaggregation in which the disaggregated parts are increasingly locked into transnational policy communities.

4. CONCLUSION

Two sets of questions associated with the tensions and tendencies of the EU's international image and self-imagining in a 'late sovereign'[54] world require further exploration.

First, what is the best overall characterisation of the EU's alternative governance model of external relations? There is a double tension at play here. On the one hand, the EU may either be seen as the key catalyst for the model it pursues, or, more modestly, as surfing upon and extending trends which are already strongly present in global governance. On the other hand, to the extent that the EU *is* self-portrayed and seen as the key player, there is an awkward relationship – for some even a performative contradiction – between, on the one hand, its 'unilateral' assumption of that position and its claimed special distinction within the role, and, on the other, the overall image of multilateral governance across a network of equal partners it seeks to project. Critiques of the EU as a hegemon (however enlightened), as paternalistic, as expressive of a Western tendency to parochial universalism, all locate and explore this tension. Here, some pre-modern political terms become relevant again. Characterisations of the EU as a new 'empire'[55] capture something of the uneasy combination of institutional interlocking, regulatory spread and asymmetry of control or direction implicit in this tension, whereas other portmanteau terms – such as, and following the Kantian tradition, 'cosmopolitan Europe',[56] are more likely to emphasise the consensual and heterarchical dimension. Clearly, Europe as it is reimagined today no more readily fits any historically received definition of an Empire or a Cosmopolitan Federation than it does that of a sovereign polity. But clearly, too, as it does with regard to the sovereign polity, the EU draws something from each of these various alternative types as it continues to finesse its sense of 'autonomy' in international law and politics.[57]

[53] AM Slaughter, *A New World Order* (Princeton NJ, Princeton University Press, 2005) 131–165.

[54] Walker (n 15).

[55] See eg J Zielonka, *Europe as Empire: the Nature of the Enlarged European Union* (Oxford, Oxford University Press, 2006); Larsen (n 7).

[56] See eg U Beck and E Grande, *Cosmopolitan Europe* (Cambridge, Polity, 2007).

[57] Marise Cremona points to the persistently 'paradoxical' way in which the efforts of the EU in general, and the CJEU in particular, to secure its identity as an international actor involve insisting on the *distinctively* autonomous (compared to other international actors) nature of its constitutional form and standing in respect of general international law. Cremona (n 3) 469. Again, the tension between fitting some recognisable template of membership of the international community and the *sui generis* nature of the underlying claim is evident.

Second, how do we reconcile the re-imagining of the world by the EU in the governance mode with the long dominant and still influential sovereignty frame? What remains of the sovereignty legacy? We have tried to develop an analysis which combines both old and new; that shows sovereignty as structuring not only in its *presence* – to the extent that the EU has to deal with states and a state system where the logic of sovereignty is still to the fore – but also in its *absence* – since it is the lack of correspondence between the EU and some of the conventional features of the sovereign system which requires or enables – and in any case releases the EU to pursue a somewhat different approach. So the logics of sovereignty and governance are bound to sit together as an uneasy hybrid, in a world in which sovereignty, while still having an important framing influence, significantly *under*specifies the detailed pattern of geopolitics.

The harder – and unanswerable – question concerns how the terms of that uneasy co-existence will continue to develop in the years to come. All elements of the present hybrid model are fluid. On the one hand, while there is ample evidence of the EU continuing to develop its 'new' governance role, the rise of other global economic powers – particularly in Asia – makes the long-term currency of the 'Brussels effect' less certain. On the other hand, there are also recurrent signs of the resurgence of a state-sovereigntist logic within many Member States,[58] and, indeed, post-Lisbon, of a more insistent presence of the EU itself in the area of 'high politics', and so aligned with a more traditional, and increasingly explicitly articulated, conception of external sovereignty.[59]

The extraordinary volatility of the current international environment only compounds the difficulty of prediction. It does so by sending sharply distinct and perhaps conflicting signals to an entity that, just because of the historical uncertainty over its role and its absence of default 'possession' goals, continually strains to demonstrate the nature of its 'relevance' to the other actors in that environment.[60] Where COVID-19 and climate change[61] have recently provided large and in some measure unanticipated new opportunities for the EU to cultivate a broader governance role as

[58] See eg Jenne (n 26).

[59] See eg 'President Jean-Claude Juncker's State of the Union Address 2018; The Hour of European Sovereignty' (*European Commission*, 12 September 2018), www.ec.europa.eu/commission/presscorner/detail/en/SPEECH_18_5808. For overviews of the intensifying recent discourse on European sovereignty, see SR Larsen 'Imagining Europe' (2023) 24 *German Law Journal* 705; SB Des Places, 'Taking the Language of "European Sovereignty" Seriously' (2020) 5 *European Papers* 287; T Verellen, 'European Sovereignty Now: A Reflection on What it Means to Speak of "European Sovereignty"' (2020) 5 *European Papers* 307.

[60] Even, somewhat paradoxically, as in the expansion of its external ambitions in the area of peace mediation over the last decade, where the policy domain is very much structured in terms of conflict over 'possession' goals; see eg SMH Nouwen, 'Exporting Peace? The EU Mediator's Normative Backpack' (2022) 1 *European Law Open* 26.

[61] See eg DA Fusiek, 'Towards Normative Power Europe: The EU as a Standard-Bearer of Multilateralism and the Role of European Norms and Values in the Post-Pandemic Geopolitical Order' (*Institute of European Democrats*, 15 December 2020), www.iedonline.eu/publications/2020/geopolitics-values/towards-normative-power-europe-the-eu-as-a-standard-bearer-of-multilateralism-and-the-role-of-european-norms-and-values-in-the-post-pandemic-geopolitical-order-fusiek; IM Marcu 'How Can the European Union Act as a Normative Power in the Green Transition?' (*Institute of European Democrats*, 16 November 2021), www.iedonline.eu/publications/2021/european-green-deal/how-can-the-european-union-act-as-a-normative-power-in-the-green-transition-marcu.

normative broker, the outbreak of war in Ukraine has also prompted a re-evaluation and, at least in some measure, a heightening of supranational capacity and expectations in the area of the 'hard' power of economic sanctions and miliary aid.[62] Whether or not we are approaching a tipping point where the EU, in response to these insistent new pressures on its Eastern border, is seen either to have reached the outer structural limits of its involvement in this most material dimension of traditional state sovereignty, or to have the political will and capacity to transcend that limitation, remains to be seen. The very vividness of that dilemma, moreover, only compounds and further advertises the difficulties of a non-state actor working out how to act 'geopolitically'[63] in a world where the other main geopolitical actors are all states.

[62] See eg J Borrell, 'It is a Matter of Life or Death: So the EU Will Provide Weapons for Ukraine's Armed Forces' *The Guardian* (27 February 2022), www.theguardian.com/commentisfree/2022/feb/27/eu-will-provide-weapons-for-ukraine-josep-borrell; see further T Hamilton 'Defending Ukraine with EU Weapons: Arms Control Law in Times of Crisis' (2022) 1 *European Law Open* 635; Larsen (n 59); G de Búrca, 'The European Union in the New Geopolitical Order' (unpublished paper, 2022).

[63] At the outset of her term as Commission President in 2019, Ursula von der Leyden explicitly framed her ambition as one of leading a 'geopolitical Commission'. 'Geopolitics' has always been concerned with the assertion of 'hard' territorial power, so the language, like that of external sovereignty, is highly suggestive of a shifting orientation. See eg N Koenig, 'The "Geopolitical" European Commission and its Pitfalls: Policy Brief' (*Hertie School Jacques Delors Centre*, 2 December 2019), www.delorscentre.eu/en/publications/detail/publication/the-geopolitical-european-commission-and-its-pitfalls.

Part III

Implementing and Resisting International Obligations and the Power of International Law

Resisting External Accountability: The European Union and Human Rights

GRÁINNE DE BÚRCA AND CLAIRE KILPATRICK

1. INTRODUCTION

1.1. A Substantial Body of EU Human Rights Law

THE EUROPEAN UNION (EU) today has an admirably robust and extensive body of human rights law. From the EU Charter of Fundamental Rights (the Charter/EUCFR), to the longstanding case law of the Court of Justice of the European Union (CJEU) on the 'general principles' of EU law, to the close relationship with the European Convention on Human Rights (ECHR) and the rulings of the European Court of Human Rights, the sources of EU human rights law and the modalities of enforcement are multiple. The content of these rights broadly reflects much of the body of international human rights law that has developed over the decades, and in some cases – for example in relation to digital rights in the EU – may be more advanced than is currently contained in international instruments or rulings.

Various EU Treaty provisions highlight the status and significance of human rights both in EU external relations and within the internal EU domain. Multiple institutions and actors, administrative and political as well as judicial, are empowered and indeed required by EU law to enforce human rights or to integrate due consideration of human rights into their respective mandates. Many EU legislative instruments implement or develop human rights principles in fields from anti-discrimination law to data protection to corporate due diligence and others. The EU Fundamental Rights Agency plays an important role in information-gathering and analysis of human rights trends across the Member States.

There is also an array of mechanisms for enforcing human rights, particularly before EU courts. Cases can be referred to the CJEU from national courts at the suit of individuals relying on human rights claims; they can be brought via direct actions to the General Court; they can be a part of infringement proceedings brought by the European Commission; and any of the three listed sources of EU human rights law in Article 6 Treaty on the European Union (TEU) can be invoked. There are also other independent mechanisms for human rights accountability including the European Ombudsman Office, which has led important investigations into EU human rights violations including in relation to the treatment of migrants and refugees at the EU's borders.[1]

Since the 1990s, which saw a busy period of constitutional and treaty consolidation of EU human rights law, an extensive academic scholarship has been dedicated to the topic of the EU and human rights, in both the internal and the external domains. Much of it is (usefully) descriptive and analytical, explaining the many sources and mechanisms and the interactions between them, while some of the scholarship is critical, pointing to shortcomings and failures in relation to the issues covered, the double-standards, hypocrisies, exclusions and blind spots, as well as the scope of legal protection and impact.

1.2. The EU and International Human Rights Accountability

One of the issues which has received comparatively little attention, however, is the engagement of the EU with the wider international human rights system beyond the European Convention on Human Rights. With the exception of a small number of excellent commentaries which have addressed aspects of the relationship of the EU's legal order to that of the international human rights system,[2] most of the scholarly analysis has examined the content, effect and development of the EU's own system of human rights, as well as its relationship with the European Convention system.[3] While there has been a certain amount of EU scholarship touching on human rights

[1] For recent examples see European Ombudsman Decision in case 1452/2022/MHZ on how the European Border and Coast Guard Agency (Frontex) ensures respect of the rights of migrants in 'debriefing' interviews (3 July 2023); European Ombudsman Own Initiative Inquiry in case OI/3/2023/MHZ on how the European Border and Coast Guard Agency (Frontex) complies with its fundamental rights obligations in the context of its search and rescue activities (24 July 2023). For a different issue area, see European Ombudsman Decision in case 1904/2021/MHZ on the Commission's failure to conduct a human rights impact assessment before assisting African governments to develop surveillance capacity (28 November 2022).

[2] The main scholars writing on the issue have been Olivier de Schutter, Israel de Jesús Butler and Bruno de Witte. See eg I de Jesús Butler and O De Schutter, 'Binding the EU to International Human Rights Law' (2008) 27 *Yearbook of European Law* 277; O De Schutter, *The Future of Europe: International Human Rights in European Integration* (Brussels, UN Human Rights Regional Office for Europe, 2020); V Kosta and B de Witte, 'Human Rights Norms in the Court of Justice of the European Union' in M Scheinin (ed), *Human Rights Norms in Other International Courts*, Studies on International Courts and Tribunals (Cambridge, Cambridge University Press, 2019) and B de Witte, 'The European Union in the International System of Human Rights Protection: Solo Singer or Voice in the Choir?' in E Bribosia and I Rorive (eds), *Human Rights Tectonics: Global Dynamics of Integration and Fragmentation* (Cambridge, Intersentia, 2018). See also the important paper by I de Jesús Butler, 'The European Union and International Human Rights Law' (Office of the High Commissioner for Human Rights 2011).

[3] For a welcome collection whose contributions focus on both dimensions, see J Wouters, M Novak, A-L Chané and N Hachez (eds), *The European Union and Human Rights: Law and Policy* (Oxford, Oxford University Press, 2020).

issues in EU external relations, this has generally focused on the extent to which the EU has or has not promoted or reflected human rights principles in its external instruments and activities,[4] including in trade, investment, diplomacy, accession and neighbourhood agreements.[5] There has been particular focus on human rights, labour, social and environmental clauses in external agreements, although these have only rarely been invoked in practice.[6]

The focus of this chapter, however, is on a less-often addressed dimension of the EU's engagement with the international human rights system, namely the external accountability of the EU. Drawing on certain arenas of EU human rights activity to help exemplify our claim, we argue that the EU has been resistant to the prospect of *external* human rights accountability. While the Court of Justice has been the most prominent actor expressing and maintaining this resistance, it is not the only EU institution which appears to consider that the EU's own mechanisms of accountability are sufficient for human rights protection. This resistance to external accountability, we argue, runs counter to one of the core commitments and expectations of the international human rights system, namely that states and polities bound by international human rights law should be subject to robust mechanisms of accountability that are not wholly internal to those polities.

Having set out the general argument on the importance of external human rights accountability, the chapter moves on to discuss a specific mechanism for external EU human rights accountability, namely the approach of the EU to the issue of accession to international human rights agreements. The record of the EU in terms of its accession to those international human rights agreements to which it could be party is examined. This is followed by a discussion of the approach of certain international human rights courts and actors in dealing with the EU, and by consideration of other possible means by which the EU may be rendered internationally accountable for its human rights performance. Finally, we discuss some reasons why the EU may have avoided external human rights accountability to date and conclude by suggesting that the EU and its various institutional actors and Member States should take active steps to improve and enhance its international human rights accountability in a range of ways.

[4] Marise Cremona's scholarship has led the way in terms of considering the role of values in the external relations of the EU, as well as in the case law of the Court. See eg M Cremona, 'Values in EU Foreign Policy' in M Evans and P Koutrakos (eds), *Beyond the Established Orders: Policy Interconnections between the EU and the Rest of the World* (Oxford, Hart Publishing, 2011) 275.

[5] See the important European Ombudsman Strategic Initiative SI/5/2021/VS concerning how the European Commission ensures respect for human rights in the context of international trade agreements (opened on 7 July 2021, decision on 15 July 2022).

[6] L Bartels, 'Assessment of the Implementation of the Human Rights Clause in International and Sectoral Agreements' (*Think Tank – European Parliament*, 15 May 2023), www.europarl.europa.eu/thinktank/en/document/EXPO_IDA(2023)702586; A Micara, 'Human Rights Protection in New Generation's Free Trade Agreements of the EU' (2019) 23 *International Journal of Human Rights* 1447. On enforcement mechanisms both by and against the EU in relation to labour and environmental standards in Free Trade Agreements, see G Marín Durán, 'Sustainable Development Chapters in EU Free Trade Agreements: Emerging Compliance Issues' (2020) 57 *CML Rev* 1031.

1.3. External Accountability as a Fundamental Expectation of the International Human Rights System

In addition to enunciating a wide range of obligations to respect, protect and fulfil an array of civil, political, economic, social, cultural and environmental rights, the international human rights system is also fundamentally premised on the idea of accountability: ie the idea that those who are responsible for respecting and protecting rights must be publicly answerable for them.[7] Accountability has been described as the '*leitmotif* of the human rights system'.[8] Comprehensive lists of human rights, even if contained in constitutions or other prominent domestic legal instruments, do not satisfy the requirements of international human rights law if there are inadequate mechanisms for holding the various duty-bearers to account for their observation of and respect for those rights. Accountability at a minimum requires that duty bearers provide to rights-holders a public account of the extent to which they have or have not fulfilled their obligations, and that some form of redress be made accessible and available to rights-holders for non-fulfillment or violation of such rights. Answerability, transparency, implementation and remedy are important dimensions of the human rights system.

While most states participating in the international human rights system have created some form of domestic or internal accountability mechanism – whether an independent judiciary, human rights commission or some other structure – to monitor observance of human rights and respond to violations, all states which are part of the international human rights system are also subject to an extensive array of *external* accountability mechanisms through which they report on their compliance. From the multiplicity of treaty-bodies which monitor the application of specific United Nations (UN) human rights treaties, to UN Special Procedures, Commissions of Inquiry, regional human rights courts and treaty-bodies, and the Universal Periodic Review, the existence of an array of mechanisms which require states to account and answer publicly in an external forum for their performance in accordance with international human rights law is a fundamental dimension of international human rights law.

There are several reasons why the existence of external accountability and not just internal accountability mechanisms are important from a human rights perspective. Consider for example the situation of a state which has ratified multiple human rights treaties, has implemented them into domestic law, and has a system of independent domestic courts to monitor compliance with those rights. Given a situation in which the state is under pressure, whether due to an economic crisis or a national security emergency, even a robustly independent domestic court may incline towards significant deference to the government's immediate priorities that is sharply at odds with or

[7] According to the United Nations (UN) Office of the High Commissioner for Human Rights (OHCHR), 'Accountability is a cornerstone of the human rights framework, itself a system of norms that govern the relationship between "duty bearers" in authority and "rights holders" affected by their actions'. See 'Who will be Accountable? Human Rights and the Post-2015 Development Agenda: Summary' (*Office of the High Commissioner for Human Rights*, 2013), www.ohchr.org/sites/default/files/Documents/Publications/WhoWillBeAccountable_summary_en.pdf.

[8] P Alston, 'Towards a Human Rights Accountability Index' (2000) 1 *Journal of Human Development* 249, 260–261.

unjustifiably overlooks the impact on rights. There are good reasons, even in the most firmly consolidated of democracies, for a system of external review to guard against the risk of neglect of due consideration of human rights in the face of other political priorities. Further, the systems of accountability established by the international human rights regime require accountability not just of duty-bearers to rights-holders, but also of duty-bearers to one another and to the international community. This kind of mutual monitoring of human rights observance is important for the human rights system as a whole, to help guard against back-sliding, to reveal outliers as far as particular contexts, communities and rights are concerned, and more generally for ongoing development and evolution across the international system. The Universal Periodic Review most clearly exemplifies this kind of peer accountability, but all kinds of UN treaty body review, special procedures and commissions of inquiry, as well as regional human rights systems reflect a basic commitment to mutual accountability in the field of human rights.[9]

In particular, as will be argued further below, given the EU's status as a complex but powerful entity which is neither a state nor a traditional international organisation, but which wields strong executive, legislative and other powers, it is clear that the EU's policy priorities and preferences can have significant effects on the economic, social, civil, political and other rights of many. With a Court of Justice which is routinely deferential to the clearly expressed political and other interests of the EU institutions, and which seems committed to asserting and enhancing the autonomy of the EU vis-à-vis the international legal order,[10] the need for robust external human rights accountability is all the more pressing and important.

2. THE EU AND ACCESSION TO INTERNATIONAL AND REGIONAL HUMAN RIGHTS INSTRUMENTS: A SNAPSHOT

2.1. The General Context

Whilst EU Member States are star global and regional pupils when it comes to ratification of treaties protecting human rights, UN human rights treaties, International Labour Organisation (ILO) Conventions and Council of Europe treaties,[11] this is

[9] On human rights monitoring and the Sustainable Development Goals (SDGs), see 'Voluntary National Reviews: OHCHR and the 2030 Agenda for Sustainable Development' (*Office of the High Commissioner for Human Rights*), www.ohchr.org/en/sdgs/voluntary-national-reviews.

[10] See J Odermatt, 'When A Fence becomes a Cage: The Principle of Autonomy in EU External Relations Law' (2016) *EUI MWP Working Paper* 2016/07; C Eckes, 'The Autonomy of the EU legal Order' (2020) 4 *Europe and the World: A Law Review* 19. On the role of the CJEU in external relations more generally see M Cremona and A Thies 'Introduction', and also B de Witte, 'A Selfish Court: The Court of Justice and the Design of International Dispute Settlement Beyond the EU' in M Cremona and A Thies (eds), *The European Court of Justice and External Relations Law: Constitutional Challenges*, Modern Studies in European Law (Oxford, Hart Publishing, 2014).

[11] Note too that the EU urges its Member States to ratify all relevant human rights treaties: Council of the European Union, 'Human Rights and Democracy: EU Strategic Framework and EU Action Plan' (2012) 11855/12, Annex II in which the EU calls on Member States '... to ratify and implement the key international human rights treaties, including core labour rights conventions, as well as regional human rights instruments'.

not the case for the EU. The EU has acceded fully to only one human rights treaty so far, the UN Convention on the Rights of Persons with Disabilities. It has made advanced steps towards accession to the European Convention on Human Rights and has acceded to the Istanbul Convention within a specific range of EU competences, both being human rights treaties of the Council of Europe. The accession gap does not primarily arise from a lack of EU capacity: the EU has legal personality and competence to conclude international agreements on its own behalf in a wide range of circumstances.[12] The very limited accession record to human rights treaties instead to some extent reflects the only recent opening of a small number of human rights treaties to non-state parties and the distinctive nature of the EU.

But the case for accession is also the case for embracing mutatis mutandis international human rights even when accession is not possible. Since EU Member States have by now transferred extensive powers to the EU to exercise, the EU clearly has the capacity to extensively affect human rights within and outside the EU. What can be drawn from this, we argue, is that accession to human rights treaties by the EU should be actively and fully pursued wherever possible and, equally crucially, the EU should act *as though* it has acceded even when it cannot. The formal absence of an accession option certainly does not mean the absence of external human rights accountability concerns or claims, but mainly reflects the traditionally state-centric nature of international law, and of international treaties. We return to this in Section 4 below.

Absent accession, EU Member States remain collectively responsible under international law for ensuring that any powers they have transferred to the EU are exercised in conformity with the ECHR or other human rights treaties.[13] Yet this is less satisfactory for several reasons, and not only because, if it were a contracting party, the EU could be directly challenged for breaches of human rights. First and foremost is the importance of external accountability through supervision of rights by international bodies and institutions. This is the most consequential contrast between internal rights guarantees, most clearly represented in the EU by the EU Charter of Fundamental Rights, and other internal human rights legislation. We explored earlier why there is a qualitative difference between internal and international rights monitoring, and why both are necessary and important. Accession also significantly enhances accountability by making clearer to human rights actors and institutions

[12] Art 216(1) Consolidated version of the Treaty on the Functioning of the European Union (TFEU) [2016] OJ C202/47: The EU may conclude an international agreement where the conclusion of a treaty is necessary, 'within the framework of the Union's policies', to achieve one of the objectives referred to in the Treaties, 'or is provided for in a legally binding Union act or is likely to affect common rules or alter their scope'. Note though that lack of competence was an issue in relation to the ECHR prior to the Lisbon Treaty with the Court of Justice finding in Opinion 2/94 that Art 352 TFEU, the 'catch-all' legal basis, would not suffice. See Opinion 2/94 *Accession of the Community to the European Convention for the Protection of Human rights and Fundamental Freedoms* ECLI:EU:C:1996:140, [1996] ECR I-1759.

[13] See eg *Matthews v UK* (1999) 28 EHRR 361, para 32 on EC failure to allow UK national from Gibraltar to vote in EP elections: 'The Court observes that acts of the EC as such cannot be challenged before the Court because the EC is not a Contracting Party. The Convention does not exclude the transfer of competences to international organisations provided that Convention rights continue to be "secured". Member States' responsibility therefore continues even after such a transfer'. Some contend that the EU has succeeded to Member States' responsibility in transferred areas: T Ahmed and I de Jesús Butler, 'The European Union and Human Rights: An International Law Perspective' (2006) 17 *EJIL* 771.

what the EU's obligations are and the relevant procedures and processes for holding it accountable. Thirdly, accession changes rights coverage, participation and responsibility. As a contracting party, the EU makes its own decisions on what exactly to ratify and any reservations to be entered. For judicial or quasi-judicial proceedings linked to human rights instruments, the EU would be a party to proceedings against it and would participate as such. The same goes for other forms of human rights monitoring. Accession would fill gaps in rights coverage when the EU acts without any Member State input, for example, in the employment of its own staff.[14] A fourth advantage of EU accession is the avoidance of conflicting obligations for EU Member States. It is particularly challenging for national courts or actors when an obligation to comply with EU law is in tension with their human rights obligations. A last and more incidental benefit is the human rights effectiveness dividend: accession by the EU has the consequence that the parts acceded to by the EU in a mixed agreement also become binding on the Member States as a matter of EU law thereby enhancing the effective enforcement of international human rights via EU law.[15]

Despite the case for EU accession to human rights treaties being ever more compelling as the EU extends its activities and areas of action, and the scope for EU human rights violations increases correspondingly, accession is only an option if the human rights treaty in question makes EU accession an option, and if the EU in turn proceeds with accession. That makes it as important to consider what happens when accession is not on the cards, as when it is. In each case, a full EU embrace of human rights instruments, including their provision of external accountability, is desirable, but must be achieved in different ways.

2.2. The EU's Record of Accession to Human Rights Treaties which are Open to it: Only One Full and One Partial Accession Out of Three

Three human rights conventions contain provisions which explicitly allow for EU accession: the 2006 UN Convention on the Rights of Persons with Disabilities (CRPD); the Council of Europe's 2011 Istanbul Convention on Violence against Women and Domestic Violence; and the European Convention on Human Rights (ECHR). A commitment to external accountability would manifest in a willingness to promptly accede, as extensively as possible, to these Conventions. By this measure, only the comprehensive EU accession to the CRPD reflects such a commitment.

[14] *Connelly v 15 Member States of the European Union*, Application No 73274/01, 9 December 2008 regarding the lack of competence of the ECtHR in employment disputes with EU institutions without involvement of a Contracting Party.

[15] Art 216(2) TFEU provides that '[a]greements concluded by the Union are binding upon the institutions of the Union and on its Member States'; Case 181/73 *Haegeman v Belgian State* ECLI:EU:C:1974:41, [1974] ECR 449, para 5; Case 104/81 *Hauptzollamt Mainz v Kupferberg & Cie.* ECLI:EU:C:1982:362, [1982] ECR 3641, para 13. The Court of Justice has interpreted this extensively to bring within EU law matters that would appear to remain within the competence of Member States: for a thorough analysis relating this jurisprudence to the CRPD see M Chamon, 'Negotiation, Ratification and Implementation of the CRPD and its Status in the EU Legal Order' in D Ferri and A Broderick (eds), *Research Handbook on EU Disability Law* (Cheltenham, Edward Elgar, 2020).

It importantly demonstrates that extensive and rapid EU accession to human rights treaties is entirely feasible, when the political will is present. By contrast, the hallmarks of accession to the Istanbul Convention and the ECHR have been substantial delay, internal opposition, and limitations on their scope. A delay of well over a decade between the time when accession could have occurred and when it has (in the case of the Istanbul Convention) or might (as in the case of the ECHR) take place, calls for further scrutiny of the states and EU institutions responsible for holding up accession. The substantial obstacles to, as well as limitations on, the scope of accession are particularly striking in both cases and underscore the importance of assessing accession not reductively as a binary yes/no issue, but rather in more qualitative terms to determine the nature, extent and limitations on the process and substance of accession.

2.2.1. The UN Convention on the Rights of Persons with Disabilities

The EU – which had been actively involved in the drafting of the CRPD – proceeded quickly to ratify the Convention without waiting for all the Member States to take that step.[16] As a party to the CRPD, the EU's compliance is monitored by the CRPD Committee, with the first reporting cycle having concluded in 2015.[17] The CRPD was innovative amongst human rights treaties in being drafted so as to permit accession by regional international organisations. To help third states clarify the respective roles of the EU and its Member States, accession had to be accompanied by a declaration of the extent of the EU's competence with respect to matters governed by the Convention.[18] On the EU side, the competence to sign the CRPD was based on the omnibus anti-discrimination legal basis (now Article 19 Treaty on the Functioning of the European Union (TFEU)) and an internal market legal basis (now Article 114 TFEU).[19] Unfortunately it now appears that the CRPD is rather the exception, slipping through before new obstacles were erected to delay and limit the EU's accession to other human rights treaties.

2.2.2. The Istanbul Convention on Violence against Women and Domestic Violence

The long and difficult path to EU accession to the Istanbul Convention contrasts with its relatively smooth accession to the CRPD. The Council of Europe's Istanbul

[16] Signature and ratification in 2010: Council Decision 2010/48/EC concerning the conclusion, by the European Community, of the United Nations Convention on the Rights of Persons with Disabilities [2010] OJ L23/35. See G de Búrca, 'The EU in the Negotiation of the UN Disability Convention' (2010) 35 *EL Rev* 174. However, the EU has been unable to accede to the Optional Protocol of the CRPD (OP-CRPD), a situation that Chamon attributes to the failure to muster the required unanimity from the Member States under Article 218(8) TFEU, given that unanimity is required under the discrimination legal basis in Article 19 TFEU, for such ratification to occur. Only 5 EU Member States have not acceded to the OP-CRPD: Bulgaria, Ireland, the Netherlands, Poland and Romania. See Chamon (n 15) 57.

[17] 'Concluding Observations on the Initial Report of the European Union' (*Committee on the Rights of Persons with Disabilities*, 2 October 2015) CRPD/C/EU/CO/1 GE.15-16705(E).

[18] Article 44(1) UN Convention on the Rights of Persons with Disabilities (New York, 13 December 2006) (CRPD).

[19] Council Decision 2010/48/EC concerning the conclusion, by the European Community, of the United Nations Convention on the Rights of Persons with Disabilities [2010] OJ L23/35.

Convention of 2011 addresses gender-based violence as a form of gender discrimination and a breach of human rights.[20] It provides explicitly for accession by the EU[21] and ratification was eventually agreed – 12 years later – by the EU Council of Ministers on 1 June 2023.[22] However, EU accession has been hobbled by the narrow legal bases for EU accession, the decision to accede only in relation to areas in which the EU has exclusive rather than shared competence, as well as by the decision not to proceed to accession without the common accord of the Member States. Most strikingly, it is an EU accession to a gender equality treaty which is not legally founded on EU commitments to gender equality. The EU has a very wide set of gender equality commitments in its Treaties, beginning with the foundational Treaty of Rome commitment to equal pay for women. Gender equality is an EU value (Article 2 TEU) and objective (Article 3 TEU), the EU has the legal competence to legislate on gender equality (Articles 19 and 157(3) TFEU), and there are mainstreaming commitments in Articles 8 and 10 TFEU,[23] as well as gender equality commitments in Articles 20, 21 and 23 of the EU Charter of Fundamental Rights. In addition, there is an extensive body of EU gender equality legislation, which includes – as far as the subject matter of the Istanbul Convention is concerned – a prohibition on sexual harassment and provisions on victim protection.[24] Yet although the EU institutions adopted a range of different views on the appropriate legal basis in EU law for ratification,[25] none of these included any of the EU's gender equality or anti-discrimination legal bases – in stark contrast with the position in relation to EU ratification of the CRPD. An additional substantial restriction, again contrasting sharply with the CRPD accession process,

[20] Council of Europe Convention on Preventing and Combating Violence against Women and Domestic Violence (Istanbul, 11 May 2011) (Istanbul Convention). See S De Vido, 'The Ratification of the Council of Europe Istanbul Convention by the EU: A Step Forward in the Protection of Women from Violence in the European Legal System' (2017) 9 *European Journal of Legal Studies* 69.

[21] Art 75 Istanbul Convention provides: 'This Convention shall be open for signature by the member States of the Council of Europe, the non-member States which have participated in its elaboration and the European Union'.

[22] Council Decision (EU) 2023/1075 on the conclusion, on behalf of the European Union, of the Council of Europe Convention on preventing and combating violence against women and domestic violence with regard to institutions and public administration of the Union [2023] OJ L143I/1; Council Decision (EU) 2023/1076 on the conclusion, on behalf of the European Union, of the Council of Europe Convention on preventing and combating violence against women and domestic violence with regard to matters related to judicial cooperation in criminal matters, asylum and non-refoulement [2023] OJ L143I/4; Declaration 2023/C 194/02 concerning the competence of the European Union with regard to matters governed by the Council of Europe Convention on preventing and combating violence against women and domestic violence [2023] OJ C194/2.

[23] De Vido usefully also points out that Art 8 TFEU is linked to the only EU declaration on gender violence in Declaration 19 on Article 8 of the TFEU [2016] OJ C202/345 which provides that among the efforts to 'eliminate inequalities between women and men', the Union will aim to combat all kinds of domestic violence in its different policies. See De Vido (n 20) 80.

[24] See, in particular, defining harassment and sexual harassment as prohibited gender discrimination Art 2(2)(a) Directive 2006/54/EC of the European Parliament and of the Council on the implementation of the principle of equal opportunities and equal treatment of men and women in matters of employment and occupation (recast) [2006] OJ L204/23.

[25] In fact, the Commission, Council and CJEU each had a distinct view on legal competences to accede to the Istanbul Convention. The Commission proposed the criminal justice competences of Art 82(2) TFEU (judicial cooperation in criminal matters) and Art 84 TFEU (crime prevention); the Council used Art 78(2) TFEU (asylum), Art 82(2) TFEU (judicial cooperation in criminal matters) and Art 83(1) TFEU (cross-border crimes) while the CJEU decided that the legal bases were Art 78(2), 82(2), 84 and 336 (for EU staff).

has been the choice of the EU to accede only in areas of its exclusive competence. One of the Istanbul Convention's ratification decisions focuses on EU institutions and public administration, that is to say, areas where the EU has an inherent exclusive competence.[26] The other focuses on judicial cooperation in criminal matters, asylum and refoulement and confines the EU only to those issues where it has acted to establish exclusive competence through the setting of common rules.[27] This is very far from the choices made in relation to the EU's accession to the CRPD, where no such restrictive competence-policing occurred.[28]

The terms of accession, including its substance and timing, follow the Court of Justice's *Opinion 1/19* in which the European Parliament asked a range of legal questions about the way in which the Istanbul Convention could be concluded by the EU.[29] The Advocate General, setting out in more detail positions on the legal basis that the Court accepted, took the position that although combating gender discrimination is undoubtedly the main purpose of the Convention, in areas of shared competence where the international agreement and the EU set minimum standards, the EU could choose which parts of the Convention it wishes or does not wish to become a party to, leaving the others to the Member States.[30] In relation to the Istanbul Convention, he argued, the EU could accordingly choose not to exercise its shared gender discrimination competence, as the EU *acquis* (its body of legislation) on gender discrimination sets only minimum rules, and it could choose instead to exercise competence only in relation to certain criminal law and asylum matters.[31] And while the Court of Justice decided that Member States could not add a new step of procedural unanimity to the qualified majority rule required to conclude the Istanbul Convention, they could nonetheless take all the time they needed to reach as broad an agreement as possible.

[26] Above n 22.

[27] Above n 22. See especially Recital (6): 'The Union should accede to the Convention only as regards the matters falling within the exclusive competence of the Union, namely insofar as the relevant provisions of the Convention may affect common rules or alter their scope. As things stand at present, this applies, in particular, to certain provisions of the Convention relating to judicial cooperation in criminal matters and to the provisions of the Convention relating to asylum and non- refoulement'.

[28] Regarding internal matters Art 3 Council Decision 2010/48/EC concerning the conclusion, by the European Community, of the United Nations Convention on the Rights of Persons with Disabilities [2010] OJ L23/35 states that the focal point required for the EU as an acceding party should be established 'With respect to matters falling within the Community's competence and without prejudice to the respective competences of the Member States'. With regard to representation within CRPD organs, the ratification decision makes clear that this will be for the EU only in matters of exclusive competence and should be agreed in areas of shared competence (Art 4). These are the only two substantive articles of the ratification decision.

[29] Opinion 1/19 *Istanbul Convention* ECLI:EU:C:2021:832. For commentaries on Opinion 1/19 and its background see P Koutrakos, 'Confronting the Complexities of Mixed Agreements – Opinion 1/19 on the Istanbul Convention' 47 (2022) *EL Rev* 247 and G Kübek, 'Facing and Embracing the Consequences of Mixity: Opinion 1/19, Istanbul Convention' (2022) 59 *CML Rev* 1465.

[30] Opinion of Advocate General Hogan in Opinion 1/19 *Istanbul Convention* ECLI:EU:C:2021:198, paras 129–130.

[31] As noted above at n 25, the Commission and Council disagreed on which limited legal bases to proceed (across different criminal justice and asylum options). As a result of this very restricted indicated exercise of EU competence, excluding gender equality, however, Advocate General Hogan considered that the EU was required to exercise its exclusive competence in relation to gender violence and gender discrimination of EU staff, a stance endorsed by the CJEU. See Opinion of Advocate General Hogan in Opinion 1/19 *Istanbul Convention* ECLI:EU:C:2021:198, paras 164–165.

Ultimately, in 2023 the Council found its way through the opposition of a minority grouping of conservative governments from Eastern European states which had hitherto blocked such a broad agreement. The agreement reached allowed ratification to proceed but, as explained here, on narrow bases excluding gender equality and only in relation to areas of exclusive EU competence.

There are important and compelling arguments against the terms chosen for EU accession to the Istanbul Convention, and the reasoning to that end in *Opinion 1/19*. The exclusion of gender equality as a legal basis for EU accession to the Istanbul Convention has been questioned by women judges at the Court of Justice.[32] It can certainly be questioned whether the EU's gender equality laws set minimum rules only and, to the extent that they do not, it could be argued that the Treaty's equality provisions are a required rather than an optional basis for EU accession to the Istanbul Convention. However, the most foundational and compelling set of arguments against the chosen terms of EU accession to the Istanbul Convention has been developed by Marise Cremona.[33] She first shows that the position adopted by the Court in *Opinion 1/19*, to allow the Council to opt for partial conclusion by the EU of the Istanbul Convention, departs from the long-established EU law position that the legal basis for conclusion of an international agreement should, as a matter of constitutional significance, be based on objective factors including the aims and contents of the international agreement as a whole. Under the established position, in other words, EU accession to the Istanbul Convention would have been based on an objective assessment of the aims and contents of the entire Convention, with gender equality at its core. She then demonstrates why this departure from the established position is deeply problematic and legally unsatisfactory. One significant issue she highlights is that the 'partial conclusion' option is generative of multiple uncertainties as regards the boundaries of EU and Member State obligations, including who might resolve them. Another, and perhaps the most serious defect, is the disconnect that partial conclusion creates in relation to the full and joint responsibility of the EU and its Member States for the Istanbul Convention under public international law.

The notable contrast with the CRPD in these three accession respects (the partial conclusion, the limitation to areas of EU exclusive competences only, and the decision to wait until common accord amongst the Member States was reached) has little to do with the EU's competence, in reality. Instead, it reflects an unfortunate EU institutional filtering of the politicised culture wars[34] in certain states of Europe around

[32] S Prechal, 'The EU's Accession to the Istanbul Convention' in K Lenaerts et al (eds), *An Ever-Changing Union? Perspectives on the Future of EU Law in Honour of Allan Rosas* (Oxford, Hart Publishing, 2019) 283: 'Given the broad approach of the Convention and in particular its emphasis on non-discrimination, it may be asked whether at least Article 19(1) TFEU should not have featured among the legal bases'.

[33] M Cremona, 'Mixed Agreements and Constitutional Gaps' in M Claes and E Vos (eds), *Making Sense of European Union Law*, Modern Studies in European Law (Oxford, Hart Publishing, 2022) 19–29. For different views see Koutrakos (n 29) (CJEU reasoning on legal basis uncontroversial and on common accord sensible blend of legal constraint and pragmatism) and Kübek (n 29) (partial conclusion 'concurs with the logic of mixity').

[34] R Kuhar and D Paternotte (eds), *Anti-Gender Campaigns in Europe: Mobilizing against Equality* (London, Rowman & Littlefield International, 2017).

status discrimination and gender equality.[35] Despite gender equality being the EU's 'first fundamental right',[36] the messy and ambivalent process of EU accession to the Istanbul convention reveals the EU taking a very weak stance indeed in defence of gender equality, and thereby also limiting the scope of its external accountability for human rights through its accession practices. The monitoring mechanism established by the Istanbul Convention will cover only a fractional part of the EU's activity in the field of gender equality, reducing the EU's international accountability to that extent.[37]

2.2.3. *The European Convention on Human Rights*

We have already noted that ECHR accession has been the predominant focus of EU human rights scholarship. On the ECHR side, EU accession was made legally possible as from 1 June 2010, with the entry into force of Protocol No 14 of 13 May 2004. By virtue of Article 17 of the Protocol, a new paragraph (2) was added to Article 59 ECHR, which simply provides that: 'The European Union may accede to this Convention.' From the EU side, the ECHR is a distinctive EU accession tale for several reasons. The ECHR is the only human rights treaty for which the EU Treaties contain a mandatory commitment to accession. Article 6(2) TEU states: 'The Union shall accede to the European Convention for the Protection of Human Rights and Fundamental Freedoms. Such accession shall not affect the Union's competences as defined in the Treaties'. The ECHR also represents a distinct accession challenge for a reason beyond those generally raised by the accession of the EU, as a non-state legal order, to human rights treaties (which generally have a non-judicial monitoring mechanism): the existence of two European courts, the European Court of Human Rights for the ECHR and the Court of Justice of the European Union. Additionally, the ECHR has historically been the human rights instrument with the strongest impact on the EU, its political institutions and the Court of Justice. This prompted a need to address questions raised, above all by the CJEU, about the co-ordination

[35] Six EU States have signed but not ratified the Convention: Bulgaria, Czechia, Hungary, Latvia, Lithuania and Slovakia. In 2021, Poland announced its intention to withdraw from the Convention as did the non-EU Member State of Turkey. See Opinion 1/19 *Istanbul Convention* ECLI:EU:C:2021:832, paras 189–190: '[Hungary maintains that] elements of the Istanbul Convention may affect the national identities of certain Member States, which the European Union is required to respect under Article 4(2) TEU. In that regard, the Republic of Bulgaria observes that according to the Konstitutsionen sad (Constitutional Court, Bulgaria), certain provisions of that convention include concepts that are incompatible with the Bulgarian Constitution and public policy, including the concepts of "socially constructed roles", "stereotypical roles" and "gender", which seek to define the concept of "sex" in a manner incompatible with the definition set out in the Bulgarian Constitution. If the European Union nevertheless acceded to that convention, the Republic of Bulgaria would risk being obliged, in order to ensure compliance with the European Union's international commitments, to implement measures contrary to its Constitution. Such an accession would therefore infringe the principle of sincere cooperation. [190] Similarly, the Slovak Republic, while taking an approach similar to that of the Council, submits that the Národná rada Slovenskej republiky (National Council of the Slovak Republic) has opposed the ratification of the Istanbul Convention by the Slovak Republic and by the European Union'.

[36] E Muir, *EU Equality Law: The First Fundamental Rights Policy of the EU*, Oxford Studies in European Law (Oxford, Oxford University Press, 2018).

[37] The Istanbul Convention has a twin-track accountability and monitoring mechanism: an independent Group of Experts on gender violence, and a political body, a Committee of the parties composed of representatives of the signatory states. The monitoring mechanism includes a country-by-country evaluation procedure with an innovative role for domestic parliaments, as well as a special inquiry procedure.

of judicial determinations in disputes concerning ECHR compatibility of EU law-related matters.[38] This was dealt with in the draft Accession Agreement of 2013 by adding two key innovations. The first, the co-respondent mechanism, is essentially the response, in a judicial system of supervision, to the concern that both the EU and its Member States can be involved in an alleged rights violation without it being clear whether one or the other, or both, is responsible.[39] The second, the prior involvement mechanism, involved a special recognition given to the CJEU, that the highest court of the EU as a contracting party should get a chance to rule on ECHR compatibility of EU law before the European Court of Human Rights (ECtHR) does.[40] Notoriously the Court of Justice has refused twice to accept that the EU can accede to the ECHR.[41] The first time, in 1994, it justified refusal on the basis that the EU Treaties at that time contained no suitable competence for a change with institutional implications as significant as those which would be brought about by ECHR accession.[42] The second time, when the Treaty had been amended in Lisbon to provide not just a competence but a mandatory commitment to accede, the draft accession agreement was found to be incompatible with EU law by the Court of Justice on 18 December 2014 in *Opinion 2/13*.[43] The refusal of the CJEU to allow accession to the ECHR seems to be explicable primarily by its reluctance to lose its exclusive role as the highest court deciding how the ECHR applies in relation to EU law.[44] This is underpinned by two imperatives for the Court of Justice, both

[38] See also Protocol (No 8) relating to Article 6(2) of the TEU on the accession of the Union to the European Convention on the Protection of Human Rights and Fundamental Freedoms (Protocol 8) [2016] OJ C202/273, which also acknowledged and addressed the need for accession to consider the 'specific characteristics' of EU law, in particular through what became the co-respondent mechanism, by requiring the agreement to provide 'the mechanisms necessary to ensure that proceedings by non-Member States and individual applications are correctly addressed to Member States and/or the Union as appropriate'. It also made clear that reservations made to the ECHR by Member States would remain unaffected by EU accession as would the exclusive competence given to the CJEU to decide inter-state disputes on EU law matters. Protocol 8 also required the accession agreement to address the co-existence of the exclusive jurisdiction of the ECtHR in Art 55 ECHR over inter-state disputes concerning the ECHR and the exclusive jurisdiction of the CJEU in Art 344 TFEU for inter-state disputes on matters concerning EU law, given that post-accession the ECHR would be part of EU law. The draft accession agreement did so by permitting states to derogate from Art 55 ECHR when a dispute raised issues of EU law, allowing Member States accordingly to comply with their EU Treaty obligation without breaching the ECHR. This was still not enough for the CJEU, however, which ruled in *Opinion 2/13* that states should, in addition to their existing EU law obligation under Art 344 TFEU, be obliged under the accession agreement to submit their disputes to the CJEU. Opinion 2/13 *Accession of the Union to the ECHR* ECLI:EU:C:2014:2454.

[39] Where alleged violations of EU secondary law are concerned, the 2013 Draft Accession Agreement provided that the relevant Member States and the EU can be co-respondents. Interestingly, where violations of primary law (the EU Treaties), all the Member States (as 'masters of the Treaties') would be co-respondents with the EU. Co-respondent status is always a choice for the Contracting Party. See Opinion 2/13 *Accession of the Union to the ECHR* ECLI:EU:C:2014:2454, paras 49–70.

[40] Hence, where the CJEU has not heard a challenge to the ECHR compatibility of EU law, and a case is lodged with the ECtHR with the EU as a co-respondent, the ECtHR proceedings will be paused to allow the 'prior involvement' of the CJEU.

[41] As a result of Opinions delivered by the Court under Art 218(11) TFEU.

[42] Opinion 2/94 *Accession of the Community to the ECHR* ECLI:EU:C:1996:140, [1996] ECR I-1759. In particular, the residual competence, Art 235 EEC (now Art 352 TFEU), which had been used for a wide range of purposes, could not, the Court found, constitute the legal basis for ECHR accession.

[43] Opinion 2/13 *Accession of the Union to the ECHR* ECLI:EU:C:2014:2454.

[44] B de Witte and Š Imamović, 'Opinion 2/13 on accession to the ECHR: Defending the EU Legal Order against a Foreign Human Rights Court' (2015) 40 *EL Rev* 683.

of which are clear in *Opinion 2/13*: to remain at the top of the judicial hierarchy for matters concerning EU law[45] and to retain its role as the filter deciding when, how, and how much of the ECHR and the ECtHR case-law should apply.[46] Yet both these imperatives go against the grain of human rights in the way they seek to close off or shrink the external accountability of the EU which, as argued in Section 1.3 above, is a central dimension and expectation of international human rights law. In acceding to the ECHR, the EU should embrace this dimension of external accountability both as regards the other parties to the ECHR, and as regards the institutional arrangements for respecting the ECHR in each of the Convention's contracting states. The essence of human rights commitments is a universal or regional, rather than polity-specific, commitment to a set of human rights standards, and a commitment by all parties to external supervision of their compliance with those human rights commitments: in other words, a commitment to external accountability. As the President of the German Constitutional Court has pointed out, '[A]s much as a uniformly high human rights standard in Europe is desirable, it is not the task of the Luxembourg court, but that of Strasbourg and the ECtHR, to safeguard it internationally'.[47]

The outcome of *Opinion 2/13* was a prolonged period of exhaustion and perplexity in the wake of the intensive work[48] and challenging diplomacy, not least within the much larger group of Council of Europe states, to reach a draft accession agreement

[45] This can be seen in several otherwise counterintuitive or overstated findings of *Opinion 2/13*: that Protocol 16 ECHR whereby (from its entry into force which occurred on 1 August 2018) highest national courts can request advisory opinions from the ECtHR requires explicit consideration in the EU-ECHR Accession Agreement to ensure its compatibility with the EU preliminary reference procedure; that EU acts that the EU has decided not to give the CJEU jurisdiction over, in CFSP measures not addressed to natural or legal persons, cannot as a result be reviewed by another court, the ECtHR; that jurisdiction for the ECtHR should be explicitly excluded for inter-state disputes relating to the application of ECHR rights which come within the scope of EU law; that allowing the ECtHR to accept a request by the EU or states to be co-respondents to cases before it would constitute ECHR overreach and fail to protect the autonomy of EU law; that only the CJEU can decide if it has already ruled on a matter before the ECHR so as to dispense with prior involvement. See Opinion 2/13 *Accession of the Union to the ECHR* ECLI:EU:C:2014:2454.

[46] This includes, most surprisingly, the CJEU's claim in *Opinion 2/13* that EU law should be allowed to go below the minimum protection of human rights required by the ECHR. This is what the CJEU claimed as regards the area of 'mutual trust' in the AFSJ (Area of Freedom, Security and Justice) (which in the TFEU is rather termed 'mutual recognition'), arguing that otherwise Member States would be hindered by (ECHR) human rights requirements from assuming the human rights compatibility of other Member States when deciding whether to return an asylum seeker or a suspected criminal. Similarly, the CJEU claimed in *Opinion 2/13* that Art 53 of the EU Charter of Rights and Article 53 ECHR require co-ordination when the ECHR sets only minimum standards and is accordingly neutral on limits set by EU law on higher Member State standards, as occurred in Case C-399/11 *Melloni* ECLI:EU:C:2013:107 in order to preserve the primacy of EU law.

[47] A Voßkuhle, 'Pyramid or Mobile? Human Rights Protection by the European Constitutional Courts' (*Council of Europe – ECtHR*, 31 January 2014), www.echr.coe.int/documents/d/echr/speech_20140131_vosskuhle_eng, cited by S O'Leary, 'The EU Charter Ten Years on: A View from Strasbourg' in M Bobek and J Prassl-Adams (eds), *The EU Charter of Fundamental Rights in the Member States*, EU Law in the Member States 7 (Oxford, Hart Publishing, 2020) 57.

[48] Accession negotiations began as a result of a Council Decision of 4 June 2010 (see Council of the European Union, 'Council Decision authorising the Commission to negotiate the Accession Agreement of the European Union to the European Convention for the protection of Human Rights and Fundamental Freedoms (ECHR)' (2010) 10817/10) resulting in a draft accession agreement on 5 April 2013 which was submitted by the Commission to the Court of Justice for an Opinion on 4 July 2013. See Opinion 2/13 *Accession of the Union to the ECHR* ECLI:EU:C:2014:2454.

in the first place.[49] A mandatory EU Treaty commitment to accede had to engage with a series of Court of Justice objections to accession, some of which appear nigh on impossible to address,[50] without undermining the essence of what accession to a human rights treaty entails. The Court of Justice administered what was almost a knock-out blow to accession, with no guarantee that any re-negotiated agreement would not suffer the same fate at its hands. In 2020, following over five years of impasse after the Court's judgment, accession negotiations between the EU and the Council of Europe were formally reopened.[51] In March 2023, after 18 meetings, a technical agreement was reached between the EU and the (now) 46 Contracting States of the Council of Europe. As with the Istanbul Convention, albeit for quite different reasons, whether accession occurs will certainly not signal the end of any need for questions about the external accountability of the EU in relation to the ECHR. Rather, the terms of any eventual accession must be carefully analysed to assess the strength and breadth of the external accountability mechanisms it provides.[52] The evident reluctance of the European Court of Justice to date to countenance external human rights accountability in relation to the European Convention on Human Rights system suggests that this set of issues should be closely watched.

[49] Hence Johan Callewaert, a member of the ECtHR registry, noted, 'Should we then go again through the pain of negotiating a new deal, which necessarily will be another compromise between the many views around the table, only to hear from the CJEU, at the end of the journey, that it is still not good enough? Who would like to take that risk?' (before going on to argue that nonetheless the efforts to accede should not be abandoned). Note also the pain expressed by one of the Council of Europe negotiating team, J Polakiewicz, 'The Future of Human Rights Protection in the EU without Accession' in Š Imamović, M Claes and B de Witte (eds) (2016), *The EU Fundamental Rights Landscape After Opinion 2/13 – Maastricht Faculty of Law Working Paper* 2016/3.

[50] For more positive views on the possibility of accession in light of *Opinion 2/13* see eg C Krenn, 'Autonomy and Effectiveness as Common Concerns: A Path to ECHR Accession after Opinion 2/13' (2015) 16 *German Law Journal* 147. Subsequent to the first wave of highly negative commentary in the immediate aftermath of *Opinion 2/13*, there has been a second more recent round of commentary on EU-ECHR accession, encouraging the various players to find a path to accession. See eg JP Jacqué, 'Encore un effort camarades … L'adhésion de l'Union à la Convention européenne des droits de l'homme est toujours à votre portée' (2020) 1 *Europe des Droits & Libertés/Europe of Rights & Liberties* 27 making the case that 'the status quo may be more dangerous for the European Union's autonomy than membership would have been on the basis of the terms of the accession agreement reached at that time'. See also J Callewaert, 'Do We still Need Article 6(2) TEU? Considerations on the Absence of EU Accession to the ECHR and its Consequences' (2018) 55 *Common Market Law Review* 1685 also arguing that the status quo is unsatisfactory but for the reasons that it does not ensure EU participation or accountability in ECtHR cases concerning EU law and threatens the longer-term consistency and stability of European human rights law, and see T Lock, 'The Future of EU Accession to the ECHR after Opinion 2/13: Is It Still Possible and Is It Still Desirable?' (2015) 11 *European Constitutional Law Review* 239.

[51] The first meeting of the 'new round' took place in September 2020 (the last negotiation meeting having been in April 2013). Meetings have taken place every few months since then. To follow the process see 'EU Accession to the ECHR ("46+1" Group)' (*Council of Europe*), www.coe.int/en/web/human-rights-intergovernmental-cooperation/accession-of-the-european-union-to-the-european-convention-on-human-rights. The draft Accession Agreement 2023 is available here: Council of Europe, '18th Meeting of the CDDH Ad Hoc Negotiation Group on the Accession of the European Union to the European Convention on Human Rights: Final Consolidated Version of the Draft Accession Instruments' (2023) 46+1(2023)36.

[52] Further, it should be noted that accession by the EU to international human rights and environmental agreements has not necessarily led to much change in the (un)willingness of the CJEU to accept the influence of external human rights standards within the EU legal system: see G de Búrca, C Kilpatrick and J Scott, 'Questioning the Principled Openness of the EU to International Law: An examination of the Court's reception of the Aarhus Convention and the Convention on the Rights of Persons with Disabilities' in M Claes and E Vos (eds), *Making Sense of EU Law* (Oxford, Hart Publishing, 2023).

3. INTERACTIONS BETWEEN THE EU AND INTERNATIONAL AND REGIONAL HUMAN RIGHTS COURTS, BODIES AND ACTORS: ANY SIGNS OF EXTERNAL ACCOUNTABILITY?

Even though the EU has not acceded to any human rights treaties apart from the CRPD and now, on narrow terms, the Istanbul Convention, international human rights courts and institutions, nevertheless, have not simply ignored the EU. States occasionally put forward their obligations as EU Member States as a reason to explain their failure to comply with international human rights obligations. Civil society actors may also organise approaches to human rights courts and institutions that highlight the roles of the EU in human rights violations. The result of such claims can be that EU institutions decide to participate in human rights proceedings, which can be seen as a first step towards external accountability. Human rights institutions may also have discretionary powers of their own that allow them to focus on the EU's role, even though it has not acceded to the relevant human rights treaties.

3.1. ECHR-EU

The ECHR in 2005 established a presumption (the '*Bosphorus* presumption') that state action taken to comply with EU obligations would be considered ECHR compliant, due to the fact that the EU legal system generally provides equivalent human rights protection to that of the ECHR.[53] This presumption would only be applied by the ECtHR in certain circumstances,[54] and can be rebutted by showing that the EU's protection for Convention rights was manifestly deficient in any given case. In the wake of the Court of Justice's refusal to allow the EU to accede to the ECHR in *Opinion 2/13*, many argued that the *Bosphorus* presumption should or could be revisited.[55] Others stated that it would be sufficient for the presumption to be applied carefully, meaning that the conditions for rebutting it could be found to be met – something which had not happened prior to *Opinion 2/13*.[56] In the event, despite the tensions produced by *Opinion 2/13*, as O'Leary has noted, 'the Bosphorus

[53] *Bosphorus v Ireland* (2006) 42 EHRR 1.

[54] The presumption applies only where the state has no discretion: *Bosphorus v Ireland* (2006) 42 EHRR 1, para 157 and where EU law supervision is fully used: *Avotiņš v Latvia*, Application No 17502/07, 23 May 2016, para 101. However, this will not necessarily require a preliminary reference to be made.

[55] M Kuijer, 'Is Accession Still Possible? Is it Desirable?' in Imamović, Claes and de Witte (eds) (n 49) 56 argued that it should be revisited; S Imamović, 'The Relationship between the Court of Justice of the EU and the European Court of Human Rights after Opinion 2/13' in Imamović, Claes and de Witte (eds) (n 49) 64 argued that it could be revisited; see also P Eeckhout, 'Opinion 2/13 on EU Accession to the ECHR and Judicial Dialogue – Autonomy or Autarky?' (2015) *Jean Monnet Working Paper* 01/15, 38. The President of the ECtHR, Dean Spielmann in the immediate aftermath suggested that, 'the principal victims will be those citizens whom this [Opinion 2/13] deprives of the right to have acts of the European Union subjected to the same external scrutiny as regards respect for human rights as that which applies to each Member State. More than ever, therefore, the onus will be on the Strasbourg Court to do what it can in cases before it to protect citizens from the negative effects of this situation,' in ECtHR Annual Report 2014, see European Court of Human rights, *Annual Report 2014* (Strasbourg, Registry of the European Court of Human Rights, 2015).

[56] Polakiewicz (n 49).

presumption survived both the obligation to accede in Article 6 TEU and the indefinite postponement of the execution of that obligation'.[57]

In many of the ECtHR cases concerning EU law, especially in justice and home affairs, the state concerned has had discretion as to how to implement the EU obligation in question, which meant that the *Bosphorus* presumption did not apply, and a state-focused human rights assessment was undertaken by the ECtHR. Internal EU law requirements, such as Article 52(3) of the Charter which refers to the correspondence between the ECHR's standards and the provisions of the Charter, also mean that the CJEU pays close attention to Strasbourg developments. In neither of these instances, however, despite the mutual references between the two courts, is the EU subject to any real external accountability vis-à-vis the ECHR. In particular, the EU's behaviour and contribution to the human rights violation is not scrutinised by the Strasbourg organs.

However, the European Commission has participated in certain cases before the Strasbourg Court, albeit only those in which it argues that the *Bosphorus* presumption should apply. This includes the case of *Bosphorus* itself,[58] and its clarificatory follow-up *Avotinš*[59] in which the European Commission made written observations and participated in the public hearing. Perhaps the most exciting example is in the pending fast-tracked ECtHR Grand Chamber case of *Duarte*.[60] This is a climate change case entailing proceedings against 33 states including all 27 EU Member States, alleging breach of the Convention's right to life, family life and non-discrimination. The Commission sought and obtained leave to intervene in the proceedings, submitting its observations on 19 May 2021.[61] Again, its observations do not argue that Member States have discretion over the issues in question (which would mean that the *Bosphorus* presumption would not apply, and the state's behaviour would be fully scrutinised) but instead that EU Member States do not have discretion so that the presumption of equivalence applies and the ECtHR should not scrutinise compliance with the ECHR. According to the Commission, 'when applying the *Bosphorus* criteria, EU law can be considered to provide for an equivalent level of protection of human rights to that of the Convention in the field of environmental protection. Therefore, Member States of the EU can be presumed not to have departed from the requirements of the Convention when they implement the legal obligations flowing from their membership to the EU'.[62]

For present purposes, the key question is whether such participation by the European Commission in these ECHR cases constitutes a step towards external accountability. In one sense, it does constitute such a step in the sense of getting EU

[57] O'Leary (n 47) 56.

[58] *Bosphorus v Ireland* (2006) 42 EHRR 1, para 125.

[59] *Avotiņš v Latvia*, Application No 17502/07, 23 May 2016, para 89.

[60] *Duarte Agostinho and Others v Portugal and Others*, Application No 39371/20.

[61] European Commission, 'Written Observations in *Duarte Agostinho and Others v Portugal and Others*, Application No 39371/20' (*Jus Mundi*, 2021), www.jusmundi.com/en/document/other/en-duarte-agostinho-others-v-portugal-and-others-third-party-intervention-of-the-european-commission-wednesday-19th-may-2021#other_document_22094.

[62] ibid para 72. For further discussion of whether EU states have discretion beyond EU law so that the *Bosphorus* presumption does not apply in Duarte, see M Pagano, 'Overcoming *Plaumann*: Environmental NGOs and Access to Justice before the CJEU' (PhD, European University Institute 2023) Section 6.2.

institutions accustomed to giving reasons for the compatibility of EU actions with human rights before an international human rights forum. On the other hand, the application of the *Bosphorus* presumption results in very substantial deference on the part of the ECtHR towards the EU's action in question in each case, which allows the EU to avoid substantive scrutiny of its laws and policies, and hence to avoid any real external accountability. Further, the fact that even the decision whether to intervene in an ECHR case dealing with EU law remains a choice for the EU which it uses to advance its preferences, rather than a duty, underlines how far it is from an external-accountability-oriented stance of the EU institutions.

3.2. European Social Charter (ESC)-EU

The European Committee of Social Rights (ECSR) took a very different approach to the EU from that of the Strasbourg Court. Rather than establishing a rebuttable presumption of human rights compliance based on the EU's supposedly equivalent level of rights protection, the ECSR adopted an approach that can be characterised as 'reasoned distancing'. The key source is a Decision of 2010 in which the ECSR took an extended view on the relationship between the ESC and EU law.[63] Most importantly, the Committee gave reasons for not adopting the same position on EU law in relation to the ESC as that adopted by the ECtHR on EU law in relation to the ECHR. The ECSR took the position that no such presumption (of compliance, and equivalent protection) could currently be established in relation to the EU and the ESC. While committing itself to reviewing whether developments in EU law post-Lisbon, including the Charter of Fundamental Rights, warranted revisiting its stance, the Committee noted as relevant to its current assessment the fact that no Treaty commitment had been made by the EU to accede to the ESC, whereas such a Treaty commitment was made in the Lisbon Treaty in relation to the ECHR. Hence, in contrast to the approach adopted by the ECtHR in *Bosphorus*, the ECSR decided that while only states are parties to the ESC, those states are required to ensure respect for the rights guaranteed by the ESC when complying with EU requirements.[64]

The sovereign debt crisis led to a series of collective complaints by Greek trade unions and pensioner associations against Greece,[65] which in turn raised the question of Greece's need to obey the requirements of the Memoranda of Understanding authored by EU institutions.[66] These Collective Complaints broke new ground by

[63] *Confédération générale du travail (CGT) v France*, Collective Complaint No. 55/2009, Decision on the Merits of 23 June 2010. For analysis of this decision see U Khaliq, 'The EU and the European Social Charter: Never the Twain shall meet?' (2013) 15 *CYELS* 169, 190–4; O De Schutter, 'The European Social Charter as the Social Constitution of Europe' in N Bruun, K Lörcher, I Schömann and S Clauwert (eds), *The European Social Charter and the Employment Relation* (Oxford, Hart Publishing, 2017) 11.

[64] See in particular *Confédération générale du travail (CGT) v France*, Collective Complaint No. 55/2009, Decision on the Merits of 23 June 2010, paras 32–37.

[65] Additional Protocol to the European Social Charter Providing for a System of Collective Complaints (Strasbourg, 9 November 1995).

[66] For details and further analysis see C Kilpatrick, 'The Human Rights Puzzle of the Euro-crisis: Why Massive Breaches of Human Rights but None of the EU Charter of Fundamental Rights?' in M González Pascual and A Torres Pérez (eds), *Social Rights and the European Monetary Union: Challenges Ahead* (Cheltenham, Edward Elgar, 2022).

being the first time the European Commission intervened before the Committee. In Collective Complaint 111/2014, the EU accepted the invitation of the European Committee of Social Rights to submit written observations,[67] pursuant to Rule 32A of the Rules of the Committee according to which 'Upon a proposal by the Rapporteur, the President may invite any organisation, institution or person to submit observations'.[68] In those observations, the Commission claimed that it had stressed to institutional creditors the need for social fairness, that it had acted in accordance with the commitments to the ESC in Article 151 TFEU and in the EU Charter of Fundamental Rights, and that commitments to social rights had been strengthened in the third Greek programme of 2015.[69] The EU was also represented in the (itself exceptional) hearing in Strasbourg of this Collective Complaint.[70] By persuading the EU to participate in proceedings before the European Committee of Social Rights, arguments for the rights-compatibility of its actions were generated and presented. Especially when juxtaposed with the multiple and severe violations of the ESC established in these Greek Collective Complaints, such participation at least provided some small but meaningful steps towards EU external accountability in relation to the ESC. It gives a sense of how important, powerful, and necessary it is to provide for much more extensive and far-ranging EU external accountability for human rights.

3.3. UN Special Procedures-EU

The UN has an extensive system of so-called special procedures, consisting primarily in a group of independent human rights experts with mandates to report and advise on human rights from a thematic perspective, or in relation to a particular country.[71] There are over 59 of these mandates, including special rapporteurs, independent experts as well as working groups, which report on a wide range of human rights issues covering economic, social, cultural, civil, and political rights, as well as the rights of specific groups and the context of particular countries. The EU itself has made submissions to some of these UN Special Procedures.[72]

[67] *Greek General Confederation of Labour (GSEE) v* Greece, Collective Complaint 111/2014, Decision on the Merits of 23 March 2017, para 6.

[68] Subsequently, the Commission made written observations on a further set of complaints brought by University Women of Europe against fifteen states on equal pay and equal opportunity (See *University Women of Europe (UWE) v various states*, Collective Complaints No. 124-138/2016).

[69] *Greek General Confederation of Labour (GSEE) v* Greece, Collective Complaint 111/2014, Decision on the Merits of 23 March 2017, paras 47–54.

[70] *Greek General Confederation of Labour (GSEE) v* Greece, Collective Complaint 111/2014, Decision on the Merits of 23 March 2017, para 17. The EU was represented by Mr Benjamin Bollendorff, Deputy to the Head of the European Union Delegation to the Council of Europe. 'The Digest of the Case-Law of the European Committee of Social Rights' (*Council of Europe*, December 2018) 33 notes that only 9 such public hearings have been held.

[71] 'Special Procedures of the Human Rights Council' (*Office of the High Commissioner for Human Rights*), www.ohchr.org/en/special-procedures-human-rights-council.

[72] See eg the submission of the EU to the Special Rapporteur on the Right to Development in 2023, in response to a call for input: 'Call for Inputs – 2023 Reports of the UN Special rapporteur on the Right to Development' (*Office of the High Commissioner for Human Rights*, 2023), www.ohchr.org/en/calls-for-input/2023/call-inputs-2023-reports-un-special-rapporteur-right-development.

While these special procedures, like most existing international human rights mechanisms, were created with states in mind, there is nothing to prevent any of these UN mandate holders from requesting a 'visit' to the European Union to investigate the situation as regards those rights which fall within the mandate of that expert. Similarly, there is nothing to prevent a study being done on the EU's compliance with particular sets of rights, or treatment of particular groups, or on another selected human rights theme or topic. To that end, recent years have seen increasing engagement by UN Special Rapporteurs with the EU in its own right, and not only via reports on or visits to particular Member States. In 2012, the Special Rapporteur for the Human Rights of Migrants undertook a study on EU border control following the migrant and refugee crisis.[73] In 2020–2021, the Special Rapporteur for Extreme Poverty and Human Rights undertook a visit to the EU and reported on his findings.[74] In 2022, the Special Rapporteur for the Rights of Persons with Disabilities undertook a visit to the EU, and reported subsequently to the Human Rights Council.[75] A complaint was made in 2021 by unions of nurses from 28 countries to the UN Special Rapporteur on the Right to Health in relation to the EU's refusal to support a waiver from the TRIPS agreement for the development of vaccines and treatments for COVID-19 during the pandemic,[76] and no less than six UN Special Rapporteurs addressed a letter to the European Union, amongst other international organisations, arguing for such a waiver and more generally for equal and universal access to COVID-19 vaccines.[77]

These examples indicate that there is interesting although certainly not yet fully tapped potential within the UN Special Procedures system for bringing about a degree of external human rights accountability on the part of the EU for many of its policies and laws which risk or harm human rights.

4. POSSIBLE REASONS FOR EU AVOIDANCE OF EXTERNAL AND INTERNATIONAL HUMAN RIGHTS ACCOUNTABILITY

In this section we briefly consider some of the possible reasons why the EU has avoided international human rights accountability to date and suggest some counter-arguments to these.[78]

[73] 'EU Border Management: UN Expert Launches one-year Study to Assess Migrants' Rights. First Stop, Brussels' (*Office of the High Commissioner for Human Rights*, 3 May 2012), c.

[74] O De Schutter, 'Report of the Special Rapporteur on Extreme Poverty and Human Rights on his Visit to the European Union' (*Human Rights Council*, 20 May 2021) A/HRC/47/36/Add.1.

[75] G Quinn, 'Report of the Special Rapporteur on the Rights of Persons with Disabilities, Gerard Quinn, on his Visit to the European Union' (*Human Rights Council*, 28 December 2022) A/HRC/52/32/Add.1.

[76] P Walker, 'Nursing Unions around World Call for UN Action on Covid Vaccine Patents' *The Guardian* (29 November 2021), www.theguardian.com/world/2021/nov/29/nursing-unions-around-world-call-for-un-action-on-covid-vaccine-patents.

[77] 'Information Note: Experts Send Pharma Companies, States, EU and WTO Letters Calling for Urgent Action on COVID-19 Vaccines' (*Office of the High Commissioner for Human Rights*, 19 October 2021), www.ohchr.org/en/press-releases/2021/10/information-note-experts-send-pharma-companies-states-eu-and-wto-letters?LangID=E&NewsID=27670.

[78] See also the excellent analysis of M de Silva, 'Accession of the European Union to the United Nations Human Rights Treaties: Explaining the Reasons for Inaction' (2020) *College of Europe EU Diplomacy Papers* 7/2020 considered further below.

A first reason that might be offered is that the EU is not a state, and since it does not have the same array of plenary powers as a state, it does not need to be subject to international human rights accountability. The argument would be that since the EU is still limited in its competences and has its own mechanisms for ensuring compliance with human rights within these, it does not need to submit itself to international or regional human rights monitoring or accountability. However, this argument is not convincing. In the first place, the EU's powers are extremely extensive and ever-growing, with or without formal treaty amendments, and the fact that they are not plenary powers over all areas of policy does not in any way mean that there is less need for external accountability for human rights compliance. The EU has vast and important powers that affect all areas of people's lives – and deaths – both within and outside of the EU, and that often affect them directly without any intermediary Member State action. Further, as we have argued above, internal mechanisms of accountability for human rights such as courts, ombudsmen and human rights agencies and commissions, although very important, are not a substitute for external mechanisms. Submission to external human rights monitoring both addresses and avoids the problem of undue deference or political control and provides a forum for international answerability and peer accountability. The current impunity of the EU and the lack of any serious internal mechanisms of accountability despite the apparent complicity of EU agencies in the pushbacks and deaths of many migrants in the Mediterranean provides just one stark example of how important adequate mechanisms of external accountability and scrutiny are.

A second reason that might be offered is that, in its capacity as an international organisation, the EU cannot at present accede to most international human rights treaty or other mechanisms. As noted above, since most international human rights treaties were drafted with only nation states in mind, they do not specifically provide for accession by an international organisation. This argument however is by no means conclusory. In the first place, this was equally true of the statute of the Council of Europe and the European Convention on Human Rights before amendment, but it did not prevent EU actors from mobilising to encourage their amendment to facilitate EU accession. The Spinelli draft constitution as early as 1984 had proposed European Community accession to the UN Covenants on Civil and Political Rights and Economic, Social and Cultural Rights, without treating the adoption of the EU's own internal charter of rights, or the need for their amendment to facilitate accession as an undue obstacle.[79] Further, even if the EU were not to pursue formal accession to international human rights instruments, there are other options for 'parallel' participation in the international human rights treaty system, as Taiwan has for example shown.[80] And even without creating elaborate parallel arrangements, the EU could in

[79] Art 4(3) Draft Treaty establishing the European Union [1984] Bull EC 2/8 (otherwise known as the Spinelli plan) provided: 'Within a period of five years, the Union shall take a decision on its accession to the international instruments referred to above and to the United Nations Covenants on Civil and Political Rights and on Economic, Social and Cultural Rights. Within the same period, the Union shall adopt its own declaration on fundamental rights in accordance with the procedure for revision laid down in Article 84 of this Treaty'. For discussion see de Silva (n 78).

[80] Y-J Chen, 'Localizing Human Rights Treaty Monitoring: Case Study of Taiwan as a Non-UN Member State' (2018) 35 *Wisconsin Law Review* 277.

all likelihood voluntarily submit itself to international human rights monitoring by the UN treaty-body system.

A third reason that might be put forward is that other international organisations, and not only the EU, have similarly rejected such human rights accountability. The World Bank,[81] the International Monetary Fund,[82] the International Financial Corporation,[83] and even the UN itself have at different times refused to accept that they should be subject to external human rights scrutiny or remedy.[84] From this perspective, the EU in avoiding external human rights accountability is merely acting like most other international organisations, and is not an outlier in that regard.[85] This argument however is seriously flawed. In the first place, the EU is a regional organisation which has declared itself to be founded on human rights and committed itself to promoting human rights both internally and externally across all of its policies. It should be leading by example amongst other international organisations, and not emulating those which have been so sharply criticised for avoiding human rights scrutiny and accountability. Further, the EU has powers which go well beyond those

[81] See P Alston, 'Report of the Special Rapporteur on Extreme Poverty and Human Rights' (*United Nations General Assembly*, 4 August 2015) A/70/274*; '"The World Bank is a Human Rights-Free Zone" – UN Expert on Extreme Poverty Expresses Deep Concern' (*Office of the High Commissioner for Human Rights*, 29 September 2015), www.ohchr.org/en/press-releases/2015/09/world-bank-human-rights-free-zone-un-expert-extreme-poverty-expresses-deep.

[82] See A Cagliari 'IMF Accountability to Human Rights: Breaking the Deadlock' (*Global Policy Forum*, May 2023), www.globalpolicy.org/sites/default/files/IMF%20Accountability_final.pdf. Note also the failure of the Managing Director of the IMF to respond to a letter sent in 2022 by six UN Special Rapporteurs raising concerns about the impact of IMF surcharges: 'IMF Continues to Disregard UN Human Rights Commission Concerns about its Surcharge Policy' (*Bretton Woods Project*, 5 April 2023), www.brettonwoodsproject.org/2023/04/imf-continues-to-disregard-un-human-rights-commission-concerns-about-its-surcharge-policy/.

[83] While the IFC claims that its Performance Standards (for borrowers) on labour, social and environmental issues 'map onto' and support some of the rights contained in the Universal Declaration on Human Rights, it has repeatedly been criticised by human rights actors and institutions for not respecting human rights including basic requirements such as the right to remedy. Compare the IFC's 'mapping' at 'The International Bill of Human Rights and IFC Sustainability Framework' (*International Finance Corporation*, January 2012), www.ifc.org/en/insights-reports/2012/ibhr-ifc-sustainability-framework, with the critiques of its funding of human rights violations and refusal to accept responsibility or provide any remedy: A Saldinger,' IFC policy for when projects cause harm lambasted as "letdown"' *Devex News* (16 March 2023), www.devex.com/news/ifc-policy-for-when-projects-cause-harm-lambasted-as-letdown-105007.

[84] R Freedman and N Lemay-Hebert, 'Towards an Alternative Interpretation of UN Immunity: A Human Rights-based Approach to the Haiti Cholera Case' (2015) 19 *Questions of International Law* 5; P Alston, 'Report of the Special Rapporteur on Extreme Poverty and Human Rights' (United Nations General Assembly, 26 August 2016) A/71/367; 'UN Human Rights Expert: "UN Lawyers Undermine a Just Solution for the Victims of Cholera in Haiti"' (*Office of the High Commissioner for Human Rights*, 25 October 2016), www.ohchr.org/en/2016/10/un-human-rights-expert-un-lawyers-undermine-just-solution-victims-cholera-haiti#:~:text=NEW%20YORK%20(25%20October%202016,caused%20in%20Haiti%20in%202010.

[85] See in this regard Ramses Wessels' criticism of the EU for aligning itself with other international organisations in arguing for extensive immunities: RA Wessel, 'Immunities of the European Union' (2013) 10 *International Organizations Law Review* 395: 'Despite its frequent claim that it should not be equated with other international organizations, it is interesting to note that in these cases the European Union often uses the argument that as an 'international organization' its claim of jurisdictional immunity is based on the rule of general (customary) international law which recognises that like States, international organizations are exempted from the local jurisdiction of municipal judicial or administrative authorities … Apart from the fact that in many other occasions the Union continues to stress its sui generis nature in comparison to other international organizations, there is simply no extensive practice to easily base the [European Commission's] claim on'.

of the international financial institutions, and even beyond those of the UN, given its character as a tightly integrated political system with executive, law-making and policy-making powers across a vast array of domains. It is much closer to a federal state in its power and influence over the rights of individuals and groups than it is to any other international organisation, and as such it should be subject to the kind of external human rights accountability that befits such a powerful entity.

Finally, de Silva has canvassed three other sets of possible reasons for the EU's failure to seek accession to UN human rights treaties.[86] These are: (1) concerns about the limits of EU competence or the likely objection of the Court of Justice; (2) possible legal problems or resistance from the side of the other parties to the UN treaties; and (3) the lack of any observable benefit to the EU. Ultimately, having conducted interviews with relevant actors as well as desk research, she rejects each of these reasons and concludes that the real explanation is a lack of 'internalisation' by the EU of the provisions of various human rights treaties (by comparison with the EU's internalisation of the provisions of the ECHR, and arguably also the CRPD), and the low priority placed by the EU on accession to these treaties. We fully agree with her conclusions in this regard.

5. CONCLUSION

We conclude with a call for the EU and its institutions and Member States to rethink their resistance to external human rights accountability. This is a call directed not only to the European Court of Justice, which was the primary actor responsible for blocking ECHR accession in *Opinion 2/13*, and also for facilitating the unjustifiably limited and partial accession to the Istanbul Convention, but also to the Council of Ministers and the Member States when it comes to their ambivalence and lack of political interest in accession to international human rights agreements. They permitted quasi-authoritarian Member States to impede initial ratification of the Istanbul Convention, and states with a regressive gender equality agenda to dilute the ultimate ratification of that Convention, and they have shown no interest in encouraging the EU to include itself in external monitoring in relation to UN human rights treaties. We join the recommendation published by the UN Office of the High Commissioner for Human Rights (OHCHR) that the EU should submit itself to the Universal Periodic Review carried out by the UN Human Rights Council, and should experiment with ways of submitting itself to UN human rights treaty body review.[87] The inconclusive and lukewarm signals towards ESC accession should be rethought particularly in the wake of the sovereign debt crisis.[88]

[86] de Silva (n 78).

[87] The 2011 Report by I de Jesús Butler, 'The European Union and International Human Rights Law' (Office of the High Commissioner for Human Rights 2011) suggested that this might be done either by analogy with the kind of treaty body review of UN Mission in Kosovo that was permitted when Kosovo was under interim UN administration, or by analogy with the EU's approach to the Refugee Convention and its cooperation in that regard with UNHCR (the UN Refugee Agency).

[88] See O De Schutter, 'Le role de la Charte sociale européenne dans le développement du droit de l'Union européenne' in O De Schutter (ed), *La Charte Sociale Européenne: une constitution sociale pour l'Europe/ The European Social Charter: A Social Constitution for Europe* (Brussels, Bruylant, 2010) 124.

We have argued that the EU currently lacks the political will or commitment to take external human rights accountability seriously, despite the many strong reasons to do so, and the inadequacy of the reasons suggested against it. Its record on accession to the human rights treaties which are open to EU access has been at best ambivalent, halting and unimpressive, and there has been little or no sign of openness to the many other possible forms of international human rights accountability available. For a powerful political and legal entity which affects the lives and rights of so many citizens both within and beyond Europe, and one which claims to be founded on the principles of respect for human rights in its internal and external domains, this is highly regrettable, and undermines the credibility and reputation of the EU as a global and regional actor.

Global EU Climate Action and the Principle of Common but Differentiated Responsibilities and Respective Capabilities

GRACIA MARÍN DURÁN* AND JOANNE SCOTT**

1. INTRODUCTION

FOLLOWING THE ADOPTION of the European Green Deal in December 2019, the European Union (EU) is becoming increasingly assertive in its use of (unilateral) trade-related measures to address its global environmental footprint, which refers to the environmental pressures 'embodied' in goods or services it imports from third countries. In this chapter, we examine two recent and closely related instances of such a global EU climate action, namely the revised Emissions Trading System (ETS) Directive and its extension to greenhouse gas (GHG) emissions from the maritime sector,[1] and the Regulation establishing a carbon border adjustment mechanism (CBAM),[2] both adopted on 10 May 2023. These measures form part of the 'Fit for 55' legislative package, which is aimed at delivering on the targets enshrined in the European Climate Law, namely: a reduction in EU GHG emissions by (at least) 55 per cent when compared to 1990 levels by 2030, and the ultimate objective of 'climate-neutrality' (net-zero GHG emissions) by 2050.[3]

However, measures of this kind that seek to mitigate the negative impact of EU consumption on the Earth's climate have often proven fiercely controversial. This

* Faculty of Laws, University College London, London, United Kingdom (gracia.marin-duran@ucl.ac.uk). Gracia gratefully acknowledges her Fernand Braudel Senior Fellowship at the EUI Law Department (October–December 2022), which enabled research and exchanges on this chapter between the authors.

** Department of Law, European University Institute, Florence, Italy (joanne.scott@eui.eu).

[1] Directive (EU) 2023/959 of the European Parliament and of the Council amending Directive 2003/87/EC establishing a system for greenhouse gas emission allowance trading within the Union and Decision (EU) 2015/1814 concerning the establishment and operation of a market stability reserve for the Union greenhouse gas emission trading system (revised ETS Directive) [2023] OJ L130/134.

[2] Regulation (EU) 2023/956 of the European Parliament and of the Council establishing a carbon border adjustment mechanism (CBAM Regulation) [2023] OJ L130/52.

[3] Arts 2(1) and (4) Regulation (EU) 2021/1119 of the European Parliament and of the Council establishing the framework for achieving climate neutrality and amending Regulation (EU) 2018/1999 (European Climate Law) [2021] OJ L243/1.

is partly because the EU's climate conservation objective is closely connected with economic competitiveness concerns about a 'level playing field' between EU and third-country producers in the context of heterogenous and asymmetrical climate action under the Paris Agreement. It is also because they give rise to what one of the authors of this chapter has called the 'territorial extension' of EU environmental law in that they use the existence of a territorial connection with the EU (eg access to its market or ports) to gain regulatory leverage over conduct or activities that take place abroad.[4] In so doing, the EU is testing the boundaries of permissible unilateral action to protect the global climate system under international law. One important constraint in this regard is ensuring the WTO-compatibility of these trade-related measures, which has been a key concern for both the EU legislator and scholars. In this chapter, we draw attention to an equally important but less explored dimension; consistency with the principle of Common but Differentiated Responsibilities and Respective Capabilities (CBDR-RC) as one of the foundational pillars of the multilateral climate change regime.

We begin with a brief account of the CBDR-RC principle under the United Nations Framework Convention on Climate Change (UNFCCC) regime, and explain *why* it is of legal significance to global EU climate action and *when* it should be taken into account (Section 2). We then turn to the selected EU trade-related climate measures, and examine whether they respect the CBDR-RC principle – and if they do not, *how* best should these measures be adjusted to ensure they do (Sections 3 and 4). Section 5 concludes.

2. CBDR-RC PRINCIPLE AND ITS SIGNIFICANCE TO GLOBAL EU CLIMATE ACTION

2.1. What is the Principle of CBDR-RC?

CBDR-RC is possibly the most widely-cited principle in the international climate architecture and has underpinned global efforts to fight climate change from the very start. It is enshrined in Article 3.1 UNFCCC, which provides that

> [t]he Parties should protect the climate system for the benefit of present and future generations of humankind, on the basis of equity and in accordance with their *common but differentiated responsibilities and respective capabilities*. Accordingly, the *developed country Parties should take the lead* in combating climate change and the adverse effects thereof.[5]

Over the past three decades, it has played a central function as a 'framework' or 'structuring' principle in the multilateral climate regime, providing the bedrock of the burden-sharing arrangements initially crafted in the UNFCCC with regards

[4] See inter alia J Scott, 'Extra-Territoriality and Territorial Extension' (2014) 62 *American Journal of International Law* 87; J Scott, 'Reducing the European Union's Environmental Footprint Through "Territorial Extension"' in V Mauerhofer, D Rupo and L Tarquinio (eds), *Sustainability and the Law* (Cham, Springer, 2020).

[5] Art 3.1 United Nations Framework Convention on Climate Change (New York, 9 May 1992) (UNFCCC) (emphasis added).

to climate change mitigation (as well as adaptation, financial assistance and technology transfer), and shaping their subsequent elaboration in the Kyoto Protocol and Paris Agreement.[6] And yet, its core content and precise meaning remain deeply contested.

The first element of the principle refers to the 'common' responsibility of States to protect the environment and is generally understood as a recognition that climate change is a matter of 'common concern' of humankind, which requires the widest possible cooperation by all States.[7] However, the exact meaning of the remainder of the principle has generated much contention over the years. Essentially, the term 'differentiated' calls for differential treatment between countries; but the basis for such a differentiation is left ambiguous. On a plain reading of Article 3.1 UNFCCC, differentiation is to be determined based on two factors: responsibility for causing climate change, and capability to address it. Yet, it does not specify how these differentiation markers should be measured and the extent to which they may be linked.

The UNFCCC itself approaches responsibility and capability as intrinsically linked rather than distinct factors, with enhanced capability being the direct result of industrialisation and *historical* responsibility for GHG emissions. This is reflected in the normative expectation on developed countries 'to take the lead' in combating climate change in Article 3.1 UNFCCC.[8] But the articulation and operationalisation of the CBDR-RC principle has markedly evolved from the UNFCCC to the Paris Agreement.[9] In particular, the so-called Lima qualifier of 'in light of national circumstances' in Article 2.2 Paris Agreement introduces a dynamic and flexible element to interpreting both responsibilities and capabilities.[10] It thereby broadens the parameters for differentiation between countries, which is no longer premised on their historical contributions alone but includes other factors (eg current and projected future GHG emissions, financial and technical capabilities, human capacity).[11]

[6] A Boyle and C Redgwell, *Bernie, Boyle, and Redgwell's International Law and the Environment*, Law Trove, 4th edn (Oxford, Oxford University Press, 2021) 150; P Cullet, 'Principle 7: Common but Differentiated Responsibilities' in JE Viñuales (ed), *The Rio Declaration on Environment and Development: A Commentary*, Oxford Commentaries on International Law (Oxford, Oxford University Press, 2015) 236; L Rajamani, 'Common but Differentiated Responsibilities' in L Krämer and E Orlando (eds), *Principles of Environmental Law*, Elgar Encyclopedia of Environmental Law 6 (Cheltenham, Edward Elgar Publishing, 2018) 298.

[7] Preamble, Recital 1 UNFCCC; J Brunnée, 'Common Areas, Common Heritage and Common Concern' in D Bodansky, J Brunnée and E Hey (eds), *The Oxford Handbook of International Environmental Law* (Oxford, Oxford University Press, 2008) 564–568.

[8] Rajamani (n 6) 295; T Deleuil, 'The Common but Differentiated Responsibilities Principle: Changes in Continuity after the Durban Conference of the Parties' 21 *Review of European Community & International Environmental Law* 271, 272. See also United Nations General Assembly, 'Rio Declaration on Environment and Development' (1992) UN Doc A/CONF.151/26 (Vol. I), Principle 7.

[9] J Peel, 'Re-evaluating the Principle of Common but Differentiated Responsibilities in Transnational Climate Change Law' (2016) 5 *Transnational Environmental Law* 245, 248–249. For a critique of this evolution, see A Rosencranz and K Jamwal, 'Common but Differentiated Responsibilities and Respective Capabilities: Did this Principle Ever Exist?' (2020) 50 *Environmental Policy and Law* 291.

[10] Art 2.2 Paris Agreement (Paris, 12 December 2015) reads: '[t]his Agreement will be implemented to reflect equity and the principle of common but differentiated responsibilities and respective capabilities, in the light of different national circumstances'.

[11] L Rajamani, 'Ambition and Differentiation in the 2015 Paris Agreement: Interpretative Possibilities and Underlying Politics' (2016) 65 *ICLQ* 493, 507–508; C Voigt and F Ferreira, '"Dynamic Differentiation": The Principles of CBDR-RC, Progression and Highest Possible Ambition in the Paris Agreement' (2016) 5 *Transnational Environmental Law* 285, 294.

At the same time, this amalgamation of country-specific responsibilities and capabilities makes it increasingly complex to determine which countries may be deemed to have a 'high' responsibility/capability and which instead possess a 'low' responsibility/capability in the global fight against climate change.

That said, there is no question that the EU itself falls within the 'high' responsibility/capability category and should, therefore, assume a leadership role in global efforts to address climate change. It seems also clear that any EU trade-related climate measure that seeks the same contribution to climate change mitigation from 'low' responsibility/capability countries would be out of step with the CBDR-RC principle. Likewise, if an 'equivalent' contribution is required of such countries, this concept should be interpreted and operationalised in line with the principle of CBDR-RC. But beyond this, the principle as generally articulated in Articles 3.1 UNFCCC and 2.2 Paris Agreement does not assist us in determining which specific forms of differentiation are needed and for which countries when adopting trade-related climate measures.[12] This is not surprising given its inherently abstract and open-ended nature as a legal principle: while it does sway decision-makers in a particular direction – differentiation between 'high' and 'low' responsibility/capability countries – it does not itself prescribe particular actions.[13] We will return below to the question of *how* the CBDR-RC principle should be integrated in the revised ETS Directive and CBAM Regulation. But it is first necessary to establish *whether* the CBDR-RC principle is legally relevant to this kind of trade-related climate measures, and if so, *when* exactly it applies.

2.2. Is the CBDR-RC Principle Legally Relevant to 'Global EU Climate Action'?

There is considerable debate over the legal status of the CBDR-RC principle under public international law, partly due to the aforementioned enduring ambiguity over its normative content. Most scholars have come to agree that CBDR-RC does not constitute a customary principle and is thus devoid of general applicability outside the confines of the treaty instrument in which it finds expression.[14] In the multilateral climate regime, CBDR-RC is explicitly expressed as an overarching principle in the operational provisions of the UNFCCC (Art 3.1) and Paris Agreement (Art 2.2) – two

[12] Note that the UNFCCC does not prohibit trade-related climate measures outright, but sets out explicit conditions on their use (Art 3.5 UNFCCC). In doing so, the UNFCCC implicitly recognises (or takes for granted) that Parties may resort to such measures, even unilaterally: see M Hertel, 'Climate-Change-Related Trade Measures and Article XX: Defining Discrimination in Light of the Principle of Common but Differentiated Responsibilities' (2011) 45 *Journal of World Trade* 653, 662.

[13] Rajamani (n 6) 293.

[14] See eg Cullet (n 6) 236; Deleuil (n 8) 275; A Gourgourinis, 'Common but Differentiated Responsibilities in Transnational Climate Change Governance and the WTO: A Tale of Two "Interconnected Worlds" or a Tale of Two "Crossing Swords"?' in P Delimatsis (ed), *Research Handbook on Climate Change and Trade Law*, Research Handbooks in Climate Law Series (Cheltenham, Edward Elgar Publishing, 2016) 36; E Hey and S Paulini, 'Common But Differentiated Responsibilities' in R Wolfrum (ed), *Max Planck Encyclopedia of Public International Law* (Oxford, Oxford University Press, 2021) para 19; Rajamani (n 6) 298; C Stone, 'Common But Differentiated Responsibilities in International Law' (2014) 98 *American Journal of International Law* 276, 299–300.

legally-binding treaties (*inter partes*) with near universal participation. The chapeau of Article 3 UNFCCC ('shall be guided') and Article 2.2 Paris Agreement ('will be implemented to respect') create normative expectations that this principle will be taken into consideration,[15] and given proper weight,[16] by the Parties in their 'actions to achieve the [temperature] objectives' of these agreements.[17] It seems clear that the CBAM Regulation qualifies as one of such actions. The EU, as the relevant international actor for present purposes, expressly accepts this proposition, recognising the CBAM is an 'essential' policy tool towards meeting the objective of 'a climate-neutral Union by 2050 in line with the Paris Agreement' and ought to 'respect CBDRRC principle'.[18]

A more complex situation is raised by the revised ETS Directive. This is because sectoral GHG emissions from international shipping, as well as from international aviation, remain outside the UNFCCC regime,[19] and are being addressed under the auspices of the International Maritime Organisation (IMO) and the International Civil Aviation Organisation (ICAO), respectively.[20] As discussed below, efforts at decarbonising the international shipping sector have been ongoing at the IMO over the past two decades, notably with the adoption of the 2018 Initial Strategy on Reduction of GHG Emissions from Ships (GHG Strategy) and its Revised GHG Strategy in July 2023.[21] While the various IMO Conventions do not explicitly recognise the CBDR-RC principle, it is nonetheless specified as a 'guiding principle' in the IMO GHG Strategies. This creates normative expectations (albeit, not treaty-based

[15] Rajamani (n 11) 508–509.

[16] This is further supported by *Gabčíkovo-Nagymaros Project (Hungary/Slovakia)* (Judgment) [1997] ICJ Rep 7, para 140, discussing the role of 'sustainable development'.

[17] Art 2 UNFCCC; Arts 2.1 and 4.1 Paris Agreement.

[18] European Commission, 'Proposal for a Regulation of the European Parliament and of the Council establishing a Carbon Border Adjustment Mechanism' (2021) COM(2021) 564 final (CBAM Proposal), Explanatory Memorandum, 1 and Preamble, Recital 9; European Commission, 'Commission Staff Working Document: Impact Assessment Report Accompanying the Document "Proposal for a Regulation of the European Parliament and of the Council establishing a Carbon Border Adjustment Mechanism"' (2021) SWD(2021) 643 final (CBAM Impact Assessment) 3–4 and 8.

[19] Art 2.2 Kyoto Protocol to the United Nations Framework Convention on Climate Change (Kyoto, 11 December 1997) provided that Annex I Parties 'shall pursue limitation or reduction of emissions of greenhouse gases not controlled by the Montreal Protocol from aviation and marine bunker fuels, working through the [ICAO] and the [IMO], respectively'. The situation under the Paris Agreement is less straightforward: while emissions from international aviation and shipping are not explicitly excluded, no Contracting Party has actually included them in nationally determined contributions. It has been argued that the commitment in Art 4.4 Paris Agreement on '*economy-wide* emission reduction or limitation targets' to ensure that the agreement's temperature goals are met implies that emissions from these two core sectors are covered by the Paris Agreement: see E Dehon, 'Legal Advice – Inclusion of Emissions from International Aviation and Shipping in Nationally Determined Contributions' (*Transport & Environment*, October 2021), www.transportenvironment.org/wp-content/uploads/2021/10/Re-Aviation-Shipping-NDC-UPDATED-Legal-Advice-Final-3-5-21-corr-1.pdf.

[20] On ICAO, see 'Carbon Offsetting and Reduction Scheme for International Aviation (CORSIA)' (*International Civil Aviation Organisation*), www.icao.int/environmental-protection/CORSIA/Pages/default.aspx.

[21] The Marine Environment Protection Committee, 'Resolution MEPC.304(72) – Initial IMO Strategy on Reduction of GHG Emissions from Ships' (*International Maritime Organisation*, 13 April 2018) MEPC 72/17/Add.1 (Initial GHG Strategy); The Marine Environment Protection Committee, 'Resolution MEPC.377(80)–2023 IMO Strategy on Reduction of GHG Emissions from Ships' (*International Maritime Organisation*, 7 July 2023) MEPC 80/17/Add.1 (Revised GHG Strategy). See further Section 3.1 below.

as in the UNFCCC/Paris Agreement context) that the principle should be duly taken into account when adopting measures to decarbonise the international shipping sector, which itself may be considered an 'action to achieve the [temperature] objectives' of the UNFCCC/Paris Agreement. Importantly again, as will be seen below, the EU does not contest this proposition and accepts the legal relevance of the CBDR-RC principle to the inclusion of GHG emissions from this sector in the revised ETS Directive.[22]

2.3. When should CBDR-RC be Taken into Account in Global EU Climate Action?

In addressing this question, we draw on the article entitled 'The Geographical Scope of the EU's Climate Responsibilities' (Climate Responsibilities article), published by one of the authors of this chapter in 2015.[23] That article analysed how far the EU's climate responsibilities ought to extend geographically. It also elaborated a framework for assessing when the principle of CBDR-RC should be relevant to EU climate action that includes GHG emissions that are generated outside of the territory of its Member States. We return to that article here because it is directly relevant for the analysis in this chapter.[24] Hence, it is necessary to provide a brief recap of the main arguments as a backdrop to the examination of the CBAM Regulation and the inclusion of maritime emissions in the revised ETS Directive.

[22] Preamble, Recital 20 revised ETS Directive; see further Section 3.2 below.

[23] J Scott, 'The Geographical Scope of the EU's Climate Responsibilities' (2015) 17 *CYELS* 92.

[24] The European Commission refers to the pre-publication version of a different article co-authored by Scott in claiming that various EU legislative proposals comply with the principle of CBDR-RC (J Scott and L Rajamani, 'EU Climate Change Unilateralism' (2012) 23 *EJIL* 469). However, the arguments concerning which share of GHG emissions the EU may include within the scope of its measures without triggering the application of the principle of CBDR-RC has been made more explicitly and comprehensively in the Climate Responsibilities article authored by Scott. See, for example, European Commission, 'Commission Staff Working Document: Impact Assessment Report Accompanying the Document "Proposal for a Directive amending Directive 2003/87/EC as regards Aviation's Contribution to the Union's Economy-wide Emission Reduction Target and Appropriately Implementing a Global Market-based Measure"' (2021) SWD(2021) 603 final, para 77 of which notes '[t]his approach has been noted as a practical way to solve the issue of Common but Differentiated Responsibilities and Capabilities, which has been a longstanding challenge in the UNFCCC context'; see, for example, J Scott and L Rajamani, 'EU Climate Change Unilateralism' (*Social Science Research Network*, 1 November 2011), papers.ssrn.com/sol3/papers.cfm?abstract_id=1952554. Identical phrasing is used in footnotes to the two Explanatory Memoranda accompanying Commission Delegated Decisions exempting incoming flights from Switzerland and the UK from the EU-ETS. See Commission Delegated Decision (EU) 2021/1416 amending Directive 2003/87/EC of the European Parliament and of the Council as regards the exclusion of incoming flights from the United Kingdom from the Union emissions trading system [2021] OJ L305/1 and Commission Delegated Decision (EU) 2020/1071 amending Directive 2003/87/EC of the European Parliament and of the Council, as regards the exclusion of incoming flights from Switzerland from the EU emissions trading system [2020] OJ L234/16. See footnote 5 in particular. In relation to shipping, there is an explicit reference to CBDR-RC and an identical formulation is used as in the above documents. However, there is no explicit reference to the article by Scott & Rajamani. Nonetheless, a Commission official closely involved in the drafting of the Directive (Damien Meadows) has confirmed that it was this article that was in mind when stating that 'this approach has been noted as a practical way to solve the issue of common but differentiated responsibilities and capabilities, which has been a longstanding challenge in the UNFCCC context'. See Preamble, Recital 20 revised ETS Directive.

Drawing on the scholarship of Simon Caney, the article draws a distinction between the EU's first-order and second-order climate responsibilities.[25] Caney explains this distinction as follows:

> First-order responsibilities, as I employ that term, are responsibilities that certain agents have to perform (or omit) certain actions. In the context of addressing climate change these *first-order* responsibilities include responsibilities to mitigate climate change (through reducing emissions and maintaining greenhouse gas sinks), to enable adaption, and to compensate people for harm done. *Second-order responsibilities*, by contrast, refer to responsibilities that some have to ensure that agents comply with their *first-order responsibilities*.[26]

When the EU exercises first-order climate responsibilities, it is regulating GHG emissions which fall, or may reasonably be viewed as falling, principally within its jurisdiction. It has primary responsibility over these emissions from the point of view of 'burden-sharing justice'.[27] These emissions 'belong' first and foremost to the EU as an entity and, hence, to an association of high responsibility/capability (EU Member) States. There is, therefore, no expectation that the EU's climate commitments should be differentiated 'downwards' to give effect to the CBDR-RC principle. On the contrary, the EU should adopt ambitious targets in relation to these emissions in keeping with the expectation in Articles 3.1 UNFCCC and 4.4 Paris Agreement that developed countries take the lead in combatting climate change.

By contrast, when the EU exercises second-order climate responsibilities, it is regulating emissions which fall, or may reasonably be viewed as falling, principally within the jurisdiction of a different State. These emissions 'belong' first and foremost to non-EU Member States, some of which will be 'low' responsibility/capability States from the perspective of the CBDR-RC principle. In stepping in, contingently, to regulate GHG emissions which ought ideally to be regulated by a different State, with a view to inducing that State to fulfil its first-order climate responsibilities, the EU ought to take the principle of CBDR-RC into consideration. Where appropriate, in keeping with this logic, the EU should impose lower burdens in relation to emissions 'belonging' to these countries. Here, the EU is acting as a surrogate regulator and should not seek to impose burdens on third countries which exceed the extent of their first-order climate responsibilities. In delineating the extent of these responsibilities, the principle of CBDR-RC should be taken into account.

This then leaves the question of how to distinguish between the EU's first- and second-order climate responsibilities, a distinction which is crucial for the application of the principle of CBDR-RC. Here, the Climate Responsibilities article looks to international standards for guidance in the form of the Guidelines adopted by

[25] S Caney, 'Two Kinds of Climate Justice: Avoiding Harms and Sharing Burdens' (2014) 22 *Journal of Political Philosophy* 125.

[26] ibid 134–135. Caney refines this definition later by observing that the exercise of second-order responsibilities can also serve to impose new first-order responsibilities on other actors by, for example, offering assistance to States, they may come to enjoy capacities to mitigate climate change that they didn't previously have (ibid 137).

[27] Caney conceives first-order climate responsibilities in terms of burden-sharing justice and second-order responsibilities in terms of harm-avoidance justice.

the Intergovernmental Panel on Climate Change (IPCC).[28] These Guidelines adopt a principally territorial approach to apportioning responsibility for GHG emissions between States. Thus, the State in which GHG emissions are generated must include them in its national inventory of GHG emissions and bears responsibility for their mitigation. For example, GHG emissions generated in the production of steel will be the responsibility of the State in which the steel is produced rather than the State in which the steel in consumed. On this basis, the starting point for our analysis is that the Union has first-order climate responsibilities for GHG emissions generated within the territory of EU Member States, and second-order responsibilities for emissions that are generated abroad. As will be further discussed below, the CBAM Regulation provides an instance of the EU exercising second-order responsibilities.

However, the Climate Responsibilities article argues that there are exceptions to this territorial approach. One category of exception arises when the IPCC Guidelines themselves endorse a departure from that approach.[29] To give just one of several possible examples, carbon dioxide emissions from commercial road vehicles are not attributed to the State in which they are generated, but to the State in which the fuel is sold to the end user, even in relation to emissions that are generated outside of that State. However, these IPCC-endorsed departures from a territorial system boundary are not pertinent for the analysis in this chapter.

Nonetheless, the Climate Responsibilities article posits the existence of a second category of exception which is directly relevant for our purposes, namely when the IPCC Guidelines leave a 'system boundary gap'.[30] Such a gap arises when the Guidelines do not settle the question of how to apportion responsibility for GHG emissions between States. To give the most pertinent example from the point of view of this chapter, the Guidelines provide for the use of fuel consumption data or ship/flight movement in apportioning GHG emissions from international aviation and shipping, but they do not specify on which basis the fuel consumed or flight/ship movements are to be attributed to particular States.[31] Hence, they do not settle the question of where primary responsibility for GHG emissions from international aviation or shipping lies. They consequently leave uncertain the issue of when a State may be considered to be exercising first-order or second-order climate responsibilities.

The Climate Responsibilities article argues that where the international 'system boundary' remains unsettled or under-specified in this way, States enjoy autonomy in determining how far their first-order climate responsibilities extend geographically.

[28] HS Eggleston, L Buendia, K Miwa, T Ngara and K Tanabe (eds), '2006 IPCC Guidelines for National Greenhouse Gas Inventories' (Intergovernmental Panel on Climate Change 2006) (2006 IPCC Guidelines for National Greenhouse Gas Inventories).

[29] Scott (n 23) 102–103. Introduction, para 1.1 of the 2006 IPCC Guidelines for National Greenhouse Gas Inventories (n 28) endorsing a principally territorial approach subject to qualifications in Section 8.2.1 of Volume 1.

[30] Scott (n 23) 103–104. It also asserts the existence of a third exception which is not relevant for this chapter. This arises 'where imported products (goods or services) are accorded a highly privileged position within the EU market as a result of an EU policy intervention that is specifically intended to reward these products due to their climate credentials, the EU should be viewed as exercising first-order climate responsibilities when it regulates the extraterritorial GHG emissions that are embodied within these products', Scott (n 23) 105.

[31] Para 8.2.1, Vol 1 and chs 3.5 (water borne transportation) & 3.6 (civil aviation), Vol 2 of the 2006 IPCC Guidelines for National Greenhouse Gas Inventories (n 28).

They should, however, be required to exercise this autonomy in a manner that is respectful of the autonomy of other States. This is in keeping with the principle of sovereign equality in international law. To this end, the gap-filling system boundary that is endorsed by a State must be susceptible to replication by all other States (or at an international level) without this resulting in the double counting of the GHG emissions.[32] It is only where this 'replication test' is met that a State may reasonably claim to be exercising first-order climate responsibilities even when they are filling a system boundary gap.

This framework helps to understand why the EU should have taken the principle of CBDR-RC into account when it adopted a Directive in 2008 to include GHG emissions from international aviation in its ETS.[33] Here, the EU was acting in a policy sphere characterised by the existence of a system boundary gap as described in the Climate Responsibilities article. Nonetheless, it exercised its autonomy in determining the geographical scope of this Directive in a manner that did not fulfil the replication test set out above. This is because it aimed to include 100 per cent of GHG emissions from flights arriving in the EU from a third country and 100 per cent of GHG emissions from flights departing from the EU for a third country.[34] If any third country were to adopt the same approach, there would result a double-counting of emissions in relation to all EU-arriving or EU-departing flights. To the extent that the replication test was not met, the EU should be considered to be exercising second-order as opposed to first-order climate responsibilities and, therefore, ought to take the principle of CBDR-RC into account. In this example, if the EU had only included the GHGs emitted in EU-arriving *or* EU-departing flights, the replication test would be met and the EU could have claimed to be exercising first-order climate responsibilities. Likewise, if the EU had only included 50 per cent of GHGs emitted in EU-arriving and EU-departing flights, the replication test would likewise have been satisfied.

It is in light of this framework that this chapter will now evaluate *how* the CBDR-RC principle should be integrated in the two selected EU climate measures. It will start by looking at the revised ETS Directive and its extension to maritime emissions (with short references to international aviation where relevant) and then turn to the best known of the EU's recent global climate measures, namely the CBAM Regulation. The next section will begin by outlining the general context for the

[32] Scott (n 23) 104. This is not to say that no double-counting will occur because non-EU Member States may exercise their system boundary autonomy in a different way. It is simply to say that double-counting would not occur if other States were to adopt the same system boundary.

[33] Directive 2008/101/EC of the European Parliament and of the Council amending Directive 2003/87/EC so as to include aviation activities in the scheme for greenhouse gas emission allowance trading within the Community (Aviation Directive) [2009] OJ L8/3. This is an additional argument to those presented by J Scott and L Rajamani in their earlier article (n 24).

[34] ibid, Annex I(1)(c). This was subject to the possibility of exempting incoming flights under Art 25a. To the extent that the emissions generated by these incoming flights fall under the EU's second-order responsibilities, it would be incumbent on the EU to take CBDR-RC into account in articulating country-specific conditions for exemption. If 100% of emissions from departing flights are regarded as falling within the EU's first-order responsibilities, then 100% of emissions from incoming flights would fall within its second-order responsibilities. If 50% of emissions from departing flights were viewed as falling within its first-order responsibilities, then 50% of emissions from incoming flights and 50% of emissions from departing flights would be viewed as falling within its second-order responsibilities.

inclusion of GHG emissions from international shipping in the EU ETS before turning to the EU initiative itself.

3. EXTENDING ETS DIRECTIVE TO MARITIME EMISSIONS AND CBDR-RC PRINCIPLE

3.1. Broader Context

The Fourth Greenhouse Gas Study adopted by the IMO estimated that shipping contributed almost 3 per cent of global GHG emissions in 2018, with international shipping contributing 2 per cent.[35] Depending on the 'plausible' economic and energy scenario' applied, maritime emissions could remain static to 2050 or rise as much as 40 per cent during this period.[36] The IMO has been active in addressing GHG emissions from shipping, for example by adopting mandatory energy efficiency requirements for new ships in 2011.[37] Nonetheless, there is widespread agreement that its level of ambition has fallen well short of what would be required for the international shipping sector to make a proportionate contribution to reaching the Paris Agreement objectives, including that of holding the increase in global temperature to well below 2°C above pre-industrial levels.[38] It is against this backdrop that the EU decision to include international maritime emissions in its ETS should be understood.

The IMO subsequently revised its Initial GHG Strategy. Its vision is set out as follows:

> [The] IMO remains committed to reducing GHG emissions from international shipping and, as a matter of urgency, aims to phase them out as soon as possible, while promoting, in the context of this Strategy, a just and equitable transition.[39]

[35] J Faber et al, 'Fourth IMO Greenhouse Gas Study: Full Report' (International Maritime Organisation 2020) 1.

[36] In 2018, international shipping emissions were 90% of 2008 levels. Using a range of 'plausible long-term economic and energy scenarios, the Fourth IMO Greenhouse Gas Study suggests that GHG emissions from international shipping could increase to as much as 130% of 2008 levels (ibid 3). Other, much higher, estimates are available. Isabelle Rojon et al in an article authored by one of the authors of the Fourth IMO Greenhouse Gas Study (Tristan Smith) suggest increases could be between 90% and 130% by 2050 compared to 2008/2018 'depending on future energy developments and economic growth prospects'. See I Rojon et al, 'The Impacts of Carbon Pricing on Maritime Transport Costs and Their Implications for Developing Economies' (2021) 132 *Marine Policy* 104653, 1.

[37] 'Resolution MEPC.203(62) – Amendments of the Annex to the Protocol of 1997 to Amend the International Convention for the Prevention of Pollution from Ships, 1973, as Modified by the Protocol of 1978 Relating Thereto' (Inclusion of regulations on energy efficiency for ships in MARPOL Annex VI) (*International Maritime Organisation*, 15 July 2011), Regs 19–21 on the Energy Efficiency Design Index (EEDI). See Appendix I of the IMO's Revised GHG Strategy (n 21) for an overview of the steps taken by the IMO. For an overview of IMO measures to date see N Wissner and S Healy, 'Raising ambition levels for the IMO for 2050: An Overview of the Key Issues at Stake at MEPC 80' (*European Parliament*, 14 June 2023), www.europarl.europa.eu/thinktank/en/document/IPOL_BRI(2023)740089.

[38] Art 2(1) Paris Agreement. It will fall further short of its objective of pursuing efforts to limit the temperature increase to 1.5°C above pre-industrial levels. B Comer, 'Zero-Emission Shipping and the Paris Agreement: Why the IMO Needs to Pick a Zero Date and Set Interim Targets in Its Revised GHG Strategy' (*International Council on Clean Transportation*, 8 September 2021), www.theicct.org/zero-emission-shipping-and-the-paris-agreement-why-the-imo-needs-to-pick-a-zero-date-and-set-interim-targets-in-its-revised-ghg-strategy/. See also S Franz et al, Requirements for a maritime transition in line with the Paris Agreement (2022) 25 *iScience* 105630.

[39] Revised GHG Strategy (n 21) part 2.

If the aspirational objectives set out in the Revised GHG Strategy were to be fully achieved, it would come much closer to meeting the well below 2°C temperature goal under the Paris Agreement, but not the more ambitious 1.5°C temperature target (see Table 1 below).[40] The level of ambition 'directing' the Revised GHG Strategy includes the objective of peaking 'GHG emissions from international shipping as soon as possible and [reaching] net-zero GHG emissions by or around, ie close to 2050'.[41] It also includes 'indicative checkpoints' to reduce emissions by 20 per cent by 2030 ('striving for 30%') and 70 per cent by 2040 ('striving for 80%').[42]

Table 1 Paris Agreement Temperature Goals and IMO Revised GHG Strategy (reductions compared to 2008/2018)

Level of Ambition	2030	2040	2050
1.5°C PA	50% reduction	Zero emissions	
1.7°C (well below 2°C) PA	33.3% reduction	66.6 % reduction	Zero emissions
IMO Revised Strategy	20% and striving for 30%	70% and striving for 80%	Net-zero by or around (close to) 2050

Looking at the content of the IMO Revised GHG Strategy, it is littered with aspiration rather than with the pursuit of clear results. The word 'should' appears 25 times compared to one appearance for the mandatory term 'shall'.[43] To give an example of the Revised GHG Strategy's aspirational nature, the document provides that 'a basket of candidate measure(s), delivering on the reduction targets, *should* be developed and finalized'.[44] This basket of measures is to be comprised of both a technical element and 'an economic element, on the basis of a maritime GHG emissions pricing mechanism'.[45] The term 'could' also puts in multiple appearances. For example, 'possible long-term measures *could* be measures finalized and agreed by the Committee beyond 2030, to be developed as part of the 2028 review of the IMO GHG Strategy'.[46]

As previously mentioned, it is significant that the Revised GHG Strategy does reference the principle of CBDR-RC.[47] This is appropriate in light of the vision animating

[40] 'Well below' is interpreted as 1.7 in the analyses conducted by the International Council on Clean Transportation (ICCT) relied upon here. It would not, however, be aligned with the more ambitious 1.5 temperature ceiling also enshrined in the Paris Agreement. See B Comer and F Carvalho, 'IMO's Newly Revised Greenhouse Gas Strategy: What it Means for Shipping and the Paris Agreement' (*International Council on Clean Transportation*, 7 July 2023), www.theicct.org/marine-imo-updated-ghg-strategy-jul23/.

[41] Revised GHG Strategy (n 21) para 2.4.

[42] ibid para 3.4.

[43] ibid para 4.3 states 'In accordance with regulations 25.3 and 28.11 of MARPOL Annex VI, a review of the mandatory goal-based technical and operational measures to reduce carbon intensity of international shipping (the "short-term GHG reduction measures") shall be completed by 1 January 2026'. Even this is a purely procedural requirement.

[44] ibid para 4.5.

[45] ibid.

[46] ibid para 4.1.4.

[47] ibid para 3.5.2.

this strategy to promote a just and equitable transition. In a somewhat convoluted formulation, it sets out 'the principles guiding' the 2023 Revised GHG Strategy which include 'the need to be cognizant of the principles enshrined in instruments already developed, such as … the principle of common but differentiated responsibilities and respective capabilities, in the light of different national circumstances'.[48] As in earlier documents, CBDR-RC is referred to alongside the long-standing IMO principles of non-discrimination and no more favourable treatment.[49] As we have argued elsewhere, while this juxtaposition may seem awkward, there is in fact no inherent incompatibility between these principles.[50]

While the Revised GHG Strategy does reference the principle of CBDR-RC, it does not specify what this concept means, nor what is required for this principle to guide the strategy or in order to be cognisant of it. Nonetheless, it places considerable emphasis upon the need to consider the impacts of measures adopted on States, including developing countries, in particular Least Developed Countries (LDCs) and Small Island Developing States (SIDS).[51] It provides for the conduct of a 'comprehensive impact assessment of the basket of candidate mid-term measures' to be adopted pursuant to the strategy by Autumn 2024.[52] It further sets out a non-exhaustive list of the kinds of impacts that should be considered and provides that measures may only be adopted after disproportionately negative impacts have been assessed and addressed, as appropriate.[53] Among the impacts to be assessed are several of particular salience for developing countries, including food security and socio-economic development and progress.[54] The concept of 'disproportionately' is not defined.

While it is not inconceivable that the rights and obligations of States could be differentiated in future measures as a way of addressing disproportionately negative impacts on especially vulnerable countries, there is nothing in the Revised GHG Strategy as it stands that demands or even acknowledges this possibility. There is likewise no attempt to formulate how CBDR-RC could be operationalised in the international shipping context. While 'impacts' may be relevant to an assessment of countries 'respective capabilities' and 'different national circumstances', this leaves entirely open the question of whether and how countries' differentiated responsibilities' for causing climate change will be taken into account.

The IMO's Revised GHG Strategy also recognises that developing countries, in particular LDCs and SIDS, have special needs with regard to capacity-building and technical cooperation.[55] It provides that '[w]hen developing candidate mid- and long-term GHG reduction measures, due account should be taken to ensure a just and equitable transition that leaves no country behind, including supportive measures'.[56]

[48] ibid para 3.5.

[49] ibid para 3.5.1.

[50] Scott (n 23) briefly at 113–114. For a discussion in the WTO context, see G Marín Durán, 'Securing Compatibility of Carbon Border Adjustments with the Multilateral Climate and Trade Regimes' (2023) 72 *ICLQ* 73, 95–100.

[51] Revised GHG Strategy (n 21) para 3.5.3.

[52] ibid para 6.2.

[53] ibid para 4.13.

[54] See, generally, Rojon et al (n 36).

[55] Revised GHG Strategy (n 21) para 5.1.

[56] ibid para 5.3.

The Marine Environment Protection Committee 'should continue to provide mechanisms for facilitating ... capacity building and technical cooperation'.[57] The IMO 'should assess periodically the provision of financial and technological resources and capacity-building to implement the Revised GHG Strategy'.[58] The IMO 'may', for example, support the implementation of existing short-term GHG reduction measures through the provision of financial and technological resources, enhanced technical cooperation, capacity-building activities and technology cooperation.[59] While it is clear that the basket of candidate mid-term measures to be developed and finalised pursuant to the strategy is to comprise 'an economic element, on the basis of a maritime GHG emissions pricing mechanism',[60] there is no discussion of the vexed question of how the revenues generated will be used and whether developing countries would stand to benefit in this respect.[61]

It is against this backdrop that this chapter now turns to look at the EU's decision to include maritime GHG emissions in its ETS, and to do so specifically from the point of view of the principle of CBDR-RC.

3.2. Respecting CBDR-RC?

The EU raised the possibility of including international shipping in the EU ETS as early as 2009. In the preamble to two key pieces of legislation, it insisted that '[a]ll sectors of the economy should contribute to achieving these emission reductions, including international shipping and aviation'.[62] It went on to stress that:

> In the event that no international agreement which includes international maritime emissions in its reduction targets through the [IMO] has been approved by the Member States or no such agreement through the UNFCCC has been approved by the Community by 31 December 2011, the Commission should make a proposal to include international maritime emissions according to harmonised modalities in the Community reduction commitment, with the aim of the proposed act entering into force by 2013.[63]

Although the Commission observed that the deadline for the conclusion of an international agreement had passed, it later decided to adopt a 'staged approach', starting

[57] ibid para 5.8.

[58] ibid para 5.10.

[59] ibid para 5.11.3.

[60] ibid para 4.5.

[61] For a discussion, see G Dominioni et al, 'Carbon Revenues From International Shipping: Enabling an Effective and Equitable Energy Transition – Technical Paper' (*World Bank*, 1 April 2022), openknowledge.worldbank.org/entities/publication/2c6a3435-b005-52a5-89d4-f66e1fe862d2; see also S Kopela, 'Climate Change, Regime Interaction, and the Principle of Common but Differentiated Responsibility: The Experience of the International Maritime Organization' (2013) 24 *Yearbook of International Environmental Law* 70.

[62] Recital 3 Decision 406/2009/EC of the European Parliament and of the Council on the effort of Member States to reduce their greenhouse gas emissions to meet the Community's greenhouse gas emission reduction commitments up to 2020 [2009] OJ L140/136. Recital 3 Directive 2009/29/EC of the European Parliament and of the Council so as to improve and extend the greenhouse gas emission allowance trading scheme of the Community [2009] OJ L140/63.

[63] ibid.

with the adoption of a Regulation on the Monitoring, Reporting and Verification (MRV) of Emissions seen as a first step.[64] This 'should serve as an example for the implementation of a global MRV with the aim [of speeding] up the international discussions'.[65] The Commission was required to review this Regulation and, where appropriate, to propose amendments to it in the event that an international agreement on global measures to reduce GHG emissions from maritime transport is reached.[66]

Despite this long build-up, it was not until 2023 that the EU decided to elaborate upon the MRV Regulation by including maritime emissions in the ETS.[67] From January 2024, shipping companies have to buy and surrender emission allowances to cover the CO_2 emitted by large ships entering EU ports.[68] Even then, the Directive adopts an incremental approach, covering only 40 per cent of maritime emissions within its scope in 2024, 70 per cent in 2025 and 100 per cent from 2026 onwards.[69] As with other similar measures, a review clause is included which requires the Commission to review the Directive in light of the adoption of a global market-based measure by the IMO.[70] Here, as elsewhere, the EU is acting as a 'contingent unilateralist' exercising second-order climate responsibilities on a contingent basis in a bid to encourage or induce third countries or international organisations to step in to regulate these GHG emissions.[71]

Unlike the original Directive aimed at including emissions from international aviation in the EU's ETS,[72] the revised ETS Directive including shipping within its scope, does refer expressly to the principle of CBDR-RC. The preamble to the Directive observes that the extension of the ETS to international maritime transport includes half of the emissions from ships performing voyages arriving at an EU port from a port outside the EU and half of the emissions from ships performing voyages departing from an EU port for a port outside the EU.[73] It, thus, covers 50 per cent of the emissions from ships arriving in and departing from the EU.[74] In the same paragraph, it goes on to note that '[t]his approach has been noted as a practical way to solve the issue of common but differentiated responsibilities and capabilities which has been a longstanding challenge in the UNFCCC context'.[75]

[64] Regulation (EU) 2015/757 of the European Parliament and of the Council on the monitoring, reporting and verification of carbon dioxide emissions from maritime transport, and amending Directive 2009/16/EC [2015] OJ L123/55.

[65] ibid Recital 1.

[66] ibid Art 25(3).

[67] Revised ETS Directive (n 1).

[68] Ships of 5000 Gross Tonnage or above. From 2026, the Directive also includes methane and nitrous oxides emitted by ships (Annex I(ix)). The aim is to incorporate acts as soon as possible after their date of entry into force in the EU, in order to ensure that the same rules apply throughout the EEA.

[69] Art 3gb revised ETS Directive.

[70] Art 3gg revised ETS Directive.

[71] Scott and Rajamani (n 24).

[72] Aviation Directive (n 33).

[73] Recital 20 revised ETS Directive.

[74] It also includes 100% of emissions generated during voyages between EU ports and within EU ports but to the extent that the measure is wholly internal to the EU, the CBDR-RC issue does not arise.

[75] Recital 20 revised ETS Directive.

This claim regarding CBDR-RC requires some unpacking, not least because it is not clear from the text where it has previously been 'noted' that this approach is a way to solve the challenge of CBDR-RC. However, it seems clear that the EU considers the fact that the revised ETS Directive includes only 50 per cent of the emissions generated during voyages to and from EU ports to support its claim to 'solve' the challenging issue of CBDR-RC. This is consistent with the argument put forward in the Climate Responsibilities article. This is because, first, the EU is taking steps to fill a system boundary gap in relation to international shipping and, therefore, has substantial autonomy in deciding which emissions to include within the scope of its responsibilities. Second, it is because the scope of the Directive is such that the replication test is met. Recall, this requires that the system boundary set by the EU must be susceptible to replication by other States without this resulting in the double counting of emissions by more than one State. This is because if third countries were to replicate the EU's scope model, each country of arrival would assert jurisdiction over 50 per cent of the emissions generated during the relevant arriving and departing voyage. This is illustrated in Table 2 below.[76]

Table 2 Revised ETS Directive and Replication Test for Shipping Emissions

Scope of EU measure	EU coverage	Third country coverage	Total coverage
Voyages departing from EU for third country	50% emissions covered	50% emissions covered	100% emissions
Voyages arriving in EU from third country	50% emissions covered	50% emissions covered	100% emissions

Before concluding this discussion of CBDR-RC in relation to the inclusion of maritime emissions in the revised ETS Directive, two additional points may be usefully made.

First, the scope of this Directive is different from that of the original Directive seeking to extend the EU ETS to emissions from international aviation. While the former includes 50 per cent of emissions generated during voyages to and from the EU, the latter included 100 per cent in both directions.[77] The critique of the original Aviation Directive from a CBDR-RC perspective therefore still stands as the EU exercised its autonomy but in a manner that did not satisfy the replication test.[78] In the case of aviation, therefore, the EU was exercising second-order as well as first-order responsibilities and, as far as the former were concerned, it ought to have taken CBDR-RC in to account.

However, the situation with aviation is evolving and the current trend is in the direction of only including outgoing but not incoming flights.[79] In 2023, the EU

[76] The same would be true if the EU had decided to include 100% of emissions generated during voyages arriving in the EU *or* departing from the EU.

[77] Aviation Directive, Art 3a and Annex I.

[78] Scott and Rajamani (n 24).

[79] See n 23.

adopted legislation amending the scope of the original Aviation Directive.[80] This requires the Commission to submit a report to the Council and the European Parliament assessing the environmental integrity of ICAO's global market-based measure (CORSIA).[81] Where appropriate, this report shall be accompanied by a legislative proposal to amend the Directive in order to exclude flights arriving in the EU (European Economic Area to be accurate) from airports situated in a third country.[82] If this were to happen, 100 per cent of emissions from EU-arriving flights would be included in the EU's ETS while no emissions from EU-departing flights destined for third countries would be included. The replication test would therefore be satisfied as there would be no double-counting of emissions.

Second, there remains a degree of ambiguity in the revised ETS Directive from the point of view of CBDR-RC. This is because it contemplates the possibility of increasing the share of shipping emissions generated during voyages to and from EU ports to more than 50 per cent.[83] The Commission is charged with reporting to the European Parliament and the Council on this issue in the event that the IMO does not adopt a global market-based measure to reduce GHG emissions from international maritime transport in line with the objectives of the Paris Agreement and at least to a level comparable to that resulting from the inclusion of maritime emissions in the EU's ETS.[84] In its report, the Commission shall consider progress at the IMO level and examine whether any third-country has a market-based measure equivalent to the Directive.[85]

If the EU were to adopt legislation to increase the scope of emissions covered by the EU's ETS to more than 50 per cent of the emissions generated during voyages arriving in *and* departing from the EU, the EU's share of global emissions would be such that the replication test could not be met. If other countries were to adopt the same approach, double counting of emissions could arise. As such, the EU would stray beyond its first-level climate responsibilities into the realm of second-order climate responsibilities and, in so doing, would trigger the need to take CBDR-RC into account. This would have at least two specific implications.

First if, as is contemplated, the EU were to adopt legislation making the inclusion of a larger share of GHG emissions conditional on the question of whether a third country has a market-based measure in place that is 'equivalent' to the EU, it would be incumbent on the EU to interpret the concept of equivalence through the lens of the principle of CBDR-RC. A country's contribution to tackling climate change should be commensurate with its level of responsibility/capability. Thus, equivalence ought not require that all countries make the same contribution, but rather that each makes

[80] Directive (EU) 2023/958 of the European Parliament and of the Council amending Directive 2003/87/EC as regards aviation's contribution to the Union's economy-wide emission reduction target and the appropriate implementation of a global market-based measure [2023] OJ L130/115.

[81] ibid, Art 28(b)(1). This report is to be published by 1 July 2026. Criteria for conducting this assessment are laid down. On CORSIA, see n 20.

[82] ibid, Art 28b(3).

[83] Art 3gg(2) revised ETS Directive.

[84] ibid.

[85] ibid. It shall also assess the risk of an increase in evasive practices, including through a shift to other modes of transport or a shift of port hubs to ports outside the Union.

a contribution that is proportionate to its relative responsibility/capability. While there is no explicit commitment to differentiation in the application of equivalence in the revised ETS Directive, the introduction of this open-ended concept together with an explicit reference to CBDR-RC in the Directive's preamble, leaves space for an interpretation of this kind. Needless to say, this interpretation would lead considerable discretion in the hands of the EU.[86]

Second, in taking CBDR-RC into account in its exercise of second-order climate responsibilities, the EU should re-visit the question of how the revenues generated from the auctioning of allowances for shipping emissions under the ETS are used. This is relevant because 'the principle of CBDR-RC finds expression' in different ways, including through 'commitments to provide, and eligibility to receive, financial and technological assistance'.[87] As things stand, revenues generated through the inclusion of international shipping in the ETS will accrue both to the EU budget in the form of 'own resources' and to the Member States.[88]

While Member States have some discretion in determining the use of their revenues, they are required to use them for one of the purposes laid down in the revised ETS Directive.[89] Commendably, even at present several of the purposes listed involve expenditure which would benefit developing countries; for example 'to finance climate actions in vulnerable third countries, including the adaptation to the impacts of climate change'.[90] Even some areas of expenditure that are not specifically targeted at developing countries would not preclude revenues being spent on projects outside the EU. This is explicit in some cases, such as in relation to expenditure in developing countries that have ratified the Paris Agreement to finance measures to avoid deforestation and support the protection and restoration of peatland, forests and other land-based ecosystems or marine-based ecosystem'.[91] In others, it is simply not precluded; for example in relation to the financing of 'research and development in energy efficiency and clean technologies'.[92] Similarly, the encouragement to Member States to increase the use of EU ETS revenues to contribute to the protection, restoration and better management of marine-based ecosystems, in particular marine protected areas, given the increase in auctioning revenues due to the inclusion of maritime transport in the ETS, is not territorially confined.[93] However, none of

[86] For an insightful discussion of the issues at stake in relation to this, see L Rajamani et al, 'National Fair Shares in Reducing Greenhouse Gas Emissions within the Principled Framework of International Law' (2021) 21 *Climate Policy* 983, 999.

[87] L Rajamani, 'The Principle of Common but Differentiated Responsibilities and Respective Capabilities in the International Climate Change Regime' in R Lyster and RRM Verchick (eds), *Research Handbook on Climate Disaster Law: Barriers and Opportunities*, Research Handbooks in Climate Law (Cheltenham, Edward Elgar Publishing, 2018) 50.

[88] Recital 41 revised ETS Directive states that 'Member States' auctioning revenues will increase as a result of the inclusion of maritime transport in the EU ETS. Therefore, Member States are encouraged to increase the use of EU ETS revenues pursuant to Article 10(3) of Directive 2003/87/EC to contribute to the protection, restoration and better management of marine-based ecosystems, in particular marine protected areas'.

[89] Art 10(1) revised ETS Directive the exception of the revenues used for the compensation of indirect carbon costs referred to in Art 10a(6) of this Directive.

[90] Art 10(3)(j) revised ETS Directive. See also sub-paragraph (a).

[91] Art 10(3)(c) revised ETS Directive.

[92] Art 10(3)(g) revised ETS Directive.

[93] Recital 41 revised ETS Directive.

these positive features compels Member States to ensure that a certain portion of the revenue generated from including international shipping in the ETS accrues to developing countries in some form. If the EU were to increase its share of maritime emissions beyond 50 per cent in both directions, the taking into account of CBDR-RC would strongly militate in favour firmer commitments in this regard.

Many of these issues will be re-visited in a different context in the next section which examines the EU's most ambitious and complex global climate measure to date, namely the CBAM.

4. THE CBAM REGULATION AND CBDR-RC PRINCIPLE

4.1. Context and Key Elements of CBAM

Border carbon adjustments such as the EU's CBAM are the climate-associated version of border tax adjustments; the latter being 'fiscal measures which put into effect, in whole or in part, the destination principle, according to which taxes are paid where products are consumed and not where they are produced'.[94] Border carbon adjustments have been a popular topic in the scholarship over the past two decades,[95] and their adoption has been contemplated by a number of jurisdictions, including the EU, in connection with domestic carbon pricing mechanisms (ie carbon taxes or ETS) to address the risk of carbon leakage.[96] Carbon leakage would occur if strong ETS-based carbon prices in the EU simply lead to a shifting of emissions abroad, through the relocation of EU industries to countries with no or less stringent carbon pricing policies and/or increased EU imports of carbon-intensive products from such countries.[97] This would result in reduced carbon emissions within the EU being offset by increasing carbon emissions outside the Union, with no net emission reduction (or even an increase) at the global level, thereby undermining the goals of the Paris Agreement.

[94] I Espa, J Francois, H van Asselt, 'The EU Proposal for a Carbon Border Adjustment Mechanism (CBAM): An Analysis under WTO and Climate Change Law' (2022) 20(1) *Oil, Gas & Energy Law Intelligence* 1, 5.

[95] See inter alia A Dias, A Nosowicz and S Seeuws, 'Border Carbon Adjustments and the WTO: Hand in Hand Towards Tackling Climate Change' (2020) 15 *Global Trade and Customs Journal* 15; R Eckersley, 'The Politics of Carbon Leakage and the Fairness of Border Measures' (2010) 24 *Ethics & International Affairs* 367; SD Ladly, 'Border Carbon Adjustments, WTO Law and the Principle of Common But Differentiated Responsibilities' (2012) 12 *International Environmental Agreements: Politics, Law and Economics* 63; M Mehling, H van Asselt, K Das, S Droege and C Verjuikl, 'Designing Border Carbon Adjustments for Enhanced Climate Action' (2019) 113 *American Journal of International Law* 433; T Meyer and TN Tucker, 'A Pragmatic Approach to Carbon Border Measures' (2022) 21 *World Trade Review* 109; J Pauwelyn, 'Carbon Leakage Measures and Border Tax Adjustments under WTO Law' in D Prévost and G Van Calster (eds), *Research Handbook on Environment, Health and the WTO*, Research Handbooks on the WTO (Cheltenham, Edward Elgar Publishing, 2012); S Sato, 'EU's Carbon Adjustment Mechanism: Will It Achieve Its Objective(s)?' (2022) 56 *Journal of World Trade* 383.

[96] For an overview of earlier proposals and CBAM legislative history, see Espa, Francois and van Asselt (n 94) 7–10; Mehling et al (n 95) 448–456.

[97] As acknowledged by European Commission itself, evidence on carbon leakage risks is mixed: CBAM Impact Assessment, 7 and Annex 11. See also K Kulovesi, 'EU Emissions Trading Scheme: Preventing Carbon Leakage Before and After the Paris Agreement' in R Leal-Arcas and J Wouters (eds), *Research Handbook on EU Energy Law and Policy*, Research Handbooks in European Law (Cheltenham, Edward Elgar Publishing, 2017) 420–421; Mehling et al (n 95) 444–446; Sato (n 95) 386–390.

In fact, concerns about carbon leakage need to be placed within the increasingly heterogenous carbon prices and other climate policies across jurisdictions stemming from the bottom-up approach to mitigation under the Paris Agreement based on self-determination and self-differentiation.[98]

It is within this context that the adoption of the CBAM Regulation in May 2023 should be understood. The Union is the first jurisdiction worldwide to extend the carbon price paid by domestic EU producers (as determined by the auctioning of emission allowances under its ETS) to emissions that are generated outside its borders but are embedded into its imports of carbon-intensive commodities. The CBAM is thus a trade-related alternative to the free allocation of emission allowances under the EU's ETS, which has been thus far used to mitigate carbon leakage risks and which levels *down* carbon prices for domestic carbon-intensive and trade-exposed industries. This free allocation method, however, has been widely criticised as ineffective from an environmental standpoint for muting the price signal for the heaviest domestic polluters and thereby damping the incentive to invest in low-carbon production.[99] By contrast, the CBAM seeks to level *up* carbon prices for imported carbon-intensive products while maintaining their full application on EU domestic firms. In this respect, it constitutes a better environmental alternative in that it allows the EU to increase its climate ambition and impose strong carbon prices on domestic enterprises while at the same time avoiding carbon leakage.[100]

The EU thus presents the CBAM primarily as a global climate measure linked to a tightening of the ETS through the gradual phased-out of free emission allowances,[101] with its overarching objective being 'to prevent the risk of carbon leakage, thereby reducing global carbon emissions and supporting the goals of the Paris Agreement'.[102] However, as was noted in the introduction, this climate-informed objective is closely intertwined with economic competitiveness concerns about a 'level playing field' between EU and third-country producers in the absence of an internationally-agreed uniform carbon price.[103] Evidently, there is an in-built economic rationale behind the carbon price equalisation logic underlying the CBAM, since the risk of carbon leakage materialises only when competitiveness concerns are not adequately addressed in the country that is imposing ambitious carbon pricing policies.[104] In other words, these climate and industrial narratives can be reconciled, at least for the EU, insofar as the CBAM is designed to ensure nothing more than

[98] Arts 4.1–4.3 Paris Agreement, and further discussion in Section 4.2.

[99] Preamble, Recitals 11-12 and Art 1(3) CBAM Regulation. For discussion, see Kulovesi (n 97).

[100] Espa, Francois and van Asselt (n 94) 6.

[101] Arts 1(3) and 31 CBAM Regulation, providing that as free allowances are expected to be gradually phased out under the revised ETS by 2034, the CBAM would be phased-in as an alternative mechanism to address carbon leakage risks.

[102] Art 1(1) CBAM Regulation.

[103] Preamble, Recital 29 CBAM Proposal, referring to 'the objective of ensuring that imports of energy intensive products into the Union are on equal footing with EU products in terms of EU ETS carbon pricing'. This reference has been removed from the adopted CBAM Regulation.

[104] Espa, Francois and van Asselt (n 94) 6. For a critical discussion of these 'Paris Agreement', 'climate leadership' and 'fair competition' narratives underlying the CBAM, see further A Pirlot, 'Carbon Border Adjustment Measures: A Straightforward Multi-Purpose Climate Change Instrument?' (2022) 34 *Journal of Environmental Law* 25, 28–35.

equalisation of carbon prices for domestic and imported products in sectors exposed to carbon leakage.

Following this carbon price equalisation logic, the CBAM (once it fully enters into force)[105] will extend the ETS-determined carbon price to emissions embodied in EU imports of carbon-intensive commodities in six sectors at 'significant risk of carbon leakage': aluminium, cement, iron and steel, fertilizers, electricity and hydrogen.[106] As of 1 January 2026, EU importers of these products would have to: (i) apply for the status of 'authorised CBAM declarant' with the competent authorities of the EU Member States where they are established and be included in the CBAM Registry;[107] (ii) submit a 'CBAM declaration' by 31 May of each year with the total (direct and indirect) emissions embedded in their imports of covered goods,[108] as verified by accredited verifiers;[109] and (iii) buy and surrender sufficient 'CBAM certificates' (whose price mirrors the weekly average price under the EU ETS) via their account in the CBAM Registry to cover these emissions.[110] However, and in line with the equalisation logic, special provisions are made for crediting explicit carbon pricing policies in trading partners, through two mechanisms: (i) the 'EU-led climate club exemption', which fully exempts from the CBAM's application imports from countries that are fully integrated into the EU ETS, or have an ETS fully linked to the EU one;[111] and (ii) the 'CBAM discount', which provides for a reduction in the number of required CBAM certificates to take account of any carbon price paid in the country of production.[112]

To further contextualise our CBDR-RC discussion in the next section, it is important to highlight that the CBAM is expected to have an uneven impact across the EU's trading partners, depending on how much of the targeted products they export to the EU and whether or not they have carbon pricing policies in place. Moreover, even within the top-twenty exporters of the covered goods, the CBAM will affect a widely heterogenous range of countries in terms of their development levels, ranging from 'developed' countries (notably Russia, Ukraine and Turkey), to 'developing' countries (including the BASIC countries, Brazil, China and India), and also several LDCs and SIDS. For instance, BASIC countries, which have voiced fierce opposition to the CBAM, feature among the top exporters for specific sectors, notably: aluminium (China and India) and iron/steel (China, Brazil and India). LDCs and SIDS generally account for a smaller share of EU imports of the targeted products, but the CBAM's impact on these countries is estimated to be considerable given the relative importance of such exports for their economies. For instance, in 2020, Mozambique was the sixth largest exporter of aluminium (accounting for nearly 7 per cent of its gross

[105] Art 32 CBAM Regulation, whereby for a transition period until December 2025, importers of covered goods will be mainly subject to reporting obligations.

[106] ibid Art 2(1).

[107] ibid Arts 4–5, 14 and 16.

[108] ibid Art 3 (21)–(22) and (34).

[109] ibid Arts 6–8.

[110] ibid Arts 20-22.

[111] ibid Art 2(4) and (6). At present, these are: Iceland, Liechtenstein, Norway (already part of the EU ETS) and Switzerland (whose ETS is linked to the EU one).

[112] ibid Art 9.

domestic product) and, in that same year, Trinidad and Tobago was the fourth largest exporter of fertilisers to the EU.[113] Furthermore, the European Commission has acknowledged that compliance costs are likely to be higher in these countries when compared to other trading partners, given their lower capacity to both decarbonise production processes as well as to measure and verify the carbon intensity of products exported to the EU.[114]

4.2. Respecting CBDR-RC?

Drawing on the framework developed in Section 2.3, in the CBAM context, the Union is clearly exercising second-order climate responsibilities, since the GHG emissions embedded in EU imports of CBAM-covered goods fall within the primary jurisdiction and responsibility of a different State pursuant to the territorial approach in the IPCC Guidelines.[115] In stepping in, contingently, to regulate these emissions, with a view to inducing the third State concerned to fulfil its first-order climate responsibilities, the EU ought to take the principle of CBDR-RC into account. Hence, unlike in the international shipping context, there is no system gap boundary for emissions from CBAM-covered sectors and the replication test is not applicable here. Instead, guidance on how to integrate CBDR-RC into the CBAM should be sought in the UNFCCC and Paris Agreement, which establish the multilateral framework for regulating emissions from CBMA-covered sectors. However, for the reasons explained in Section 2.2, the abstract articulation of the CBDR-RC principle in Articles 3.1 UNFCCC and 2.2 Paris Agreement does not help us in determining which specific kinds of differentiation ought to be introduced into the CBAM. A more adequate benchmark are the mitigation provisions in these agreements, which are of direct relevance to the CBAM as a carbon-reduction measure, and which implement in more precise terms the CBDR-RC principle through a set of differentiated obligations among State Parties. Given that these substantive commitments are conventional norms that are legally-binding on the EU,[116] our position is that the CBAM can only be in spirit with the CBDR-RC if it does *not* (unilaterally) undercut the differentiation balance (multilaterally) established in the mitigation pillar of the (currently applicable) Paris Agreement.[117]

It is rather odd for a measure that is purposely aimed at achieving the Paris Agreement's goals that the CBAM Regulation makes no explicit reference to the CBDR-RC principle. It does nonetheless acknowledge it implicitly, by justifying the

[113] CBAM Impact Assessment, Annex 3, 20-21; Annex 10, 100–1.

[114] ibid, 21. With a focus on African countries, see also E Gergondet, 'The European Union's Proposed Carbon Border Adjustment Mechanism and its Impact on Trade with Africa' (2021) 16 *Global Trade and Customs Journal* 564, 567–570.

[115] Volume 2 ('Energy') and Volume 3 ('Industrial Processes and Product Use') of the 2006 IPCC Guidelines for National Greenhouse Gas Inventories (n 28).

[116] Albeit the legal character or strength does vary across individual provisions: see generally D Bodansky, 'The Legal Character of the Paris Agreement' (2016) 25 *Review of European, Comparative & International Environmental Law* 142.

[117] On this point, see further Marín Durán (n 50) 81–84.

CBAM as a tool to enable the EU to 'continue playing a leading role in global climate action'.[118] To the extent that the prospect of carbon leakage is genuine, it is true that the CBDR-RC principle places the EU in a dilemma. On the one hand, the EU is called upon to meet its first-order climate responsibilities and increase its own mitigation efforts (*in casu*, by phasing-out ETS free emission allowances), but it is hard to see why and how the EU should lead in this manner if it would simply result in a shifting of carbon emissions abroad. On the other hand, the EU should consider the CBDR-RC principle when exercising second-order climate responsibilities through the CBAM and recognise that not all countries are to contribute in equal measure to the common goal of mitigating climate change, in view of their differentiated responsibilities and capabilities. The preceding Commission legislative proposal goes some way in recognising this,[119] but maintains the CBAM respects the CBDRC-RC principle without need for any form of differentiation. In what follows, we appraise the Commission's position against the CBDR-RC principle as operationalised in the mitigation provisions of the Paris Agreement.

The Commission's main reason as to why the CBAM respects the CBDR-RC principle is that it has been 'designed in such a manner that it does not directly depend on the *overall level of ambition* of a country nor on the *policy choices* made by a country'.[120] This statement is partly correct,[121] if we consider emission reduction targets as the most obvious quantitative indicator of each Party's overall level of climate ambition under the Paris Agreement. In this regard, the EU's emission reduction target is *economy-wide*,[122] whereas the CBAM would only apply to selected sectors and only insofar as the foreign products are exported to the EU.[123] Hence, the CBAM would not harmonise emission reduction targets between the EU and the exporting countries through the backdoor. But this should not mask the fact that, for *particular* sectors/products, the CBAM is clearly aimed at incentivising (or arguably, forcing) a reduction of carbon emissions in exporting countries. So, the question is whether this emission-reduction effect of the CBAM defies the balance of differentiated obligations on mitigation under the Paris Agreement. As elaborated below, we believe this is the case to some extent.

In broad terms, an exemption from the CBAM for *all* developing (non-Annex I) countries no longer appears justifiable on CBDR-RC grounds under the Paris Agreement, as it was at the time of the Kyoto Protocol when developing countries were not be expected to reduce GHG emissions at all.[124] By contrast, the Paris

[118] Preamble, Recital 8 CBAM Regulation.

[119] CBAM Proposal, 1; see also CBAM Impact Assessment, 4.

[120] CBAM Impact Assessment, 8 (emphasis added).

[121] The claim regarding 'policy choices' is simply incorrect, given the nature of the CBAM as carbon price equalisation measure, which undercuts the substantial flexibility provided in the Paris Agreement with regards to the choice of means to pursue decarbonisation. For further discussion, see Marín Durán (n 50) 89; and Pirlot (n 104) 33.

[122] See 'Nationally Determined Contributions Registry' (*United Nations Framework Convention on Climate Change*), www.unfccc.int/NDCREG.

[123] Note that, in these sectors, the ETS applies instead to all domestic production (whether domestically consumed or exported) and emissions are also subject to an EU-wide cap that decreases every year through a linear reduction factor: para 11 revised ETS Directive.

[124] See Marín Durán (n 50) 85–86. This point is independent of more pragmatic considerations relating to the risk of carbon leakage.

Agreement does not allocate an exclusive responsibility for reducing GHG emissions to developed countries (or Annex I countries). Instead, in order to achieve the agreement's temperature goals, *all* Parties are committed to 'reach global peaking of [GHG] emissions as soon as possible, recognizing that peaking will take longer for developing country Parties, and to undertake rapid reductions thereafter … so as to achieve a balance between anthropogenic emissions by sources and removals by sinks of [GHGs by 2050]'.[125] More specifically, the Paris Agreement embraces a bounded self-differentiation model to mitigation commitments,[126] which imposes a binding obligation of conduct on each Party to 'prepare, communicate and maintain nationally determined contributions (NDCs) that it intends to achieve', coupled with strong normative expectations on 'progression' and 'highest possible ambition' for each successive NDC, 'in light of different national circumstances'.[127]

Within this global mitigation trajectory, the Paris Agreement still assigns a leadership role to developed countries by undertaking economy-wide absolute reduction targets, but 'developing countries should continue enhancing their mitigation efforts, and are encouraged to move over time towards economy-wide emission reduction or limitation targets in the light of different national circumstances'.[128] Such a normative expectation has been met in practice with several developing countries committing to economy-wide reduction or limitation targets, including the BASIC countries.[129] However, there are two important qualifications to this general proposition which, contrary to what the Commission claims, do call for introducing specific forms of differentiation in the CBAM.

The first relates to developing countries and stems from Article 4.5 Paris Agreement, which clearly requires ('shall') developed countries to provide financial support to developing countries to assist their mitigation efforts, 'recognizing that *enhanced support* for developing country Parties will allow for *higher ambition in their actions*'.[130] The Paris differentiation balance thus reflects a critical understanding of the relationship between greater overall ambition with developing countries assuming responsibility for lowering carbon emissions (which the CBAM encourages), on the one hand, and increased financial resources by developed countries to

[125] Art 4.1 Paris Agreement.

[126] Rajamani (n 11) 509, rightly noting that the 'Paris Agreement operationalises the CBDRRC principle not by tailoring commitments to categories of Parties as the UNFCCC and the Kyoto Protocol do, but by tailoring differentiation to the specificities of each of the Durban pillars – mitigation, adaptation, finance, technology, capacity-building and transparency'.

[127] Arts 4.2 and 4.3 Paris Agreement; see further Rajamani (n 11) 500–501; Voigt and Ferreira (n 11) 295–297.

[128] Art 4.4 Paris Agreement.

[129] For instance, in its second update NDC (April 2022), Brazil commits to an absolute economy-wide reduction in emissions by 37 per cent below 2005 levels in 2025, and by 50 per cent below 2005 levels in 2030. China, in its first updated NDC (October 2021), commits to emission-peaking before 2030, an emission-reduction target of 65 per cent below 2005 levels by 2030 and achieving carbon neutrality before 2060. India, in its first NDC (October 2016, not updated), commits to reduce the emission intensity of its GDP by 33 to 35 per cent from 2005 levels by 2030. South Africa, in its updated NDC (September 2021), commits to economy-wide emission limitation targets for 2025 and 2030. All NDCs are available at: 'Nationally Determined Contributions Registry' (*United Nations Framework Convention on Climate Change*), www.unfccc.int/NDCREG. See also, Rajamani et al (n 86) 1000.

[130] Art 4.5 Paris Agreement (emphasis added), read in conjunction with Art 9 Paris Agreement.

support such mitigation efforts, on the other hand (which the CBAM ignores).[131] From this perspective, both the CBAM Regulation and the earlier Commission legislative proposal are disappointing and strikingly silent on the use of revenue generated through the sale of CBAM certificates. They just contain preambular provisions declaring that the Union:

> is committed to working with and supporting [including through financial assistance] low and middle-income third countries towards the decarbonisation of their manufacturing industries as part of the external dimension of the European Green Deal and in line with the Paris Agreement … The Union is working towards introducing a new own resource based on the revenues generated by the sale of CBAM certificates.[132]

But there are no firmer commitments or guidance on revenue use in their operative texts. In line with the Paris burden-sharing arrangements, CBAM-generated revenue ought to be recycled back to affected developing countries to support their own decarbonisation efforts.[133]

The second form of differentiation concerns LDCs and SIDS, whose specific situation is acknowledged in the mitigation and other provisions of the Paris Agreement.[134] Of most relevance is Article 4.6, which provides that these countries '*may* prepare and communicate strategies, plans and actions for low greenhouse gas emissions development reflecting their special circumstances'.[135] This provision follows those applicable to all Parties seen above, and its permissive character is clearly significant. It differentiates LDCs/SIDS from all other Parties (including other developing countries), in that these countries can – but are under no obligation to – undertake emission-reduction action. This special treatment of LDCs/SIDs reflects the fact that they bear the least (historical and current) responsibility for the climate emergency (ie, presently accounting for only 7 per cent of global GHG emissions) and have the least capacity to adapt to new climate conditions,[136] thus being the most vulnerable countries to the adverse effects of climate change. Insofar as the EU's CBAM would incentivise (or arguably, pressure) producers in LDCs/SIDS to lower carbon emissions, it is out of step with the CBRDDC principle as operationalised in Article 4.6 Paris Agreement.

The EU, however, has rejected from the start the possibility of an LDCs/SIDS exemption on grounds that it would run counter the overarching objective of the CBAM by encouraging a growth of emissions in these countries and be counterproductive in potentially locking them into high-carbon development paths.[137] The first

[131] Rajamani (n 11) 494.

[132] Preamble, Recital 55 CBAM Proposal.

[133] Similarly, see Mehling et al (n 95) 478–479; Pirlot (n 104) 45; UNCTAD, 'A European Union Carbon Border Adjustment Mechanism: Implications for Developing Countries' (*United Nations Conference on Trade and Development*, 2021), www.unctad.org/system/files/official-document/osginf2021d2_en.pdf, 24.

[134] See also Arts 9(4), 9(9), 11(1) and 13(3) Paris Agreement.

[135] Emphasis added.

[136] UNDP, 'The State of Climate Ambition – Global Outlook Report 2021' (*United Nations Development Programme*, October 2021), www.undp.org/sites/g/files/zskgke326/files/2021-11/UNDP-NDC-Global-Outlook-Report-2021-The-State-of-Climate-Ambition.pdf, 13.

[137] CBAM Impact Assessment, 30.

concern is an overstatement, given that the risk of carbon leakage associated with LDCs/SIDS has been estimated to be negligible,[138] while the second argument is not entirely misplaced. However, as seen above, the Paris differentiation balance does give LDCs/SIDS full discretion ('may') as to whether they embrace the decarbonisation of energy-intensive industries in light of their special circumstances –and ultimately, this autonomous choice ought to be respected by the EU when designing the CBAM in spirit with the CBDR-RC principle.

To sum up, contrary to what the Commission claims, the EU's CBAM as presently designed is *not* compatible with the CBDR-RC principle as given effect in the mitigation provisions of the Paris Agreement. To be brought in spirit with this principle, the CBAM needs to be adjusted through two kinds of differentiation: (i) an LDCs/SIDS exemption (based on Article 4.6 Paris Agreement) and (ii) a revenue-recycling provision applicable to imports originating in developing countries (based on Article 4.5 Paris Agreement).

5. CONCLUSIONS

This chapter has appraised global EU climate action, as manifested in two recent trade-related climate measures, from the point of view of the principle of CBDR-RC and has made four key points.

First, it has argued that the CBDR-RC principle is legally relevant to these EU measures and has clarified when it should be taken into consideration by the Union. Second, the chapter has found that, overall, the EU has acted consistently with the CBDR-RC principle when exercising first-order climate responsibilities. In relation to international shipping, this is because the EU has filled a system boundary gap left by the UNFCCC regime and because in the design of the revised ETS Directive, the 'replication' test elaborated by Scott has been met. This test has been met because if other countries were to adopt the same approach as the EU, no double counting of carbon emissions would arise. In relation to the CBAM, this is because it arguably enables the EU to fulfil its leadership role in the global battle against climate change called by the CBDR-RC principle, by increasing its ambition through the phasing-out of (environmentally inefficient) free emission allowances under the ETS while avoiding carbon leakage risks.

Third, and conversely, the chapter has argued that the EU has not acted consistently with the principle of CBDR-RC when exercising second-order climate responsibilities in the CBAM context. In view of this, it has proposed two adjustments to the design of the measure to bring it in line with this principle. The first is the introduction of a full exemption from the CBAM's application for LDCs and SIDS in order to duly recognise their special status under Article 4.6 Paris Agreement. In addition, the EU must ensure that CBAM-generated revenue is used to support decarbonisation efforts in other affected developing countries, pursuant to its obligation under Article 4.5 Paris Agreement.

[138] Mehling et al (n 95) 475; UNCTAD (n 133).

Fourth, and finally, the chapter has observed that while the EU has not yet exercised second-order climate responsibilities in the ETS/international shipping context, if it were to do so in the future, specific forms of differentiation would need to be introduced in relation to emissions that fall within the purview of the first-order climate responsibilities of non-EU Member States. This would arise, for example, if the EU were to include more than 50 per cent of the emissions generated during voyages starting and ending in the EU. In this situation, in evaluating the 'equivalence' of third-country measures in the shipping sector, the principle of CBDR-RC ought to be considered. In keeping with this, a country's contribution to tackling the climate change impacts of shipping should be differentiated in accordance with that country's relative degree of responsibility/capability.

Environmental Information and 'External Pressure': Assessing EU Compliance with its International Obligations under the Aarhus Convention

PÄIVI LEINO-SANDBERG*

1. INTRODUCTION

SHOULD THE QUESTION of the EU's compliance with its international obligations be subject to public scrutiny and debate? Based on an empirical analysis of the thinking of the Council and the Commission presented in this Chapter, the EU institutions seem to take it for granted that transparency and public debate harm the EU interest in international relations. I suggest that this presumption should be reconsidered – there are situations where in fact the opposite may be true.

Under Article 216(2) Treaty on the Functioning of the European Union (TFEU) 'Agreements concluded by the Union are binding upon the institutions of the Union and on its Member States', and as the Court established already in *Haegeman* – something that Marise taught me in London in 2000–2001 – the provisions of such agreements 'form an integral part of Community law'.[1] International agreements concluded by the EU thus 'bind its institutions and consequently prevail over acts of secondary EU legislation'.[2] The EU Treaties establish a specific objective for the EU's external action to contribute to the 'respect for the principles of the United Nations Charter and international law'[3] and under Article 3(5) Treaty on European Union (TEU), the EU is also to contribute to the strict observance and the development of international law, even if the relevance of Article 3(5) TEU continues to be debated.[4] The Court has further specified that the EU is 'bound to observe international law in

* Professor of Transnational European Law, University of Helsinki. This chapter is written in the context of the Academy of Finland Strategic Research Council consortium project 2035Legitimacy. I am grateful to Laurens Ankersmit, Sebastian Bechtel, Christina Eckes and Joanne Scott for comments on an earlier draft, and to Onno Brouwer and Anne Friel for many discussions around the theme.

[1] Case 181/73 *Haegeman v Belgian State* ECLI:EU:C:1974:41, [1974] ECR 449, para 5.

[2] Case C-308/06 *Intertanko and Others* ECLI:EU:C:2008:312, [2008] ECR I-4057, para 42.

[3] Art 21(1) Consolidated version of the Treaty on European Union (TEU) [2016] OJ C202/13.

[4] R Dunbar, 'Article 3(5) TEU a Decade On: Revisiting "Strict Observance of International Law" in the Text and Context of Other EU Values' (2021) 28 *Maastricht Journal of European and Comparative Law* 479.

its entirety … which is binding upon the institutions of the European Union'[5] and that 'Treaty obligations must be performed in good faith, which nevertheless constitutes a binding principle of general international law applicable to subjects of that law who are contracting parties to a treaty'.[6] It is thus clear that the EU needs to comply with international law in general and its own international commitments specifically. Yet, the approach of the EU courts in admitting international law into the EU's legal order is not exactly *völkerrechtsfreundlich* as Jan Klabbers has pointed out,[7] and it remains understudied how these general principles turn into institutional action.

One context where EU's compliance has proved particularly tricky is that of the United Nations Economic Commission for Europe (UNECE) Convention on Access to Information, Public Participation in Decision-Making and Access to Justice in Environmental Matters (the Aarhus Convention). The Convention builds on three pillars: the *rights of access to information*, *public participation* in decision-making, and *access to justice* in environmental matters.[8] It is a mixed agreement that the EU approved in 2005,[9] and thus consented to be bound by its provisions.[10] The provisions of the Aarhus Convention dealing with access to environmental information were subsequently implemented in EU law and made applicable to Union institutions and bodies through the Aarhus Regulation.[11] Its Article 3 [further] directs requests for access to environmental information held by Community institutions and bodies to be decided under Regulation No 1049/2001. Regulation No 1049/2001 and the Aarhus Regulation, and thus also the Aarhus Convention, are intended to be read consistently.[12] Since then, the Aarhus Convention Compliance Committee (ACCC) has found that the EU has failed to properly implement Articles 9(3) and 9(4) of the Convention concerning access to justice by members of the public.[13] According to the ACCC, compliance with these obligations was not secured by the Aarhus Regulation, the preliminary reference procedure or by existing jurisprudence of the Court of Justice of the European Union (CJEU) on Article 263 TFEU.

[5] Case C-366/10 *Air Transport Association of America and Others* ECLI:EU:C:2011:864, para 101.

[6] Case C-104/16 P *Council v Front Polisario* ECLI:EU:C:2016:973, para 124.

[7] J Klabbers, 'Straddling the Fence: The EU and International Law' in A Arnull and D Chalmers (eds), *The Oxford Handbook of European Union Law* (Oxford, Oxford University Press, 2015) 63.

[8] Art 1 Convention on Access to Information, Public Participation in Decision-Making and Access to Justice in Environmental Matters (Aarhus, 25 June 1998) (Aarhus Convention).

[9] Council Decision 2005/370/EC on the conclusion, on behalf of the European Community, of the Convention on access to information, public participation in decision-making and access to justice in environmental matters [2006] OJ L124/1.

[10] Art 216(2) Consolidated version of the Treaty on the Functioning of the European Union (TFEU) [2016] OJ C202/47. See also Arts 2(1)(b) and 14 Vienna Convention on the Law of Treaties (Vienna, 23 May 1969) (VCLT), generally understood as an expression of customary international law.

[11] Regulation (EC) No 1367/2006 of the European Parliament and of the Council on the application of the provisions of the Aarhus Convention on Access to Information, Public Participation in Decision-making and Access to Justice in Environmental Matters to Community institutions and bodies (Aarhus Regulation) [2006] OJ L264/13.

[12] Recital 15 of the Aarhus Regulation makes clear that '[w]here Regulation (EC) No 1049/2001 provides for exceptions, these should apply subject to any more specific provisions in this Regulation concerning requests for environmental information'.

[13] On this, see I Hadjiyianni, 'Judicial Protection and the Environment in the EU Legal Order: Missing Pieces for a Complete Puzzle of Legal Remedies' (2021) 58 *CML Rev* 777; I Hadjiyianni, 'Multi-Level Governance in Action: Access to Justice in Light of the Aarhus Convention and its Implementation in the EU Legal Order' (2020) 26 *European Public Law* 889.

Limited access to EU Courts is a well-known fact. While some adjustments (considered insufficient by the ACCC) were made in the Treaty of Lisbon, opening the Treaties has been excluded – even if is a basic point of international law that 'a party may not invoke the provisions of its internal law as justification for its failure to perform a treaty'.[14] This has over the years led to widespread concern among non-governmental organisations (NGOs) and also legal academics, many of whom joined in a call on the institutions to bring the EU's compliance with the Aarhus Convention in line with its international obligations.[15] Over the years, the EU has been accused of not taking its procedural human rights obligations under the Aarhus Convention seriously.[16] This is problematic, keeping in mind its ambition to 'lead by example'.[17] At the same time, the European Court of Justice (ECJ) has insisted that the Aarhus Convention cannot 'have primacy over EU primary law, with the result that derogation from the fourth paragraph of Article 263 TFEU cannot be accepted on the basis of that agreement'.[18] Furthermore, individuals cannot rely directly on Article 9(3) of the Aarhus Convention before the EU Courts,[19] as the Article does not, according to the Court, 'contain any unconditional and sufficiently precise obligation capable of directly regulating the legal position of individuals' and is 'subject, in its implementation or effects, to the adoption of a subsequent measure'.[20] Therefore, the EU's compliance is dependent on the Aarhus Regulation. The 2021 reform of the Aarhus Regulation introduced a mechanism of administrative review by means of secondary legislation, which is also a possible way of redress approved by the Convention.[21] While the problem regarding access to justice has thus been recently addressed – even if not necessarily satisfactorily solved[22] – the negotiation process highlighted other problematic aspects in EU compliance that have so far received less attention as regards access to environmental information and participatory rights, which both are core rights secured under the same Convention.

[14] Art 27 VCLT.

[15] 'Aarhus Convention – The EU Urged to Stop Violating International Rules' (*The Good Lobby*, 14 April 2021), www.thegoodlobby.eu/the-legal-community-urges-the-eu-to-stop-violating-international-rules-on-access-to-justice-in-environmental-matters/.

[16] O Kelleher, 'Systemic Climate Change Litigation, Standing Rules and the Aarhus Convention: A Purposive Approach' (2022) 34 *Journal of Environmental Law* 107.

[17] See A Cassese et al, 'Leading by Example: A Human Rights Agenda for the European Union for the Year 2000 – Agenda of the Comité des Sages and Final Project Report' (European University Institute 1998). This was a core theme of my doctoral thesis 'Universality as Particularity: The Politics of Human Rights in the European Union' (PhD, University of Helsinki 2005). Marise acted as the faculty opponent during the public defence.

[18] Case T-600/15 *PAN Europe and Others v Commission* ECLI:EU:T:2016:601, para 56.

[19] ibid para 59.

[20] See Case C-240/09 *Lesoochranárske zoskupenie* ECLI:EU:C:2011:125, [2011] ECR I-1255, para 45 and Joined Cases C-402/12 P to C-403/12 P *Council and Others v Vereniging Milieudefensie and Stichting Stop Luchtverontreiniging Utrecht* ECLI:EU:C:2015:4, para 55.

[21] See Art 9 of the Aarhus Convention: 'The provisions of this paragraph 2 shall not exclude the possibility of a preliminary review procedure before an administrative authority and shall not affect the requirement of exhaustion of administrative review procedures prior to recourse to judicial review procedures, where such a requirement exists under national law'.

[22] See eg GC Leonelli, 'Access to the EU Courts in Environmental and Public Health Cases and the Reform of the Aarhus Regulation: Systemic Vision, Pragmatism, and a Happy Ending' (2021) 40 *Yearbook of European Law* 230; A Hough, 'Final Report: Analysis of the Revised Proposal to Amend the Aarhus Regulation Agreed 12.07.21' (*Environmental Justice Network Ireland*, September 2021), www.ejni.net/wp-content/uploads/2021/09/AJO-Final-Report.pdf.

The Aarhus Convention stands out from many other international settings because of its objectives and the way they have been integrated into the working arrangements of the regime, which provides publicly accessible and inclusive processes that enable and encourage participation by non-state actors. This is the direct opposite of the traditional foreign policy paradigm that I have described in my earlier writings.[23] As I described in a book chapter included in Marise's *Structural Principles of EU External Relations Law*, a new more transparent paradigm has, however, been slowly breaking in the context of agreements relating to data protection (the Society for Worldwide Interbank Financial Telecommunications (SWIFT)) and broad regulatory agreements such as the Transatlantic Trade and Investment Partnership (TTIP) and the Anti-Counterfeiting Trade Agreement (ACTA) that have a direct impact on individuals and their rights. In cases brought by academics, NGOs and Members of the European Parliament (MEPs), the Court has had the opportunity to address the appropriate limits of secrecy in external relations. Also, the Ombudsman has taken an active role in the discussions, following which the Commission has agreed to more proactive disclosure policies, for example, as regards its recommendations for negotiating directives. For the Commission, this allows the public 'to have a better informed view and to discuss issues of interest and concern right from the start of preparations for a negotiation'.[24] As Marise has observed, the release of information on the TTIP is remarkable, and has signalled a new approach to transparency in trade negotiations;[25] the publication of the EU's positions at different stages of elaboration and thinking, together with openness to consultation and debate, helps to fill a gap which is becoming evident as international agreements are increasingly quasi-legislative in nature.[26] However, it is equally evident that rights of public access and participation in

> the democratic life of the Union is coming under increasing pressure as a result of the increased scope of the EU's international activities. More and more documents that concern citizens' daily lives potentially fall within the scope of the international relations exception.[27]

These discussions have, however, been limited to negotiations for new agreements. But how about existing agreements and compliance with them?

In this chapter, I describe how the EU institutions 'think' about the need for secrecy in external relations and the participation of civil society in such discussions, and how this thinking affects the legal argumentation that they use. I mirror this argumentation against the objectives of the Aarhus Convention and EU Treaties that

[23] P Leino-Sandberg, 'The Principle of Transparency in EU External Relations Law: Does Diplomatic Secrecy Stand a Chance of Surviving the Age of Twitter?' in M Cremona (ed), *Structural Principles in EU External Relations Law* (Oxford, Hart Publishing, 2018) 202. See also P Leino-Sandberg, 'Secrecy, Efficiency, Transparency in EU Negotiations: Conflicting Paradigms?' (2017) 5 *Politics and Governance* 6.

[24] European Commission, 'Factsheet on the Transparency Policy in DG Trade', circabc.europa.eu/ui/group/7fc51410-46a1-4871-8979-20cce8df0896/library/ebae888d-6243-48a2-a766-e21923793a71/details.

[25] M Cremona, 'Guest Editorial: Negotiating the Transatlantic Trade and Investment Partnership (TTIP)' (2015) 52 *CML Rev* 351, 361.

[26] ibid 362.

[27] L Ankersmit and J Peters, 'Public Access to Documents in EU External Relations' (2022) *Amsterdam Law School Legal Studies Research Paper* 2022-08/*Amsterdam Centre for European Law and Governance Research Paper* 2022–02, 3.

opt for a model of participatory democracy where civil society participation on the substance of legislative processes forms the essence of what democratic participation is about.[28] I was particularly interested in institutional legal opinions (and other less formal legal analyses) and their impact on the outcome, against the background of my earlier work on legal services[29] and an ongoing research project relating to public access to environmental information and participatory rights in the EU.[30] My past research had shown that legal advice is hardly ever proactively disclosed by the institutions. Requesting access and appealing negative decisions seldom makes much of a difference.[31] Thus, I was eager to find out how the question of EU compliance with its various obligations under the Aarhus Convention had been assessed and prepared on the EU side. With that in mind, I submitted a request for the analyses of the legal services of the Commission and the Council since the EU joined the Convention.[32] Their responses provided the empirical evidence for my investigation into the institutional thinking in the EU.

In this chapter, I first describe the story of EU compliance with Aarhus and then discuss the relationship between the EU's international commitments under the Aarhus Convention and its internal law-making procedures from the perspective of EU's transparency law, which emphasises transparency in legislative procedures. The earlier case law on external relations suggests that what in particular merits protection is the EU's strategic objectives or elements of the negotiations – but what exactly are the strategic considerations that can be protected under Regulation No 1049/2001 and should they be protected? Finally, the Council justified non-disclosure with the risk of 'external pressure' by civil society, indicating that the institutions should be protected from their 'interference'. What is the role of civil society and legal academia in conducting a public debate about the way in which the EU complies with its international obligations? Is this not the core of what Aarhus was supposed to be about?

In the next section, I describe my empirical enquiry into how the legal services of the Council and the Commission have analysed the EU's compliance with its Aarhus obligations.

2. MY EMPIRICAL ENQUIRY: ASSESSING AARHUS COMPLIANCE

Regulation No 1049/2001 provides the principles, conditions and limits governing the right of access to documents held by the EU institutions. While '[i]n principle, all

[28] P Leino-Sandberg, 'Disruptive Democracy: Keeping EU Citizens in a Box' in I Govaere, S Garben and P Nemitz (eds), *Critical Reflections on Constitutional Democracy in the European Union*, Modern Studies in European Law 94 (Oxford, Hart Publishing, 2019) 295.

[29] P Leino-Sandberg, *The Politics of Legal Expertise in EU Policy Making*, Cambridge Studies in European Law and Policy (Cambridge, Cambridge University Press, 2021) ch 4.

[30] 'Issues Related to Justice of Climate Policies' (2035Legitimacy), www.2035legitimacy.fi/about-the-project/.

[31] See Leino-Sandberg (n 29) ch 4.

[32] On the research ethical questions relating to my involvement in transparency cases, see P Leino-Sandberg, 'Transparency as a Critical Research Agenda: Engaging with the EU Institutions on Access to Documents' in M Hillebrandt, P Leino-Sandberg and I Koivisto (eds), *(In)visible European Government: Critical Approaches to Transparency as an Ideal and a Practice*, Routledge/UACES Contemporary European Studies (Abingdon, Routledge, 2023).

documents of the institutions should be accessible to the public', it also contains limited exceptions, and several of them come to play in the context of this matter. Article 4(1)(a) states that the 'institutions shall refuse access to a document where disclosure would undermine the protection of: (a) the public interest as regards international relations'. Article 4(2) enables them to 'refuse access to a document where disclosure would undermine the protection of (…) legal advice'. Finally, Article 4(3) establishes a possibility to protect a document in matters where the final decision has yet to be taken, if its disclosure would seriously undermine the institution's decision-making process. The latter two exceptions contained in Article 4(2) and 4(3) may only be applied if there is no overriding public interest in transparency. The Union Courts have consistently maintained that derogations to the Regulation must be applied and interpreted strictly.[33] A decision refusing access to documents must also set out how access to the requested documents 'could specifically and actually undermine the interest protected by the exception'.[34] The interest being undermined must further be 'reasonably foreseeable and not purely hypothetical'.[35] Moreover, the exceptions in Regulation No 1049/2001 must be interpreted with further strictness in the event that the document at issue relates to the legislative processes of the Union.[36]

The Commission proposed in 2008 to align the exceptions in Regulation No 1049/2001 more carefully with the requirements of the Aarhus Convention,[37] including its basic premiss that the 'aforementioned grounds for refusal shall be interpreted in a restrictive way, taking into account the public interest served by disclosure and taking into account whether the information requested relates to emissions into the environment'.[38] As the Commission later withdrew its proposal after a long legislative stalemate, a safe presumption is that the exceptions and their application remain to be fully reconciled with the Convention.[39]

Exercising my right of public access, I approached the Council in March 2021[40] and learned that its legal service had addressed the issue of EU compliance with the Aarhus Convention twice. First, its legal service contributed to the discussions in the Environment Working Party in 2004 when it addressed the proposed Aarhus Regulation, in particular as regards the access to justice aspects. I was granted access to the parts describing the legal framework, while the actual analysis was

[33] Case C-64/05 P *Sweden v Commission* ECLI:EU:C:2007:802, [2007] ECR I-11389, para 66; Joined Cases C-39/05 P and C-52/05 P *Sweden and Turco v Council* ECLI:EU:C:2008:374, [2008] ECR I-4723, para 36; Case C-57/16 P *ClientEarth v Commission* ECLI:EU:2018:660, para 80.

[34] Case C-57/16 P *ClientEarth v Commission* ECLI:EU:2018:660, para 51.

[35] Case C-506/08 P *Sweden v MyTravel and Commission* ECLI:EU:C:2011:496, [2011] ECR I-6237, para 76; Case C-280/11 P *Council v Access Info Europe* ECLI:EU:C:2013:671, para 31.

[36] Case C-57/16 P *ClientEarth v Commission* ECLI:EU:C:2018:660, para 101.

[37] European Commission, 'Proposal for a Regulation of the European Parliament and of the Council regarding Public Access to European Parliament, Council and Commission Documents' (2006) COM(2008) 299 final.

[38] Art 4(4) second paragraph Aarhus Convention.

[39] An often-cited example are the general presumptions of confidentiality that according to the Court may also apply to environmental information in the context of infringement proceedings. See Case C-514/11 P *LPN and Finland v Commission* ECLI:EU:C:2013:738.

[40] 'Legal Advice on the EU's Compliance with the Aarhus Convention: Reply Adopted by the Council on 11 June 2021 to Confirmatory Application 16/c/01/21' (*AskTheEU.org*, 14 June 2021), www.asktheeu.org/en/request/9189/response/32032/attach/5/ANNEX.pdf?cookie_passthrough=1.

blanked out.[41] The second occasion was an opinion of the legal service addressed to the Working Party on International Environment Issues on 'Aarhus Convention – findings of the Compliance Committee: preparation for the MoP and next steps (2017)'.[42] Again, I received a number of quotes of various legal provisions but none of the actual analysis. According to the Council, even if the Aarhus regulation (EC) No 1367/2006 had now been adopted, the legal advice contained in the two opinions was relevant for assessing EU compliance and for the revision process of the Regulation.[43] The Council also made the specific point that 'should the documents be released, third parties may attempt to influence or exert pressure on the policy choices to be made by the institutions'.

I appealed the decision through a confirmatory application, and pointed out that the justification that the advice continues to be relevant for the ongoing revision seemed to be a highly general justification. If legal advice could be withheld simply because the EU act in question might later be subject to a revision process, this argument that would apply generally to all legal advice adopted in legislative matters, and is as such too broad and hypothetical to fulfil the criteria set in Court jurisprudence. It seemed disproportionate that the Council has not disclosed the opinion during the following 15 years. As to the Council's argument about the complexity of the legal issues concerned, I pointed out that many topics indeed are complex, but the legal questions involved are well known and broadly debated in civil society. Finally, I stressed that the possibility for third parties to influence policy choices is a fundamental aspect of democratic debate in any society governed by the rule of law, which the Council should not undermine, and stressed the reality of pressure must be confirmed.[44] It is difficult to see how a legislative document that relates to access to information and public participation could be sensitive. In its final decision, the Council maintained its position but granted slightly extended partial access to the later opinion. In both rounds, the Council also extended the time limit significantly from the 15 working days prescribed in the regulation, so the final decision was taken in June 2021, three months after my request.

In March 2021, I also approached the Commission for 'documents which contain the analysis of the Commission Legal Service concerning the EU's compliance with the Aarhus Convention'. Rather than fifteen working days, the Commission took four months and one week to give its first decision. When a document request deals with a topical issue, ignoring the time limits seems to be par for the course with the Commission, as the applicant will have more difficulty appealing a decision that has

[41] Council of the European Union, 'Contribution of the Legal Service to the Proceedings of the "Environment Working Party" on Proposal for a Regulation of the European Parliament and of the Council on the Application of Provisions of the Aarhus Convention on Access to information, Public participation in Decision-making and Access to Justice in Environmental Matters to EC Institutions and Bodies (Doc. 14152/03 of 30.10.2003)' (2004) 15435/04.

[42] Council of the European Union, 'Opinion of the Legal Service to Working Party on International Environment Issues on Aarhus Convention – Findings of the Compliance Committee: Preparation for the MoP and Next Steps' (2017) 8445/17.

[43] Letter from the Directorate-General Communication and Information dated 19 April 2021, Ref. 21/0651-mj/jl.

[44] On this, see Case T-252/19 *Pech v the Council* ECLI:EU:T:2021:203, para 92.

not formally been taken.[45] When the response finally came, the Commission Legal Service identified six documents and denied access to all of them, as they, in its view, dealt with highly sensitive issues and were in any case internal documents intended for other Commission's services.[46]

Of the six documents, five were older and concerned the way in which the EU had, under the original Aarhus Regulation, complied with the Convention, sometimes from a rather general angle. The Commission described their contents as follows:

1. Note of the Legal Service of 22 February 2008 for the Director General of DG ENV,[47] which reveals the Commission's practice regarding the EU representation before ACCC procedures and contains legal assessment of the legal aspects and implications of the institutional arrangements followed to represent the EU at the international level.
2. Note of the Legal Service of 27 February 2008 for the Director of DG ENV[48] explaining its position on the question of the applicability of Title IV of the Aarhus Regulation to decisions on co-financing under regional policy and on the issue of the applicability of the Aarhus instruments to Euratom law.
3. Note of the Legal Service of 27 June 2012 for its own Director-General,[49] which sums up the views of the different teams of the Legal Service and the other Directorate Generals concerning both the issue of the disclosure of information relating to 'business secrets', and the 'problematic notion' of 'emissions into the environment'.
4. Note of the Legal Service of 29 January 2013 for the attention of the Directors-General of DG CLIMA, DG AGRI, DG ENTR, DG ENV, DG SANCO, DG MOVE and DG ENER[50] explaining the position defended by the Commission in Case T-545/117 and several other arguments concerning the implications for the EU institutions of granting access to environmental information concerning emissions into the environment.
5. Note of the Legal Service of 27 May 2015 for its own Director-General,[51] which is an 'assessment both on sensitive and highly political issues' such as 'establishing a new horizontal and sectorial legislative instrument' and the 'management of infringement proceedings on access to justice'.

The sixth document was more recent and concerned directly the draft proposal amending the Aarhus Regulation. It was a Note of the Legal Service of 4 June 2020,[52] provided within the inter-service consultation launched by DG ENV on the proposal for a regulation amending the Aarhus Regulation and with an attachment where the Legal Service provides track-changes comments on the draft, including on the

[45] On this, see also C Eckes and P Leino-Sandberg, 'The European Commission's Assessment of EU Withdrawal from the Energy Charter Treaty: Legal Analysis or Confidential Strategy?' (*European Law Blog*, 28 September 2022), www.europeanlawblog.eu/2022/09/28/the-european-commissions-assessment-of-eu-withdrawal-from-the-energy-charter-treaty-legal-analysis-or-confidential-strategy/.

[46] 'Legal Advice on the EU's Compliance with the Aarhus Convention: The Director-General of Legal Service of the European Commission on Your Request of 12 March 2021 Registered on 15 March 2021 under Reference GestDem 2021/1560' (*AskTheEU.org*, 23 July 2021), www.asktheeu.org/en/request/9188/response/32729/attach/3/LS%20reply%20to%20GestDem2021%201560.pdf?cookie_passthrough=1.

[47] Document reference Ares(2015)5156891.

[48] Document reference Ares(2015)5157745.

[49] Document reference Ares(2012)776625.

[50] Document reference Ares(2013)132146.

[51] Document reference Ares(2015)2200028.

[52] Document reference Ares(2020)2895997.

question of whether the proposal ensures conformity with the conclusions of the ACCC. The Commission notes that the 'proposal is the subject of ongoing discussions on very sensitive issues, which are at the level of the first reading [and] will certainly be followed by a political repositioning of the Commission'. According to the Commission, none of these documents could be made publicly available to any extent, which made filing a further confirmatory application seem like a waste of time. As a result, none of the legal analyses made either in the Council or the Commission concerning the compliance of the EU with its obligations under the Aarhus regime was made public by either of the two institutions.

In assessing my request, the Commission relied on the exceptions that protect legal advice and decision-making process ('space to think'). The Council also put much emphasis on international relations and the Court's early case law presenting that specific provision as a rather categorical exception.[53] This is somewhat curious keeping in mind that the Council's input into actual EU negotiations is significantly smaller than that of the Commission; the Council formulates the broad frame of the mandate while the Commission operationalises it. The case law that the Commission chose to rely on was carefully selected; there would have been other more recent case law on the international relations exception, albeit relating to document requests that concerned matters where the EU was still engaged in negotiations. The most notable example is the international Anti-Counterfeiting Trade Agreement. In response to a request by the Foundation for a Free Information Infrastructure for 12 documents,[54] the Council denied access because

> … disclosure of this information could impede the proper conduct of the negotiations, … would weaken the position of the European Union in these negotiations and might affect relations with the third parties concerned.[55]

In March 2010, the European Parliament passed a resolution demanding greater transparency and calling on the Commission to make public all documents relating to the negotiations.[56] Public access to documents produced during the ACTA negotiations was eventually taken to Court by Ms in 't Veld MEP in her case against the Commission.[57] The General Court proved responsive to the Commission concerns. It emphasised the 'particularly sensitive and essential nature of the interests' relating

[53] See Case C-266/05 P *Sison v Council* ECLI:EU:C:2007:75, [2007] ECR I-1233, para 34; Case T-63/10 *Jurašinović v Council* ECLI:EU:T:2012:516, para 32; Case T-331/11 *Besselink v Council* ECLI:EU:T:2013:419, para 32; Case T-851/16 *Access Info Europe v Commission* ECLI:EU:T:2018:69, para 40.

[54] The Council identified Commission recommendations for negotiating mandates, to which it granted partial access. In addition, it denied access to Commission working documents, the Presidency notes and an outcome of consultations with Justice and Home Affairs counsellors concerning one of the negotiation rounds. 'FFII Opposes Stealth Legislation, Demands ACTA Documents' *FFII Press Releases* (Brussels, 3 November 2008), www.web.archive.org/web/20090503123622/http:/press.ffii.org/Press_releases/FFII_opposes_stealth_legislation%2C_demands_ACTA_documents.

[55] Council of the European Union – General Secretariat (5 November 2008) 08/1835ws/jj, available at www.web.archive.org/web/20110409015547/http://action.ffii.org/acta/Analysis?action=AttachFile&do=get&target=08-1835en.wes.ws-jj.pdf.

[56] European Parliament, 'Resolution on the Transparency and State of Play of the ACTA Negotiations' (2010) P7_TA(2010)0058.

[57] Case T-301/10 *In 't Veld v Commission* ECLI:EU:T:2013:135.

to international relations.[58] It noted that EU positions naturally change during negotiations, depending on concessions and compromises made by others, and accepted that 'the formulation of negotiating positions may involve a number of tactical considerations of the negotiators, including the European Union itself'.[59] It accepted that unilateral disclosure of EU negotiating positions might have negative effects and seriously undermine the maintenance of mutual trust, which is essential to the effectiveness of negotiations and a very delicate exercise.[60] Finally, since the exception involved no public interest test, such arguments were rejected as 'ineffective'.[61] However, while the Court thus approved the institutional strategy of broad non-disclosure, ACTA is today famous for being rejected by the European Parliament, which refused to give its consent to the agreement, partly due to concerns over its impact on democracy.[62] These experiences suggest that there might occasionally exist a public interest in access to timely information that overrides the dominant mindset of confidentiality.

I did not appeal any of these decisions rejecting my access, as the old legal opinions seemed less relevant at the point when the legislative proposal amending the Aarhus regulation was already being negotiated.[63] The Commission proposal indicates that it:

> aims to improve the implementation of the Aarhus Convention following the adoption of the Lisbon Treaty and to address the concerns expressed by the Aarhus Convention Compliance Committee (the Committee) regarding the EU's compliance with its international obligations under the Convention. It aims to do so in a way that is compatible with the fundamental principles of the EU legal order and with its system of judicial review.[64]

Following the publication of the proposal, the Commission accepted an offer from the ACCC for advice on whether the proposal would bring the EU into compliance with the Aarhus Convention.[65] In February 2021, ACCC advice concluded that the Commission proposal fell short of compliance on four points.[66] The European

[58] ibid para 108.
[59] ibid para 125.
[60] ibid paras 125–126.
[61] ibid para 131.
[62] M Horten, 'Wow What a Scorcher! ACTA Slaughtered 478 to 39' (*Iptegrity.com*, 4 July 2012), www.iptegrity.com/index.php/acta/781-wow-what-a-scorcher-acta-slaughtered-478-to-39.
[63] European Commission, 'Proposal for a Regulation of the European Parliament and of the Council on Amending Regulation (EC) No 1367/2006 of the European Parliament and of the Council of 6 September 2006 on the Application of the Provisions of the Aarhus Convention on Access to Information, Public Participation in Decision-making and Access to Justice in Environmental Matters to Community Institutions and Bodies' (2020) COM(2020) 642 final.
[64] ibid 1.
[65] 'Request for Advice: Reply by the European Commission Services to the Invitation of the Aarhus Convention Compliance Committee (ref: ACCC/M/2017/3)' (*United Nations Economic Commission for Europe*, 5 November 2020), www.unece.org/fileadmin/DAM/env/pp/compliance/Requests_from_the_MOP/ACCC-M-2017-3_European_Union/Correspondence_with_the_Party_concerned/frPartyM3_05.11.2020.pdf.
[66] 'Advice from the Committee to the Party Concerned: Advice by the Aarhus Convention Compliance Committee to the European Union concerning the implementation of request ACCC/M/2017/3' (*United Nations Economic Commission for Europe*, 12 February 2021), www.unece.org/sites/default/files/2021-02/M3_EU_advice_12.02.2021.pdf.

Parliament subsequently adopted a position that sought to implement the ACCC's recommendations,[67] in enabling review of all administrative decisions taken by the EU institutions if they break environmental laws.[68] Trilogues started in early June 2021,[69] and while they were ongoing, the ACCC published a draft report – based on an EU progress report – in which it reiterated the EU's non-compliance with the Aarhus Convention and repeated its earlier recommendations.[70] In July, the three EU institutions reached an agreement on the reform. The compromise text was communicated to the ACCC,[71] which found in its final report that the 'co-legislator's agreement to amend the Aarhus Regulation … would fulfil the requirements'[72] and recommended the Meeting of Parties to endorse the trilogue agreement as bringing EU legislation in compliance with the Aarhus Convention.[73]

In the Council, discussions were informed by a new opinion by the Council Legal Service[74] concerning the scope of the Commission proposal and the ACCC advice of 12 February 2021. I requested public access to the opinion under Regulation No 1049/2001 and the Aarhus Regulation No 1367/2006. As the Court of Justice has consistently held that legislative transparency is of paramount importance in the democratic process of the European Union,[75] I stressed that the legal opinion

[67] European Parliament, 'Amendments adopted on the Proposal for a Regulation of the European Parliament and of the Council Amending Regulation (EC) No 1367/2006 of the European Parliament and of the Council of 6 September 2006 on the Application of the Provisions of the Aarhus Convention on Access to Information, Public Participation in Decision-making and Access to Justice in Environmental Matters to Community Institutions and Bodies (COM(2020)0642 – C9-0321/2020–2020/0289(COD))' (2021) P9_TA(2021)0254.

[68] 'EU Parliament Champions Compliance with International Rule of Law' (*ClientEarth*, 20 May 2021) www.clientearth.org/latest/press-office/press/eu-parliament-champions-compliance-with-international-rule-of-law/.

[69] Council of the European Union, 'Proposal for a Regulation of the European Parliament and of the Council on amending Regulation (EC) No 1367/2006 of the European Parliament and of the Council of 6 September 2006 on the Application of the Provisions of the Aarhus Convention on Access to Information, Public Participation in Decision-making and Access to Justice in Environmental Matters to Community Institutions and Bodies – Preparation for the Trilogue' (2021) 9672/21, 2.

[70] Aarhus Convention Compliance Committee, 'Draft Report of the Compliance Committee: Compliance by the European Union with its Obligations under the Convention' (*United Nations Economic Commission for Europe*, July 2021) ECE/MP.PP/2021/XX, available at www.unece.org/sites/default/files/2021-07/M3_EU_draft_report_to_MOP7_for_comment.docx.

[71] Council of the European Union, 'Proposal for a Regulation of the European Parliament and of the Council on amending Regulation (EC) No 1367/2006 of the European Parliament and of the Council of 6 September 2006 on the Application of the Provisions of the Aarhus Convention on Access to Information, Public Participation in Decision-making and Access to Justice in Environmental Matters to Community Institutions and Bodies – Letter to the Chair of the European Parliament Committee on the Environment, Public Health and Food Safety (ENVI)' (2021) 11044/21.

[72] Aarhus Convention Compliance Committee, 'Draft Report of the Compliance Committee' ECE/MP.PP/2021/XX, para 146. Emphasis added.

[73] ibid para 148.

[74] Council of the European Union, 'Opinion of the Legal Service on the Commission Proposal for a Regulation amending the "Aarhus Regulation" (Regulation (EC) No 1367/2006) – Scope of Application of the Proposal, and 2021 Advice of the Aarhus Convention Compliance Committee on the Proposal' (2021) 8721/21.

[75] Council of the European Union – General Secretariat, 'Communication: Public Access to Documents – Confirmatory Application No 29/c/02/21 – Launch of Written Procedure' (2021) CM 4164/21; Council of the European Union – General Secretariat, 'Public Access to Documents – Confirmatory Application No 29/c/02/21' (2021) 10266/21.

relates to a legislative file. A similar request was also made by ClientEarth – the NGO that had also initiated the Aarhus compliance procedure that led the ACCC to conclude that the EU is in breach of its obligations (see below Section 4). We only gained restricted access to some general parts of the opinion, such as a description of the main elements of the current internal review system provided for by the Aarhus Regulation and the existing case-law related to the definition of an 'administrative act'.[76]

One fundamental issue at stake in these requests is also the meaning of 'environmental information', which is defined broadly under the Aarhus Regulation[77] but interpreted narrowly by the EU institutions. In its decision, the Council considered that a legal opinion related to the implementation of the Aarhus Convention does not constitute environmental information. Yet, the Commission proposal indicates that:

> The legal basis for action in this area is Article 192(1) TFEU. … The proposal aims to improve the protection of the environment, by improving the administrative review procedure available to NGOs as regards administrative acts and omissions of EU institutions and bodies where those contravene environmental law.[78]

Any legislative procedure aimed at modifying the Aarhus Regulation thus seems to logically to fall under the Aarhus definition, as would a legal opinion addressing these changes.

In its reply to my request, the Council stressed ongoing negotiations within the EU and the external dimensions context of the matter, but also the risk of 'external pressure' created by civil society, which would hinder efficient decision making.[79] Importantly, however, by the time the Council took its final decision on these requests, the EU institutions had already adopted the trilogue agreement, and the ACCC had published its finding that the agreement would bring the EU into compliance with its obligations. I – and in a separate appeal, Client Earth – appealed the denial decision to the General Court.[80] The matter breaks new ground also in other respects, as the following section demonstrates by placing the argumentation used by the Council in the context of existing transparency jurisprudence.

[76] Council of the European Union, 'Public Access to Documents – Confirmatory Application No 29/c/02/21' (2021) 10266/21; Council of the European Union – General Secretariat, 'Communication on Public Access to Documents – Confirmatory Application No 29/c/02/21 – Outcome of the Written Procedure Initiated by CM 4164/21' (2021) CM 4165/21; see also Council of the European Union, 'Opinion of the Legal Service on the Commission Proposal Amending the "Aarhus Regulation"' 8721/21.

[77] Under Art 2(1)(d)(iii) Aarhus Regulation, 'environmental information' also includes information on 'measures (including administrative measures), such as policies, legislation, plans, programmes, environmental agreements, and activities affecting or likely to affect the elements and factors referred to in points (i) and (ii) as well as measures or activities designed to protect those elements'.

[78] European Commission, 'Proposal for a Regulation Amending Regulation (EC) No 1367/2006' COM(2020) 642 final.

[79] 'Reply Adopted by the Council on 11 June 2021 to Confirmatory Application 16/c/01/21' (n 40) para 37.

[80] Case T-683/21 *Leino-Sandberg v Council*. See also Case T-682/21 *ClientEarth v Council*. The Court annulled the Council's decisions in Joined Cases T-682/21 and T-683/21 ClientEarth and Leino-Sandberg v Council, after completion of this chapter.

3. THE INTERNAL-EXTERNAL PARADIGMS IN ASSESSING PUBLIC ACCESS TO LEGAL OPINIONS

In its case law the Court has made a clear distinction between public access to legal opinions in legislative matters and legal opinions relating to external relations. According to the Court, legal advice linked to a legislative procedure mandates a particularly high standard of transparency. The legal opinion I requested belongs formally to a legislative file decided on the basis of the ordinary legislative procedure (Article 192(1) TFEU). However, the Council saw the transparency requirement differently. It recycles its old argumentation from other cases, stressing that the:

> possibility that the legal advice in question be disclosed to the public during the negotiations on the Commission's proposal may weaken the Council's position in those negotiations. Moreover, it could expose the Council Legal Service [CLS] to external pressure, which in turn, could affect the way in which legal advice is drafted and hence prejudice the possibility to express views free from external influences. Indeed, disclosure in such context would run counter the ability of the [CLS] to continue offering a honest and frank opinion, ultimately undermining the decision-making autonomy of the Council.[81]

The Council's arguments have remained essentially unchanged despite a sequence of Court rulings on similar matters.[82] In the recent *Budgetary Conditionality* case, the ECJ repeated that:

> the disclosure of documents containing the advice of an institution's legal service on legal issues arising when legislative initiatives are being debated increases the transparency and openness of the legislative process and strengthens the right of EU citizens to scrutinise the information which has formed the basis of a legislative measure. The Court has concluded that there is no general need for confidentiality as regards the opinions of the Council Legal Service relating to a legislative process and that Regulation No 1049/2001 imposes, in principle, an obligation to disclose them. It is precisely openness in that regard which, by allowing divergences between various points of view to be openly debated, contributes to reducing doubts in the minds of citizens, not only as regards the lawfulness of an isolated legislative measure but also as regards the legitimacy of the legislative process as a whole.[83]

As the Court has accepted exceptional non-disclosure where an opinion is of a sensitive nature and has a wide scope, the Council argues that the Aarhus opinion is indeed sensitive because it concerns the findings of the ACCC[84] and also wide in scope as it discusses the ACCC's findings with respect to 'the EU's system of legal remedies'.[85] Finally, the Council was not convinced of the existence of a public interest in disclosure as, in its opinion, participation in the legislative process by NGOs and civil society to ensure the correct transposition of the Aarhus Convention is of

[81] 'Reply Adopted by the Council on 11 June 2021 to Confirmatory Application 16/c/01/21' (n 40) para 58.

[82] See on this, Leino-Sandberg (n 29) ch 4.

[83] Case C-156/21 *Hungary v Parliament and Council* ECLI:EU:C:2022:97, paras 58–59.

[84] 'Reply Adopted by the Council on 11 June 2021 to Confirmatory Application 16/c/01/21' (n 40) para 45.

[85] ibid paras 48–51.

a 'very general nature'.[86] Given that the process will determine the extent to which citizens can exercise their rights in relation to environmental matters at the EU level in the future, this is a curious claim. It appears less a statement of fact than a statement of wish, reflecting the desire to keep any public participation indeed 'very general'.

However, the external dimension of the Aarhus legal opinion is not irrelevant: the EU legislative reform was launched due to the findings of the ACCC. Legal questions are equally relevant in external relations as they are in the internal sphere, and the negotiation position of the EU and its institutions is necessarily constrained by the Treaties.[87] In *Kadi*, the ECJ held that 'an international agreement cannot affect the allocation of powers fixed by the Treaties or, consequently, the autonomy of the Community legal system, observance of which is ensured by the Court'.[88] Institutional legal opinions often address questions of competence in the realm of external relations and compatibility of international arrangements with primary law – questions that have featured in many negotiations in recent years. Documents setting out the legal limits for international agreements concluded by the EU set out views on the law to be observed. Depending on when the advice is given, they can also describe and react to proposals on the international negotiation agenda.

The Council has consistently relied on the international relations exception, which from the institutional perspective offers more possibilities to limit disclosure. In the early cases, the Court accepted that international relations have a complex and delicate nature which calls for the exercise of particular care and requires a margin of appreciation.[89] However, secrecy would need to be justified by an analysis of the relevant content and context and the specific circumstances, not just by any abstract or distant connection with international relations.[90] One of the more recent Court cases concerns a Council Legal Service opinion on the proposed legal basis of the draft Council decision to authorise the Commission to launch negotiations for the so-called SWIFT Agreement.[91] The applicant, Sophie In't Veld MEP, received partial access, with the Council invoking the exceptions relating to the protection of international relations and legal advice. The Council argued that disclosure would not only reveal information on certain provisions in the envisaged Agreement but also have a negative impact on the EU negotiating position and damage the climate of confidence. The legal basis issue was sensitive, since it had an

[86] ibid para 81.

[87] Case 294/83 *Les Verts v Parliament* ECLI:EU:C:1986:166, [1986] ECR 1339, para 23; Joined Cases C-402/05 P and C-415/05 P *Kadi and Al Barakaat International Foundation v Council and Commission* ECLI:EU:C:2008:461, [2008] ECR I-6351, paras 281–282.

[88] Joined Cases C-402/05 P and C-415/05 P *Kadi and Al Barakaat International Foundation v Council and Commission* ECLI:EU:C:2008:461, [2008] ECR I-6351, paras 281–282.

[89] Case C-266/05 P *Sison v Council* ECLI:EU:C:2007:75, [2007] ECR I-1233, para 35; Case T-63/10 *Jurašinović v Council* ECLI:EU:T:2012:516, para 26.

[90] Case T-211/00 *Kuijer v Council* ECLI:EU:T:2002:30, [2002] ECR II-485, paras 60–61; Case C-350/12 P *Council v in't Veld* ECLI:EU:C:2014:2039, para 51.

[91] Case T-529/09 *In't Veld v Council* ECLI:EU:T:2012:215.

impact on the Parliament's prerogatives, and was subject to disagreement between the institutions.[92]

On appeal, the CJEU stressed that the principle of transparency applies to decision-making also in the field of EU international activity.[93] While the considerations relating to citizen participation and the legitimacy of administration are of a particular relevance where the Council is acting in its legislative capacity, the substance of the envisaged agreement had potential implications for EU legislative activity and the protection of fundamental rights.[94] The General Court also considered the effect of the on-going procedure for concluding the international agreement and established that:

> Indeed, the public interest in the transparency of the decision-making process would become meaningless if, as the Commission proposes, it were to be taken into account only in those cases where the decision-making process has come to an end.[95]

The Court accepted the non-disclosure of those elements in the document that could reveal the strategic objectives pursued by the EU in the negotiations, but emphasised that the risk to international relations 'must be reasonably foreseeable and must not be purely hypothetical.'[96] Such a risk could only be established for those elements of the CLS opinion 'relating to the specific content of the agreement envisaged or the negotiating directives capable of revealing the strategic objectives pursued by the European Union in the negotiations'.[97]

Similar elements were also present when ClientEarth requested the Commission legal analysis of the investor-state dispute settlement (ISDS) and the new Investment Court System (ICS) in light of CJEU case law on the autonomy of EU law. The request covered various kinds of legal opinions. Some of the advice concerned specific provisions in the TTIP agreement, the negotiations for which had already halted; some discussed legal options that were relevant for several agreements under negotiation (EU-Canada Comprehensive Economic and Trade Agreement (CETA) and TTIP), while other documents concerned the ISDS mechanisms more generally.[98] At the time of the decision, a great deal of information about the results of the negotiations was already available in the public domain.[99]

[92] See Council of the European Union, 'Public Access to Documents – Confirmatory Application No 22/c/01/09' (2009) 13802/09, paras 10 and 15 as discussed in Case T-529/09 *In't Veld v Council* ECLI:EU:T:2012:215, para 7.

[93] Case C-350/12 P *Council v in't Veld* ECLI:EU:C:2014:2039, para 76.

[94] Case T-529/09 *In't Veld v Council* ECLI:EU:T:2012:215, paras 89, 92.

[95] Case T-529/09 *In't Veld v Council* ECLI:EU:T:2012:215, para 101.

[96] Case C-350/12 P *Council v in't Veld* ECLI:EU:C:2014:2039, paras 52 and 63–64.

[97] Case T-529/09 *In't Veld v Council* ECLI:EU:T:2012:215, para 59. Upheld on appeal in Case C-350/12 P *Council v in't Veld* ECLI:EU:C:2014:2039, paras 42–69.

[98] See the Commission decision of 9 March 2016, Ref. Ares(2016)1202343 (as discussed in Case C-612/18 P *ClientEarth v Commission* ECLI:EU:C:2020:223).

[99] The Commission had approved and published its proposal for an Investment Court System in its negotiations over TTIP with the United States and it had completed the negotiations with Canada over CETA (that included ICS) and published the text of that agreement. Similarly, information on well-known and publicly available provisions in international investment agreements, such as the International Convention on the Settlement of Investment Disputes (ICSID) could not reveal strategic objectives. See L Ankersmit and J Peters, 'Public Access to Documents'.

Despite this, the ECJ accepted that the request covered legal analysis that may give 'an insider look into the European Union's strategy and negotiating margin of manoeuvre' and that its disclosure could negatively affect the negotiating position of the EU.[100] Again, the Court emphasised that:

> the legal options on open sensitive issues relating to ISDS, including the creation of an ICS, *which were still under negotiation* in the framework of the Transatlantic Trade Investment Partnership and other agreements, and that the disclosure of the requested documents could undermine the public interest as regards international relations – in that their disclosure would have revealed the legal considerations *underpinning the Commission's negotiating proposals in ongoing negotiations* and would thereby have weakened the Commission's negotiating position by giving to the Commission's negotiating partners an *insider look into the European Union's strategy and negotiating margin of manoeuvre* – with the result that that disclosure would have negatively affected the Commission's effectiveness in the negotiations, in a realistic and non-hypothetical way.[101]

A legal opinion is never the EU's 'negotiating position', but a document that may discuss the legal aspects of matters on the negotiating agenda. The repeated references to the 'ongoing' negotiations with third parties leave little doubt that the Court considered this a central element of the reasoning behind its ruling.[102]

Legal opinions can also be used in a highly instrumentalist fashion internally to promote an institutional agenda or an 'EU interest' in negotiations, as was the case in the context of the recently concluded negotiations over the EU-UK trade and cooperation agreement.[103] The deal was closed urgently in a matter of days as an EU-only agreement, excluding alternative scenarios that would have involved national parliaments in a more meaningful fashion. The solution was justified by a Council Legal Service opinion, which remains formally confidential though publicly available on a popular website.[104] So far, no detailed analysis concerning the competence structure of the agreement and the implications of the EU-only agreement has been made publicly available. The Council received a request for access to the legal opinion from one of my Master's students, who was writing her thesis about the EU-UK TCA at the time. The request was refused on the basis that the 'legal advice contained in the requested document relates to a decision-making process of non-legislative nature, which is still ongoing'.[105] It argued more specifically that 'the requested opinion touches upon horizontal issues (conclusion of EU-only agreements by the exercise by the EU of its potential EU competence, effects for the Member States of the exercise

[100] Case C-612/18 P *ClientEarth v Commission* ECLI:EU:C:2020:223, para 41.

[101] ibid para 41 (emphasis added).

[102] ibid para 42.

[103] We have analysed this in depth in C Eckes and P Leino-Sandberg, 'The EU-UK Trade and Cooperation Agreement – Exceptional Circumstances or a New Paradigm for EU External Relations?' (2022) 85 *Modern Law Review* 164.

[104] The leaked opinion of the Council Legal Service is available at S Peers, 'The Brexit Deal – Council Legal Service Opinion' (*EU Law Analysis*, 27 January 2021), www.eulawanalysis.blogspot.com/2021/01/the-brexit-deal-council-legal-service.html?m=1. The relevant Annex B of Doc 6239/20 to which the opinion refers is not publicly available.

[105] Council of the European Union, 'Public Access to Documents – Confirmatory Application No 07/c/01/21' (2021) 6418/21, para 5.

by the EU of its potential competence etc.) that have broad implications going beyond the decision-making process in question'.[106] The refusal to grant access was appealed to the European Ombudsman who concluded that:

> the type of trade agreements that can be concluded is part of EU law and therefore known by third parties. Most of the information contained in the opinion is already publicly available. The Ombudsman therefore takes the view that disclosing the opinion is unlikely to undermine the EU's negotiation position or reveal its strategy, either now or in future trade negotiations. … the Ombudsman noted that the information contained in the opinion at issue cannot be regarded as sensitive.[107]

In this case, I believe that the publicity of legal opinions could also have improved its quality and presentation of arguments in a more balanced manner. However, the Council has continued to refuse to disclose the opinion until this day.

The CJEU has later specified that the way in which external parties, like third countries, perceive the decisions of the EU, is a component of the international relations of the Union for the purposes of Regulation No 1049/2001.[108] This issue came up in the *Bankwatch* case, which concerned a Commission decision to grant an Euratom loan to the National Nuclear Energy Generating Company of Ukraine (Energoatom), secured by the Ukrainian Government. CEE Bankwatch Network, an association of NGOs, requested access to various documents relating to the granting decision. The Court accepted that disclosure of the agreement might undermine the quality of EU-Ukraine relations by hurting the confidence or trust of the authorities of a third country: 'Indeed, the pursuit and the quality of those relations depend on that perception'.[109] Willingness to protect EU strategic objectives and the climate of negotiations has also been visible in the European Ombudsman's own-initiative inquiry on the TTIP where she set three criteria for evaluating harm in this context, building on an evaluation of disclosure would:

> i) damage mutual trust between the negotiators; ii) inhibit the development of free and effective discussions in the context of the negotiations and/or iii) reveal strategic elements of the negotiations either to the other negotiating party or to third parties.[110]

These criteria would seem to exclude questions that are entirely internal to EU decision-making, such as questions of competence and other Treaty limitations.[111]

[106] ibid para 28.

[107] European Ombudsman Recommendation in case 717/2021/DL on the Council of the European Union's refusal to give full public access to a legal opinion related to the EU trade agreement with the United Kingdom (24 February 2022), paras 17–18.

[108] Case T-307/16 *CEE Bankwatch Network v Commission* ECLI:EU:T:2018:97.

[109] ibid para 90.

[110] European Ombudsman Letter in case IO/11/2014/RA to the Council of the EU requesting an opinion in the European Ombudsman's own-initiative inquiry OI/10/2014/MMN concerning transparency and public participation in relation to the Transatlantic Trade and Investment Partnership (TTIP) negotiations (29 July 2014); European Ombudsman Letter in Case IO/10/2014/RA to the European Commission requesting an opinion in the European Ombudsman's own-initiative inquiry OI/10/2014/MMN concerning transparency and public participation in relation to the Transatlantic Trade and Investment Partnership (TTIP) negotiations (29 July 2014).

[111] Decision of the European Ombudsman in case 90/2009/(JD)OV closing his inquiry into complainant 90/2009/(JD)OV against the Council of the European Union (23 July 2010), para 33.

While public access is primarily decided on the basis of content, context also matters. When assessing 'harm from disclosure', a negotiation process that has come to an end is not the same as an ongoing negotiation process. The Aarhus situation relates to compliance with an already existing international agreement and where the Union's political room for manoeuvre is already limited by the obligations that it is bound by under Article 216 TFEU, which are not subject to negotiation. Such a setting has to my knowledge not been addressed by the Court.

4. STRATEGY AND EXTERNAL PRESSURE IN COMPLYING WITH THE AARHUS CONVENTION

In its decision on my confirmatory application, the Council claims that international relations would be undermined because disclosure of the legal opinion would affect the ability of the EU to defend its position in the international framework set up by the Aarhus Convention.[112] As explained above, the Aarhus regime is exceptional in its transparency and inclusiveness that reflect its main ambition to promote public access and participation by civil society. It therefore provides excellent means to examine the merits of the Council claim against how the question of EU compliance was assessed in the Aarhus framework.

Article 15 of the Aarhus Convention presumes the setting up of 'optional arrangements of a non-confrontational, non-judicial and consultative nature for reviewing compliance with the provisions of the Convention', which has led to the setting up of the ACCC in 2002.[113] Of particular interest for this chapter are the two procedures that led to the ACCC concluding that the EU is not in compliance with the Convention.[114] The first one was brought by NGO ClientEarth, which argued that 'if the jurisprudence of the European Courts is not altered, the European Community will fail to comply with article 9 paragraphs 2 to 5, of the Aarhus Convention by preventing NGOs and individuals from having access to justice with respect to decisions of EC institutions'.[115] This procedure ended in a finding of non-compliance and a draft decision for the Sixth Meeting of the parties in 2017 to endorse those findings.[116] At that meeting the only Parties to take issue with the draft Decision were

[112] 'Reply Adopted by the Council on 11 June 2021 to Confirmatory Application 16/c/01/21' (n 40) para 70.

[113] In 2002 the Parties adopted decision I/7 on review of compliance to monitor compliance with the Convention. See Meeting of the Parties to the Convention on Access to Information, Public Participation in Decision-making, and Access to Justice in Environmental Matters, 'Report of the First Meeting of the parties: Addendum Decision I/7 Review of Compliance' (*United Nations Economic Commission for Europe*, 2 April 2004) ECE/MP.PP/2/Add.8.

[114] Aarhus Convention Compliance Committee, 'Findings and Recommendations of the Compliance Committee with regard to Communication ACCC/C/2008/32 (Part II) concerning Compliance by the European Union Adopted by the Compliance Committee on 17 March 2017' (*United Nations Economic Commission for Europe*, 2 June 2017) ECE/MP.PP/C.1/2017/7.

[115] All of the documents and communications relevant to this procedure are available at 'ACCC/C/2008/32 European Union' (*United Nations Economic Commission for Europe*), www.unece.org/env/pp/cc/accc.c.2008.32_european-union.

[116] Draft Bureau Decision VI/8f, available at: The Bureau of the Meeting of the Parties to the Convention on access to Information, Public Participation in Decision-making and Access to Justice in Environmental Matters, 'Draft Decision VI/8f concerning Compliance by the European Union with its Obligations under the Convention' (*United Nations Economic Commission for Europe*, 10 July 2017) ECE/MP.PP/2017/25.

the EU and certain of its Member States while all of the other Parties were ready to endorse the ACCC's findings at that time, as is the practice.[117] Since opposition to the findings existed on the EU side, the meeting decided to postpone the decision and specifically requested the ACCC 'to review any developments that had taken place regarding the matter and to report to the Meeting of the Parties accordingly'.[118] This led to a second procedure dealing with the ACCC's follow-up to its findings of non-compliance against the EU.[119]

What is notable with the Aarhus regime is that all of the ACCC's procedures are published on its website, along with all of the communications and submissions that are exchanged.[120] While the Meeting of the Parties formally decides on matters of compliance, interested third parties to a compliance case, for example a member of the public or another Contracting Party, have the right to submit observations on the substance of the dispute and be involved in all stages of the procedure. They are registered by the Secretariat as observers and receive invitations to comment each step of the procedure.[121]

Certain NGOs participated in the two EU procedures, but no other Contracting Parties expressed interest in becoming official observers.[122] Therefore, it would seem the need to protect trust of other parties (a possible ground for invoking the international relations exception accepted by the Court in its earlier case law) was absent, as there were no other parties to the proceedings. All the documents and communications that are relevant to this procedure can be found online,[123] including the ACCC advice given to the EU after the adoption of the Commission proposal.[124] The EU's comments on the ACCC's draft report were circulated among the Communicant and observers and made public on the ACCC's website. These comments provided information on the trilogue agreement and requested that the ACCC would confirm that the result will end the non-compliance.[125] At the end of the process, the ACCC

[117] Meeting of the Parties to the Convention on access to Information, Public Participation in Decision-making and Access to Justice in Environmental Matters, 'Report on the Sixth Session of the Meeting of the Parties' (*United Nations Economic Commission for Europe*, 21 December 2017) ECE/MP.PP/2017/2, paras 55–65.

[118] ibid para 63.

[119] ibid.

[120] See Aarhus Convention Compliance Committee, *Guide to the Aarhus Convention Compliance Committee*, 2nd edn (Geneva, United Nations Economic Commission for Europe, 2019) para 23.

[121] See eg the letter inviting communicants and observers to comment on the UNECE website, accessible at: F Marshall, 'Request ACCC/M/2017/3 by the Meeting of the parties concerning Compliance by the European Union with its Obligations under the Aarhus Convention' (*United Nations Economic Commission for Europe*, 2 July 2012), www.unece.org/sites/default/files/2021-07/toCommM3_02.07.2021.pdf.

[122] The only Parties listed as observers are Germany and Portugal, who represented the Council.

[123] All the documents and communications that are relevant to this procedure can be found online with reference ACCC/M/2017/3. See 'ACCC/C/2008/32 European Union' (*United Nations Economic Commission for Europe*), www.unece.org/env/pp/cc/accc.c.2008.32_european-union.

[124] 'Advice from the Committee to the Party Concerned: Advice by the Aarhus Convention Compliance Committee to the European Union concerning the implementation of request ACCC/M/2017/3' (*United Nations Economic Commission for Europe*, 12 February 2021), www.unece.org/sites/default/files/2021-02/M3_EU_advice_12.02.2021.pdf.

[125] EU comments regarding the Aarhus Convention Compliance Committee's final report pursuant to request ACCC/M/2017/3 (EU) in case ACCC/C/2008/32 of 16 July 2021, available at 'Comments on the Committee's Draft Report: Aarhus Convention/ACCC/M/2017/3 (European Union)/EU Comments on the committee's Draft Report' (*United Nations Economic Commission for Europe*, 16 July 2021), www.unece.org/sites/default/files/2021-07/frPartyM3_16.07.2021_comments.pdf.

essentially agreed with the EU's position and considered that the 'co-legislator's agreement to amend the Aarhus Regulation, if enacted in that form prior to the opening of the seventh session of the Meeting of Parties, would fulfil the requirements …'.[126] Its Report indicates that the Meeting of the Parties would adopt a decision endorsing its findings and concluding that the EU amendment to the Aarhus Regulation brings it into compliance with Articles 9(3) and 9(4) of the Aarhus Convention.[127] There were no changes of substance to the Bureau's draft decision and the report from the Meeting of the Parties shows that there was no discussion in relation to the EU's compliance with the findings.[128] Therefore, the EU's compliance was confirmed, and the situation was made known to anyone interested in the process.

This is relevant because the exceptions in Regulation No 1049/2001 only 'apply for the period during which protection is justified on the basis of the content of the document'.[129] At the time I requested the legal opinion, there remained no realistic prospect that any Contracting Party would raise objections to the ACCC's recommendations or that even a substantive discussion would take place. To my knowledge, in the history of the Aarhus Convention the situation has never arisen that *another* Contracting Party has objected to the recommendation in the ACCC's Report.[130] In any case, there is another procedure that allows Contracting Parties to contest compliance by another Contracting Party with the Convention. If a Contracting Party had been seriously concerned about the EU's failure to grant environmental NGOs adequate access to justice in environmental matters, it could have made a submission to the ACCC,[131] which would not have made much sense, since the latter had already found non-compliance. This kind of submissions have so far been made twice in the Convention's history, once by Romania concerning compliance by Ukraine in the context of the construction of a navigation canal in the Danube Delta[132] and once by Lithuania concerning compliance by Belarus in the context of the construction

[126] Aarhus Convention Compliance Committee (n 70) para 146.

[127] This is reflected in the Bureau to the Aarhus Convention's draft Decision VII/8f published on the same day that the Contested Decision was adopted (Annex B.8 to the Council's Defence), see The Bureau of the Meeting of the Parties to the Convention on access to Information, Public Participation in Decision-making and Access to Justice in Environmental Matters, 'Draft Decision VII/8f concerning Compliance by the European Union with its Obligations under the Convention' (*United Nations Economic Commission for Europe*, 9 August 2021) ECE/MP.PP/2021/29, points 3–6.

[128] See Meeting of the Parties to the Convention on access to Information, Public Participation in Decision-making and Access to Justice in Environmental Matters, 'Report on the Seventh Session of the Meeting of the Parties' (*United Nations Economic Commission for Europe*, 17 February 2022) ECE/MP.PP/2021/2, paras 54–59.

[129] Art 4(7) Regulation (EC) No 1049/2001 of the European Parliament and of the Council regarding public access to European Parliament, Council and Commission documents [2001] OJ L145/43.

[130] Parties have in the past objected to parts of recommendations directed at them, for example with the UK at the 2017 Meeting of the Parties regarding the specific modalities of how to involve the public located abroad in decision-making on specific activities in a case concerning the permitting of Hinkley Point C nuclear power plant and the EU at the 2021 Meeting of the Parties in relation to questions of state aid.

[131] See Meeting of the Parties to the Convention on Access to Information, Public Participation in Decision-making, and Access to Justice in Environmental Matters, 'Decision I/7 Review of Compliance' ECE/MP.PP/2/Add.8, paras 15–16.

[132] Case ACCC/S/2004/1, available at Aarhus Convention Compliance Committee, 'Report on the Seventh Meeting: Addendum Findings and Recommendations' (*United Nations Economic Commission for Europe*, 14 March 2005) ECE/MP.PP/C.1/2005/2/Add.3.

of Ostrovets nuclear power plant.[133] Evidently, both cases arose in circumstances in which the submitting Party was concerned about the potential transboundary impact. For this reason, the alarming claim presented by the Council that the EU's 'international relations would be undermined because disclosure of the legal opinion would affect the ability of the EU to defend its position' seems completely hypothetical.

A somewhat similar setting was at stake when Professor Besselink requested access to the negotiation mandate concerning EU Accession Agreement to the European Convention of Human Rights.[134] Unlike the EU, the Council of Europe had placed all its negotiating directives on the internet. The Court did not consider this fact but found that the Council had interpreted the international relations exception too broadly and stressed that it could only be used to protect objectives that were subject to concrete negotiations. The Court accepted that when the positions of the EU and its negotiating partners change:

> it cannot be precluded that disclosure by the Union, to the public, of its own negotiating positions, when the negotiating positions of the other parties remain secret, could, in practice, have a negative effect on the negotiating capacity of the Union.[135]

However, those parts of the directives which merely referred to the principles included in the EU Treaties or the list of questions to be addressed in the negotiations were to be handed out.

The Aarhus Convention and this particular compliance procedure concern the rights of civil society and their enforcement by the EU. In this specific context, the Council's insistence that disclosure of legal analysis on the effect of Treaty constraints would result in 'external interference' is particularly worrisome. In its response to my request, the Council argues that:

> if the analysis carried out by the [CLS] had to be fully disclosed, certain of the arguments developed therefore would give rise to external interference. After the Commission presented its proposal amending Regulation 1367/2006, several NGOs have actively run campaigns urging the institutions 'to amend EU access to justice law and comply with international law' and 'to close the loopholes identified [in the Commission proposal] and ensure an internal review mechanism that is finally fit for purpose'. These NGOs consider that the ongoing revision of the Aarhus Regulation as proposed by the Commission last year is 'still not strong enough to ensure compliance with international law'.[136]

As evidence, the Council refers to a small number of blog posts written by NGOs.[137] The Council then goes on to elaborate that:

> The reality of this external pressure is therefore not purely hypothetical, if not to say certain, and the evidence set out in the previous paragraph shows that there is a

[133] Case ACCC/S/2015/2, available at Aarhus Convention Compliance Committee, 'Findings and Recommendations with regard to Submission ACCC/S/2015/2 concerning Compliance by Belarus Adopted by the Compliance Committee on 23 July 2021' (*United Nations Economic Commission for Europe*, 25 August 2021) ECE/MP.PP/C.1/2021/13.

[134] Case T-331/11 *Besselink v Council* ECLI:EU:T:2013:419.

[135] ibid para 72.

[136] 'Reply Adopted by the Council on 11 June 2021 to Confirmatory Application 16/c/01/21' (n 40) para 37.

[137] The Council did not mention my own post in the European Law Blog around the same time entitled 'Watering Down the Aarhus Regulation – Time to Deliver an "Adequate and Effective Remedy"'.

> reasonable risk that the decision to be taken would be substantially affected as a result of that pressure.[138]

It seems astonishing and, from the viewpoint of democratic participation, chilling, that the Council sees such modest civil society participation as a threat to its decision making. If NGOs writing blog posts is not an appropriate way of democratic participation, then what is? That democratic society relies on the engagement of civil society, is at the core of the normative choice made in Article 10 TEU for participatory democracy. In every functioning democracy, legislative processes are (and should be!) subject to pressures, which should have capacity to affect the outcome. In this context, debate taking place before decisions are taken would also provide a means for the Council to ascertain that the legal analysis that it bases its position on is solid and survives external scrutiny. This is of a particular importance also given that the question concerns obligations that are already binding on the EU. Timely disclosure of a legal opinion discussing the EU law boundaries to solutions that the European Union could implement to remedy non-compliance with the Aarhus Convention could inform the public and trigger debate concerning the revision process of the Aarhus Regulation. Debate among citizens, NGOs and academics might actually contribute to reaching results that are sustainable and thus avoid subsequent legal challenges. Institutional legal services have no monopoly of legal expertise. In her conclusions on the inquiry to the TTIP, the European Ombudsman also suggests that there may be situations in international negotiations where it makes sense to engage with public opinion early:

> Responses to the Ombudsman's public consultation have made clear the importance that stakeholders attach to documents, such as consolidated texts containing EU and US positions. … Early publication of common negotiating texts would allow for timely feedback to negotiators in relation to sections of the agreement that pose particular problems. The Ombudsman assumes that it is preferable to learn of such problems sooner rather than later, so that they can be tackled effectively.[139]

Also the EU Courts have addressed similar arguments by the Council many times and stressed that:

> in a system based on the principle of democratic legitimacy, co-legislators must be held accountable for their actions to the public. If citizens are to be able to exercise their democratic rights they must be in a position to follow in detail the decision-making process within the institutions taking part in the legislative procedures and to have access to all relevant information. … Thus, the expression of public opinion in relation to a particular provisional legislative proposal or agreement … forms an integral part of the exercise of EU citizens' democratic rights ….[140]

T Paloniitty and P Leino-Sandberg, 'Watering Down the Aarhus Regulation – Time to Deliver an "Adequate and Effective Remedy"' (European Law Blog, 11 March 2021) www.europeanlawblog.eu/2021/03/11/watering-down-the-aarhus-regulation-time-to-deliver-an-adequate-and-effective-remedy/.

[138] 'Reply Adopted by the Council on 11 June 2021 to Confirmatory Application 16/c/01/21' (n 40) para 37.

[139] European Ombudsman Decision in case OI/10/2014/RA closing her own-initiative inquiry OI/10/2014/RA concerning the European Commission (6 January 2015), paras 22–23.

[140] Case T-540/15 *De Capitani v Parliament* ECLI:EU:T:2018:167, paras 98–99.

The Council's argumentation is troubling for journalists, academics, and NGOs, who rely on access to public documents to fulfil their role as 'public watchdogs'. The Grand Chamber of the European Court on Human Rights has stressed their role in democratic society, and that:

> the manner in which public watchdogs carry out their activities may have a significant impact on the proper functioning of a democratic society. … Given that accurate information is a tool of their trade, it will often be necessary for persons and organisations exercising watchdog functions to gain access to information in order to perform their role of reporting on matters of public interest.[141]

In this jurisprudence the 'watchdog' function also extends to academic researchers,'[142] who exercise their academic freedom protected under Article 13 the Charter of Fundamental Rights of the European Union.[143] When asking for the legal opinion, Neither ClientEarth nor I ask out of private interest, but in our respective roles as a civil society representative and a researcher, exercising a right that the public access to documents regime is specifically meant to serve.[144] And there are seldom contexts where recycling the argument of 'external pressure' would be more inappropriate than that of the Aarhus Convention framework.

5. CONCLUSIONS

Given the subject matter of the Aarhus Convention, the travails of the EU first in properly implementing it in EU law and then in living up to its scriptures in its institutional practices provides a rather delicious case study into the troubled relation of EU institutions with transparency and citizen participation. It also illustrates a number of more general themes of EU transparency research. Notwithstanding some proactive policies in the form of 'a new approach to transparency in trade negotiations', the transparency regime in Regulation No 1049/2001 remains unchanged, and its international-relations exception is arguably one of the elements in most urgent need of update.[145] Despite its public promises, the Commission has done little to improve access to documents relating to trade agreements under negotiation.[146] Now that negotiating mandates are more frequently disclosed, one also wonders about the actual transparency gain, since they generally contain very little information. Often they rather include a list of elements that the agreement should cover.[147] Strategic information about EU negotiation objectives is rather included in documents

[141] *Magyar Helsinki Bizottság v Hungary*, Application No 18030/11, 8 November 2016, para 167.

[142] ibid para 168.

[143] 'The arts and scientific research shall be free of constraint. Academic freedom shall be respected.' See Article 13 Charter of Fundamental Rights of the European Union [2016] OJ C202/389.

[144] Case T-561/12 *Beninca v Commission* ECLIEU:T:2013:558, para 58.

[145] D Curtin and P Leino-Sandberg, 'Openness, Transparency and the Right of Access to Documents in the EU. In-Depth Analysis' (2016) *EUI RCAS Working Paper* 2016/63.

[146] Ankersmit and Peters (n 27).

[147] See eg Council of the European Union, 'Negotiating Directives for a Free Trade Agreement with Australia' (2018) 7663/18; Council of the European Union, 'Negotiating Directives for the Modernisation of the Energy Charter Treaty – Adoption' (2019) 10745/19 ADD 1.

produced during the negotiations that concern negotiation tactics or that reveal the areas in which the Commission, acting on behalf of the EU, would be willing to compromise in any negotiation. The Commission website includes some reports from negotiation rounds and text proposals, but their number is more limited.[148] Despite some more proactive gestures of providing access to negotiation mandates or selected negotiations documents, EU's external negotiations continue to provoke great public interest beyond these snapshots made available at the Commission's own discretion, which is reflected in access to documents requests.[149] Very few negative decisions have been appealed, as a result of which institutional choices remain unchallenged.

The reform of the Aarhus Regulation may have addressed a troubling point in EU compliance with its international obligations under the Aarhus Convention. But while access to justice is significantly improved, it is not clear that even these rights granted under the Convention are now properly secured. In particular, Article 9 of the Convention creates an obligation to ensure that 'members of the public have access to administrative or judicial procedures to challenge acts and omissions by private persons and public authorities' and that such procedures 'shall … be fair, equitable, timely and not prohibitively expensive'. The last element, the right to affordable justice, was dealt serious blows by the Court's recent decisions. Stichting Greenpeace Nederland, an NGO that lost a case, was ordered to pay not only its own legal costs and those of the Commission, but also the costs of intervening private parties.[150] In another case, civil society activists going to Court in an access to documents case against Frontex were ordered to pay a massive lawyer's fee after losing the case.[151] These are not minor events – they are likely to have a major chilling effect on the ability of NGOs and citizens to seek judicial remedies. An online petition calling for the payment to be dropped was signed by more than 87,000 people.[152] To my knowledge, the ACCC has not addressed these questions. The Commission Communication from 2023 refers to 'weaknesses and obstacles for NGOs at national level, including insufficient standing and high litigation costs', but frames them as problems that primarily concern the Member State level.[153] Yet, the EU is as a Contracting Party in its own

[148] 'Transparency in EU Trade Negotiations' (*European Commission*), policy.trade.ec.europa.eu/eu-trade-relationships-country-and-region/transparency-eu-trade-negotiations_en.

[149] DG Trade reports that in 2021 it handled 291 requests covering 1,200 documents that had not been proactively disclosed originating from law firms (about 33%), citizens (17%), journalists (17%), NGOs (12%), academic institutions (12%), companies and associations (7%), and others (2%). 76% of these requests led to full access to the requested documents, 'Transparency in EU Trade Policy: 2021 Statistics for DG TRADE' (*European Commission*), policy.trade.ec.europa.eu/eu-trade-relationships-country-and-region/transparency-eu-trade-negotiations/transparency-eu-trade-policy-2021-statistics-dg-trade_en.

[150] Case T-545/11 RENV *Stichting Greenpeace Nederland and PAN Europe v Commission* ECLI:EU:T:2018:817.

[151] Case T-31/18 *Izuzquiza and Semsrott v Frontex* ECLI:EU:T:2019:815.

[152] 'Petition: Luisa and Arne vs Frontex' (WeMoveEurope), act.wemove.eu/campaigns/luisa-arne-vs-frontex-en.

[153] European Commission, 'Communication from the Commission to the European Parliament, the Council, the European Economic and Social Committee and the Committee of the Regions on the Findings Adopted by the Aarhus Convention Compliance Committee in Case ACCC/C/2015/128 as regards State Aid: Analysing the Implications of the Findings and Assessing the Options Available' (2023) COM(2023) 307 final.

right equally bound to guarantee review that is 'fair, equitable, timely and not prohibitively expensive'.

As to the other two objectives of the Convention, transparency and participatory rights, EU institutions still have a long way to go to make them reality. This is partly due to the legal framework which remains incomplete, but partly to the way the Court has applied it. But, without doubt, the most important obstacle to transparency and participatory rights remains the institutions' steadfast refusal to properly apply the framework, a refusal that seems to be rooted in a peculiar understanding of the role of NGOs and researchers in democratic life. Both in the internal and the external sphere of decision making, different viewpoints, and even vocal criticism, are not 'external interference' but rather lie at the very heart of democratic participation. Trying to insulate EU decision-making from such external scrutiny is depriving it of a key part of its democratic credentials. The EU desperately needs that external interference and scrutiny, and the media attention it brings, to gradually grow into a genuine democratic political entity. Until the institutions recognise this, the EU is doomed to remain a distant and obscure bureaucracy that few outside the Brussels square mile understand.

Part IV

Strategic International Ambitions and the Power of EU Instruments

Enhancing European Technological Sovereignty: The Foreign Investment Screening Regulation and Beyond

SARA POLI AND DANIELE GALLO*

PROLOGUE

MARISE CREMONA HAS been a leading scholar and a guide for many academics who have known her at the European University Institute (EUI) or in other academic contexts. She is a great example of someone who has left a mark on the professional and personal lives of those who are lucky enough to work with her. When you talk to Marise, she is always able to give you useful suggestions and help in finding new research leads. She was the inspiration for Sara Poli deciding to study EU external relations at the EUI. Sara learnt so much from her both during her course and in their conversations at Villa Schifanoia. In 2008–2009, they worked together on the '*Kadi* legacy' and on the external dimension of the area of freedom, security, and justice. Marise also accepted Sara's invitation to events organised in Pisa on other topics related to external relations. During her year at the EUI, Sara also met Daniele Gallo, Jean Monnet Fellow at the EUI at that time, who was also inspired by Marise's classes – including those offered at Luiss for several years – and writings.

We would like to thank Marise for her words of advice and encouragement, but also for her human touch, which is such a rare quality. In this chapter, devoted to the EU's ability to protect critical infrastructure and critical technologies, we cover some of the themes on which Marise has written extensively. These include the boundaries between the EU's internal market-based regulatory competence and the common commercial policy, the choice of the legal basis of EU acts, the EU regulation of new technologies, and the EU's approach to foreign direct investments.

* Sara Poli is Full Professor of EU Law at the University of Pisa; Daniele Gallo is Full Professor of EU Law and Jean Monnet Chair at Luiss University (2020–2023), Rome. Although the article was a product of common efforts of the authors, Sara Poli focused on Sections 1–3 and 5–7 while Daniele Gallo is the author of the whole of Section 4. Section 8 and the Addendum were written by both authors. The authors are grateful to Dr Valeria Vinci for her editorial assistance.

1. INTRODUCTION

In recent years, four sources of major concern regarding the use of key enabling technologies[1] have been the focus of the EU institutions' attention: (1) the EU has accumulated technological gaps and lost competitiveness in the global market;[2] (2) foreign direct investments (FDI) may affect Member States' security and public order where foreign operators take control of critical infrastructure[3] and technologies;[4] (3) foreign subsidised companies may take over EU-based companies of strategic importance; (4) the EU is dependent on third countries for critical raw materials which are essential in technology-related industries and digital infrastructure. In order to address the four interconnected challenges mentioned above, the Commission,[5] the Council[6]

[1] T Ramahandry et al, 'Key Enabling Technologies for Europe's Technological Sovereignty' (*European Parliamentary Research Service*, 16 December 2021), www.europarl.europa.eu/thinktank/en/document/EPRS_STU(2021)697184.

[2] 'Europe can hardly compete with its main rivals (USA and China), especially in the fields of micro/nano-electronics and artificial intelligence' in Ramahandry et al (n 1) 38.

[3] There are different definitions of this notion. Regulation (EU) 2019/452 of the European Parliament and of the Council establishing a framework for the screening of foreign direct investments into the Union (Regulation 2019/452) [2019] OJ L79I/1 offers the following one: '(a) critical infrastructure, whether physical or virtual, including energy, transport, water, health, communications, media, data processing or storage, aerospace, defence, electoral or financial infrastructure, and sensitive facilities, as well as land and real estate crucial for the use of such infrastructure (Art 4(1)(a))'. Elsewhere critical infrastructure is defined as: 'An asset, system or part thereof located in Member States which is essential for the maintenance of vital societal functions, health, safety, security, economic or social well-being of people, and the disruption or destruction of which would have a significant impact in a Member State as a result of the failure to maintain those functions.' Art 2(a)Directive 2008/114/EC on the identification and designation of European critical infrastructures and the assessment of the need to improve their protection [2008] OJ L345/75. This Directive, which applied to energy and transport infrastructures only, also defines a 'European Critical Infrastructure' and lays down a procedure for the designation of 'ECI' whose disruption would have cross-border effects and aims to protect those infrastructures that enable the provision of essential services or functions for society or economic activities. It was a first step to identify and designate ECIs whose disruption caused by attacks had significant cross-border impacts (on at least two Member States). For comments on this Directive and on its revision, see I Anglmayer, 'European critical infrastructure Revision of Directive 2008/114/EC' (*European Parliamentary Research Service*, 3 February 2021), www.europarl.europa.eu/thinktank/en/document/EPRS_BRI(2021)662604. However, this piece of legislation has been repealed by Directive (EU) 2022/2557 of the European Parliament and of the Council on the resilience of critical entities and repealing Council Directive 2008/114/EC (Directive 2022/2577) [2022] OJ L333/164. The new act, which will be briefly discussed in Section 7, has expanded the scope of application to include 'critical entities', that is to say entities operating critical infrastructure. See Recital 3.

[4] Art 4(1)(b) Regulation 2019/452 states: 'Critical technology and dual use items are defined in point 1 of Article 2 of Council Regulation (EC) No 428/2009 (15), including artificial intelligence, robotics, semiconductors, cybersecurity, aerospace, defence, energy storage, quantum and nuclear technologies as well as nanotechnologies and biotechnologies'.

[5] The President of the European Commission has stressed the importance of investing in 'Our European tech sovereignty' in her speech '2021 State of the Union Address by President von der Leyen' (*European Commission*, 15 September 2021), www.ec.europa.eu/commission/presscorner/detail/en/SPEECH_21_4701. Furthermore, in her political guidelines of 2019 it was stated that it was not too late to achieve technological sovereignty in some critical technology areas. See Ursula von der Leyen, 'A Union That Strives for More: My Agenda for Europe (Political Guidelines for the Next European Commission 2019–2024)' (*European Commission*, 9 October 2019), commission.europa.eu/system/files/2020-04/political-guidelines-next-commission_en_0.pdf. See also European Commission, 'Shaping Europe's Digital Future' (2020) COM(2020) 67 final; European Commission, 'A New Industrial Strategy for Europe' (2020) COM(2020) 102 final; European Commission, 'Updating the 2020 New Industrial Strategy: Building a Stronger Single Market for Europe's Recovery' (2021) COM(2021) 350 final.

[6] See eg Council Conclusions on the significance of 5G to the European Economy and the need to mitigate security risks linked to 5G [2019] OJ C414/7.

and the Parliament[7] have often advocated the need to strengthen European technological sovereignty and the EU's strategic autonomy.[8] In this context we concentrate on the second of the four listed concerns and in particular on Regulation 2019/452 establishing a framework for the screening of foreign direct investments (FDIs) into the Union (Regulation 2019/452),[9] which was enacted to enable the Member States to take restrictive measures relating to FDIs on grounds of security or public order. Most notably, in this chapter we discuss whether or not this piece of legislation can be considered an instrument that reinforces the Union's strategic autonomy and technological sovereignty. The need to protect critical infrastructure[10] and critical technologies,[11] which lies at the roots of Regulation 2019/452, is linked to the debate on the strengthening of EU's strategic autonomy and European technological sovereignty (ETS), even if there is no mention of these notions in the Regulation. Given that Member States are sovereign in the protection of national security and public order,[12] we reflect on whether the Regulation is a step forward toward the enhancement of EU's powers in safeguarding the Union dimension of security and public order and whether it represents as such an advancement of the EU's integration process. We also consider whether the EU has been capable of enacting other legal instruments that were designed to support Member States in preserving critical technologies and critical infrastructure, despite it having limited conferred competences to do so.

The chapter proceeds as follows. In Section 2 we set Regulation 2019/452 in the wider context of the debate on the strengthening of the EU's *technological sovereignty and strategic autonomy* in the protection of critical infrastructure and technology. We attempt to define the contours of the two concepts (in italic) and identify the broad spectrum of EU policies relevant to the achievement of the underlying objectives. The authors take the view that the scale of the challenges requires a European rather than an exclusively national approach. In Sections 3 and 4 we shift attention to Regulation 2019/452. The existence of a clear nexus between FDIs and technology is undisputed, as shown by the Explanatory Memorandum attached to the Proposal for Regulation 2019/452,[13] whereby it is stated that the Commission, while considering

[7] See eg European Parliament, 'Resolution on a New Industrial Strategy for Europe (2020/2076(INI))' P9_TA(2020)0321 [2021] OJ C425/43.

[8] See above n 3.

[9] Regulation 2019/452.

[10] For a definition see above n 3. Examples of these infrastructures are ports, roads, telecommunication networks, and energy networks. See W Zwartkruis and B de Jong, 'The EU Regulation on Screening of Foreign Direct Investment: A Game Changer?' (2020) 31 *European Business Law Review* 447, 451.

[11] For a definition see above n 4.

[12] Under Article 4(2) Treaty on European Union (TEU), the Union 'shall respect […] essential State functions, including ensuring the territorial integrity of the State, maintaining law and order and safeguarding national security. In particular, national security remains the sole responsibility of each Member State.'

[13] European Commission, 'Proposal for a Regulation of the European Parliament and of the Council establishing a framework for screening of foreign direct investments into the European Union' (2017) COM(2017) 487 final, para 3. See also European Commission, 'Report From The Commission to The European Parliament and the Council: First Annual Report on the Screening of Foreign Direct Investments into the Union' (2021) COM(2021) 714 final; European Commission, 'Report from the Commission to the European Parliament and the Council: Second Annual Report on the Screening of Foreign Direct Investments into the Union' (2022) COM(2022) 433 final; European Commission, 'Commission Staff Working Document: Screening of FDI into the Union and its Member States accompanying the document "Report from the Commission to the European Parliament and the Council Second Annual Report on the Screening of Foreign Direct Investments into the Union"' (2021) SWD(2021) 334 final.

that openness to foreign investment remains a key principle for the EU and a major source of growth, acknowledges the existence of risks 'about foreign investors, notably state-owned enterprises, taking over European companies with key technologies for strategic reasons'.[14] In addition, in the Explanatory Memorandum, it is asserted that the Regulation is complementary to EU policies 'in the fields of electronic communications, cybersecurity, critical infrastructure protection, and industrial competitiveness in cybersecurity products and services'.[15] In Section 3 we highlight the different objectives of Regulation 2019/452 while in Section 4 attention is devoted to the functioning of the screening mechanism of FDIs, the sectors in respect of which the screening is performed, the cooperation between the European Commission and national authorities, and the special treatment reserved for sovereign investments. In Section 5 we assess whether in the context of Regulation 2019/452 the EU has been granted sufficiently robust powers to limit the risk of foreign investors acquiring control over critical infrastructure and critical technologies in the Member States. Furthermore, we discuss whether or not the mentioned Regulation has the effect of fostering the EU's technological sovereignty. In Section 6 we examine whether, given the limits of EU's competences, the EU has been capable of taking effective action to meet the challenges of protecting technology that is vital for the internal market and for the Union and Member States' security. In this Section an overview of the measures that were adopted to ensure that national authorities may safeguard critical infrastructure and technologies is provided. Section 7 contains an example of national export control measure of key enabling technology, that was enacted by a Member State but may be considered a contribution to the reinforcement of the EU's technological sovereignty (ETS). Finally, Section 8 provides some concluding remarks.

2. THE DEBATE ON STRENGTHENING EUROPEAN TECHNOLOGICAL SOVEREIGNTY AND THE EU'S STRATEGIC AUTONOMY

Before turning to the examination of Regulation 2019/452, it is necessary to briefly clarify the meanings of EU's strategic autonomy and ETS.[16] The former term refers to the ability of the EU to act autonomously, that is, without being dependent[17] on

[14] European Commission, 'Proposal for a Regulation of the European Parliament and of the Council establishing a framework for screening of foreign direct investments into the European Union' (2017) COM(2017) 487 final, para 1.

[15] ibid.

[16] On the nexus between trade, investment and strategic autonomy see the reflections in T Verellen and A Hofer, 'The Unilateral Turn in EU Trade and Investment Policy' (2023) 28 *European Foreign Affairs Review* 1.

[17] Editorial Comments, 'Keeping Europeanism at Bay? Strategic Autonomy as a Constitutional Problem' (2022) 59 *CML Rev* 313; M Damen, 'EU Strategic Autonomy 2013–2023: From Concept to Capacity' (*European Parliamentary Research Service*, 8 July 2022), www.europarl.europa.eu/thinktank/en/document/EPRS_BRI(2022)733589. A scholar argues: 'Si la revendication d'indépendance s'inscrit dans des enjeux de souveraineté, la recherche d'autonomie semble aussi être une façon dépolitisée de parler de souveraineté, un peu à la manière de la jurisprudence de la Cour de justice qui défend l'autonomie de l'Union européenne à l'égard des ordres juridiques extérieurs.' See B Bertrand, 'La souveraineté numérique européenne: une "pensée en acte"?' (2021) 2 *Revue trimestrielle de droit européen* 249, 253. See also the contributions in B Bertrand (ed), *La politique européenne du numérique* (Bruxelles, Bruylant, 2023).

other countries. This does not necessarily imply that the EU is seeking to expand its competences. In contrast, in the latter notion of ETS the use of the word 'sovereignty' next to 'European' may be taken as an indication that the EU institutions are pursuing the federalist objective of reinforcing the sovereignty of the EU. In this respect, a precise definition of the concept is missing in the EU's official documents.[18] The Commission's working programme Horizon Europe (2023–2024) 'digital, industry and technology'[19] is useful in shedding light on this notion. Strengthening ETS requires consolidating the EU's capacity to use existing technologies, and to develop new technologies, to protect the integrity and security of the Union and its Member States.[20] Therefore, there seems to be a link between attempting to avoid situations of technological dependence and common foreign and security policy objectives.[21] Technological sovereignty also refers to EU Member States' capacity to be self-sufficient in crucial technology-intensive sectors which are the basis of the provision of core services for a modern economy. Thus, reducing dependence on third countries is necessary not only to enhance the EU and Member States' security but also to ensure the functioning of the internal market. This link is well captured by the roll out of 5G technology.[22] Dependence on countries such as China for the supply of 5G connectivity is considered both a concern for EU security and for the functioning of the internal market; this is why the European Council has highlighted the need to apply restrictions to high-risk suppliers for key assets defined as critical[23] and to strengthen the capacity of the Union in this area.[24]

[18] In academia the notion of 'European Sovereignty' has been debated. For example, an author claims that European Sovereignty has an internal and external dimension: the first consists in taming national sovereignty of Member States; the second one is defined as the EU's 'attempt to restore and expand the "rule of law" not only by harnessing market forces but by using them in order to promote "home-grown" legal standards'. A Bailleux, 'The Two Faces of European Sovereignty' (2020) 5 *European Papers* 303.

[19] European Commission, 'Commission Implementing Decision on the Adoption of the Work Programme for 2023–2024 within the Framework of the Specific Programme implementing Horizon Europe – the Framework Programme for Research and Innovation and on its Financing: Annex VII Horizon Europe Work Programme 2023–2024 "7. Digital, Industry and Space"' (2022) C(2022) 7550 final.

[20] ibid 15. The enhancement of the European technological sovereignty partly overlaps with the effort to strengthen 'digital sovereignty'. This overlap is clear from the Commission Communication, 'Shaping Europe's Digital Future' in which it is stated: 'European technological sovereignty starts from ensuring the integrity and resilience of our data infrastructure, networks and communications. It requires creating the right conditions for Europe to develop and deploy its own key capacities, thereby reducing our dependency on other parts of the globe for the most crucial technologies. Europe's ability to define its own rules and values in the digital age will be reinforced by such capacities'. European Commission, 'Shaping Europe's Digital Future' (2020) COM(2020) 67 final, 2.

[21] Art 21(2)a) Regulation 2019/452.

[22] The latest technology in wireless connectivity. B Akcali Gur, 'Cybersecurity, European Digital Sovereignty and the 5G Rollout Crisis' (2022) 46 *Computer Law & Security Review* 3.

[23] European Council, 'Special Meeting of the European Council (1 and 2 October 2020) – Conclusions' (2020) EUCO 13/20. As of 2017 the US government restricted the use of equipment sold by the Chinese company that was the main developer of 5G, Huawei. Security reasons were the justifications provided for such a move. See JC Gallagher, 'The U.S. Restrictions on Huawei Technologies: National Security, Foreign Policy, and Economic Interests' (*Congressional Research Service*, 5 January 2022), www.everycrsreport.com/files/2022-01-05_R47012_65c5c54827b8fef912a19079f10e144b3b88d009.pdf.

[24] China has also complained at World Trade Organization (WTO) level about the discriminatory market access prohibition enacted by Sweden on 5G equipment. Council for trade in Goods, 'Minutes of the meeting of the Council for Trade in Goods 31 March and 1 April 2021' (*World Trade Organisation*, 16 June 2021) G/C/M/139, ss 13 and 38. For a comment and more details see G Adinolfi, 'States' economic

It is worth noting that the importance of ETS[25] is advocated in various contexts, including in the Common Foreign and Defence Policy. For example, in the 'Strategic Compass',[26] it is stated that: '[r]educing strategic dependencies and enhancing our technological sovereignty is critical if we are to meet the challenges of a more dangerous world'.[27] There is no doubt that the outbreak of the conflict in Ukraine has made this need even more compelling.

Technological dependence is also risky in the field of space.[28] Indeed, the delivery of digital services, on which many economic activities are based, is possible thanks to space services and data from the Galileo, EGNOS and Copernicus programmes. The EU attempted to gain independence from third countries early on in this area.[29] It should be added that space data and technology have a dual use: they can be exploited for both civil and foreign policy purposes.[30]

measures to counter cyberattacks: disentangling their (il)legitimacy under international law' (2022) 3 *Rivista di diritto internazionale privato e processuale* 513, 523.

[25] Some scholars define 'technological sovereignty' as the ability of a country (or a group of countries) 'to generate autonomously technological and scientific knowledge or to use technological capabilities developed outside through the activation of reliable partnerships'. F Crespi, S Caravella, M Menghini and C Salvadori, 'European Technological Sovereignty: An Emerging Framework for Policy Strategy' (2021) 56 *Intereconomics* 348, 349. Think tanks have also started a reflection on this concept. It is defined as 'The ability for Europe to develop, provide, protect, and retain critical technologies required for the welfare of European citizens and prosperity of businesses, and the ability to act and decide independently in a globalised environment'. Ramahandry et al (n 1) 3. In other contexts 'technological sovereignty' refers to 'an ability of states, or a community of states, to provide the technologies it deems critical for its existence and operation, as well as for maintaining its "capabilities", and to be able to develop these technologies or source them from other economic areas without one-sided structural dependency'. J Edler, K Blind, R Frietsch, S Kimpeler, H Kroll, C Lerch, T Reiss, F Roth, T Schubert, J Schuler and R Walz, 'Technology Sovereignty: From Demand to Concept' (2020) *Fraunhofer Institute for Systems and Innovation Research ISI* 2.

[26] Council of the European Union, 'A Strategic Compass for Security and Defence – For a European Union that Protects its Citizens, Values and Interests and Contributes to International Peace and Security' (2022) 7371/22 approved by European Council, 'European Council Meeting (24 and 25 March 2022) – Conclusions' (2022) EUCO 1/22. On the new strategy see L Mola, 'Fostering "European Technological Sovereignty" Through the CSDP: Conceptual and Legal Challenges. First Reflections Around the 2022 Strategic Compass' (2023) 8 *European Papers* 459.

[27] European External Action Service, 'Working Document of the European External Action Service: A Strategic Compass for Security and Defence – For a European Union that Protects its Citizens, Values and Interests and Contributes to International Peace and Security' (2021) *EEAS(2021)* 1169, 20.

[28] This is clear, for example, in a speech delivered by Thierry Breton at the launch event of the European Space Programme: 'Europe must be able to monitor space by its own. This is a question of strategic autonomy, both for the security of our critical infrastructure, but also for Europe's access to space'. The speech available at: 'Launch Event of the New European Union Space Programme' (*European Commission*, 22 June 2021), www.ec.europa.eu/commission/presscorner/detail/en/speech_21_7635. See also D Fiott, 'The European space sector as an enabler of EU strategic autonomy' (*European Parliamentary Research Service*, 16 December 2020), www.europarl.europa.eu/thinktank/en/document/EXPO_IDA(2020)653620.

[29] The idea of European independence from American or Russian technology dates back to the creation of the Copernicus programme. Galileo is the 'first public infrastructure owned by the European institutions' and operates independently of other existing systems; it thus contributes, among other things, to the strategic autonomy of the Union, particularly for environmental data that are essential for monitoring. The EGNOS (European Geostationary Navigation Overlay Service) programme uses and enhances the information transmitted by the signals from the satellite constellations of the American GPS and Russian GLONASS systems by means of three satellites in geostationary orbit and is linked to air navigation.

[30] Space is also crucial for defence purposes, as highlighted in the Card report. '2020 Coordinated Annual Review on Defence (CARD) Report: Executive Summary' (*European Defence Agency*, 2020), www.eda.europa.eu/docs/default-source/reports/card-2020-executive-summary-report.pdf, 7.

The effort to strengthen technological sovereignty overlaps with that of making the EU strategically autonomous not only to preserve itself but also to become more competitive in the world market. It is useful to give a few examples. The EU is lagging behind other countries and has accumulated competitive disadvantages in key technology-intensive sectors of the economy such as robotics and nanotechnology. These gaps affect the functioning of the internal market but also the EU's competitiveness in the global market. The COVID-19 pandemic contributed to exacerbating dependence on foreign countries. The shortage of 'critical products' such as semiconductors and recent initiatives adopted by the EU in this area illustrate how the EU has sought to preserve its industrial and technological base. As a matter of fact, the EU has an overall share of only 10 per cent in the global semiconductors market, as reported in a study quoted by a Commission document.[31] EU Member States rely on third-country suppliers: Taiwan and Singapore are where the most advanced chips are manufactured.

The Commission has proposed the adoption of the so-called EU Chips Act, which was preannounced by its President,[32] with a view to making the EU strategically autonomous as far as critical technologies are concerned. The proposal[33] includes, among others, Article 114 Treaty on the Functioning of the European Union (TFEU) as its legal basis since, as the Commission convincingly argues, it aims at creating a harmonised legal framework for increasing the Union's resilience and security of supply in the area of semiconductors. At the same time, the proposed Act is also based on other multiple legal bases related to the EU's complementary competences.[34] Indeed, the EU measure aims at supporting actions taken by Member States to foster innovation and adjust the semiconductor industry to structural changes and to accelerate production. The proposed Chips Act further advocates boosting cooperation with like-minded partners, such as the United States, Japan, South Korea, Singapore, Taiwan and others, and establishing strong cooperation with neighbouring countries.[35] In addition, the EU has also supported the conclusion of partnerships with the private sector in order to fill its technological gaps.[36]

[31] European Commission, 'Proposal for a Regulation of the European Parliament and of the Council establishing a Framework of Measures for Strengthening Europe's Semiconductor Ecosystem (Chips Act)' (2022) COM(2022) 46 final.

[32] 'Statement by European Commission President von der Leyen on her visit to ASML, together with Dutch Prime Minister Rutte' (*European Commission*, 15 November 2021), www.ec.europa.eu/commission/presscorner/detail/en/statement_21_6050.

[33] European Commission, 'Proposal for a Regulation of the European Parliament and of the Council establishing a Framework of Measures for Strengthening Europe's Semiconductor Ecosystem (Chips Act)' (2022) COM(2022) 46 final.

[34] Arts 173 (3), 182(1) and 183 Consolidated version of the Treaty on the Functioning of the European Union (TFEU) [2016] OJ C202/47.

[35] European Commission, 'Proposal for a Regulation of the European Parliament and of the Council establishing a Framework of Measures for Strengthening Europe's Semiconductor Ecosystem (Chips Act)' (2022) COM(2022) 46 final, 21.

[36] For example, in December 2020, 22 Member States committed to work together to reinforce Europe's capabilities in semiconductor technologies and offering the best performance for applications in a wide range of sectors. They joined the European Alliance for Industrial Processors and Semiconductor Technologies. See 'Digital sovereignty: Commission kick-starts Alliances for Semiconductors and Industrial Cloud Technologies' (*European Commission*, 19 July 2021), www.ec.europa.eu/commission/presscorner/detail/en/ip_21_3733. It should be noted that as of February 2022, the Commission has also approved

There are other strategic areas in which the EU is set to become autonomous. These comprise pharmaceuticals[37] and 'critical raw materials'.[38] In certain fields, where the EU cannot achieve complete autonomy, it is currently preparing to reduce its 'strategic dependencies'.[39] Yet in some areas the latter cannot be eliminated altogether. This is the case in relation to access to critical raw materials, the list of which has grown from 14 in 2011 to 30 in 2020.[40] Indeed, due to the lack of these resources in the EU,[41] the latter is dependent on imports from third countries and is bound by the export restrictions of the countries holding these materials.[42] The Union has sought to react to this vulnerability by concluding bilateral agreements with key trade partners.[43]

3. THE OBJECTIVES OF THE 2019 FOREIGN DIRECT INVESTMENTS SCREENING REGULATION AND ITS AMBIGUITIES

Having sketched out the debate on ETS and EU's strategic autonomy, we will now explore whether Regulation 2019/452 is subject mainly to a supranationalist or intergovernmentalist logic, ie, whether by reinforcing EU's powers in the field it challenges to a great extent Member States' sovereignty.[44]

three Important Projects of Common European Interest (IPCEIs): one on microelectronics and two on batteries. These projects 'can make a very important contribution to sustainable economic growth, jobs, competitiveness and resilience for industry and the economy in the Union and strengthen its open strategic autonomy, by enabling breakthrough innovation and infrastructure projects through cross-border cooperation and with positive spill-over effects on the internal market and the society as a whole'. European Commission, 'Communication from the Commission: Criteria for the Analysis of the Compatibility with the Internal Market of State Aid to Promote the Execution of Important Projects of Common European Interest' [2021] OJ C528/10, para 2.

[37] As the Commission highlights in a recently published document: 'Building up EU's open strategic autonomy in the area of medicines requires actions to identify strategic dependencies in health, and to propose measures to reduce them, possibly including by diversifying production and supply chains, ensuring strategic stockpiling, as well as fostering production and investment in Europe'. European Commission, 'Pharmaceutical Strategy for Europe' (2020) COM(2020) 761 final, 17.

[38] See for the current list European Commission, 'Critical Raw Materials Resilience: Charting a Path towards greater Security and Sustainability' (2020) COM(2020) 474 final, 3–4.

[39] See European Council, 'European Council Meeting (24 and 25 March 2022) – Conclusions' (2022) EUCO 1/22, point 20.

[40] 2020 COM (2020) 474 final, 3.

[41] European Commission, 'Critical Raw Materials Resilience: Charting a Path towards greater Security and Sustainability' (2020) COM(2020) 474 final, 15.

[42] M Szczepański, 'Critical Raw Materials in EU External Policies: Improving Access and Raising Global Standards' (*European Parliamentary Research Service*, 12 May 2021), www.europarl.europa.eu/thinktank/en/document/EPRS_BRI(2021)690606.

[43] Two examples of instruments designed to guarantee the supply of critical goods are represented by partnership on raw materials and batteries with Ukraine (13 July 2021, see 'EU and Ukraine kick-start Strategic Partnership on Raw Materials' (*European Commission*, 13 July 2021), single-market-economy.ec.europa.eu/news/eu-and-ukraine-kick-start-strategic-partnership-raw-materials-2021-07-13_en) and with Canada (15 June 2021, see 'EU and Canada set up a Strategic Partnership on Raw Materials' (*European Commission*, 21 June 2021), single-market-economy.ec.europa.eu/news/eu-and-canada-set-strategic-partnership-raw-materials-2021-06-21_en), signed with the view to diversify the EU's sources of supply thus decreasing its dependence on 'difficult' third countries. These initiatives are designed to bolster Europe's resilience and open strategic autonomy in key technologies needed for the transition towards a green and digital economy.

[44] In contrast, the European Parliament is clear since it refers to 'Union's sovereignty' rather than to 'European sovereignty'. In European Parliament, 'Resolution on a New Industrial Strategy for Europe

The Regulation is ambiguous regarding the subjects whose sovereignty is strengthened. Adopted pursuant to Articles 3(1)(e) TEU and 207(1) TFEU,[45] it was intended to pursue two different objectives. On the one hand, it was designed to make it possible for *Member States* to exercise their sovereign right to oppose FDIs from third countries on the grounds of public policy or public security. This right is protected under Article 65(1)(b) TFEU which regulates the derogations from free movement of capitals. However, after the Lisbon Treaty included FDIs within the scope of the common commercial policy, Member States were prevented from autonomously opposing capital movements from third countries, since these restrictions fell within the scope of an exclusive competence of the Union.[46] As the Commission emphasises, 'investment screening mechanisms may represent a restriction on the free movement of capital which, however, may be justified when necessary and proportionate for the achievement of the objectives defined in the Treaty'.[47] Therefore, the measure under examination is conceived to restore Member States' sovereignty, while legitimately derogating from the law of EU internal market. On the other hand, the concerned instrument was aimed at establishing a *Union's framework* that applies in case foreign direct investments affect Member States' critical infrastructure and critical technologies in a way that jeopardises security or public order.

The underlying preoccupation of the Regulation on FDIs is that EU Member States may lose control of critical infrastructure and technologies as a result of inbound FDIs of foreign operators.[48] This concern is well expressed in the Commission proposal which is the basis of Regulation 2019/452, where it is stated:

> Recently, a series of take-overs of European companies involved foreign investors with strong ties to their home governments which strategy focus on the purchase of European companies that develop technologies or maintain infrastructures that are essential to perform critical functions in society and the economy. The ultimate risk is that such

(2020/2076(INI))' P9_TA(2020)0321 [2021] OJ C425/43, point O, it is stated: '[…] For the *Union's sovereignty* [emphasis added] and strategic autonomy, an autonomous and competitive industrial base and a massive effort in research and innovation are needed to develop leadership in key enabling technologies and innovative solutions and to ensure global competitiveness'.

[45] On the interlinkages between investment screening and the Common Commercial Policy (CCP)'s exclusive competence, and the related controversy in the literature also in light of the Court of Justice's opinion on the FTA with Singapore, see M Blungenberg and F Blandford, 'Investment Screening – a New Era of European Protectionism?' in M Hahn and G Van der Loo (eds), *Law and Practice of the Common Commercial Policy: The First 10 Years after the Treaty of Lisbon*, Studies in EU External Relations 18 (Leiden, Brill Nijhof, 2021) 167–168; A Dimopoulos, 'EU Investment Agreements: A New Model for the Future' in J Chaisse, L Choukroune and S Jusoh (eds), *Handbook of International Investment Law and Policy* (Singapore, Springer, 2019).

[46] For a full discussion of the topic see M Cremona, 'Regulating FDI in the EU Legal Framework' in JHJ Bourgeois (ed), *EU Framework for Foreign Direct Investment Control*, European Monographs 111 (Alphen aan den rijn, Wolters Kluwer, 2020) 31, 35. See also Opinion of Advocate General Ćapeta in Case C-106/22 *Xella Magyarország* ECLI:EU:C:2023:267.

[47] European Commission, 'Proposal for a Regulation of the European Parliament and of the Council establishing a framework for screening of foreign direct investments into the European Union' (2017) COM(2017) 487 final, 4.

[48] For a conceptualisation of the first steps to be taken toward the establishment of a possible outbound investment screening mechanism within the EU, designed first and foremost to preserve ETS, see European Commission and High Representative of the Union for Foreign Affairs and Security Policy, 'European Economic Security Strategy' (2023) JOIN(2023) 20 final, para 32.

investment could be detrimental to security and public order of the Union or its Member States.[49]

The implicit reference in the Commission's words is to Chinese investors.[50] In the light of these concerns, it is necessary for investments from operators of third countries to be scrutinised before being authorised.

The issue to which we turn our attention in Sections 4–5 is whether the European Commission is endowed with powers by Regulation 2019/452 apt to achieve the second of its objective, which is to protect Member States' critical infrastructure and critical technologies from FDIs that threaten security or public order. After a scrutiny of the different aspects of the Union's framework on FDI, we will attempt to provide a final answer in Section 5.

4. THE COMMISSION'S ROLE IN THE PROCESS OF INVESTMENT SCREENING: THE EMERGENCE OF A EUROPEANISED SOVEREIGNTY IN THE AREA OF FDIs?

The EU has to reconcile its efforts to acquire autonomy in key sectors of the economy with the goal of being open to trade and investments. As the Commission acknowledges in its Communication on 'A New Industrial Strategy for Europe', while the openness of Europe's economy is the source of its prosperity and competitiveness, EU industry being integrated in global value chains, EU institutions 'should not be naïve to threats to fair competition and trade'.[51] Regulation 2019/452 is destined to address this challenge in relation only to FDIs,[52] not portfolio investments, being the former 'investments of all kinds by natural persons or commercial, industrial, or financial undertakings' that aim at establishing or maintaining 'lasting and direct links between the person providing the capital and the entrepreneur to whom or the undertaking to which the capital is made available to carry on economic activity'.[53] As clarified by the CJEU, FDIs are linked 'to a form of participation in an undertaking through the holding of shares which confers the possibility of effectively participating in its management and control'.[54] Moreover, as recently noted by the Court, the concept of foreign investor enshrined in Regulation 2019/452 encompasses that of an 'undertaking of a third country', which refers to 'an undertaking constituted or

[49] European Commission, 'Proposal for a Regulation of the European Parliament and of the Council establishing a framework for screening of foreign direct investments into the European Union' (2017) COM(2017) 487 final, 10.

[50] See below Section 6.

[51] European Commission, 'A New Industrial Strategy for Europe' (2020) COM(2020) 102 final, 6.

[52] On the notion of FDIs in light of EU primary and secondary law, as well as of the EU case law, see in particular LS Otto, 'What Is a Foreign Direct Investment? Understanding Third Country Direct Investments Conceptually and in Practise' in S Hindelang and A Moberg (eds), *2020 YSEC Yearbook of Socio-Economic Constitutions: a Common European Law on Investment Screening (CELIS)* (Cham, Springer, 2021) 516–522.

[53] See C Herrmann and M Hoffmann, 'Investment in the European Union: Competences, Structures, Responsibility and Policy' in Chaisse, Choukroune and Jusoh (eds) (n 45) 2213, 2234.

[54] Case C-35/11 *Test Claimants in the FII Group Litigation* ECLI:EU:C:2012:707, para 102; Opinion 2/15 *Free Trade Agreement between the European Union and the Republic of Singapore* ECLI:EU:C:2017:376, para 227, cited in Herrmann and Hoffmann (n 53) 2234.

otherwise organised under the laws of a third country'. It follows that the scope of Regulation 2019/452 is limited only to investments in the EU made by undertakings constituted or otherwise organised under the laws of a third country. The Regulation, by contrast, does not apply to the situation 'where investments are made by undertakings registered in Hungary or in another Member State over which an undertaking registered in a third country has [a] majority control'.[55]

The Regulation, whose adoption was anything but uncontroversial,[56] must be examined in the light of the 2021 Trade Policy Review – An Open, Sustainable and Assertive Trade Policy,[57] whereby it is affirmed that Member States are encouraged to set up and enforce a full-fledged FDIs screening mechanism to contrast cases where the acquisition or control of a particular business, infrastructure or technology would challenge security and/or public order in the EU.[58]

From the analysis of the relevant EU secondary law measures[59] enacted by the European Commission in the last two and a half years aimed at specifying the scope of Regulation 2019/452,[60] it can be inferred that such measure, by setting up a new, coordinated (between the Commission and the Member States) screening mechanism in the field of FDIs, grants the Commission the power to both check that Member States do not unduly restrict extra-EU investors' access to the market and ensure that national authorities are not acquiescent vis-à-vis disruptive extra-EU investors who target companies operating across Member States in politically or strategically sensitive areas. To this end, the Regulation sets up a cooperation mechanism between Member States and between Member States and the Commission, which may lead to

[55] Case C-106/22 *Xella Magyarország* ECLI:EU:C:2023:568, para 33. On this matter see the Addendum.

[56] See S Hindelang and A Moberg, 'The Art of Casting Political Dissent in Law: The EU's Framework for the Screening of Foreign Direct Investment' (2020) 57 *CML Rev* 1427, 1428. See also S Vellucci, 'The New Regulation on the Screening of FDI: The Quest for a Balance to Protect EU's Essential Interests' (2019) 1 *Diritto del commercio internazionale* 123, 142–143.

[57] European Commission, 'Trade Policy Review – An Open, Sustainable and Assertive Trade Policy' (2021) COM(2021) 66 final.

[58] ibid 23.

[59] See also European Commission, 'Guidance to the Member States concerning Foreign Direct Investment from Russia and Belarus in view of the Military Aggression against Ukraine and the Restrictive Measures laid down in recent Council Regulations on Sanctions' [2022] OJ C151I/1, on which see S Pugliese, 'Toward a New EU strategic Dimension: Common Purchase and Investment Screening Mechanisms as a Means of Crisis Preparedness and Management' (2022) 2 *Il Diritto dell'Unione Europea* 391, 409–415.

[60] See the following measures: European Commission 'Guidance to the Member States concerning Foreign Direct Investment and Free Movement of Capital from Third Countries, and the Protection of Europe's Strategic Assets, ahead of the Application of Regulation (EU) 2019/452 (FDI Screening Regulation) 2020/C 99 I/01' [2020] OJ C 99I/1; Commission Delegated Regulation (EU) 2020/1298 amending the Annex to Regulation (EU) 2019/452 of the European Parliament and of the Council establishing a framework for the screening of foreign direct investments into the Union [2020] OJ L304/1; Commission Delegated Regulation (EU) 2021/2126 amending the Annex to Regulation (EU) 2019/452 of the European Parliament and of the Council establishing a framework for the screening of foreign direct investments into the Union [2021] OJ L432/1; European Commission, 'Report From The Commission to The European Parliament and the Council: First Annual Report on the Screening of Foreign Direct Investments into the Union' (2021) COM(2021) 714 final; European Commission, 'Report from the Commission to the European Parliament and the Council: Second Annual Report on the Screening of Foreign Direct Investments into the Union' (2022) COM(2022) 433 final; European Commission, 'Commission Staff Working Document: Screening of FDI into the Union and its Member States accompanying the document "Report from the Commission to the European Parliament and the Council Second Annual Report on the Screening of Foreign Direct Investments into the Union"' (2021) SWD(2021) 334 final.

the issuance by the Commission of opinions concerning the investments at stake.[61] On the other hand, the Regulation is explicitly without prejudice to Member States' competence in defining national security, as referred to in Article 65(1)(b) TFEU, Article 4(2) TEU, and Article 346 TFEU, according to domestic legal systems.[62] As a matter of fact, national security remains the sole responsibility of each Member State since different countries have different perceptions of security threats, as reflected in their different economic and geopolitical situations.[63]

Against this background, Regulation 2019/452 represents both the crystallisation of a trend and a novelty. It confirms and crystallises, in the aftermath of the 2008 economic crisis, the twofold idea that globalisation *without ifs and buts* is not always beneficial and international markets are not *per se* neutral. It is a novelty because, after decades of indifference towards the screening of FDIs, the EU has at last acted. For the first time, the Commission has been granted a role in the process of investment screening within the EU, and this happened for two reasons, as recalled by Hindelang and Moberg.[64] The first reason was to react, in terms of reciprocity, to the protectionist activism of several third countries, especially China.[65] Indeed, on 12 March 2019, the Commission and the EU's High Representative for Foreign Affairs and Security Policy defined the country as a 'systemic rival' and sought to promote a more balanced and reciprocal trade and investment relationship, as well as the protection of critical infrastructure and the technological base in Europe.[66] More generally, an unfair situation was deemed to be caused by the fact that major trading partners subjected EU outward FDIs to screening, while FDIs were not regularly subject to a review process within the EU. The second reason was to mitigate fragmentation and excessive decentralisation caused by heterogeneous national legislations.[67]

[61] See Arts 1, 6, 7, and 8 Regulation 2019/452.

[62] See Art 1(2) Regulation 2019/452. On this point see S Korte, 'Exploring the Possibilities and Limits of the EU and Member States to Set Up an Investment Screening Mechanism in the Light of Union Law' in Hindelang and Moberg (eds) (n 52) 439 and 445.

[63] See G Napolitano, 'Il regolamento sul controllo degli investimenti esteri diretti: alla ricerca di una sovranità europea nell'arena economica globale' (2019) 1 *Rivista della Regolazione dei mercati* 2; J Snell, 'EU Foreign Direct Investment Screening: Europe qui protege?' (2019) 44 *EL Rev* 137.

[64] See also Hindelang and Moberg (n 56) 1430.

[65] See also L Lonardo, 'EU Law Against Hybrid Threats: A First Assessment' (2021) 6 *European Papers* 1075, 1082; M Demertzis and G Wolff, 'Hybrid and Cybersecurity Threats and the European Union's Financial System' (2019) *Bruegel Policy Contribution* Issue No 10; J de Kok, 'Towards a European Framework for Foreign Investment Reviews' (2019) 44 *EL Rev* 24, 25; M Misra, 'Thinking Past Naivete: Investment Screening by the EU as a Problem of (Mis)trust in International Relations' (2023) 28 *European Foreign Affairs Review* 117.

[66] European Commission and High Representative of the Union for Foreign Affairs and Security Policy, 'EU-China – A Strategic Outlook' (2019) JOIN(2019) 5 final.

[67] For historical background see Cremona (n 46); A Dimopolous, 'European Union' in M Krajewski and RT Hoffmann (eds), *Research Handbook on Foreign Direct Investment*, Research Handbooks in International Law Series (Cheltenham, Edward Elgar, 2019); A Bakker, 'The Political Economy of Capital Controls and Liberalization in the European Union' in Hindelang and Moberg (eds) (n 52); SF Wernicke, 'Investment Screening: The Return of Protectionism? A Business Perspective' in Hindelang and Moberg (eds) (n 52); S Simon, 'Investment Screening: The Return of Protectionism? A Political Account' in Hindelang and Moberg (eds) (n 52); J Warchol, 'The Birth of the EU Screening Regulation' in Hindelang and Moberg (eds) (n 52); B Thorbjørn Daniel, 'Comment on "In Search for an EU Competence to Establish an Investment Screening Mechanism and Restricting Effects Flowing from Fundamental Freedoms, Fundamental Rights, and Other EU Primary Law"' in Hindelang and Moberg (eds) (n 52).

In this context, the EU has elevated and promoted at the European level, through the adoption of a horizontal, (thus not sectorial)[68] measure, the objectives of national security and public order. The Union has therefore intervened by transforming national public interests into an EU *positive* rule that conceptualises security as a *common* rather than merely a *national* notion.[69] It has done so by acknowledging that FDIs in strategic companies or companies of general interest operating in a Member State potentially pose a threat to the Union as a whole and to its strategic interests, not only to the host State of the companies targeted by the investment.

In this respect, the Union has seized the space that individual States had been overseeing autonomously for decades. And it is precisely this process of sharing control among domestic authorities and the EU that has triggered an unprecedented development, namely the emergence of Europeanised sovereignty in the area of FDIs. As will be shown in the following sections, this Europeanised sovereignty takes shape in a variety of sectors, including technological, in which extra-EU investments penetrate more frequently and incisively.

4.1. The Screening Mechanism

Regulation 2019/452 includes a definition – unusual within the international landscape – of screening mechanism, meant as an 'instrument of general application',[70] accompanied by implementing measures and administrative procedures allowing to assess, investigate, authorise, condition, and prohibit FDIs on grounds of security or public order.[71] Not only does the Regulation explain the meaning of 'screening mechanism', but it also sets forth the principles that govern the latter, beginning with transparency and non-discrimination. To that end, Member States will lay down the circumstances that are to trigger screening, the grounds for screening, and the detailed applicable procedural rules, including the relevant timeframes, the rules on confidentiality and those on the right to seek recourse against domestic screening decisions.[72]

[68] See, in particular, in the energy sector, Art 11 Directive 2009/73/EC of the European Parliament and of the Council concerning common rules for the internal market in natural gas and repealing Directive 2003/55/EC [2009] OJ L211/94; Art 53 Directive (EU) 2019/944 of the European Parliament and of the Council on common rules for the internal market for electricity and amending Directive 2012/27/EU (recast) [2019] OJ L158/125; Regulation (EU) 2017/1938 of the European Parliament and of the Council concerning measures to safeguard the security of gas supply and repealing Regulation (EU) No 994/2010 [2017] OJ L280/1. For an overview on the plurality of regulatory approaches see H Berger, 'The Banking and Insurance Sector' in Hindelang and Moberg (eds) (n 52); D Eisenhut, 'The Defence, Military and Dual-Use Sector' in Hindelang and Moberg (eds) (n 52); H Jessen, 'The Transport Sector' in Hindelang and Moberg (eds) (n 52); BOG Mortensen, 'The Energy Sector' in Hindelang and Moberg (eds) (n 52); M Fehlin, 'The Telecommunications and IT Infrastructure Sector' in Hindelang and Moberg (eds) (n 52).

[69] In that regard, see the critical observations in T Verellen, 'When Integration by Stealth Meets Public Security: The EU Foreign Direct Investment Screening Regulation' (2021) 48 *Legal Issues of Economic Integration* 19, 39.

[70] Art 2(4) Regulation 2019/452.

[71] See the observations in G Napolitano, 'I golden powers italiani alla prova del Regolamento europeo' in G Napolitano (ed), *Foreign Direct Investment Screening – Il controllo sugli investimenti esteri diretti* (Bologna, il Mulino, 2020).

[72] See Art 3(2) Regulation 2019/452.

Meanwhile, national authorities should ensure that the host Member State gives due consideration to the observations of the other Member States potentially affected by the impact of the investment on their own territory, and to the Opinion of the Commission, if adopted.[73] Furthermore, while the procedural participation of third parties is not specifically regulated, Recital 14 expressly provides that Member States and the Commission might consider information received from economic operators, civil society organisations, or social partners such as trade unions.[74] All these provisions give rise to a European architecture regulating the operation of screening mechanisms.

As for the national layer of governance, first, while it is true that a Member State which has established a screening mechanism in its domestic legal order is subject to the partially harmonising rules provided for in the Regulation,[75] it is also true that there is no obligation to establish such a mechanism. The process, thus, is voluntary, which means that its settlement is at the discretion of each national government. So far, 19 Member States have taken action. In Estonia, Greece, Ireland, Luxembourg, Croatia, and Sweden a consultative or legislative process for introducing specific legislation was initiated in 2021. As for Bulgaria and Cyprus, no publicly reported initiatives are known.[76] In any case, for those Member States currently deprived of a screening mechanism, or whose screening mechanisms do not cover all the relevant transactions, the Commission advocates for 'a full-fledged screening mechanism' and in the meantime for the use of 'all other available options to address cases where the acquisition or control of a particular business, infrastructure or technology would create a risk to security or public order in the EU, including a risk to critical health infrastructures and supply of critical inputs'.[77]

Second, the way in which the mechanism functions in practice varies from country to country since the principles and rules of administrative law that apply to screening mechanisms are normally designed differently across Member States. Moreover, the asymmetries that may derive from different conceptions of national security and public order at the domestic level must be taken into account. In particular, the Regulation's non-interference with the organisational structures chosen by the States to regulate their screening mechanisms entails that national authorities are not compelled to allocate adequate personal and financial resources for its enforcement,

[73] See Art 6(9) Regulation 2019/452.

[74] See Recital 14 Regulation 2019/452.

[75] As pointed out by Snell (n 63) 137; Hindelang and Moberg (n 56) 1446.

[76] See European Commission, 'Report from the Commission to the European Parliament and the Council: Second Annual Report on the Screening of Foreign Direct Investments into the Union' (2022) COM(2022) 433 final; European Commission, 'Commission Staff Working Document: Screening of FDI into the Union and its Member States accompanying the document "Report from the Commission to the European Parliament and the Council Second Annual Report on the Screening of Foreign Direct Investments into the Union"' (2021) SWD(2021) 334 final. For an update, which has been released after the completion of this article, see the Economic Security Factsheet – Proposal for a new regulation on the screening of foreign investments of 24 January 2024, where a reference is made to 22 EU Member States with screening mechanisms already in force.

[77] European Commission 'Guidance to the Member States concerning Foreign Direct Investment and Free Movement of Capital from Third Countries, and the Protection of Europe's Strategic Assets, ahead of the Application of Regulation (EU) 2019/452 (FDI Screening Regulation) 2020/C 99 I/01' [2020] OJ C 99I/1, para 3.

nor do they have to set up specific forms of separation between politics and administration. There are thus negative implications, from that point of view, especially for those countries where the autonomy of the latter from the former seems to be not sufficiently developed.[78]

4.2. National and European Interests

As anticipated, in Regulation 2019/452 it is established that the protected interests at both national and European levels are limited to security and public order. It goes without saying that this limitation serves to avoid the screening of FDIs undertaken by the States from becoming a mere protectionist tool of industrial policy. On the other hand, the two interconnected concepts of security and public order are inherently broad, not being tied 'only' to military and police security but to a variety of different domains. Moreover, *de facto*, the choice to hinder FDIs may be frequently rooted in the protection of strategic industrial sectors, which means that screening mechanisms today could constitute a disguised, possibly illegitimate, form of socio-economic protectionism.[79]

Regulation 2019/452 includes a particularly wide, far-reaching, unfinished catalogue of areas within which the investment may be subject to controls and limitations. Such a list is notably wider than that envisaged in the majority of national legislations until 2019 – the date of the entry into force of the Regulation – and is non-exhaustive:[80] (a) 'critical infrastructure, whether physical or virtual, including energy, transport, water, health, communications, media, data processing or storage, aerospace, defence, electoral or financial infrastructure, and sensitive facilities, as well as land and real estate crucial for the use of such infrastructure'; (b) critical technologies and dual use items as defined in point 1 of Article 2 of Council Regulation (EC) No 428/2009,[81] including 'artificial intelligence, robotics, semiconductors, cybersecurity, aerospace, defence, energy storage, quantum and nuclear technologies as well as nanotechnologies and biotechnologies'; (c) 'supply of critical inputs, including energy or raw materials, as well as food security'; (d) 'access to sensitive information, including personal data, or the ability to control such information'; and (e) 'the freedom and pluralism of the media'.

The notion of 'public good' assumes, therefore, a supranational, instead of an exclusively national, connotation, as already remarked in the previous sections. This is a dynamic that often occurs in the EU legal order: that is to say, systemic upheavals and paradigm shifts, which affect the very logic of the European legal system, take place more or less *en souplesse* in acts of an apparently technical nature. Indeed, while

[78] One might think, today, of Hungary.

[79] M Nettesheim, 'Screening for What Threat: Preserving "Public Order and Security", Securing Reciprocity in International Trade, or Supporting Certain Social, Environmental, or Industrial Policies?' in Hindelang and Moberg (eds) (n 52) 483.

[80] See Art 4(1) Regulation 2019/452.

[81] Council Regulation (EC) No 428/2009 setting up a Community regime for the control of exports, transfer, brokering and transit of dual-use items (recast) [2009] OJ L134/1.

Member States remain sovereign in enforcing the screening mechanism to protect their national critical infrastructure and technologies, the EU, through the Commission, is directly involved in the control over FDIs and can object to them when it deems that security and public order, at national and European level, are threatened.

As to the content and extent of the reasons of security and public order, two issues shall be raised with regard to Articles 63–66 TFEU.

The first relates to the role of economic considerations in the justification invoked by a Member State to subject the FDI to its domestic screening mechanism. In this respect, it is likely that economic concerns will slip into the assessment performed by the host Member State. But is this circumstance in conflict with the case law of the CJEU, especially with the so-called doctrine of non-economic considerations, according to which economic aims are precluded as justifications for restrictions on free movement?[82] The answer is that restrictive measures taken on the basis of economic objectives could be permitted thanks to a case-by-case analysis if such objectives are instrumental to the pursuit, ultimately, of non-economic goals. Indeed, a close view of EU jurisprudence shows that the prohibition at the core of the approach adopted by the CJEU concerns only 'aims of a purely economic nature'.[83] As stated in *Essent*, grounds of a purely economic nature cannot constitute overriding reasons in the public interest justifying a restriction of a fundamental freedom guaranteed by the Treaties unless those grounds pursue 'an objective in the public interest'.[84] Hence, it may be alleged that the objective of safeguarding EU technological security falls within this notion,[85] thus making it possible for a Member State to invoke this justification to object to an FDI.

[82] See, *ex multis*, Case 7/61 *Commission v Italia* ECLI:EU:C:1961:31, [1961] ECR 317, para D; Case 95/81 *Commission v Italy* ECLI:EU:C:1982:216, [1982] ECR 2187, para 27; Case 238/82 *Duphar* ECLI:EU:C:1984:45, [1984] ECR 523, para 23; Case 352/85 *Bond van Adverteerders v State of the Netherlands* ECLI:EU:C:1988:196, [1988] ECR 2085, para 34; Case C-288/89 *Stichting Collectieve Antennevoorziening Gouda v Commissariaat voor de Media* ECLI:EU:C:1991:323, [1991] ECR I-4007, para 11; Case C-55/94 *Gebhard v consiglio dell'Ordine degli Avvocati e Procuratori di Milano* ECLI:EU:C:1995:411, [1995] ECR I-4165, para 37; Case C-224/97 *Ciola* ECLI:EU:C:1999:212, [1999] ECR I-2517, para 17; Case C-398/95 *Syndesmos ton en Elladi Touristikon kai Taxidiotikon Grafeion v Ypourgos Ergasias* ECLI:EU:C:1997:282, [1997] ECR I-3091, para 23; Case C-158/96 *Kohll v Union des caisses de maladie* ECLI:EU:C:1998:171, [1998] ECR I-1931, para 50; Case C-35/98 *Verkooijen* ECLI:EU:C:2000:294, [2000] ECR I-4071, paras 47–48; Case C-388/01 *Commission v Italy* ECLI:EU:C:2003:30, [2003] ECR I-721, para 22; Case C-109/04 *Kranemann* ECLI:EU:C:2005:187, [2005] ECR I-2421, para 34; Case C-137/04 *Rockler* ECLI:EU:C:2006:107, [2006] ECR I-1441, para 24; Case C-444/05 *Stamatelaki* ECLI:EU:C:2007:231, [2007] ECR I-3185, para 31; Case C-171/08 *Commission v Portugal* ECLI:EU:C:2010:412, [2010] ECR I-6871, para 52; Case C-563/17 *Associação Peço a Palavra and Others* ECLI:EU:C:2019:144, para 70. In the literature, see J Snell, 'Economic Aims as Justification for Restrictions on Free Movement' in AAM Schrauwen (ed), *Rule of Reason: Rethinking Another Classic of European Legal Doctrine*, Hogendorp Papers 4 (Groningen, Europa Law Publishing, 2005); NA Georgiadis, *Derogation Clauses: The Protection of National Interests in EC Law*, Publications of the Hellenic Institute of International and Foreign Law 23 (Athènes, Ant N Sakkoulas, 2006) 199–203; recently, C Barnard, *The Substantive Law of the EU: The Four Freedoms*, 7th edn (Oxford, Oxford University Press, 2022) 145–196, 472–512.

[83] Amongst others, *cf* Case 95/81 *Commission v Italy* ECLI:EU:C:1982:216, [1982] ECR 2187, para 22; Case C-35/98 *Verkooijen* ECLI:EU:C:2000:294, [2000] ECR I-4071, paras 47–48; Case C-141/07 *Commission v Germany* ECLI:EU:C:2008:492, [2008] ECR I-6935, para 60; Joined Cases C-105/12 to C-107/12 *Essent and Others* ECLI:EU:C:2013:677, paras 51–52.

[84] Joined Cases C-105/12 to C-107/12 *Essent and Others* ECLI:EU:C:2013:677, paras 51–52.

[85] The CJEU has recognised that the security of energy supply is a public interest which justifies a derogation from the free movement of goods. Case 72/83 *Campus Oil* ECLI:EU:C:1984:256, [1984] ECR 2727, paras 34–35.

The second issue is to understand whether FDIs can be treated differently from intra-EU direct investments and, ultimately, to what extent. In this regard, in the Guidance it is explicitly observed that 'in the analysis of justification and proportionality, restrictions on the movement of capital to and from third countries take place in a different legal context compared to restrictions to intra-EU capital movements'. Consequently, the Commission points out that, under the Treaty, 'additional grounds of justification may be acceptable in the case of restrictions on transactions involving third country', such as transparency in the governance of the investor, and that the permissible grounds of justification may 'be interpreted more broadly', that is, the host State's derogatory reasoning on security and public order will be less strict.[86] Therefore, the Commission, inspired by the CJEU case law on taxation,[87] makes it clear that, under the free movement of capital, a divide between extra-EU and intra-EU investments can be drawn[88] insofar as justifications for restrictions on the former could be permitted, while restrictions on the latter would be rejected.[89]

4.3. Cooperation between the Commission and the Member States

We turn our attention now to the core operative part of Regulation 2019/452, namely the techniques of cooperation on multiple institutional levels. These rules represent an important innovation, marking a shift towards a higher degree of communitarisation of procedures and the involvement of the Commission, as well as of the Member States other than the FDI's host Member State.

Cooperation differs depending on whether direct investments are scrutinised by Member States with a national mechanism in place, or not subject to any mechanism.[90] In any event, information-sharing requirements are imposed on all Member States, regardless of whether they have put a mechanism in place or not. In the (more frequent) case of Member States with such a mechanism, they are required to notify the Commission and the other Member States without undue delay of any foreign investment that is undergoing screening.[91] Regulation 2019/452 became applicable in October 2020 and by September 2022, 679 notifications were made by

[86] European Commission 'Guidance to the Member States concerning Foreign Direct Investment and Free Movement of Capital from Third Countries, and the Protection of Europe's Strategic Assets, ahead of the Application of Regulation (EU) 2019/452 (FDI Screening Regulation) 2020/C 99 I/01' [2020] OJ C 99I/1, para 4. The existence of a clear divide between EU and non-EU is clear in the recent practice of the Commission, as briefly observed in the Addendum.

[87] Case C-35/11 *Test Claimants in the FII Group Litigation* ECLI:EU:C:2012:707, para 171, but also Case C-101/05 *A* ECLI:EU:C:2007:804, [2007] ECR I-11531, para 67, and Case C-194/06 *Orange European Smallcap Fund* ECLI:EU:C:2008:289, [2008] ECR I-3747, para 65.

[88] See, on SWFs and soes, the reflections by H Schweitzer, 'Sovereign Wealth Funds: Market Investors or "Imperialist Capitalists"? The European Response to Direct Investment by Non-EU State-Controlled Entities' in C Herrmann and JP Terhechte (eds), *European Yearbook of International Economic Law*, Vol 2 (Berlin, Springer, 2011) 103–108; D Gallo, 'On the Content and Scope of National and European Solidarity Under Free Movement Rules: The Case of Golden Shares and Sovereign Investments' (2016) 1 *European Papers* 823, 844–845.

[89] Snell (n 63) 137.

[90] See, respectively, Arts 6 and 7 Regulation 2019/452.

[91] Art 6(1) Regulation 2019/452.

various Member States pursuant to Article 6 of the Regulation.[92] While the notified transactions varied in terms of sectors of the investment target, the origins of the ultimate investor and the value of the transaction, it can be pointed out that the highest number of transactions concerned information and communication technologies.

As highlighted in the Commission's 2nd Annual Report, Regulation 2019/452 foresees that an assessment of FDI transactions is undertaken in two possible phases.[93] While all notified transactions are assessed under Phase 1, only some proceedings reach Phase 2, which implies a more detailed assessment of cases that could possibly affect security or public order in more than one Member State, or create risks for projects or programmes of Union interest.[94] Such a phase could ultimately be concluded by the Commission issuing an Opinion on the case in question pursuant to Article 7. In 2021, of the 414 cases notified, 86 per cent were closed by the Commission in Phase 1, with the remaining 14 per cent proceeding to Phase 2 with additional information being requested from the notifying Member State. The information and technologies sector accounted for 32 per cent of the sectors concerned. As for the adoption of the Commission's opinions, in the period 2020–2021, they were issued in fewer than 3 per cent of all cases notified.

It is for the State undertaking the screening to disclose information with its notification, including the ownership structure of the foreign investor and of the target undertaking and the approximate value of the FDI. At this point, two layers intersect: if a Member State considers that an FDI, undergoing screening in another Member State, is likely to affect security or public order, it may provide observations to that Member State;[95] if the Commission considers that an FDI undergoing screening is likely to affect security or public order in more than one Member State, it may issue an Opinion addressed to the Member State undertaking the screening and notified also to the other Member States.[96] The Opinion, which could also suggest potential mitigating measures to address specific risks, is thus issued only if required by the circumstances of the case, first and foremost in the light of the investor's 'risk profile'[97] and the criticality of the investment target.[98] Furthermore, on one hand, the Opinion must be rendered following comments from other Member States, 'after

[92] See European Commission, 'Report From The Commission to The European Parliament and the Council: First Annual Report on the Screening of Foreign Direct Investments into the Union' (2021) COM(2021) 714 final; European Commission, 'Report from the Commission to the European Parliament and the Council: Second Annual Report on the Screening of Foreign Direct Investments into the Union' (2022) COM(2022) 433 final. As clarified in the Addendum, notifications to the Commission grew in the years and in three years have reached the number of 1200.

[93] European Commission, 'Report from the Commission to the European Parliament and the Council: Second Annual Report on the Screening of Foreign Direct Investments into the Union' (2022) COM(2022) 433 final. On the number/percentage of opinions rendered see the Commission Staff Working Document mentioned in the Addendum.

[94] With regard to projects and programmes, see Art 8 Regulation 2019/452 and the Annex 'List of Projects or Programmes of Union Interest referred to in Article 8(3)'.

[95] Art 6(2) Regulation 2019/452.

[96] Art 6(3) Regulation 2019/452.

[97] European Commission, 'Report from the Commission to the European Parliament and the Council: Second Annual Report on the Screening of Foreign Direct Investments into the Union' (2022) COM(2022) 433 final.

[98] Art 8 Regulation 2019/452.

at least one third of Member States consider that a foreign direct investment is likely to affect their security or public order'; on the other hand, the Commission may issue the Opinion 'irrespective of whether other Member States' have provided such comments.[99]

As already mentioned, those Member States without a screening mechanism in place are also concerned by the Regulation's peer-review mechanism. If a Member State or the Commission becomes aware of a planned or completed investment that affects, respectively, its own security or public order, or that of other Member States, the latter can provide comments and the Commission may issue an Opinion, despite the absence of a national screening mechanism in the host Member State.[100]

In this framework the State hosting the investment, albeit not being subject to the veto power of the Commission, is bound to give 'due consideration' to the observations of the other Member States and to the Opinion of the Commission.[101] This means also that, should the State hosting the investment and/or also undertaking the screening depart from the assessments carried out in the comments by the other States and in the Opinion, it shall duly justify its decision. Yet, the Regulation does not supply the other Member States and the Commission with specific tools in a case where the host State does not give due consideration to the observations and the Opinions, or somehow departs from them: hence the limits of the competence exercised by the Commission. However, Recital 17 of the Regulation affirms that the Member State must give due consideration 'through, where appropriate, measures available under its national law, or in its broader policy-making, in line with its duty of sincere cooperation laid down in Article 4(3) TEU'. Indeed, the duty of sincere cooperation requires the EU institutions and the Member States to cooperate in good faith pursuant to Article 4(3) TEU and may also impose a duty on Member States to undertake or refrain from undertaking certain actions.[102]

In this connection, what measures can the Member States and the Commission adopt when faced with a State that is reluctant to cooperate? With regard to the former, the State which feels threatened may autonomously activate its own screening mechanism as regards the effects of the investment on its territory, and do so while simultaneously communicating its observations to the Commission. National authorities might also refer to Article 259 TFEU, as has happened in only a few cases brought before the CJEU.[103] The Commission, instead, could rely on infringement proceedings *ex* Article 258 TFEU, yet with all its well-known limits concerning timing, which are particularly problematic if the investment at stake constitutes a threat for the country and the Union as a whole. For the time being, there is, to the best of our knowledge, no relevant practice.

[99] Art 6(3) Regulation 2019/452.

[100] Art 7(2) Regulation 2019/452. See eg Verellen (n 69) 26.

[101] See Arts 6(9) and 7(7) Regulation 2019/452. The 'due consideration' becomes 'utmost account' when the foreign investment is likely to affect projects or programmes of Union interest, such as the European defence industrial development programme, Galileo, Horizon, as provided by Art 8(2)(c). On this matter see Zwartkruis and de Jong (n 10) 468.

[102] See eg Case C-246/07, *Commission v Sweden* ECLI:EU:C:2010:203, [2010] ECR I-3317, paras 71–77.

[103] No rulings yet; see Verellen (n 69) 26.

4.4. Review of Legality and the Opinions of the Commission

A further question, which has so far not been addressed either by the CJEU or in the literature,[104] is whether the Opinions issued by the Commission under Regulation 2019/452 can be directly or indirectly reviewed by the Court, pursuant to Article 263 TFEU (action for annulment) and Article 267(1)(b) TFEU (preliminary reference on validity), respectively.

Arguably, the act which concretely produces adverse effects on interests vis-à-vis third parties is the national decision adopted following the Opinion, and not the Opinion itself. Opinions are, therefore, intraprocedural acts, of a non-binding nature and are not susceptible of *de jure* limiting Member States' discretion, enacted within the context of a composite procedure which ends with an act of the national authority, not of the Commission. Hence, the conclusion that the opinions cannot be subject to an action for annulment brought either by the concerned States (where the investment is carried out) or, *a fortiori*, by the extra-EU investors or the target companies, the latter being an action whose preconditions, as enshrined in Article 263(4) TFEU, are even stricter, as is well known. This notwithstanding, it could be argued that national judges may refer to the Court of Justice *ex* Article 267(1)(b) TFEU, within the context of a preliminary reference on validity, to verify whether the Opinions comply with Regulation 2019/452 and EU law as a whole. In brief, the extra-EU investor, as well as the target undertaking, could rely on an indirect action, grounded in national procedures and remedies, rather than follow the path provided by Article 263 TFEU.[105] At the time of writing, also in this respect, to the best of our knowledge, there is no relevant practice.

4.5. Special Treatment of Sovereign Investments

Regulation 2019/452 states that the Member State and the Commission may take into account 'whether a foreign investor is controlled directly or indirectly … by the government of a third country'.[106] It refers to so-called sovereign investors, in particular state-owned enterprises and sovereign funds,[107] some of which are linked

[104] But see Blungenberg and Blandford (n 45) 173.

[105] On the different topic of the recourse against Member States' screening see TM Hagemeyer, 'Access to Legal Redress in an EU Investment Screening Mechanism' in Hindelang and Moberg (eds) (n 52) 806–807.

[106] See Recital 13 Regulation 2019/452.

[107] On sovereign investors in international and/or EU law, see LC Backer, 'The Private Law of Public Law: Public Authorities as Shareholders, Golden Shares, Sovereign Wealth Funds, and the Public Law Element in Private Choice of Law' (2008) 82 *Tulane Law Review* 1801; K Barysch, S Tilford and P Whyte, 'State, money and rules: An EU policy for Sovereign Investments' (*Centre for European Reform*, 1 December 2008) www.cer.eu/publications/archive/essay/2008/state-money-and-rules-eu-policy-sovereign-investments; SM Carbone, '"Golden Share" e fondi sovrani: lo Stato nelle imprese tra libertà comunitarie e diritto statale' (2009) 23 *Diritto del commercio internazionale* 503; J Cooke, 'Finding the Right Balance for Sovereign Wealth Fund Regulation: Open Investment vs. National Security' (2009) *Columbia Business Law Review* 728; E Mostacci, 'Stati finanziari e mercati sovrani: la crisi economica e gli strumenti per fronteggiarla' (2009) 9 *Diritto pubblico comparato ed europeo* 305; A Gigante and A Ligustro, 'Il diritto internazionale degli investimenti di fronte alla sfida dei fondi sovrani' (2010) *Diritto pubblico comparato ed europeo* 1179; Schweitzer (n 88); F Bassan, *The Law of Sovereign Wealth Funds* (Cheltenham, Edward Elgar, 2011);

to governments of third countries where the rule of law, euphemistically, shows different nuances from those it tends to have in the (great majority of the Member States) of the Union.

In this regard, on the one hand, it is well known that the EU order is characterised by the principle of neutrality of property ownership, pursuant to Article 345 TFEU. It follows that the public nature of the investor-undertaking, in various forms and degrees, cannot be an obstacle per se to its participation in other undertakings. On the other hand, this is not an absolute principle because, as clarified by the Court of Justice, it must always be interpreted, at a systematic level, in the light of the internal market's freedoms of movement.[108] Now, it is clear that the *longa manus* of State capitalism, when it comes to sovereign investors, often directly involved in critical technological sectors, traceable, more or less formally, to third countries, may cause concern. It is, therefore, clear that there is a reverse presumption with respect to these investors when compared to investors who are not sovereign: if the non-EU investor is controlled by a third country's government, the principle of legal neutrality does not come into play, with the consequence that the investment will be treated prima facie as potentially harmful and, thus, unwelcomed in the European territory.

5. DOES THE FOREIGN DIRECT INVESTMENTS SCREENING REGULATION HELP PROTECT CRITICAL INFRASTRUCTURE AND CRITICAL TECHNOLOGIES, THUS REINFORCING EUROPEAN TECHNOLOGICAL SOVEREIGNTY?

In Section 4.3 we have seen that Regulation 2019/452 represents a new important legal evolution for the EU in the field of trade since for the first time the EU institutions take a cautious approach towards FDI of third country investors. This instrument has the merit of providing common rules on how Member States may protect their companies from FDIs threatening security and public order, thus reducing the legal fragmentation as far as the screening of FDIs is concerned in the EU.

M Lamandini, 'Temi e problemi in materia di contendibilità del controllo, fondi sovrani e investimenti diretti stranieri nei settori strategici tra libera circolazione dei capitali e interesse nazionale' (2012) 3 *Rivista di diritto societario* 510; V Michel, 'Golden shares, fonds souverains et mission d'intérêt économique général' (2012) *Europe* 30; the contibutions in KP Sauvant, LE Sachs and WPF Schmit Jongbloed (eds), *Sovereign Investment: Concerns and Policy Reactions* (New York, Oxford University Press, 2012) 24 ff, including, in particular, J Chaisse, 'The Regulation of Sovereign Wealth Funds in the European Union: Can the Supranational Level Limit the Rise of National Protectionism?'; the contributions in P Bodeau-Livinec (ed), *Les fonds souverains et l'Union européenne: les liaisons dangereuses du marché et du politique* (Paris, Pedone, 2014), including, in particular, F Martucci, 'Les fonds souverains et l'Union européenne: les liaisons dangereuses du marché et du politique'; A Cummine, 'Ethical Sovereign Investors: Sovereign Wealth Funds and Human Rights' in JP Bohoslavsky and JL Černič (eds), *Making Sovereign Financing and Human Rights Work* (Oxford, Hart Publishing, 2014); the contributions in F Bassan, *Research Handbook on Sovereign Wealth Funds and International Investment Law* (Cheltenham, Edward Elgar, 2015), including, in particular, A De Luca, 'The EU and Member States: FDI, Portfolio Investments, Golden Powers and SWFs'; D Gallo,' The Rise of Sovereign Wealth Funds (SWFs) and the Protection of Public Interest(s): The Need for a Greater External and Internal Action of the European Union' (2016) 27 *European Business Law Review* 459; M Thatcher and T Vlandas, *Foreign States in Domestic Markets: Sovereign Wealth Funds and the West* (Oxford, Oxford University Press, 2021).

[108] See, *ex multis*, Joined Cases C-105/12 to C-107/12 *Essent and Others* ECLI:EU:C:2013:677, para 36.

Turning to the issue of whether the new Regulation reinforces ETS, the answer is mixed. It is negative if we consider that the Commission is not empowered to prevent an EU Member State from hosting an investment likely to affect security or public order beyond its borders. Indeed, as analysed in Section 4, although the EU has exclusive competences in respect of FDIs, the Member State where the FDI is planned enjoys a wide margin of discretion in deciding whether or not to authorise it. This means that foreign investors, 'including those controlled directly or indirectly, for example through significant funding, including subsidies, by the government of a third country or are pursuing State-led outward projects or programmes', may be able to take over critical infrastructure and critical technologies. In addition, Member States are not obliged to set up screening mechanisms.[109] The measure under consideration does not even require a minimum harmonisation of national legislations concerning screening mechanisms of FDIs.

Furthermore, the legislators could have endowed the Commission with wider powers,[110] especially in screening FDIs likely to affect 'projects or programmes of Union interest'. Indeed, to protect key enabling technologies, such as artificial intelligence, robotics and semiconductors, telecommunication infrastructure or Galileo, it is probably not enough that Member States take the Opinion of the Commission into 'the utmost consideration'.[111]

The EU review process of FDI described in the previous Section is not as centralised or robust as that existing in the US,[112] which was recently complemented by

[109] 'Nothing in this Regulation shall limit the right of each Member State to decide whether or not to screen a particular foreign direct investment within the framework of this Regulation'. The Commission encouraged all Member States 'to set up and enforce a fully fledged FDI screening mechanism to address cases where the acquisition or control of a particular business, infrastructure or technology would create a risk to security or public order in the EU'. See European Commission, 'Report From The Commission to The European Parliament and the Council: First Annual Report on the Screening of Foreign Direct Investments into the Union' (2021) COM(2021) 714 final, 7. For a list of screening mechanisms see the document available at 'Investment Screening' (*European Commission*), policy.trade.ec.europa.eu/enforcement-and-protection/investment-screening_en.

[110] See eg S Robert, 'Foreign Investment Control Procedures as a Tool to Enforce EU Strategic Autonomy' (2023) 8 *European Papers* 513.

[111] Art 8(2)(c) Regulation 2019/452.

[112] The Committee on foreign investment in the US (CFIUS) is a multi-agency government body chaired by the Secretary of the Treasury that, amongst other things, reviews transactions involving foreign investment in the US. The powers of this committee were expanded in 2018 with the Foreign Investment Risk Review Modernization Act of 2018 (FIRRMA), HR 5515–538. See 'FIRRMA FAQs' (*US Department of the Treasury*), home.treasury.gov/system/files/206/FIRRMA-FAQs.pdf. It is noteworthy that the number of factors affecting national security that CFIUS takes into consideration was expanded in September 2022. See Executive Order 14083 Ensuring Robust Consideration of Evolving National Security Risks by the Committee on Foreign Investment in the United States [2022] Federal Register Vol 87, No 181 and 'Statement by Secretary of the Treasury Janet L. Yellen on President Biden's Executive Order on the Committee on Foreign Investment in the United States' (*US Department of the Treasury*, 15 September 2022), home.treasury.gov/news/press-releases/jy0951. The Committee reviews the effects that a given transaction has 'on U.S. technological leadership in areas affecting U.S. national security, including but not limited to microelectronics, artificial intelligence, biotechnology and biomanufacturing, quantum computing, advanced clean energy, and climate adaptation technologies'. See 'FACT SHEET: President Biden Signs Executive Order to Ensure Robust Reviews of Evolving National Security Risks by the Committee on Foreign Investment in the United States' (*The White House*, 15 September 2022), www.whitehouse.gov/briefing-room/statements-releases/2022/09/15/fact-sheet-president-biden-signs-executive-order-to-ensure-robust-reviews-of-evolving-national-security-risks-by-the-committee-on-foreign-investment-in-the-united-states/.

further investment restrictive measures on sensitive technologies addressed to foreign investors from 'countries of concern,' including China, the Special Administrative Region of Hong Kong and the Special Administrative Region of Macau.[113] A scholar compares the type of screening mechanism set up by the Regulation under examination and the merger Regulation[114] and reaches this conclusion:

> … The fact acknowledged by Regulation 2019/452 is that FDI screening for public interest or national security reasons is a quintessentially national competence at the core of state sovereignty. This makes it impossible at the current stage of EU law to have a unified or EU legal instrument such as the EUMR [European Merger Regulation]. For business, it would no doubt be convenient to have the equivalent of an EUMR applicable to FDI screening, but that would require the willingness of EU Member States to give up sovereignty in a core area, a radical shift which does not seem likely in the foreseeable future.[115]

Despite the mentioned weaknesses, the Regulation under scrutiny shows potential to strengthen the Union's technological sovereignty since it reinforces the Commission's role in screening FDIs and makes an FDI in one Member State 'a matter of common interest' for the other Member States if such an investment may affect security and public order. We do not share the view expressed by an author that the mentioned act 'may paradoxically contribute to the emergence or further consolidation of many national as opposed to a common EU conception of public security'.[116]

Regulation 2019/452 favours transparency and exchange of information between Member States and the Commission; this act encourages a trialogue between the EU Member State undertaking the screening of an investment, the Member State (or

[113] On 9 August 2023 an executive order entitled 'Addressing United States Investments in Certain National Security Technologies and Products in Countries of Concern' was enacted by President Biden. The program is described as an instrument 'that complements the United States' existing export control and inbound screening tools with a "small yard, high fence" approach to address the national security threat posed by countries of concern advancing such sensitive technologies'. 'President Biden Signs Executive Order on Addressing United States Investments In Certain National Security Technologies And Products In Countries Of Concern' (*The White House*, 9 August 2023), www.whitehouse.gov/briefing-room/statements-releases/2023/08/09/president-biden-signs-executive-order-on-addressing-united-states-investments-in-certain-national-security-technologies-and-products-in-countries-of-concern/. 'Countries of concern' are defined as 'engaged in comprehensive, long-term strategies that direct, facilitate, or otherwise support advancements in sensitive technologies and products that are critical to such countries' military, intelligence, surveillance, or cyber-enabled capabilities. Moreover, these countries eliminate barriers between civilian and commercial sectors and military and defense industrial sectors, not just through research and development, but also by acquiring and diverting the world's cutting-edge technologies, for the purposes of achieving military dominance'. The measure has a clear national security component and, amongst other things, it prohibits US persons from engaging in transactions that involve national security technologies and products that are considered to pose a particularly acute national security threat because of their potential to significantly advance the military, intelligence, surveillance, or cyber-enabled capabilities of countries of concern. The objects of the prohibited transactions have to be identified in future Regulations. See 'Executive Order on Addressing United States Investments in Certain National Security Technologies and Products in Countries of Concern' (*The White House*, 9 August 2023), www.whitehouse.gov/briefing-room/presidential-actions/2023/08/09/executive-order-on-addressing-united-states-investments-in-certain-national-security-technologies-and-products-in-countries-of-concern/.

[114] Council Regulation (EC) 139/2004 on the control of concentrations between undertakings (EC Merger Regulation) [2004] OJ L24/1.

[115] P Callol, 'Protectionist Trends in Cross-Border Mergers and Acquisitions in Europe: National Interest, FDI and other Ingredients of the Growing Regulatory Maze' (2021) 42 *European Competition Law Review* 117, 126–127.

[116] Verellen (n 69) 21.

Member States) affected by the proposed investment, and the Commission. The latter enjoys the right to issue an Opinion on a proposed investment both in cases where the investment is subject to a screening mechanism and where there is no screening mechanism. Member States may consult the Commission when they consider that an investment may raise security or public order concerns. It is true that Member States are free to disregard possible objections to the investment made by the Commission or by the other Member States. However, as recalled in the Regulation,[117] the EU Member State of the investment is bound to respect the duty of loyal cooperation when it receives comments from the Commission or the other EU Members. This obligation applies even when Member States exercise a national competence, as happens in the context of the screening of FDI on the grounds of security or public order. As a result, the bar to disregard the Opinion of the Commission or that of other Member States is set at a relatively high level. A further positive aspect of the screening mechanism is that the scope of the Regulation is broad in terms of the 'critical infrastructure' and 'critical technology' covered. Furthermore, the range of factors that the Commission and the Member States (other than the one hosting the FDI) may take into consideration in determining the extent to which the investment poses a threat to security or public order is wide and of a non-exhaustive nature. These factors include, among other things, 'whether the foreign investor is directly or indirectly controlled by the government of a third country'. Finally, the projects and programmes with a 'European dimension' are also broadly defined[118] and it is up to the Commission to examine whether FDI affect security or public order. Therefore, this institution has its own role to perform in determining whether the Union's public order and security are affected.

6. PROTECTING CRITICAL INFRASTRUCTURE AND CRITICAL TECHNOLOGIES AND THE QUESTION OF EU COMPETENCE: THE RANGE OF MEASURES ENACTED ON THE BASIS OF A FLEXIBLE USE OF ARTICLE 114 TFEU

In this Section we explore whether the EU is equipped with sufficient powers to strengthen its technological sovereignty and is capable of adopting measures that enable Member States to preserve their technological leadership or to protect their security and integrity. One scholar takes a negative view; in his words:

> Without a competence that would correspond with the EU's novel, rather prescriptive political and policy ambitions, the task of protecting European sovereignty in the

[117] See Recital 17 Regulation 2019/452.

[118] They are so defined if they are supported by 'a substantial amount or a significant share of Union funding' or if they are covered by Union law 'regarding critical infrastructure, critical technologies or critical inputs which are essential for security or public order.' A non-exhaustive list is included in the Annex I Regulation 2019/452 and has been expanded with the Commission Delegated Regulation (EU) 2021/2126 amending the Annex to Regulation (EU) 2019/452 of the European Parliament and of the Council establishing a framework for the screening of foreign direct investments into the Union [2021] OJ L432/1. For example, this Regulation lists the Space Programme, the EU's Global Navigation Satellite System (Galileo), the European Geostationary Navigation Overlay Service (EGNOS) as well as the Union's free and openly accessible Earth Observation programme (Copernicus).

technological domain will, in a decisive part, fall onto the Member States acting within national competences. The EU's role may therefore be reduced to coordinating the expectedly diverse efforts of the Member States as dictated by their diverse interests.[119]

In the authors' view, the Union can claim to be better placed than its single Member States to tackle the current situation of technological dependency. Indeed, enhancing ETS requires action in the fields of trade, the internal market, including the free movement of capital, industrial policy, research and space. The EU enjoys exclusive (trade), concurrent (internal market) and coordination and supporting (industry and space) competence, and the contribution of the EU institutions is therefore necessary to achieve the mentioned objective, while respecting Member States' exclusive competence in protecting their own security. At the same time, the EU may deploy financial resources in pursuit of this goal. In September 2022 the Commission's President launched the idea of setting up a European Sovereign Fund, and the Commissioner for the Internal Market, Thierry Breton is considering financing this Fund 'through common debt, like we successfully did with NextGeneration EU'.[120]

It is noteworthy that the EU has adopted a number of measures to protect critical infrastructure and technologies. In order to do so the EU institutions have made good use of Article 114 TFEU which provides a very flexible legal basis[121] considering the practice and case law of the CJEU.[122]

The EU has relied on Article 114 TFEU to enact measures with three objectives: the first is to avoid distortions of the level playing field caused by foreign subsidised investment in all economic sectors, including strategic industries, critical assets and technologies. The second is to ensure the resilience of critical infrastructure and critical technologies, which are essential for both the functioning of the internal market and the EU's and Member States' security, and which are vulnerable since they are exposed to disruption[123] or destruction. The third objective is to increase the cyber security of network and information systems used to provide essential services in key sectors of economic activities. The latter purpose is clearly more related to

[119] M Varju, 'The Protection of Technology Sovereignty in the EU: Policy, Powers and the Legal Reality' (2022) 47 *EL Rev* 568, 583. For an overview of the legal hurdles that make it difficult for the EU to achieve technological sovereignty see S Poli, 'Il rafforzamento della sovranità tecnologica europea e il problema delle basi giuridiche' (2021) 5 *Atti convegni AISDUE* 69; E Fahey and S Poli, 'The Strengthening of the European Technological Sovereignty and its Legal Bases in the Treaties' (2022) 2 *Eurojus* 147.

[120] 'A European Sovereignty Fund for an industry "Made in Europe" I Blog of Commissioner Thierry Breton' (*European Commission*, 15 September 2022), www.ec.europa.eu/commission/presscorner/detail/en/STATEMENT_22_5543.

[121] In *Tobacco advertising* (Case C-376/98 *Republic of Germany v Council* ECLI:EU:C:2000:544, [2000] ECR I-8419), the CJEU made it clear that it can be used to adopt a measure where it is genuinely intended to improve the conditions for the establishment and the functioning of the internal market and it had that effect. ML Flear, 'Regulating New Technologies: EU Internal Market Law, Risk and Socio-Technical Order' in M Cremona, *New Technologies and EU Law*, Collected Courses of the Academy of European Law 24/2 (Oxford, Oxford University Press, 2017) 93. After the ruling mentioned above, the trend of widely interpreting the conditions that justify reliance on Art 114 TFEU has continued. See Case C-58/08 *Vodafone and Others* ECLI:EU:C:2010:321, [2010] ECR I-4999.

[122] 'It [the legislature] is able to exploit the broad and fuzzy contours of Article 114 TFEU to convert compliance with the principle of conferral into little more than a drafting exercise'. S Weatherill, 'The Limits of Legislative Harmonization Ten Years after Tobacco Advertising: How the Court's Case Law has become a "Drafting Guide"' (2011) 12 *German Law Journal* 827, 848.

[123] In particular, in case of cyberattacks.

the security of these systems than to the functioning of the internal market. Yet, Article 114 TFEU was used as the sole legal basis (without relying on Article 352 TFEU), despite the clear objective of the measure to ensure the resilience of these systems. Indeed, the smooth operation of network and information systems is necessary to ensure both security and the functioning of the internal market.

Turning to the first measure, Regulation 2022/2560 on foreign subsidies distorting the internal market was recently adopted as a complementary measure to Regulation 2019/452.[124] Both acts have in common the objective of countering first and foremost China's industrial policy embodied by the ten years 'Made in China 2025 Key Technology Roadmap'[125] and its wide use of subsidies to make acquisitions of strategic infrastructure and critical technologies or to participate in public procurement bids in strategic sectors.[126] Indeed, even though the two mentioned Regulations apply to all foreign companies, they are particularly intended to respond to China's industrial policy which is aimed at 'making the country an industrial leader by providing favourable conditions for growth to a number of industrial and hi-tech sectors such as robotics, electric vehicles, medical equipment, aerospace, maritime and railway'.[127] Chinese acquisitions of EU operators account for 95 per cent of Chinese FDIs in the EU.[128]

The Commission gives several examples of EU-based companies that were acquired by state-owned companies (SOE) as in the case of the acquisition of Pirelli by ChemChina, or even private companies which received direct or indirect financial support from the State that may be qualified as subsidies.[129]

In addition to takeovers, bids by subsidised Chinese companies are problematic in specific situations. An example is when they concern 'public concession contracts having as their object the operation and exploitation of large infrastructures

[124] Regulation (EU) 2022/2560 of the European Parliament and of the Council on foreign subsidies distorting the internal market [2022] OJ L330/1 on which, see JJ Piernas López, 'The Foreign Subsidies Regulation: an Ambitious Instrument that Raises Significant Challenges' (2023) 2 *CPI Antitrust Chronicle* 44; L Hornkohl, 'Protecting the Internal Market From Subsidisation With the EU State Aid Regime and the Foreign Subsidies Regulation: Two Sides of the Same Coin?' (2023) 14 *Journal of European Competition Law & Practice* 137; T Mülleribold, 'The Draft Foreign Subsidies Regulation: Relationship with Other Instruments' (2022) 3 *Zeitschrift für Europarechtliche Studien* 431; J Kuhling, P Reinhold and T Weck, 'State Capitalism and Level Playing Field: The Need for a "Third-Country State Aid Instrument" to Restore a Level Playing Field in the EU's Internal Market' (2020) 19 *European State Aid Law Quarterly* 403; J Blockx and P Mattiolo, 'The Foreign Subsidies Regulation: Calling Foul While Upping the Ante?' (2023) 28 *European Foreign Affairs Review* 53.

[125] See A Gabriele, *Enterprises, Industry and Innovation in the People's Republic of China Questioning Socialism from Deng to the Trade and Tech War* (Singapore, Springer, 2020) 171–178.

[126] For comments on the white paper that was published before the Regulation was enacted see Editorial Comments, 'Protecting the EU's Internal Market in Times of Pandemic and Growing Trade Disputes: Some Reflections about the Challenges posed by Foreign Subsidies' (2020) 57 *CML Rev* 1365.

[127] European Commission, 'Commission Staff Working Document: Impact Assessment accompanying the Proposal for a Regulation of the European Parliament and of the Council on Foreign Subsidies Distorting the Internal Market' (2021) SWD(2021) 99 final, 5.

[128] ibid 15. From 2008 to 2017, the stock of EU FDI in China grew from EUR 54 billion to EUR 178 billion. See Ramahandry et al (n 1) 8.

[129] European Commission, 'Commission Staff Working Document: Impact Assessment accompanying the Proposal for a Regulation of the European Parliament and of the Council on Foreign Subsidies Distorting the Internal Market' (2021) SWD(2021) 99 final, 12–13.

(e.g. railways, telecommunications and utilities)'.[130] It is clear that subsidised companies create unfair competition against non-subsidised companies in public procurement procedures. The latter procedures are open in the EU but there is a lack of reciprocity in the treatment reserved for EU operators in China. This is one of the reasons that led to the negotiation of the Comprehensive Agreement on Investment with China.[131]

Until the Regulation on foreign subsidies was adopted, it was not possible for the EU to react when subsidised foreign operators sought to acquire shares of EU companies and force technology transfer or participated in public procurement procedures, thus creating unfair competition for EU companies. As the Commission states, the new instrument is conceived specifically for tackling 'the issue of distortions to the level playing field caused by foreign subsidised investments in the internal market, including strategic industries, critical assets and technologies'.[132] There was a regulatory gap in this field which was neither covered by internal measures in the field of state aids, nor by the anti-subsidy Regulation.[133] The new instrument goes beyond the trade measures enabling the Commission to react to subsidised goods and is presented as an instrument that enhances the resilience of the internal market against distortions caused by foreign subsidies and thereby contributes to the Union's open strategic autonomy.

In contrast with the FDIs Regulation, Regulation 2022/2560 envisages a central role for the Commission in examining whether foreign subsidies distort the internal market; indeed, this institution is able to tackle subsidised investments and impose redressive measures in order to remedy the distortion in the internal market actually or potentially caused by a foreign subsidy; it may also accept commitments from the undertaking under investigation (Articles 7(1) and (2)). The Commission enjoys wide powers of investigation (which may also be carried out in the territory of a third country, if the latter raises no objections) and may impose fines and periodic penalty payments.

It is interesting that the new act is simultaneously based on Articles 114 and 207(1) TFEU. The use of this dual legal basis is possible but uncommon in practice.[134] In particular, the objectives of the new Regulation can be divided into two categories: a general objective, that is, the creation of a level playing field for EU operators, and two specific ones, which consist in identifying the most distortive subsidies and

[130] ibid 18.

[131] The text of the agreement is available at 'EU and China Reach Agreement In Principle on Investment' (*European Commission*, 30 December 2020), www.ec.europa.eu/commission/presscorner/detail/en/ip_20_2541.

[132] See European Commission, 'Proposal for a Regulation of the European Parliament and of the Council on Foreign Subsidies Distorting the Internal Market' (2021) COM(2021) 223 final, 5; Recital 3 Regulation (EU) 2022/2560 of the European Parliament and of the Council on foreign subsidies distorting the internal market [2022] OJ L330/1.

[133] European Commission, 'Commission Staff Working Document: Impact Assessment accompanying the Proposal for a Regulation of the European Parliament and of the Council on Foreign Subsidies Distorting the Internal Market' (2021) SWD(2021) 99 final, 29.

[134] For a proposal for Regulation based on Art 114 and 207 TFEU, see eg European Commission, 'Proposal for a Regulation of the European Parliament and of the Council on Prohibiting Products made with Forced Labour on the Union Market' (2022) COM(2022) 453 final.

in removing the subsidies in order to ensure the proper functioning of the internal market.[135] It is here submitted that the measure in question seems more an internal market measure than a trade instrument. Article 207 may be used as a legal basis when there is a link with international trade.[136] The Regulation on foreign subsidies does have such a link, but does not seek to promote trade, within the meaning of *Opinion 2/15*;[137] in contrast, it is intended to react to 'foreign subsidies that take the form of subsidised investments'. In addition, even if it is possible to argue that the measure has the objective of regulating trade, the new unilateral[138] measure does not seek to regulate trade as its primary objective.[139] This seems to be in contrast to measures based on Article 207 TFEU. In the light of the aim and the content of the measure, it may be thought that Article 114 TFEU could have been the only appropriate legal basis.

The second interesting measure, adopted on the basis of the internal market provision of the TFEU, is Directive 2022/2557 on the resilience of 'critical entities'[140] which repeals Council Directive 2008/114/EC.[141] Critical entities are defined as entities providing services essential to the functioning of the internal market.[142] They operate in many sectors, such as energy, transport, banking, drinking water, waste water, production, processing and distribution of food, health, space, financial market infrastructure and digital infrastructure sectors and in certain aspects of the public administration sector. The space sector falls within the scope of the critical entities Directive with respect to the provision of certain services that depend on ground-based infrastructure owned, managed and operated either by Member States or by private parties. Since there is fragmentation in respect of the characterisation of these entities amongst the Member States, the new measure aims at achieving a solid level of harmonisation in sectors and categories of entities falling within the scope of

[135] European Commission, 'Commission Staff Working Document: Impact Assessment accompanying the Proposal for a Regulation of the European Parliament and of the Council on Foreign Subsidies Distorting the Internal Market' (2021) SWD(2021) 99 final, 38.

[136] Case C-414/11 *Daiichi Sankyo and Sanofi-Aventis Deutschland* ECLI:EU:C:2013:520, paras 50–52; Case C-137/12 *Commission v Council* ECLI:EU:C:2013:675, para 58. For comments on the latter judgment see R Mastroianni and G Lo Tauro, 'Common Commercial Policy or Internal Market Rules as the Legal Basis for the Conclusion of International Agreements after Lisbon: *Commission v Council (Conditional Access Convention)*' in G Butler and RA Wessel (eds), *EU External Relations Law: The Cases in Context* (Oxford, Hart Publishing, 2022). For studies on the internal market see generally M Cremona, 'The External Dimension of the Single Market: Building (on) the Foundations' in C Barnard and J Scott (eds), *The Law of the Single European Market: Unpacking the Premises* (Oxford, Hart Publishing, 2002) 357–358; P Eeckhout, *The European Internal Market and International Trade: A Legal Analysis* (Oxford, Clarendon Press, 1994).

[137] Opinion 2/15 *Free Trade Agreement between the European Union and the Republic of Singapore* ECLI:EU:C:2017:376.

[138] In contrast, an international agreement that concerns investment protection must be based on Art 207 TFEU. See on this issue M Cremona, 'Defining the Scope of the Common Commercial Policy' in Hahn and Van der Loo (eds) (n 45) 56.

[139] A Rosas, 'Mixity and the Common Commercial Policy after Opinion 2/15' in Hahn and Van der Loo (eds) (n 45) 33.

[140] Directive (EU) 2022/2557 of the European Parliament and of the Council on the resilience of critical entities and repealing Council Directive 2008/114/EC (Directive 2022/2577) [2022] OJ L333/164.

[141] See for a comment A Lazari, *European Critical Infrastructure Protection* (Cham, Springer, 2014).

[142] Recital 2 Directive 2022/2577.

the Directive. The aim of this measure is to enhance the resilience[143] of entities in the Member States which are critical for the provision of services essential for the maintenance of vital societal functions or economic activities in the internal market in a wide number of sectors.[144] The idea behind the new measure is that considering the increased interdependence between Member States in relation to services provided by using critical infrastructure, a disruption in one Member State may have implications in other Member States or in the whole of the EU. The divergence of laws at a national level is a factor that obstructs the functioning of the internal market and makes the Union more vulnerable to natural or man-made, accidental or intentional hazards. The new Directive harmonises the security requirements to be respected by critical entities providing essential services. It lays down obligations on Member States and on critical entities. The former is required to identify critical entities on the basis of common criteria and take measures aimed at ensuring that services which are essential for the maintenance of vital societal functions or economic activities are provided in an unobstructed manner in the internal market. National authorities must also support critical entities in meeting the obligations imposed on them.

An interesting aspect of the Directive under examination is that it lays down rules with respect to 'critical entities of European significance'.[145] This notion is new and its inclusion in the text of the act shows that the EU uses Article 114 TFEU to protect a 'common good' and is not merely coordinating Member States' efforts in protecting their own critical entities. This is an indication that the EU is seeking to strengthen the ETS, which means that it has developed regulatory measures to strengthen the capacity of the EU to preserve the internal market whose functioning is its '*raison d'être*'.

The third act based on Article 114 TFEU is Directive 2022/2555 on measures for a high common level of cybersecurity across the Union[146] to protect Network and Information Systems (NIS) from cyber threats. These systems are used by 'essential' and 'important' entities that provide services in the internal market. It is therefore of fundamental importance for their functioning that cybersecurity is protected. Uniform criteria are established to identify such entities. The purpose of Directive 2022/2555 is to achieve a high level of cybersecurity (sic![147]) in the context of the EU.

[143] This is defined as 'the ability to prevent, resist, mitigate, absorb, accommodate to and recover from an incident that disrupts or has the potential to disrupt the operations of a critical entity'. Art 2(2) Directive 2022/2577.

[144] Commission, 'Proposal for a Directive of the European parliament and of the Council on the Resilience of Critical Entities' (2020) COM(2020) 829 final, 4.

[145] These entities provide the same or similar essential services to or in six or more Member States. Art 17(1)(b) Directive 2022/2577.

[146] Directive (EU) 2022/2555 of the European Parliament and of the Council on measures for a high common level of cybersecurity across the Union, amending Regulation (EU) No 910/2014 and Directive (EU) 2018/1972, and repealing Directive (EU) 2016/1148 (NIS 2 Directive) [2022] OJ L333/80.

[147] Recital 4 NIS 2 Directive. It may be thought that in consideration of the purpose of enhancing cyber security of the NIS, the Directive had to be based on an additional legal basis which in the absence of explicit powers of the EU to harmonise security requirements, could have been Art 352 TFEU. The reason why Art 114 TFEU is used as a legal basis is that the review of Directive (EU) 2016/1148, based on the same provision, has shown a wide divergence in its implementation by Member States, including in relation to its scope, the delimitation of which was very largely left to the discretion of the Member States.

It applies to a wide range of 'sectors and services of vital importance to key societal and economic activities in the internal market',[148] such as energy, transport, banking, financial market infrastructure, drinking water, waste water, digital infrastructure, ICT service management, public administration and space.[149] All entities identified as critical entities under Directive (EU) 2022/2557 are considered to be 'essential entities' under this Directive.[150] However, the latter category of entities goes beyond that of critical entities. The measure under examination complements the Directive on the resilience of critical entities insofar as the latter addresses the physical security of entities whereas the former tackles cybersecurity.[151]

It is noteworthy that the mentioned Directive considers foreign ownership of critical infrastructure within the Union as a potential threat because 'services, the economy and the free movement and safety of Union citizens depend on the proper functioning of critical infrastructure'.[152]

The three measures briefly presented above are examples of how the EU is able, through Article 114 TFEU, to achieve different objectives which are at the heart of the functioning of the internal market: countering subsidised investments and protecting the cyber security of technology and infrastructure. The reason why the EU institutions were able to rely on Article 114 TFEU in such a flexible manner is due to the case law of the CJEU which has managed to gradually transform the EU's harmonisation power into a regulatory power that is de facto independent of the existence of national legislation.[153]

7. AN EXAMPLE OF NATIONAL MEASURE THAT ENHANCES EU'S TECHNOLOGICAL SOVEREIGNTY: THE DUTCH EXPORT CONTROL MEASURE OF CHIP MACHINES

Member States have recently contributed to the achievement of 'Europe's technological sovereignty' through export control of advanced semiconductor technology.[154] In particular, in March 2023 the Dutch government announced the export of 'chips machines capable of producing transistors that measure under seven manometers'. The Dutch export control measure subjects to authorisation the export of this type of advanced semiconductor manufacturing equipment, starting from 1 September 2023.[155]

[148] Recital 6 NIS 2 Directive.

[149] Operators of ground-based infrastructure, owned, managed and operated by Member States or by private parties, that support the provision of space-based services, excluding providers of public electronic communications networks.

[150] Recital 30 NIS 2 Directive.

[151] ibid.

[152] Recital 19 NIS 2 Directive. In this context reference is made to Regulation 2019/452.

[153] R Schütze, 'Limits to the Internal Market Competence(s): Constitutional Comparisons,' in L Azoulai (ed), *The Question of Competence in the European Union* (Oxford, Oxford University Press, 2014) 232.

[154] The content of this section was published in the framework of another contribution written by one of the authors. See S Poli, 'Reinforcing Europe's Technological Sovereignty Through Trade Measures: The EU and Member States' Shared Sovereignty, (2023) 8 *European Papers* 429.

[155] See 'Government Publishes Additional Export Measures for Advanced Semiconductor Manufacturing Equipment (*Government of the Netherlands*, 30 June 2023), www.government.nl/latest/news/2023/06/30/

This very specific technology (the most advanced deep ultraviolet (DUV) immersion lithography and deposition) is manufactured by ASML and is necessary, in combination with certain other advanced technologies produced outside The Netherlands, in playing a crucial role in the manufacture of advanced semiconductors. This measure, which is country neutral,[156] was taken on grounds of 'national and international security' and is justified in the name of these public interests since the technology used to make semiconductors is constantly advancing, potentially changing the impact that the export of these products has on security. However, security concerns were not the only justification as the basis of this measure.

In a letter from the Minister of Foreign Trade and Development Cooperation to the Dutch Parliament, Ms Schreinemacher, it is stated that the trade restriction is part of a strategy inaugurated in December 2022 to control exports of the semiconductor technology in order to achieve three objectives:

1. preventing a situation in which Dutch goods contribute to undesirable end use, such as military deployment or weapons of mass destruction;
2. preventing undesirable long-term strategic dependencies; and
3. preserving the Netherlands' technological leadership position.[157]

It is clear from this statement that the Member State concerned has acted on the basis of a mixture of trade-related and non-trade related concerns, including security. Ms Schreinemacher is acting to preserve her country's technological leadership, to prevent its strategic dependency and protect national and international security. The Dutch initiative is crucial to protecting not only the mentioned national interests but also those of EU Member States. There is a common European interest in the enactment of the said export control measure. Each Member State has the power to autonomously determine whether or not to introduce export restrictions. Indeed, Member States are sovereign in protecting essential security interests, under Article 4(2) TEU. Yet, Member States must exercise their powers in full respect of those of the EU and in particular of the Union regime on dual use goods which is currently regulated by Regulation (EU) 2021/821.[158] It is submitted that when export control measures are enacted vis-à-vis a third country, concerning strategic technologies (regardless of whether they are dual use goods or not), Member States should coordinate their action with the Union since this is required by the principle of conferral and by the exclusive nature of the EU competence in the field of trade. Even if a given technology

government-publishes-additional-export-measures-for-advanced-semiconductor-manufacturing-equipment.

[156] Although the measure at stake is country neutral, China's run to achieve technological leadership in the chip sector is affected by the export restriction. See Poli (n 154) 441–442.

[157] L Schreinemacher, 'Letter of 8th March 2023 from the Minister for Foreign Trade and Development Cooperation to the President of the House of Representatives of the States General Announcing Forthcoming Export Control Measures concerning Advanced Semiconductor Manufacturing Equipment' (*Government of the Netherlands*, 10 March 2023), www.government.nl/documents/parliamentary-documents/2023/03/10/letter-to-parliament-on-additional-export-control-measures-concerning-advanced-semiconductor-manufacturing-equipment.

[158] Regulation (EU) 2021/821 of the European Parliament and of the Council setting up a Union regime for the control of exports, brokering, technical assistance, transit and transfer of dual-use items (recast) [2021] OJ L206/1.

is available in a single Member State, decisions to sell or not to sell to Chinese operators should be discussed at EU level.

It is submitted that The Netherlands seems to have acted within the limits of its exclusive competence in full respect of EU exclusive competence in trade matters as defined in the Union regime on dual use goods. Indeed, while announcing the setting up of a national control list by public ministerial order, the Dutch Minister for Foreign Trade and Development cooperation shows a clear intention to act within the framework of Regulation (EU) 2021/821 on dual-use items and even at multilateral level in the context of the Wassenaar arrangements. Ms Schreinemacher announces that it will notify the European Commission and the EU Member States about the national control measure, under Articles 9 and 10 of the mentioned Regulation. At this point, the Dutch Minister observes that a new legal issue will emerge for the other EU Member States: will they impose an authorisation requirement similar to that of The Netherlands, considering that the dual good concerned is not available in other EU countries? As it is emphasised in the letter of 8 March 2023,

> the provision in the Dual-Use Regulation on member states adopting another country's national control measures is new, and has not previously been applied. The Netherlands has recently held close consultations with the European Commission and EU member states to explain the importance of this specific control measure in the light of national security, and to gain support for it. In the months ahead, the government will continue these efforts with a view to establishing the national control list in the EU landscape as effectively as possible.[159]

Export controls similar to those enacted by the Netherlands should also be adopted by other Member States, even if they do not manufacture the technology at stake. This is necessary to ensure the unity and effectiveness of the export control system, thus avoiding any loopholes in the EU export control of dual use goods. The possibility for EU Member States to amend their national control lists in light of the Dutch decision is provided for by Article 9(4) of the dual use good Regulation.

In a recent Communication entitled 'European Economic Security Strategy', we learn that 'the provisions that allow one Member State to introduce export controls based on another Member State's legislation, amounting to a coordinated and cross-border effect, among EU Member States and supported by the Commission, of export controls whose implementation is a national prerogative'[160] are currently being tested. At the beginning of 2024, after our chapter had been submitted, the white paper on export controls was published by the Commission. The latter highlights important shortcomings of Regulation (EU) 2021/821, including the risk that national export controls adopted by one Member State may be circumvented if an exporter of a Member State, say the Netherlands, sells the dual use good to customers in another Member State, which does not apply a similar control. Such a customer could then legally re-export the goods concerned from there to the third country.[161]

[159] Schreinemacher (n 157).

[160] European Commission and High Representative of the Union for Foreign Affairs and Security Policy, 'European Economic Security Strategy' (2023) JOIN(2023) 20 final, 10.

[161] White paper on export controls (2024) COM(2024) 25 final, 8.

In the future it is likely that the current Regulation on export control systems will be changed to ensure greater coordination amongst Member States in export controls thus making them more effective.

The case of the Dutch export restriction of chipmaking equipment shows that the EU and its Member States can act together to strengthen Europe's technological sovereignty, according to a model which can be defined as 'shared sovereignty'. The Netherlands has relied on its exclusive powers to protect national and international security, to safeguard its technological leadership and to prevent the emergence of new dependencies on semi-conductors. At the same time, the government has consulted with the Commission, in line with its duty of sincere cooperation and with the EU regime for the control of export of dual use items.

8. CONCLUSIONS

In this chapter three different modes of strengthening European technological sovereignty in the protection of critical infrastructure and technologies were explored.

Regulation 2019/452 can be considered an expression of the first mode, which is based on the decentralised review of FDIs by Member States and on the coordinating powers of the Commission. Even if the latter, unlike the Committee on Foreign Investment in the United States (CFIUS),[162] does not have the authority to autonomously review FDIs in a Member State, the FDIs Regulation is a step forward in protecting the EU's technological assets and critical infrastructure. Indeed, it makes it possible that in time the Commission's ability to influence Member States' decisions regarding FDI will grow. The context in which this Regulation operates nowadays has changed with respect to 2017 when the proposal at the basis of the Regulation was submitted by the Commission. The Regulation was adopted before the pandemic and the outbreak of the war in Ukraine. The former emergency exposed with particular acuteness the EU's vulnerability with respect to goods (ie, vaccines) at the early stage of the pandemic. The outbreak of the Ukraine war provoked a 'security earthquake' in the EU. When the FDI screening measure was proposed by the Commission, the new trade measure was conceived as an instrument to 'restore the level playing field in the area of investment'. This is an area which was upset by China's industrial policy[163]. China aimed at exploiting the EU's openness to investment for gaining influence and/or control over European companies, while EU operators continue(d) to be subject to obstacles in investing in the Chinese market.[164] Regulation 2019/452 entrusted Member States with significant powers for the screening of FDIs, including those

[162] See above n 112.

[163] This is inferred from the letter written by Germany, Italy and France to the Commission requesting the latter to 'develop an appropriate instrument' which could complement existing national measures that could not exclude on the basis of security and public order that 'European companies were acquired as part of other countries' strategic industrial policies.' The reference is clearly to China. See 'European Investment Policy: A Common Approach to Investment Control' (*Politico*, 28 July 2017), www.politico.eu/wp-content/uploads/2017/08/170728_Investment-screening_non-paper.pdf.

[164] See M Leonard, J Pisani-Ferry, E Ribakova, J Shapiro and GB Wolff, 'Redefining Europe's Economic Sovereignty' (2019) 9 *Bruegel Policy Contribution*.

enabling a foreign investor to take over key technologies that affect national industrial policy.[165] However, the competence of the Commission vis-à-vis unwelcome non-EU FDIs was supposed to remain limited.

After the outbreak of war in Ukraine, we have witnessed new vigour in the Commission's initiatives designed to protect critical infrastructure and critical technologies from FDIs of non-EU operators. Guidelines to the Member States concerning FDIs from Russia and Belarus were adopted to steer national authorities' decisions on authorising FDIs coming from operators of these countries. The Commission has taken the position that

> there is a heightened risk that any investment directly or indirectly related to a person or entity associated with, controlled by or subject to influence by the Russian or Belarusian government into critical assets in the EU may give reasonable grounds to conclude that the investment may pose a threat to security or public order in Member States.[166]

This is an attempt to ensure convergence in Member States' assessments of risks related to FDIs for essential security reasons.

Now, in view of the new security environment and of the degree of sensitivity concerning dependence on third countries as a result of the war, the Commission may be able to persuade Member States to take greater care in authorising inbound FDIs not only in respect of Russian investors but also of those investors coming from other trading partners with authoritarian governments. Furthermore, in a recent Communication on European economic security strategy, the Commission has stated that it will examine security *risks* (emphasis added) that result from outbound investments, liaising with Member States.[167] The setting up of a Committee of national experts is also announced. According to the Commission, on the one hand, the mentioned investments may entail 'technology and know-how leaking as part of that investment'.[168] On the other hand, European companies' capital, expertise and knowledge may be used by investors of third countries to enhance the latter's military and intelligence capabilities, thus undermining international peace and security. Furthermore, in early January 2024, while working on the proof of this chapter, the White Paper on Outbound Investments has been issued.[169]

Depending on how the FDI screening mechanism is applied in the future by the Commission, the Union may become an actor in transition toward technological sovereignty rather than merely a witness to fragmented efforts by individual Member States to preserve national technological sovereignty in Europe.

In this chapter we have also reflected on how the Union, despite its limited competences, has been capable of enacting other measures to protect critical infrastructure and technology on the basis of Article 114 TFEU; the latter provision has been used as

[165] Zwartkruis and de Jong (n 10) 464.

[166] European Commission, 'Guidance to the Member States concerning Foreign Direct Investment from Russia and Belarus in view of the Military Aggression against Ukraine and the Restrictive Measures laid down in recent Council Regulations on Sanctions' [2022] OJ C151I/1.

[167] European Commission and High Representative of the Union for Foreign Affairs and Security Policy, 'European Economic Security Strategy' (2023) JOIN(2023) 20 final, 11.

[168] ibid.

[169] White Paper on Outbound Investments (2024) COM/2024/24 final.

a 'strategic' legal basis to ensure a level playing field for EU operators (ie, Regulation on foreign subsidies) but also to support Member States' efforts to enhance the security of critical infrastructure and technologies. The stretch of the EU's competence in the field of internal market may be considered as the second mode of strengthening the ETS.

In addition to EU unilateral trade measures such as the Regulations on FDI and that on anti-subsidies, other security-related trade measures were taken by a Member State in pursuit of its economic interests as well as to promote international security. The Dutch export restriction of chip machines of March 2023 is such a measure: in principle, it is designed to strengthen national technological sovereignty: it was based on the need to preserve this country's technological leadership and on security concerns. This measure can be considered as the third mode of strengthening the EU's technological sovereignty: by enacting export restrictions vis-à-vis third countries' operators, Member States also serve EU's economic interests and security at a global level, thus contributing to indirectly preserving the EU's technological leadership and security.

In conclusion, this chapter has shown that globalisation is receding in favour of the opposite phenomenon of progressive deglobalisation. It is against this backdrop that a new legal order is beginning to assert itself in the European context, one that does more than simply frame and, where necessary, direct the market. A legal order that aims to limit, in particularly innovative terms, the market access of non-EU actors and that seems to be the result of three trends within the Union. First: the current policies on foreign subsidies and foreign direct investment reveals the tendency to approach trade relations, especially with China, in terms of reciprocity, given the substantial collapse of the World Trade Organization (WTO). Second: such policies, together with the State aid policy conducted by the Commission in the aftermath of the COVID-19 outbreak, are also a sign of the tendency to do what the US and China, among other countries, have been doing for a long time, that is designing an industrial policy aimed at benefiting domestic operators and, at the same time, countering the expansionism of third countries of both a commercial and strategic kind. Third: those policies also reveal the tendency to break away from certain dogmas of the past, inspired by a vision of free market *without ifs and buts*. Moreover, when the foreign investment is made by companies (as often happens), active mainly (but not only) in the technology sector, that act as the *longa manus* of a third state and enjoy significant State subsidies (or at least a special relationship with public authorities), the underlying priority of the emerging new legal order of the market is to counter State-generated distortions rather than market-generated distortions. From this perspective, the threat is posed by a globalisation with new contours; it is, therefore, State capitalism, rather than capitalism *tout court*, that is under indictment.

ADDENDUM

As mentioned in our chapter, after the submission of our piece to the Editors, while working on the proofs, on 24 January 2024 the European Commission adopted five initiatives to strengthen the EU's economic security 'at a time of growing geopolitical tensions and profound technological shifts', in line with the June 2023 European Economic Security Strategy as stated in the Commission's website (ec.europa.eu/commission/presscorner/detail/en/ip_24_363). The package includes the Proposal for a Regulation of the European Parliament and of the Council on the screening of foreign investments in the Union and repealing Regulation (EU) 2019/452 of the European Parliament and of the Council (COM(2024) 23 final), complemented by an Explanatory Memorandum and a Staff Working Document. The proposal aims at further strengthening the protection of EU security and public order by proposing improved screening of foreign investment into the EU through a revision of Regulation 2019/452, in the light of the practice undertaken in the last three years involving over 1,200 FDI transactions notified by Member States under the existing FDIs Regulation. As clarified by the Commission in the Explanatory Memorandum, the proposal pursues the following goals: ensuring that all Member States have a screening mechanism in place; identifying sectors where all Member States must screen foreign investments; and applying EU screening not only to non-EU investors but also to investments by EU investors that are ultimately controlled by non-EU countries' entities. Amongst relevant features of such a proposal lies one that has been already stressed in our article, whereby the Commission affirms, in the Explanatory Memorandum, that 'it is possible to make a distinction between the application of internal market freedoms to investments within the EU where the EU entity is controlled by a non-EU country investor and pure intra-EU situations. Consequently, under the Treaty, restrictions on transactions involving a non-EU country may be based on different considerations. This is also appropriate considering that these transactions are screened as part of a Union-wide cooperation mechanism'.

EU Trade Policy and the Promotion of Gender Equality: Disseminating International Law and Mobilising Internal Stakeholders

ANNE THIES

1. INTRODUCTION

IN 2004, Marise Cremona, recognising the power of law in the EU's external relations, identified five roles for the EU as a global actor: laboratory and model; market player; rule generator; stabiliser; magnet and neighbour.[1] The EU as a global actor has been exercising these various roles by relying on its internal and external competences,[2] often simultaneously pursuing internal and external objectives,[3] acting in collaboration with its Member States and other global actors,[4] concluding international treaties[5] and adopting unilateral measures.[6] In so doing, the EU has had to accommodate the voices of various stakeholders within the EU to legitimise its action legally and politically, and to achieve the shared objectives the

[1] M Cremona, 'The Union as a Global Actor: Roles, Model and Identity' (2004) 41 *CML Rev* 553.

[2] M Cremona, 'EU External Relations: Unity and Conferral of Powers' in L Azoulai (ed), *The Question of Competence in the European Union* (Oxford, Oxford University Press, 2014); M Cremona, 'The Principle of Conferral and Express and Implied External Competences' in R Schütze and T Tridimas (eds), *Oxford Principles of European Union Law – Volume 1: The European Union Legal Order* (Oxford, Oxford University Press, 2018); M Cremona, 'Balancing Union and Member State Interests: Opinion 1/2008, choice of legal base and the common commercial policy under the Treaty of Lisbon' (2010) 35 *EL Rev* 678.

[3] M Cremona, 'The European Neighbourhood Policy: More than a Partnership?' in M Cremona (ed), *Developments in EU External Relations Law*, The Collected Courses of the Academy of European Law XVII/1 (Oxford, Oxford University Press, 2008).

[4] M Cremona, 'Member States as Trustees of the Union Interest: Participating in International Agreements on Behalf of the European Union' in A Arnull, C Barnard, M Dougan and E Spaventa (eds), *A Constitutional Order of States? Essays in EU law in Honour of Alan Dashwood* (Oxford, Hart Publishing, 2011).

[5] M Cremona, 'Making Treaties and Other International Agreements: The European Union' in CA Bradley (ed), *Comparative Foreign Relations Law* (Oxford, Oxford University Press, 2019); M Cremona, 'The Doctrine of Exclusivity and the Position of Mixed Agreements in the External Relations of the European Community' (1982) 2 *Oxford Journal of Legal Studies* 393.

[6] M Cremona, 'EC Competence, "Smart Sanctions", and the Kadi Case' (2009) 28 *Yearbook of European Law* 559.

Member States agreed on when establishing and empowering the EU as a rules-based actor. Such balancing acts have often been submitted to the Court of Justice of the European Union for judicial review.[7] Law has been instrumental in developing the constitutional framework for the EU's international action,[8] with a crucial role given to structural principles in particular.[9] The role of values in EU foreign policy has been subject to debate,[10] and the significance of the global reach of EU law (achieved through unilateral, bilateral and multilateral legal instruments) for EU external relations and its identity as an international actor has been analysed.[11]

Building on the outstanding and comprehensive scholarship produced by Marise Cremona, and wholeheartedly thanking her for her commitment to gender equality in academia, this chapter turns to the field of trade and gender. The promotion of gender equality through EU external action has gained some attention by political scientists,[12] while political economists and trade policy experts have analysed the gendered impact of trade.[13] Linked to this volume's focus on the 'power of law' in the EU's external relations, this chapter explores the ways in which the EU as a global actor has weaved its commitment to 'integrate a gender perspective in all major Commission initiatives' and the recognition of 'gender equality and women's empowerment [as] a core objective of EU external action', which it aims to promote also in its trade policy,[14] into its trade policy-making, treaty-making and domestic law-making related to trade with non-EU actors.

The objective of this chapter is two-fold: first, it analyses the EU's current ways of advancing gender equality and the economic empowerment of women in its interaction with *non-EU* actors. More specifically, it analyses the extent to which the EU has helped to increase the reach of international law on gender equality

[7] M Cremona and A Thies (eds), *The European Court of Justice and External Relations: Constitutional Challenges*, Modern Studies in European Law (Oxford, Hart Publishing, 2014); M Cremona, A Thies and RA Wessel (eds), *The European Union and International Dispute Settlement* (Oxford, Hart Publishing, 2017); M Cremona, 'The Opinion Procedure under Article 218(11) TFEU: Reflections in the Light of Opinion 1/17' (2020) 4 *Europe and the World: A Law Review* 11.

[8] M Cremona, 'External Relations of the European Union: The Constitutional Framework for International Action' in P Craig and G de Búrca (eds), *The Evolution of EU Law*, 3rd edn (Oxford, Oxford University Press, 2021).

[9] M Cremona (ed), *Structural Principles in EU External Relations Law* (Oxford, Hart Publishing, 2018).

[10] M Cremona, 'Values in EU Foreign Policy' in M Evans and P Koutrakos (eds), *Beyond the Established Orders: Policy Interconnections between the EU and the Rest of the World* (Oxford, Hart Publishing, 2011).

[11] M Cremona, 'Extending the Reach of EU Law: The EU as an International Legal Actor' in M Cremona and J Scott (eds), *EU Law beyond EU Borders: The Extraterritorial Reach of EU Law*, The Collected Courses of the Academy of European Law XXVII/1 (Oxford, Oxford University Press, 2019).

[12] See for a recent discussion of the development of the field in political sciences, with reference to relevant literature, P Debusscher and I Manners, 'Understanding the European Union as a Global Gender Actor: The Holistic Intersectional and Inclusive Study of Gender+ in External Actions (2020) 18 *Political Studies Review* 542. See also T Väyrynen, E Féron, P Medie, S Parashar, C Confortini (eds), *Handbook of Feminist Peace Research* (London, Routledge, 2020); R Guerrina, L Chappell and KA Wright, 'Transforming CSDP? Feminist Triangles and Gender Regimes' (2018) 56 *Journal of Common Market Studies* 1036; G Allwood, 'Gender Mainstreaming and Policy Coherence for Development: Unintended Gender Consequences and EU Policy' (2013) 39 *Women's Studies International Forum* 42.

[13] A Frohmann, 'Gender Equality and Trade Policy' (2017) *SECO Working Paper* 24/2017.

[14] European Commission, 'A Union of Equality: Gender Equality Strategy 2020–2025' (2020) COM(2020) 152 final, 15, 17.

(eg UN Convention on the Elimination of All Forms of Discrimination against Women (CEDAW), International Labour Organization (ILO) Conventions) and contributed to the creation of tailored gender equality obligations through external trade action (ie trade agreements, Generalised Scheme of Preferences (GSP), international initiatives). Hence focusing on the dissemination and potential enforcement of international law on gender equality through EU trade action, the chapter complements legal scholarship that focuses on the EU's international (trade) agreements and human rights,[15] the implications of EU's foreign policy objectives for its external action more broadly,[16] and the gender-responsiveness of EU trade agreements.[17]

Second, and acknowledging the significance of the global impact of individual EU Member States and private actors, the chapter analyses the extent to which the EU has invited and obliged them to promote gender equality in interaction with trading partners outside the EU. The need to 'mobilise' EU internal stakeholders to promote the enforcement of gender equality commitments (established by trade agreements, international and EU law) has been recognised by the EU, non-governmental organisations and academics.[18] However, to date no scholarly attention has been given to the anchoring of such mobilisation in the EU legal order with a particular focus on trade and gender. The chapter thus is the first to analyse: (a) the EU tools to involve Member States and private actors in the enforcement of international legal obligations of the EU's treaty partners (ie Single Entry Point, Access2Market), and (b) the scope of legal obligations fostering gender equality imposed on EU stakeholders interacting with

[15] V Kube, *EU Human Rights, International Investment Law and Participation: Operationalizing the EU Foreign Policy Objective to Global Human Rights Protection*, Interdisciplinary studies in Human Rights 4 (Cham, Springer, 2019); L Bartels, *Human Rights Conditionality in the EU's International Agreements*, Oxford Studies in European Law (Oxford, Oxford University Press, 2005); L Bartels, 'The EU's Human Rights Obligations in Relation to Policies with Extraterritorial Effects' (2014) 25 *EJIL* 1071; J Harrison, 'The Labour Rights Agenda in Free Trade Agreements' (2019) 20 *Journal of World Investment and Trade* 705.

[16] J Larik, *Foreign Policy Objectives in European Constitutional Law*, Oxford Studies in European Law (Oxford, Oxford University Press, 2016).

[17] C Gammage, 'Empowering Women in Trade: How Gender Responsive are the EU's Trade Agreements?' in E Fahey and I Mancini (eds), *Understanding the EU as a Good Global Actor: Ambitions, Values and Metrics*, Elgar Studies in European Law and Policy (Cheltenham, Edward Elgar, 2022); A Thies, 'The EU's Law and Policy Framework for the Promotion of Gender Equality in the World' in T Giegerich (ed), *The European Union as Protector and Promoter of Equality*, European Union and its Neighbours in a Globalized World 1 (Cham, Springer, 2020), 429–454, 443, 446f; J True, 'Trading-Off Gender Equality for Global Europe? The European Union and Free Trade Agreements' (2009) 14 *European Foreign Affairs Review* 723.

[18] See eg European Commission, 'Communication on Decent Work Worldwide for a Global Just Transition and a Sustainable Recovery' (2022) COM(2022) 66 final, 4, with reference to GAP III, 'Gender Action Plan – Putting Women and Girls' Rights at the Heart of the Global Recovery for a Gender-Equal World' (*European Commission*, 25 November 2020), www.ec.europa.eu/commission/presscorner/detail/en/IP_20_2184; and European Commission, 'A Union of Equality: Gender Equality Strategy 2020–2025' (2020) COM(2020) 152 final; 'Implementation and Enforcement of EU Trade Policy: Issues Paper' (*European Commission*, 22 September 2022), circabc.europa.eu/ui/group/7fc51410-46a1-4871-8979-20cce8df0896/library/7103f3c9-2dc5-4bc5-be52-210c133802ca/details?download=true%5D; which refers to 'Mobilising EU stakeholders abroad on Market Access and Trade and Sustainable Development issues' on p 5; Gammage, 'Empowering Women in Trade' 173, with reference to 'CONCORD's Analysis of the European Commission Gender Equality Strategy' (*CONCORD*, March 2020), www.concordeurope.org/wp-content/uploads/2020/05/CONCORD-analysis-of-Gender-Equality-Strategy-FINAL-updated-version-19.05.2020.pdf, 2.

trading partners outside the EU (eg due diligence, procurement). The chapter thereby complements existing work on the 'global reach'[19] and the 'Brussels effect'[20] of EU substantive regulation relevant for trade (eg environmental protection, chemicals, data protection).

The chapter is structured as follows. After Section 2 reminding the reader of the global challenge of gender in/equality and the relevance of trade, the chapter in Section 3 outlines the EU's legal framework for advancing gender equality through trade. Subsequently, in Section 4 the chapter evaluates examples of recent EU practice at global and in Section 5 at domestic level to assess the extent to which the EU's commitment to (globally) advance gender equality and the economic empowerment of women has gone beyond mere political statements and strategy documents. The chapter analyses explicitly 'external trade' measures (ie trade agreements, GSP, international initiatives) as well as EU internal measures that address and oblige actors within the EU, but have – even if pursuing, at least partially, internal market objectives – an external reach or effect (ie due diligence, procurement).

2. TRADE AND GENDER

'Women and girls represent half of the world's population, and, therefore, also half of its potential'.[21] Gender equality is recognised as a fundamental human right and as 'essential to achieve peaceful societies, with full human potential and sustainable development'.[22] The Sustainable Development Agenda has included gender equality as one its goals (Goal 5),[23] and there is evidence that 'empowering women spurs productivity and economic growth'.[24] However, as highlighted also by the UN, UN Women and the World Bank, girls and women around the globe continue to suffer from discrimination and inequality with regard to education, health and related services, economic structure, participation and access to resources and economic opportunities, public life and decision-making.[25] Women around the globe remain more affected by poverty than men. According to the *Global Gender Gap Report*

[19] Cremona and Scott (eds) (n 11); see also on the EU as 'global regulatory power', focusing on environmental law J Scott, 'Extraterritoriality and Territorial Extension in EU Law' (2014) 62 *American Journal of Comparative Law* 87, and on 'internal measures with extraterritorial implications' in the field of environmental protection I Hadjiyianni, *The EU as a Global Regulator for Environmental Protection*, Modern Studies in European Law (Oxford, Hart Publishing, 2019) 92.

[20] A Bradford, *The Brussels Effect: How the European Union Rules the World* (Oxford, Oxford University Press, 2020).

[21] 'Global Issues: Gender Equality' (*United Nations*), www.un.org/en/global-issues/gender-equality.

[22] ibid; see also World Bank Group, *The Little Data Book on Gender* (Washington, International Bank for Reconstruction and Development/The World Bank, 2019) V.

[23] 'Sustainable Development Goals – Goal 5: Achieve Gender Equality and Empower All Women and Girls' (*United Nations*), www.un.org/sustainabledevelopment/gender-equality/.

[24] See n 21.

[25] See for an analysis of global indicators and country specific developments, providing comparable statistics for men and women 2010–2017 World Bank Group, *The Little Data Book on Gender*. For a historical overview of UN and UN Women work related to gender equality as well as links to relevant documents and treaties see n 21.

2023 published by the World Economic Forum, the economic participation and opportunity gender gap will close in 169 years.[26]

Trade policy and trade liberalisation have been employed to give access to markets and reduce poverty in developed and in developing countries; yet, it remains a challenge to make trade beneficial also for the poorest and most vulnerable.[27] As observed by Peters, many persons have not only not benefitted from global trade and investment but also suffered due to technical and demographic change and pollution caused by it; 'debates on poverty, inequality, and social exclusion as global concerns accompany the timid expressions of a "more social", and more individualised international legal framework which is in the making'.[28]

International organisations, states, advocacy groups and scholars have highlighted that trade is not gender neutral. Trade policy needs to become 'more responsive to the specific needs of women and instrumental to gender equality and women's empowerment',[29] and decrease economic and social disadvantage that women experience as workers, consumers, and family members.[30]

Acknowledging the link between trade and gender has led to gender impact assessments and the inclusion of gender equality provisions in trade instruments.[31] In 2016, the first chapter on gender equality was included in the trade agreement between Chile and Uruguay, followed by Chile's updated FTA with Canada and ongoing negotiations between the EU and Chile of their modernised Strategic Partnership.[32] The importance of assessing 'all likely gender impacts' for making trade agreements genuinely gender-responsive has been explained in the 2020 report published by the World Trade Organization (WTO)'s Trade Impact Group by using the following example.

[26] 'Global Gender Gap Report 2023' (*World Economic Forum*, 20 June 2023), www3.weforum.org/docs/WEF_GGGR_2023.pdf, 6; the Report and an interactive data platform are also available at www.weforum.org/publications/global-gender-gap-report-2023/.

[27] See eg *The Role of Trade in Ending Poverty* (Washington/Geneva, World Bank and World Trade Organization, 2015), and *Trade and Poverty Reduction: New Evidence of Impacts in Developing Countries* (Washington/Geneva, World Bank and World Trade Organization, 2018).

[28] A Peters, 'Global Constitutionalism: The Global Dimension' (2017) *MPIL Research Paper Series* No 2017-25, 8f.

[29] UN Inter-Agency Network on Women and Gender Equality, 'Gender Equality & Trade Policy' (*United Nations*, 2011) www.un.org/womenwatch/feature/trade/gender_equality_and_trade_policy.pdf.

[30] *Women and Trade: The Role of Trade in Promoting Gender Equality* (Washington, World Bank and World Trade Organization, 2020); 'Gender Equality and Trade: Recent Developments and Ways Forward' (*The Trade Justice Movement and The Gender and Development Network*, June 2018), www.tjm.org.uk/documents/briefings/Gender-equality-and-trade-recent-developments-and-ways-forward.pdf.

[31] See eg United Nations Conference on Trade and Development, 'Implementing Gender-Aware Ex Ante Evaluations to Maximize the Benefits of Trade Reforms for Women' (2016) Policy Brief No 51; United Nations Conference on Trade and Development, 'Trade and Gender Toolbox' (2017) UNCTAD/DITC/2017/1; 'Report: Trade and Social Sustainability – An Overview and Analysis' (*National Board of Trade Sweden*, 2017), www.kommerskollegium.se/en/publications/reports/2017/trade-and-social-sustainability/; 'Trade and Gender Equality – The Role of Trade Policy' (*National Board of Trade Sweden*, 2020), www.kommerskollegium.se/en/publications/reports/2020/trade-and-gender-equality--the-role-of-trade-policy/; JA Monteiro, 'Gender-Related Provisions in Regional Trade Agreements' (*World Trade Organization*, 18 December 2018) Staff Working Paper ERSD-2018-15; JA Monteiro, 'Gender-related Provisions in Regional Trade Agreements Database' (*WTO Economic Research and Statistics Division*, July 2020), www.wto.org/english/res_e/reser_e/ersd202108_e.htm.

[32] Frohmann (n 13) 17 et seq. See for text of the 2022 politically concluded EU-Chile Interim Trade Agreement: 'EU-Chile: Text of the Agreement' (*European Commission*), policy.trade.ec.europa.eu/eu-trade-relationships-country-and-region/countries-and-regions/chile/eu-chile-agreement/text-agreement_en.

> For example, if food prices go down following trade liberalization, women may win as consumers since they can secure their household's food with a smaller share of household income; but women food producers may be unable to compete with imported products because of price or quality and be crowded out of the market.[33]

Increased global awareness of gender inequality and the potential role for trade to induce positive change, has led to country/region specific data collection to assess how states and regional actors tackle inequality at the national/regional level.[34] In 2017, 118 WTO members, including the EU, supported a Joint Declaration on Trade and Women's Economic Empowerment (Buenos Aires Declaration).[35] The Buenos Aires Declaration affirmed WTO members' commitment to make trade 'more gender-responsive', the 'sharing of best practice of gender-based analysis of trade policies and monitoring their effects', sharing 'ways of data collection and analysing gender-focused statistics', collaborating to 'remove barriers to women's economic empowerment and increase their participation in trade', and 'ensuring that Aid for Trade supports efforts to analyse, design and implement more gender-responsive trade policies'; the Declaration has by now been endorsed by 127 members and observers.[36] The WTO's informal working group (IWG) on trade and gender has been operating since 2020, supported also by the EU.[37]

In 2020, the World Bank and WTO presented disaggregated labour data by gender at the industry level for a large number of countries and highlighted the capacity of trade to increase women's share in the labour force, increase their own skills and wages, and find ways to achieve better work–life balance, enhancing their countries' productivity and incomes.[38]

In short, the potential role of trade in promoting gender equality has been asserted, and tools have been developed at international, regional and national level to work towards gender equality through trade policy and agreements. The need to make trade policy more gender-responsive has thus been recognised not only as a moral but also economic imperative, framed by international, regional and national legal obligations and political commitments related to the promotion of gender equality.

[33] *Delivering on the Buenos Aires Declaration on Trade and Women's Economic Empowerment* (Geneva, International Trade Centre, 2020) 31.

[34] See eg the World Bank's Data Portal, which holds data for countries and regions related to economic opportunities, health, education, public life and decision-making, agency and inequality by wealth: 'Gender Data Portal' (*The World Bank*), genderdata.worldbank.org.

[35] 'Buenos Aires Declaration on Women and Trade Outlines Actions to Empower Women' (*World Trade Organization*, 12 December 2017), www.wto.org/english/news_e/news17_e/mc11_12dec17_e.htm; 'Joint Declaration on Trade and Women's Economic Empowerment on the Occasion of the WTO Ministerial Conference in Buenos Aires in December 2017' (*World Trade Organization*, 12 December 2017), www.wto.org/english/thewto_e/minist_e/mc11_e/genderdeclarationmc11_e.pdf.

[36] 'Buenos Aires Declaration on Trade and Women's Economic Empowerment' (*World Trade Organization*), www.wto.org/english/tratop_e/womenandtrade_e/buenos_aires_declaration_e.htm#:~:text=In%20December%202017%2C%20in%20the,in%20entering%20the%20global%20marketplace.

[37] Trade Policy Review Body, 'Trade Policy Review Report by the European Union' (*World Trade Organization*, 11 April 2023) WT/TPR/G/442, s 5.45.

[38] *Women and Trade: The Role of Trade in Promoting Gender Equality* (Washington, World Bank and World Trade Organization, 2020).

Being a significant global trade power,[39] the EU's stance and action matters. The EU has the capacity to engage with, and influence other international partners,[40] using instruments for trade liberalisation and its own regulatory regime as leverage to increase gender equality not only within the EU but also at a global level.

3. EU LEGAL AND POLICY FRAMEWORK FOR THE PROMOTION OF GENDER EQUALITY THROUGH TRADE

The EU holds exclusive competence for most areas of external trade.[41] Gender equality and non-discrimination have been on the EU's legislative agenda for many years, leading to internal legal integration to advance equality.[42] The equality of men and women and the prohibition of discrimination have deep roots in the EU's internal market as well as the EU's fundamental rights regime (see now Articles 20, 21 and 23 Charter of Fundamental Rights of the European Union (Charter)). According to Article 2 Treaty on European Union (TEU), '[t]he Union is [inter alia] founded on the values of respect for […] equality, the rule of law and respect for human rights'; and EU values are recognised as 'common to the Member States in a society in which pluralism, non-discrimination, tolerance, justice, solidarity and equality between women and men prevail'.

The EU Treaties now make explicit also the EU's obligation to promote gender equality in its external action. According to Article 8 Treaty on the Functioning of the EU (TFEU), the EU shall 'in all its activities […] aim to eliminate inequalities, and to promote equality, between men and women'. Article 10 TFEU clarifies that '[i]n defining and implementing its policies and activities, the Union shall aim to combat discrimination based on sex, racial or ethnic origin, religion or belief, disability, age or sexual orientation'. According to Article 205 TFEU, '[t]he Union's [external] action on the international scene […] shall be guided by the principles, pursue the objectives and be conducted in accordance with the general provisions laid down in Chapter 1 of Title V of the Treaty on European Union'. The external objectives, principles and values referred to in Article 21 TFEU include the commitment to advance equality, foster multilateralism, consolidate and support principles of international law, and promote good global governance. In the context of the common commercial policy,

[39] In the EU's Trade Review Report adopted in 2023, the WTO called the EU 'the world's top trader, with EUR 6.28 trillion traded in goods and services in 2021', international trade being the equivalent of 21.5% of EU GDP; see Trade Policy Review Body, 'Trade Policy Review Report by the European Union' (*World Trade Organization*, 11 April 2023) WT/TPR/S/442.

[40] See chapter by N Walker, Section 3. 'Reimagining the World' for discussion of the EU's global influence and governance model, and text at note 39.

[41] Arts 3(1)(e), 206, 207 (3)–(6), 218 Consolidated version of the Treaty on the Functioning of the European Union (TFEU) [2016] OJ C202/47. See already Opinion 1/75 *OECD Understanding on a Local Cost Standard* ECLI:EU:C:1975:145, [1975] ECR 1355 and Case 41/76 *Donckerwolke and Others v Procureur de la République and Others* ECLI:EU:C:1976:182, [1976] ECR 1921.

[42] According to the Commission, since the 1970s, 13 pieces of legislation have been adopted, covering equal treatment when applying for work, working, or concerning the protection of pregnant workers and breastfeeding mothers, as well as rights to maternity and parental leave, see 'European Employment Strategy: Tackling Discrimination at Work' (*European Commission*), www.ec.europa.eu/social/main.jsp?catId=158&langId=en.

the EU Treaty has made explicit that it 'shall be conducted in the context of the principles and objectives of the Union's external action', which include the commitment to equality just mentioned.[43] As a consequence, it is on the basis of the EU's own legal order established by the EU Treaties that the EU is under the obligation to promote gender equality in its trade policy and action, including the negotiation of trade agreements and other trade-related measures.

The EU has further cemented its commitment to the promotion of gender equality and the advancement of women's empowerment in various action plans and strategies. Most recently, the EU adopted its Gender Action Plan III (GAP III), 2020–2025,[44] and Gender Equality Strategy 2020–2025.[45] Recognising also the link between trade and gender, the Gender Equality Strategy 2020–2025 specified that

> [t]he Commission will continue to actively promote gender equality through its trade policy, including through its active engagement on the issue in the World Trade Organisation. It will continue to gather gender-disaggregated data, to ensure that trade-related aspects of gender are adequately addressed in trade agreements and to consider gender impact in trade initiatives.[46]

The Commission announced that '[i]n partner countries, the EU will make use of the External Investment Plan to promote women's entrepreneurship and labour market participation', and the Commission refers to the example of 'the Women's Financial Inclusion Facility alone aim[ing] to leverage EUR 100 million for women's access to finance'.[47] Moreover, the Commission announced that '[t]he EU Strategy with Africa in 2020 will also focus on gender equality and women's empowerment'.[48] In 2022, the EU and Africa published their 'Joint Vision for 2030'. Accordingly, the envisaged renewed Partnership 'aims to be the driving force in promoting our common priorities, shared values, international law, and preserving together our interests and common public goods', which includes 'the protection of human rights for all, gender equality and women's empowerment in all spheres of life [...], sustainable and inclusive economic growth, the fight against inequalities [...] and the inclusion of women'.[49] The EU's Gender Equality Strategy 2020–2025 also envisaged that '[i]n the EU's external policies, gender mainstreaming is used in the budget process through the commitment of ensuring that 85% of all new programmes contribute to gender equality and women's empowerment'.[50]

[43] Art 207(1) TFEU.

[44] 'EU Gender Action Plan II: How EU Delegations Contribute to Gender Equality Worldwide' (*Capacity4dev*, 17 April 2019), capacity4dev.europa.eu/articles/eu-gender-action-plan-ii-how-eu-delegations-contribute-gender-equality-worldwide_en.

[45] European Commission, 'A Union of Equality: Gender Equality Strategy 2020-2025' (2020) COM(2020) 152 final, 18.

[46] ibid.

[47] ibid. Please note that while the EU External Investment Plan is a tool of external action that the EU employs also to advance gender equality, it is part of the EU development policy and will thus not be analysed further in this chapter, see 'EU External Investment Plan' (*European Commission*, 13 November 2019), commission.europa.eu/system/files/2019-11/factsheet_eip_en.pdf.

[48] European Commission, 'A Union of Equality: Gender Equality Strategy 2020-2025' (2020) COM(2020) 152 final, 18.

[49] 'Sixth European Union – African Union Summit: Joint Vision for 2030' (*European Council*, 18 February 2022), www.consilium.europa.eu/media/54412/final_declaration-en.pdf, 1.

[50] European Commission, 'A Union of Equality: Gender Equality Strategy 2020–2025' (2020) COM(2020) 152 final, 18, making reference to the measurement being done according to the OECD Gender Equality

Gender equality specific instruments were complemented in 2021 by the Commission's 'Trade Policy Review' (TPR), entitled 'An Open, Sustainable and Assertive Trade Policy', which promulgated a fair, sustainable, and green transition through 'Open Strategic Autonomy'.[51] Accordingly, 'the EU works with partners to ensure adherence to universal values, notably the protection of human rights', including gender equality.[52] Moreover, the EU referred to its commitment made in the 2017 Buenos Aires Joint Declaration on Trade and Women's Economic Empowerment to 'carry out work to develop a better understanding of the gender equality implications of various parts of trade policy and inform actions for improved gender awareness in trade policy'.[53] In 2021, the Commission also published 'The European Pillar of social rights Action Plan', listing gender equality as the second of its 20 principles.[54]

In her political guidelines, the President of the Commission Ursula von der Leyen found clear words, stating that she 'want[ed] Europe to strive for more by strengthening our unique brand of responsible global leadership'.[55] In February 2022, the Commission published its Communication on 'Decent Work Worldwide for a global just transition and a sustainable recovery'.[56] Accordingly, the 'EU is committed to shaping the global agenda on decent work and promoting a human-centred future of work' and 'aspires to champion decent work both at home and around the world, in line with the UN 2030 Agenda for Sustainable Development'.[57] The Commission emphasised that the EU's 'comprehensive approach aims at effective promotion of decent work for all', and that it, inter alia:

> aim[ed] to promote gender equality including through women's economic empowerment, increasing women's participation on the labour market in all sectors and at all levels and ensuring equal pay for work of equal value.[58]

Importantly for the focus of this chapter, the Commission added that

> this comprehensive approach addresses workers in domestic markets in third countries and in global supply chains. It includes all relevant stakeholders: governments, social partners, civil society, business actors and consumers. The comprehensiveness of EU

Policy Maker, and the Commission applying its own humanitarian Gender-Age marker for humanitarian aid.

[51] European Commission, 'Trade Policy Review – An Open, Sustainable and Assertive Trade Policy' (2021) COM(2021) 66 final.

[52] ibid 6, with reference to the Gender Equality Strategy 2020–2025 and the GAP III.

[53] ibid 22.

[54] European Commission, 'The European Pillar of Social Rights Action Plan' (2021) COM(2021) 102 final.

[55] 'Commission Document on EU Involvement in the Promotion of Decent Work Published' (*European Commission*, 26 October 2020), www.ec.europa.eu/social/main.jsp?langId=en&catId=158&furtherNews=yes&newsId=9813.

[56] European Commission, 'Communication on Decent Work Worldwide for a Global Just Transition and a Sustainable Recovery' (2022) COM(2022) 66 final.

[57] ibid 1.

[58] ibid 4, with reference to GAP III, 'Gender Action Plan – Putting Women and Girls' Rights at the Heart of the Global Recovery for a Gender-Equal World' (*European Commission*, 25 November 2020), www.ec.europa.eu/commission/presscorner/detail/en/IP_20_2184; and European Commission, 'A Union of Equality: Gender Equality Strategy 2020-2025' (2020) COM(2020) 152 final.

action is expressed by different EU initiatives in the area [[59]], including the proposal for a Corporate Sustainability Due Diligence Directive [[60]] that is adopted together with this Communication, and the ongoing review of the 15-point Action Plan on Trade and Sustainable Development in the EU's trade policy [[61]].[62]

In April 2023, the European Commission (in the EU's Trade Policy Review Report submitted to the WTO) considered the 'promotion of gender equality a *priority* of all external policies and actions' (emphasis added), with GAP III and the Gender Equality strategy offering a '*roadmap for working together with stakeholders at national, regional and multilateral levels*' (emphasis added). Moreover, it was announced that the EU 'steps up action in strategic thematic areas; calls for the institutions to lead by example and; ensures the transparency of the results.'[63] The Commission reiterated the EU's commitment to work 'with partners to ensure adherence to universal values, including the promotion and advancement of gender equality'.[64] In collaboration with the International Trade Centre (ITC) the EU initiated a project that 'looks at applying a gender lens to the work of the WTO', which has led to four webinars on topics such as e-commerce, trade facilitation, investment facilitation and government procurement.[65]

In addition to its involvement in gender equality work undertaken within the WTO and the ITC, the EU has also entered strategic partnerships with UN Women and the ILO. Since 2012, the EU and UN Women have been 'working jointly for gender equality and women's empowerment worldwide to reach a Planet 50-50 by 2030'.[66] The EU has contributed and subscribed to the G7 Roadmap for a Gender-Responsive Economic Environment of 2017,[67] which includes states' external action as an important area

[59] See European Commission, 'Communication on Decent Work Worldwide for a Global Just Transition and a Sustainable Recovery' (2022) COM(2022) 66 final, s 3 and also European Commission, 'Commission Staff Working Document: Promote Decent Work Worldwide Responsible Global Value Chains for a Fair, Sustainable and Resilient Recovery from the COVID-19 Crises' (2020) SWD(2020) 235 final.

[60] European Commission, 'Proposal for a Directive of the European Parliament and of the Council on Corporate Sustainability Due Diligence and Amending Directive (EU) 2019/1937' (2022) COM(2022) 71 final.

[61] 'EU Trade Meetings with Civil Society' (*European Commission*), trade.ec.europa.eu/dialogue/meetdetails.cfm?meet=11601.

[62] European Commission, 'Communication on Decent Work Worldwide for a Global Just Transition and a Sustainable Recovery' (2022) COM(2022) 66 final, 4, with reference to GAP III, 'Gender Action Plan – Putting Women and Girls' Rights at the Heart of the Global Recovery for a Gender-Equal World' (*European Commission*, 25 November 2020), www.ec.europa.eu/commission/presscorner/detail/en/IP_20_2184; and European Commission, 'A Union of Equality: Gender Equality Strategy 2020-2025' (2020) COM(2020) 152 final.

[63] Trade Policy Review Body, 'Trade Policy Review Report by the European Union' (*World Trade Organization*, 11 April 2023) WT/TPR/G/442, s 5.48.

[64] ibid s 5.44.

[65] ibid s 5.45.

[66] 'Joint Statement on the Memorandum of Understanding between the European Union and the United Nations Entity for Gender Equality and the Empowerment of Women' (*UN Women*, 15 June 2016), www.unwomen.org/en/news/stories/2016/6/joint-statement-on-the-mou-between-the-eu-and-un-women.

[67] While the EU is not itself one of the seven members (Canada, France, Germany, Italy, Japan, UK, US), it has observer status. The Commission, together with the EEAS and on behalf of the EU has played an important role in preparing the G7 Roadmap; see 'Questions and Answers: What is the EU Doing for Women's Rights and Gender Equality' (*European Commission*, 6 March 2018), ec.europa.eu/commission/presscorner/detail/en/MEMO_18_1602. See for full text of Roadmap 'G7 Roadmap for a Gender-Responsive Economic Environment' (*European Council*, 27 May 2017), www.consilium.europa.eu/media/23560/g7-gender-roadmap.pdf.

for further action. According to the Roadmap, states should 'intensify [their] efforts and consider strengthening the mainstreaming of gender equality and women's rights and empowerment in [their] external action and programs targeting economic and productive sectors, and in development cooperation policies'. In accordance with this commitment, the EU, UN Women and the ILO entered a strategic partnership working towards economic empowerment of women at work.[68]

The ongoing EU-ILO partnership aims at 'bringing labour law and practice in line with International Labour Standards (ILS), building the institutional capacity of public administrations, social partners and other relevant stakeholders to support law reform and reporting, and strengthening institutional frameworks to facilitate social dialogue and conflict resolution'.[69] Between 2019 and 2022, the EU provided more than EUR 7.5 million in funding for the project 'Trade and Decent Work', which is carried out by the ILO and aims at improving working conditions for women and the application of fundamental ILO fundamental conventions in EU trading partner countries, in particular related to equal remuneration and non-discrimination.[70]

The EU's commitment to the promotion of gender equality through trade thus is deeply anchored in the legal and policy framework of the EU. Moreover, the EU has regularly endorsed international law aimed at advancing gender equality in its policy documents, trade agreements and as contributor to international initiatives.[71] Such unilateral commitment to existing international law has included international legal obligations originally imposed on the EU Member States individually rather than the EU itself.[72] The EU committed itself to the 2030 Agenda for Sustainable Development of 2015 that contains Goal 5, according to which states are committed 'to achieve gender equality and the empowerment of all women and girls'.[73]

4. EU EXTERNAL TRADE MEASURES AND ENFORCEMENT OF GENDER EQUALITY OBLIGATIONS

Having discussed trade and gender as well as the EU's framework for the promotion of gender equality through trade, this section turns to selected EU external trade-related

[68] 'Promoting Women's Economic Empowerment at Work through Responsible Business Conduct in G7 Countries' (*International Labour Organization*), www.ilo.org/empent/Projects/WCMS_646572/lang--en/index.htm; see also 'About' (*Women's Empowerment Principles*), www.weps.org/about.

[69] 'Trade for Decent Work Project' (*International Labour Organization*), www.ilo.org/global/standards/WCMS_697996/lang--en/index.htm.

[70] '2023 Report on Gender Equality in the EU' (*European Commission*, April 2023), commission.europa.eu/system/files/2023-04/annual_report_GE_2023_web_EN.pdf, 74. For further detail see 'Trade for Decent Work Project' (n 69).

[71] eg Convention on the Elimination of All Forms of Discrimination against Women (New York, 18 December 1979) (CEDAW); see Global Call to Action of the UN SG's High Level Panel for Women's Economic Empowerment of 2016, 'Final Report of the UN High-Level Panel on Women's Economic Empowerment Calls on Leaving No One Behind' (*UN Women*, 14 March 2017), www.unwomen.org/en/news/stories/2017/3/new-final-report-of-the-un-high-level-panel-on-womens-economic-empowerment.

[72] eg ILO Conventions targeting non-discrimination in employment (including the ratification and implementation of ILO Conventions 100 and 111 on equal remuneration and non-discrimination) (NB: ILO Conventions have been ratified only by EU Member States as ILO Members, not the EU itself).

[73] See eg GAP II, para 3; Council of the European Union, 'Gender Action Plan 2016-2020 – Council Conclusions (26 October 2015)' (2015) 13201/15.

measures as tools for doing so. It analyses recent examples of EU practice regarding the incorporation of gender equality provisions in EU trade agreements with third states, and the EU's Generalised Scheme of Preference. Moreover, it examines the extent to which gender equality obligations integrated or created by such measures have been made subject to monitoring and enforcement on the international level. Focusing here on the interaction between the EU and third countries (within the framework provided by international law) will provide the background for the subsequent analysis on the role of Member States and private stakeholders in advancing gender equality through trade due to EU *internal* measures (Section 5).

4.1. Treaty-Making

The EU's commitment to advance gender equality and the economic empowerment of women has become visible in relation to the preparation, wording and monitoring of trade agreements with non-EU states. The EU undertakes gender impact assessments and includes gender equality provisions in agreement texts.[74] The discussion in the following paragraphs demonstrates, however, that though there has been some recognition of the EU's (procedural) efforts to take account in treaty negotiations of the potential impact trade agreements have on gender equality and the economic empowerment of women, the robustness and implications of (substantive) treaty provisions have been more controversial.

In 2015, The Commission adopted 'Guidelines on the analysis of human rights impacts in impact assessments for trade-related policy initiatives', which: (a) focus on the methodology of impact assessment when proposing a new policy initiative and when negotiating a bilateral or plurilateral trade agreement; and (b) describe the principles and approach applicable to the entire cycle of a policy, and hence also in the context of ex post evaluations.[75] In 2016, the Commission published the second edition of its *Handbook for Trade Sustainability Impact Assessment*, which included the assessment of human rights impacts and underlined 'the importance of close dialogue with all relevant stakeholders, including the more vulnerable ones'.[76] The EU's sustainable impact assessment integrates international standards, as it 'includes an assessment, based on the latest methodology available – the United Nations Conference on Trade and Development (UNCTAD) Trade and Gender

[74] For a list of Sustainability Impact Assessments (SIA) reports, the respective Commission position paper in response to the SIA, and information about the methodological framework for SIAs, see 'Sustainability Impact Assessments' (*European Commission*), policy.trade.ec.europa.eu/analysis-and-assessment/sustainability-impact-assessments_en; for discussion of impact assessment and treaty provisions see Thies (n 17) 429–454, 443, 446f.

[75] Directorate-General for Trade, 'Guidelines on the Analysis of Human Rights Impacts in Impact Assessments for Trade-Related Policy Initiatives' (*European Commission*, 2015), circabc.europa.eu/ui/group/7fc51410-46a1-4871-8979-20cce8df0896/library/991d8e1d-dbaa-49d6-8582-bb3aab2cab48/details.

[76] Directorate-General for Trade, 'Handbook for Trade Sustainability Impact Assessment: 2nd Edition' (Publications Office, 18 August 2016), op.europa.eu/en/publication-detail/-/publication/8b3a2b37-1028-11e6-ba9a-01aa75ed71a1; with reference to the full list of SIAs conducted, see Sustainability Impact Assessments' (*European Commission*), policy.trade.ec.europa.eu/analysis-and-assessment/sustainability-impact-assessments_en.

Toolbox[77] – of the impact on women in their roles as workers, entrepreneurs, traders, and consumers'.[78]

Some scholars have criticised the EU's institutional lack of awareness of the details of EU human and fundamental rights obligations and the lack of coherence in its approach in the promotion of human rights through trade and investment policy.[79] Also the 'analytical framing of gender in EU trade policy' in particular has been criticised for failing 'to adopt an intersectional or critical understanding of the diverse ways in which social, economic, political and cultural factors contribute to and sustain structural inequalities and vulnerabilities that in turn constrain the transformative potential of trade law and policy'.[80]

From a global institutional perspective, the EU's commitment to, and undertaking of impact assessment regarding gender equality has fared rather well. In the WTO's 2020 Report 'Delivering on the Buenos Aires Declaration on trade and women's economic empowerment', the EU was mentioned in the section on 'Models for Impact', as having 'systematically considered the impact of trade policy initiatives on gender equality and women's rights in its evaluations', using 'impact assessments before negotiations, sustainability impact assessments during negotiations, and ex post evaluations after a trade agreement has been in force for a sufficient amount of time'.[81]

Separately from questioning the scope and quality of the EU's impact assessment (ie what could be classified as a procedural aspect of the promotion of gender equality), attention shall be given here also to the gender equality provisions and chapters incorporated in trade agreements. The following analysis includes the integration or incorporation of existing international law obligations related to gender equality and the mainstreaming of gender throughout various sections of EU trade agreements, both aiming to make trade under the agreement more gender-responsive. It is also regarding both types of gender equality commitments or obligations, that we shall examine the EU and its treaty partners' commitment to their monitoring and enforcement.

EU trade agreements refer to international conventions on gender equality (eg CEDAW, ILO Conventions) and the UN's Fourth World Conference on Women in Beijing (1995), and they sometimes include clear objectives, such as the strengthening of dialogue and cooperation to promote gender equality.[82] The Cotonou Agreement

[77] United Nations Conference on Trade and Development, 'Trade and Gender Toolbox' (2017) UNCTAD/DITC/2017/1.

[78] '2019 Report on Equality Between Women and Men in the EU' (*European Commission*, March 2019), commission.europa.eu/system/files/2019-03/annual_report_ge_2019_en_1.pdf, ch5, 54.

[79] V Kube, 'The Polisario Case: Do EU Fundamental Rights Matter for EU Trade Policies?' (*EJIL: Talk!*, 3 February 2017), www.ejiltalk.org/the-polisario-case-do-eu-fundamental-rights-matter-for-eu-trade-polices; Kube (n 15); S Velluti, 'The Promotion and Integration of Human Rights in EU External Trade Relations' (2016) 32 *Utrecht Journal of International and European Law* 41.

[80] Gammage (n 17) 160.

[81] *Delivering on the Buenos Aires Declaration on Trade and Women's Economic Empowerment* (Geneva, International Trade Centre, 2020) 3 and 4.

[82] 'Report: Trade and Social Sustainability – An Overview and Analysis' (*National Board of Trade Sweden*, 2017), www.kommerskollegium.se/en/publications/reports/2017/trade-and-social-sustainability/, 42, with reference to the EU's Association Agreements/Deep and Comprehensive Free Trade Areas (DCFTAs) with Georgia, Moldavia, Ukraine, Chapter on Employment, Social and Equal Opportunities.

between the EU and the members of the African, Caribbean and Pacific Group of States has been considered particularly significant, as it 'prescribes the integration of gender equality into all areas of the agreement'.[83]

Chapter 13 of the EU-Vietnam Trade and Investment Agreement is dedicated to 'trade and sustainable development'.[84] According to Article 13.1(1), the objective of the chapter is 'to promote sustainable development, notably by fostering the contribution of trade and investment related aspects of labour and environmental issues'. Having recalled international initiatives, including UN and ILO agendas, Article 13.1(2) 'integrates' the objective of sustainable development in the parties 'bilateral relationship'. A 'cooperative approach' is embodied, which is 'based on common values and interests, taking into account the differences in the Parties' respective levels of development' (Art 13.1(5)).

In 2022, the EU and New Zealand concluded negotiations for a comprehensive trade agreement that includes a trade and sustainable development chapter; the trading countries committed to advance relevant UN and ILO conventions advancing women's economic empowerment and gender equality, including promoting cooperation in international fora to advance these objectives.[85] In June 2023, the EU and Kenya concluded the negotiations of their trade agreement (though still subject to potential modifications and signatures) and included Article 4 on Trade and Gender Equality, in which the parties recognise the link between inclusive trade policies and the empowerment of women, commit to effective provision of equal opportunities and implementation of relevant obligations under international agreements, also through the aligning of domestic laws.[86] The EU and Kenya commit to bilateral and multilateral cooperation 'on trade-related aspects of gender equality policies and measures, including activities designed to improve the capacity and conditions for women, including workers, businesswomen and entrepreneurs, to access and benefit from the opportunities created by this Agreement' and agree on the importance of monitoring and assessing the impact of its implementation.[87]

The EU has started to negotiate also entire chapters on gender equality, again anchoring international law and standards in the wording of trade agreements. For instance, Chapter 27 has been included in the EU-Chile Interim Trade Agreement,

On the 'promotional' approach to compliance see also G Marín Durán, 'Sustainable Development Chapters in EU Free Trade Agreements: Emerging Compliance Issues' (2020) 57 *CML Rev* 1031, 1033; see for response M Bronckers and G Gruni, 'Retooling the Sustainability Standards in EU Free Trade Agreements' (2021) 24 *Journal of International Economic Law* 25.

[83] 'Report: Trade and Social Sustainability – An Overview and Analysis' (*National Board of Trade Sweden*, 2017), www.kommerskollegium.se/en/publications/reports/2017/trade-and-social-sustainability/, 42.

[84] Chapter 13 Free Trade Agreement between the European Union and the Socialist Republic of Viet Nam (EU-Vietnam FTA) [2020] OJ L186/3 (see especially [2020] OJ L186/132).

[85] Trade Policy Review Body, 'Trade Policy Review Report by the European Union' (*World Trade Organization*, 11 April 2023) WT/TPR/G/442, s 5.46. For the full text of the chapter, including Art 19.4 on gender equality, see: 'The EU-New Zealand Trade Agreement' (*European Commission*), policy.trade.ec.europa.eu/eu-trade-relationships-country-and-region/countries-and-regions/new-zealand/eu-new-zealand-agreement_en.

[86] 'EU-Kenya: Text of the Agreement' (*European Commission*), policy.trade.ec.europa.eu/eu-trade-relationships-country-and-region/countries-and-regions/east-african-community-eac/eu-kenya-agreement/text-agreement_en, Annex V.

[87] ibid Annex V, Art 4, paras 6 and 7.

which the Council adopted on 4 December 2023;[88] this chapter was drafted following an ex-post evaluation of the impact of the current agreement and an assessment of the potential impact of a modernised agreement with a chapter on gender equality to address, for example, workforce inequalities.[89]

In line with the EU's values-based trade strategy, the focus has been on *cooperation* between the treaty partners, rather than the establishment of legally binding obligations or commitments.[90] Even where Trade and Sustainable Development chapters include labour, environmental and human rights, they have traditionally not been made subject to the dispute settlement mechanism of the trade agreement, limiting the enforceability of such obligations to government consultations and (non-binding) reports of experts.[91] As a consequence, if a contracting party does not comply with its gender equality obligations under international law incorporated in EU trade agreements, it remains questionable to what extent treaty parties are in a position to suspend trade concessions to induce compliance.[92]

The recent agreement negotiated with Kenya (mentioned above) is an interesting recent example, in that it includes the use of temporary measures to enforce environmental protection and climate change commitments but not gender equality ones, while including both in the agreement's dispute settlement mechanism. Gender equality is addressed in Article 4 of the draft Annex V on trade and sustainable development and thus placed prominently in the Annex, following only provisions on 'Context and Objectives' (Art 1), the parties 'Right to Regulate and Levels of Protection' (Art 2) and 'Multilateral Labour Standards and Agreements' (Art 3). Article 4 precedes provisions on environmental matters and climate change (Arts 5 and 6). However, it is noticeable that the provisions on trade and climate change, in particular obligations related to the implementation of the Paris Agreement, enable the parties to 'take appropriate measures relating to this Agreement in the event of a violation of the obligation under paragraph 3', relying on procedures established in the 'Cotonou Agreement or the corresponding provisions of its successor agreement' (Art 6(3), (4)).[93]

[88] 'EU-Chile: Council Adopts Decisions for a Modernised Association Agreement' (*Council of the European Union*, 4 December 2023), www.consilium.europa.eu/en/press/press-releases/2023/12/04/eu-chile-council-adopts-decisions-for-a-modernised-association-agreement/.

[89] See for full text at 'EU-Chile: Text of the Agreement' (*European Commission*), policy.trade.ec.europa.eu/eu-trade-relationships-country-and-region/countries-and-regions/chile/eu-chile-agreement/text-agreement_en. For an overview and regular updates, see 'Chile' (*European Commission*), policy.trade.ec.europa.eu/eu-trade-relationships-country-and-region/countries-and-regions/chile_en.

[90] Gammage (n 17) 168, with reference to C Gammage, 'Social Norms and Free Trade Agreements: Justiciable or Not?' in C Gammage and T Novitz (eds), *Sustainable Trade, Investment, and Finance: Toward Responsible and Coherent Regulatory Frameworks?* (Cheltenham, Edward Elgar, 2019).

[91] See eg Art 13.16 EU-Vietnam FTA; Art 13.16 Free Trade Agreement between the European Union and its Member States, of the one part, and the Republic of Korea, of the other part (EU-South Korea FTA) [2011] OJ L127/6.

[92] For further discussion of the consequences of incompliance see Marín Durán (n 82); Bronckers and Gruni (n 82); P Van Elsuwege, 'The Nexus between the Common Commercial Policy and Human Rights: Implications of the Lisbon Treaty' in M Hahn and G Van der Loo (eds), *Law and Practice of the Common Commercial Policy: The First 10 Years after the Treaty of Lisbon*, Studies in EU External Relations 18 (Leiden, Brill Nijhof, 2021).

[93] 'EU-Kenya: Text of the Agreement' (*European Commission*), policy.trade.ec.europa.eu/eu-trade-relationships-country-and-region/countries-and-regions/east-african-community-eac/eu-kenya-agreement/text-agreement_en, Annex V.

There is, however, no such provision included in the Article on gender equality. According to Article 4, the parties are 'commit[ted] to implement the provisions of this Agreement in a manner that promotes and enhances gender equality' (para 1), to 'effectively implement [their] obligations under international agreements' (para 3), they 'shall strive to ensure that its relevant law and policies provide for, and encourage, equal rights, treatment and opportunities between men and women' (para 4), 'work together' (para 6) and agree 'on the importance of monitoring and assessing, in accordance with their domestic procedures, the impact of the implementation of this Agreement on gender equality and equal opportunities provided for women in relation to trade'.

In case of disagreement between the Parties regarding the application of the Annex, the Parties have access to the dispute resolution procedures laid down in Article 16 et seq of the Annex, namely consultations and mediation (Art 17) and Dispute Settlement (Art 18). Resolutions reached between the parties through consultation or mediation shall be made publicly available (Art 17(4)). Relying on cross-referencing to the Agreement, it seems possible for the parties to have recourse to arbitration, resulting in an arbitration panel ruling (Art 115) and possibly a review of compliance. However, parties seem not to be authorised to retaliate for breaches of obligations established in the Annex on Trade and Sustainability, except for the climate change exception discussed above. Article 18 of the Annex does not include Article 117 of the Agreement, which is the basis for parties to employ 'Temporary remedies in case of non-compliance'. In other words, the parties are not in a position to constrain access to other (trade-related) rights under the Agreement in response to non-compliance with gender equality commitments made in the Annex on Trade and Sustainable Development.

Admittedly, the existing procedures established with the Cotonou Agreement and its successor have facilitated the inclusion of temporary remedies in the context of environmental matters.[94] However, there would have been an opportunity to also include the compliance with gender equality and other human rights obligations in the catalogue of obligations, the noncompliance with which can lead to temporary measures, increasing pressure on treaty partners to comply.[95]

To conclude this section of the chapter, gender equality impact assessment and the inclusion of gender equality provisions in trade agreements are to be welcomed in principle. Impact assessments have increased the EU's active engagement with the implications of trade agreements for gender equality and the economic empowerment of women, even if the EU needs to increase its engagement with the criticism put forward to further improve the quality of impact assessments.

[94] See for Art 96 of the Cotonou Agreement: 'Post-Cotonou Agreement: Consultation Procedure (Article 96)' (*European Council*, 25 October 2018), www.consilium.europa.eu/en/policies/cotonou-agreement/article-96-cotonou-agreement/.

[95] See 2018 Non paper of Commission services, making the case for 'more assertive enforcement', Commission Services, 'Non Paper of the Commission Services*: Feedback and Way Forward on Improving the Implementation and Enforcement of Trade and Sustainable Development Chapters in EU Free Trade Agreements' (*Politico*, 26 February 2018), www.politico.eu/wp-content/uploads/2018/02/TSD-Non-Paper.pdf, 3.

The inclusion of gender equality provisions and chapters has made the EU's commitment to gender equality more visible on the global stage. However, the actual impact of gender equality provisions in EU trade agreements on women will need to be continuously assessed to confirm the EU's nature as role model in the field of trade and gender.[96] While recognising the political challenge the EU might face when advocating enforceable legal obligations related to gender equality within the context of trade agreements, it remains unsatisfactory that not all EU trade agreements contain gender equality provisions. For instance, the recent EU-Japan Economic Partnership Agreement (2019) does not even mention gender equality in its Chapter 16 on Trade and Sustainable Development,[97] while, noticeably, the Japan UK Comprehensive Economic Partnership Agreement (2020), concluded post-Brexit, contains an entire chapter on trade and women's economic empowerment (even if excluded from the agreement's dispute settlement).[98]

Moreover, as long as gender equality chapters remain excluded from the dispute settlement mechanism of trade agreements that can lead to the suspension of trade concessions in response to the infringement of gender equality obligations, it remains controversial if the incorporation of international law in EU agreements is more than symbolic in nature. It should be added, however, that other not-strictly enforceable commitments have been considered in recent disputes, which has given rise to hope that gender equality will also be included in dispute settlement.[99] Moreover, there is hope that further mainstreaming of gender equality commitments in EU trade agreements – both in the form of non-discrimination obligations and commitment to remove barriers for women to access the benefits of trade through sharing of good practice and collaboration (eg access to finance, digital inclusion, domestic regulation) – will further advance gender equality and the economic empowerment of women.[100]

4.2. The EU's Generalised Scheme of Preferences

The EU has established a Generalised Scheme of Preferences to reduce or remove import duties from products coming onto the EU market from vulnerable developing

[96] See Cremona (n 1); *Delivering on the Buenos Aires Declaration on Trade and Women's Economic Empowerment* (Geneva, International Trade Centre, 2020). One analysis of EU FTA's and recent evaluation reports has led to the conclusion that there is 'no evidence yet to show a positive correlation between the inclusion of gender clauses in FTAs and the empowerment of women', see Gammage (n 17) 160.

[97] 'EU-Japan Economic Partnership Agreement' (*European Commission*), policy.trade.ec.europa.eu/eu-trade-relationships-country-and-region/countries-and-regions/japan/eu-japan-agreement_en.

[98] See for Chapter 27 Agreement between the United Kingdom of Great Britain and Northern Ireland and Japan for a Comprehensive Economic Partnership (*UK Government*, October 2020) CP311 Volume 1.

[99] Gammage (n 17) 168, with reference to 'Restrictions Applied by Ukraine on Exports of Certain Wood Products to the European Union: Final Report of the Arbitration Panel of 11 December 2020' (*European Commission*, 12 December 2020), circabc.europa.eu/rest/download/89749bde-3615-413c-8834-0110021e6522 and 'Report of the Panel of Experts of the EU–Korea Free Trade Agreement of 20 January 2021' (*European Commission*, 25 January 2021), circabc.europa.eu/ui/group/09242a36-a438-40fd-a7af-fe32e36cbd0e/library/d4276b0f-4ba5-4aac-b86a-d8f65157c38e/details; for discussion of the EU-Korea case see also Van Elsuwege (n 92) 431f.

[100] See eg Art 19.4 of the EU-New Zealand Free Trade Agreement (2023) at 'EU-New Zealand: Text of the Agreement' (*European Commission*), policy.trade.ec.europa.eu/eu-trade-relationships-country-and-region/

countries.[101] The objective of such trade facilitation is to help 'developing countries to alleviate poverty and create jobs based on international values and principles, including labour and human rights, environment and climate protection, and good governance'.[102] The EU's system is complex, and Regulation 2012/24 identifies three different layers of tariff preferences in Article 1: (a) a general arrangement, (b) a special incentive arrangement for sustainable development and good governance (GSP+), and (c) a special arrangement for the least-developed countries (Everything But Arms (EBA)).[103] The EU is one of 13 trade actors currently using a GSP system; the EU and the US are the only trade actors that make access to preferential treatment under their GSP system conditional on compliance, at least to some degree, with human rights standards.[104]

Article 9 of the Regulation is specifying details of the EU's 'Special Incentive Arrangement for Sustainable Development and Good Governance' (GSP+), making reference to the need to have ratified all 27 international conventions listed in Annex VIII to the Regulation.[105] These conventions include those relevant for the present discussion, namely the UN Convention on the Elimination of All Forms of Discrimination Against Women (CEDAW, 1979), the ILO Convention concerning Equal Remuneration of Men and Women Workers for Work of Equal Value, No 100 (1951), and the Convention concerning Discrimination in Respect of Employment and Occupation, No 111 (1958).[106] Beneficiary countries need to commit to the implementation of the Conventions and need to agree to reporting and being monitored by the EU (Article 9). Importantly, preferential access can be withdrawn in case of non-compliance (Article 15), linking trade preferences to parties' compliance with international conventions on other matters.

What is worth adding here is that the abovementioned Conventions related to gender equality are listed in Part A of Annex VIII of the Regulation. They are thus relevant not only for GSP+ beneficiary countries and their access to preferential treatment. Instead, Chapter V of the Regulation contains 'Temporary Withdrawal Provisions Common to All Arrangements'. According to Article 19(1)(a), 'serious and systematic violation of principles laid down in the conventions listed in Part A of

countries-and-regions/new-zealand/eu-new-zealand-agreement/text-agreement_en; Art 27.1(1) of the Advanced Framework Agreement between the EU and Chile (2023) at 'EU-Chile: Text of the Agreement' (*European Commission*), policy.trade.ec.europa.eu/eu-trade-relationships-country-and-region/countries-and-regions/chile/eu-chile-agreement/text-agreement_en.

[101] For a detailed discussion of the motivation and historical development of Generalised Systems of Preference see O de Schutter, *Trade in the Service of Sustainable Development: Linking Trade to Labour Rights and Environmental Standards* (Oxford, Hart publishing, 2015) ch 4, 102–123.

[102] 'Generalised Scheme of Preferences' (*European Commission*), policy.trade.ec.europa.eu/development-and-sustainability/generalised-scheme-preferences_en.

[103] On the three layers of the EU's GSP Scheme, examples and case-law see de Schutter (n 101) ch 4, 110–123.

[104] J Zerk and R Beacock, 'Advancing Human Rights through Trade: Why Stronger Human Rights Monitoring is Needed and How to Make it Work' (*Chatham House*, 26 May 2021), www.chathamhouse.org/2021/05/advancing-human-rights-through-trade/03-human-rights-monitoring-and-gsp-schemes, 28.

[105] Regulation (EU) No 978/2012 of the European Parliament and of the Council applying a scheme of generalised tariff preferences and repealing Council Regulation (EC) No 732/2008 [2012] OJ L303/1.

[106] See Art 9(1)(b) and Annex VIII Regulation (EU) No 978/2012 of the European Parliament and of the Council applying a scheme of generalised tariff preferences and repealing Council Regulation (EC) No 732/2008 [2012] OJ L303/1.

Annex VIII' 'may be withdrawn temporarily, in respect of all or of certain products originating in a beneficiary country'.[107]

In January 2019 the European Parliament concluded that the conditionality established by the EU's unilateral preference GSP system has in practice 'been applied or considered only for very grave human and labour rights violations, not specifically related to women rights'.[108] It further observed that the 'impact of GSP+ has been mixed', making reference to Pakistan – being the biggest GSP+ beneficiary country due to its textile exports to the EU – which 'remains widely dominated by men, and working women are exposed to multiple forms of discrimination'.[109]

In its Resolution of 14 March 2019 on the implementation of the GSP Regulation, the European Parliament stressed that

> the improved, constant and systematic monitoring of the implementation process is of paramount importance, and can be achieved by stepping up cooperation between all actors so as to improve information gathering and in-depth analysis by using all the available information and resources, such as the reports from international monitoring bodies, including the UN, the ILO, the Organisation for Economic Cooperation and Development (OECD), and including direct involvement of civil society and social partners in the process

and that

> [it was] necessary in order to ensure the full potential of the GSP+ scheme to improve the situation with regard to workers' rights, *promotion of gender equality* and the abolition of child and forced labour through the effective implementation of the 27 conventions (emphasis added).[110]

Another example of the European Parliament's attempts to increase visibility of non-compliance with the conditionality provisions established in the GSP system, as well as its commitment to request the Commission, the High Representative, EU Delegations and Member States' representations to react is with regard to the Philippines as GSP+ country. In February 2022, the European Parliament published a resolution identifying human rights violations, including against women, and calling on the Commission to set clear GSP+ benchmarks, to initiate the procedure that could lead to temporary withdrawal of trade preferences and to monitor progress.[111]

The Commission's proposal for a new GSP Regulation for 2024–2034 has included 32 conventions, regarding children's rights, rights of persons with disabilities, labour inspection and tripartite consultations.[112] While CEDAW and the abovementioned

[107] See for an 'Overview of EU GSP Scheme Layers: Human Rights Conditions and Compliance Checks' also Table 2 in Zerk and Beacock (n 104) 29.

[108] I Zamfir, 'At a Glance: Gender Equality and Trade' (*European Parliamentary Research Service*, January 2019), www.europarl.europa.eu/RegData/etudes/ATAG/2019/633163/EPRS_ATA(2019)633163_EN.pdf, 2.

[109] ibid, with reference to an EP Study: B Richardson, J Harrison and L Campling, 'Labour rights in Export Processing Zones with a Focus on GSP+ Beneficiary Countries' (*European Parliament*, June 2017), www.europarl.europa.eu/RegData/etudes/STUD/2017/603839/EXPO_STU(2017)603839_EN.pdf.

[110] European Parliament, 'Resolution on the Implementation of the GSP Regulation (EU) No 987/2012 (2018/2107(INI))' (2019) P8_TA(2019)0207, Recital 9.

[111] European Parliament, 'Resolution on the Recent Human Rights Developments in the Philippines (2022/2540(RSP))' (2022) P9_TA(2022)0049, Recitals M, P, paras 7, 12, 21 et seq.

[112] 'Commission Proposes New EU Generalised Scheme of Preferences to Promote Sustainable Development in Low-Income Countries' (*European Commission*, 22 September 2021), policy.trade.ec.europa.eu/news/

relevant ILO Conventions (No 100, No 111) remain listed in what is now Annex VI, the ILO Violence and Harassment Convention, No. 190 (2019) is currently missing in the Commission's proposal,[113] which might be due to the lack of ratification by all EU Member States.[114] In June 2023, the negotiations stalled as the European Parliament 'reiterated its position that preferential trade access under the GSP should not be made conditional on the readmission of third-country nationals' (which had been suggested by the Council).[115] This recent development shows how the GSP system is subject to political priorities and objectives, with the European Parliament monitoring the negotiations – here aiming to keep migration policy out of a system that is meant to improve beneficiary countries commitment to international conventions in exchange for trade preferences.

In April 2023, in its Trade Policy Review Report submitted to the WTO, the EU confirmed its commitment to

> monitor … respect by beneficiary countries for the principles of core international conventions on promoting women's rights and gender equality, notably the UN Convention on the Elimination of All Forms of Discrimination against Women the Convention concerning Equal Remuneration of Men and Women Workers for Work of Equal Value, and the Convention concerning Discrimination in Respect of Employment and Occupation.[116]

Again, the EU missed the opportunity to also endorse the ILO Violence and Harassment Convention, No. 190 (2019) in that context, which can only be explained by the mixed ratification record of the EU Member States.[117]

In sum, the EU has established conditionality as an integral part of its unilateral GSP system, committing itself to monitor beneficiary countries' respect for international law on women's rights and gender equality. What remains noticeable, however, is that the European Parliament has highlighted that to date a country's lack of respect for women's rights and gender equality has not led to the suspension of trade concessions (see above). It would go beyond the scope of this chapter to collect and analyse data on the effect the GSP system has had on advancing gender equality in all beneficiary countries, even in absence of the suspension of trade concessions. In November

commission-proposes-new-eu-generalised-scheme-preferences-promote-sustainable-development-low-income-2021-09-22_en. The additional conventions included are the Optional Protocol to the Convention on the Rights of the Child on the Involvement of Children in Armed Conflict (2000), the Convention on the Rights of Persons with Disabilities (2007), Convention on Labour Inspection No 81 (1947), and the Convention on Tripartite Consultations No 144 (1976).

[113] European Commission, 'Proposal for a Regulation of the European Parliament and of the Council on Applying a Generalised Scheme of Tariff Preferences and Repealing Regulation (EU) No 978/2012 of the European Parliament and of the Council' (2021) COM(2021) 579 final.

[114] 'Ratifications of C190 – Violence and Harassment Convention, 2019 (No. 190): Countries that Have Not Ratified this Convention' (*International Labour Organization*) www.ilo.org/dyn/normlex/en/f?p=NORMLEXPUB:11310:0::NO:11310:P11310_INSTRUMENT_ID:3999810:NO.

[115] 'MEPs Pause GSP Negotiations as Council Hijacks Scheme for Migration Agenda' (*European Parliament*, 27 June 2023), www.europarl.europa.eu/news/en/press-room/20230626IPR00816/meps-pause-gsp-negotiations-as-council-hijacks-scheme-for-migration-agenda.

[116] Trade Policy Review Body, 'Trade Policy Review Report by the European Union' (*World Trade Organization*, 11 April 2023) WT/TPR/G/442, s 5.47.

[117] 'Ratifications of C190 – Violence and Harassment Convention, 2019 (No. 190): Countries that Have Not Ratified this Convention' (*International Labour Organization*) www.ilo.org/dyn/normlex/en/f?p=NORMLEXPUB:11310:0::NO:11310:P11310_INSTRUMENT_ID:3999810:NO.

2023, the joint report by the European Commission and the High Representative for the Common Foreign and Security Policy on the GSP to Parliament, covering the period 2020–22, highlighted that GSP+ has been effective in, inter alia, advancing women's rights.[118]

5. MOBILISING EU STAKEHOLDERS

As discussed above, an ongoing challenge in the promotion of gender equality through trade remains the limited effect and enforcement of gender equality obligations in the EU's interaction with third countries, even where gender equality provisions are included in trade agreements and the EU's GSP(+) system. Complementing efforts to improve the impact of such measures at the global level, the EU has increasingly envisaged the mobilisation of EU domestic stakeholders to play a fuller and more proactive role in the implementation and enforcement of EU trade policy.[119] The aspect of 'mobilisation' of interest for this chapter concerns the EU's internal efforts to make domestic actors – who are engaging in extra-EU trade (eg Member States, EU institutions, private actors) or being interested in trade-related matters (eg trade organisations, non-governmental organisations, citizens) – help monitor third countries' compliance with international gender equality obligations and/or advance gender equality in their own trade relations.

The subsequent analysis thus distinguishes between two types of EU internal measures of mobilisation. First, it analyses EU measures that have *invited or encouraged* Member States and private stakeholders to contribute to the enforcement of third countries' obligations under international law related to the promotion of gender equality and the economic empowerment of women (ie Single Entry Point, Access2Markets). Second, it examines the extent to which EU domestic measures have begun to create *legal obligations* for private stakeholders, Member States and EU institutions to advance gender equality in their own interaction with trading partners outside the EU (ie public procurement, due diligence).

5.1. Member State and Private Enforcement of Third Country Obligations?

In 2020, the role of a 'Chief Trade Enforcement Officer' (CTEO) was established by the EU Commission. The CTEO assists the Commission in implementing and

[118] European Commission and High Representative of the Union for Foreign Affairs and Security Policy, 'Joint Report to the European Parliament and the Council on the Generalised Scheme of Preferences covering the Period 2020-2022' (2023) JOIN(2023) 34 final.

[119] See eg European Commission, 'Communication on Decent Work Worldwide for a Global Just Transition and a Sustainable Recovery' (2022) COM(2022) 66 final, 4, with reference to GAP III, 'Gender Action Plan – Putting Women and Girls' Rights at the Heart of the Global Recovery for a Gender-Equal World' (*European Commission*, 25 November 2020), www.ec.europa.eu/commission/presscorner/detail/en/IP_20_2184; and European Commission, 'A Union of Equality: Gender Equality Strategy 2020-2025' (2020) COM(2020) 152 final; 'Implementation and Enforcement of EU Trade Policy: Issues Paper' (*European Commission*, 22 September 2022), circabc.europa.eu/ui/group/7fc51410-46a1-4871-8979-20cce8df0896/library/7103f3c9-2dc5-4bc5-be52-210c133802ca/details?download=true%5D, 5.

enforcing trade rules within the EU and its trading partners.[120] More specifically the CTEO is meant to strengthen the implementation of the EU's multilateral, regional and bilateral trade agreements, and to ensure that third countries meet their commitments established in EU trade agreements with them, including those related to trade and sustainable development.[121]

In addition to their own monitoring function and other tasks, the CTEO is in charge of managing the 'Single Entry Point' where 'EU companies, trade organisations or non-governmental organisations can submit complaints', which was also introduced in 2020.[122] Such complaints can be brought by stakeholders not only if they face barriers to trade in non-EU countries, but also be about non-EU countries not meeting their sustainable development commitments established in EU trade agreements or the GSP.[123] As clarified in the 2022 operating guidelines for the Single Entry Point and complaints mechanism, individual or collective complaints related to third countries' non-compliance with commitments made in chapters dedicated to Trade and Sustainability Development (TSD) Chapters or the GSP can also be brought by Member States, Domestic Advisory Groups (DAGs) formed in accordance with EU trade agreements (for TSD complaints), and even by citizens or permanent residents.[124]

In terms of a substantive benchmark for any of such TSD or GSP complaints however, the just mentioned operating guidelines limit the number of complaints, employing the wording of Article 19(1)(a) of the Regulation and stating that

> [t]he Commission would like to draw the complainant's attention to the fact that the violation of TSD or GSP obligations must be *systematic* in the third country. This means that the violation should *not consist in an isolated case of non-compliance, but should consist of a widespread practice in the third country that is not properly addressed by the competent authorities*. In that respect, a practice may be identified as the systemic misapplication of legislation as well as the systemic failure to apply a law or regulation that would be compliant with the TSD or GSP obligation of the third country (emphasis added).[125]

It should be added here that in addition to the establishment of the CTEO and the Single Entry Point, the Commission Directorate General for Trade has introduced the 'Access2Markets' platform online, which is designed to provide comprehensive information and support to EU business trading with third countries.[126] The platform is meant to enable companies to access key information needed for 'trade in services as well as for investment and procurement in 3rd countries'; moreover, the platform has been set up to enable EU actors to 'learn about EU trade agreements, how to

[120] 'Chief Trade Enforcement Officer' (*European Commission*), policy.trade.ec.europa.eu/enforcement-and-protection/chief-trade-enforcement-officer_en.

[121] ibid.

[122] ibid.

[123] 'Single Entry Point' (*European Commission*, 31 May 2022), circabc.europa.eu/ui/group/7fc51410-46a1-4871-8979-20cce8df0896/library/d8d14d98-a915-4d8b-a6da-39e711c903d2/details.

[124] Directorate-General for Trade, 'Operating Guidelines for the Single Entry Point and Complaints Mechanism for the Enforcement of EU Trade Agreements and Arrangements' (*European Commission*, 22 June 2022), trade.ec.europa.eu/access-to-markets/en/form-assets/operational_guidelines.pdf, 2.

[125] ibid 12.

[126] 'Access2Markets' (*European Commission*), trade.ec.europa.eu/access-to-markets/en/home.

benefit from them and read stories on successful companies using them'.[127] The Access2Markets platform also gives actual access to the 'Single Entry Point' discussed above.[128] At the time of finalising this chapter, however, the sites on guidance on GSP and trade and sustainable development complaints are under construction,[129] which makes it difficult to assess what role EU stakeholders are expected to play in the enforcement of trade agreements' sustainable development chapters, including gender equality provisions.

In sum, the Commission has established a mechanism that invites stakeholders to contribute to the enforcement of third country commitments to trade and sustainable development, including gender equality. The threshold for complaints, namely to challenge only 'systematic' violations of TSD or GSP obligations, might be high. However, providing channels and support for EU stakeholders to voice their concerns related to trade and sustainable development must be welcomed.

5.2. Due Diligence Obligations

The previous paragraphs have demonstrated the EU's willingness to facilitate EU stakeholders helping to enforce the sustainability obligations of third countries, aiming to support them where such incompliance affects their own interests and competitiveness. As a consequence, Member States, private stakeholders and others can play a role in increasing the monitoring of *third country compliance* with international law and other gender equality obligations established in EU trade agreements concluded with such third country. What needs to be distinguished from such, what could be called 'voluntary' and arguably self-focused, involvement of EU stakeholders is the scope for *EU internal regulation of EU private stakeholders, EU institutions and Member States* trading with partners outside the EU, aiming to enforce gender equality obligations or standards to be met by them.

International organisations and non-governmental organisations (NGOs) have long recognised the potential impact of market participants on the protection and promotion of human rights, including gender equality.[130] Efforts have been made to establish obligations imposed on private actors through domestic legislation shaped by international law and standards, including the need to exercise due diligence when engaging with other business actors.[131]

For instance, the garment sector is one that has received the EU's attention and is relevant for our discussion of trade and gender. According to the Commission's

[127] ibid.

[128] ibid.

[129] 'Single Entry Point: Trade and Sustainable Development' (*European Commission*), trade.ec.europa.eu/access-to-markets/en/content/trade-and-sustainable-development.

[130] D Bilchitz, *Fundamental Rights and the Legal Obligations of Business*, Cambridge Studies in Constitutional Law (Cambridge, Cambridge University Press, 2021).

[131] See eg the Report of the Special Representative of the Secretary-General on the issue of human rights and transnational corporations and other business enterprises, J Ruggie, 'Protect, Respect and Remedy: A Framework for Business and Human Rights' (*Human Rights Council*, 7 April 2008) A/HRC/8/5, discussing due diligence as part of the 'corporate responsibility to respect', paras 56–64.

Communication of February 2022 on 'decent work worldwide for a global just transition and a sustainable recovery', the EU has developed a set of policies and supported actions to address decent work in the garment sector and reduce vulnerabilities, making supply chains more sustainable.[132] The EU has supported Better Work[133] to improve working conditions in the garment industry and the Vision Zero Fund[134] to improve occupational health and safety in the garment sector.[135] The Communication also refers to the EU's contribution to 'interventions to increase knowledge and awareness aiming to improve working conditions in the garment sector through responsible production and consumption'.[136] Moreover, the Commission refers to its effort in the framework of the Circular Economy Action Plan, 'preparing a strategy for sustainable textiles, focusing on a sustainable recovery from the COVID-19 crisis[137] and to reduce the sector's environmental and social impacts'.[138] The EU is committed to 'tak[ing] into account current challenges in the textiles value chain, including the need to protect human rights, including labour rights, and promote due diligence across supply chains in the textile sector', placing its currently proposed Corporate Sustainability Due Diligence Directive at the core of its efforts.[139]

As discussed above,[140] the EU's comprehensive approach 'aims to promote gender equality including through women's economic empowerment, increasing women's participation on the labour market in all sectors and at all levels and ensuring equal pay for work of equal value'.[141] Addressing 'workers in domestic markets in third countries and in global supply chains', the EU's approach is said to 'include … all relevant stakeholders: governments, social partners, civil society, business actors and

[132] European Commission, 'Communication on Decent Work Worldwide for a Global Just Transition and a Sustainable Recovery' (2022) COM(2022) 66 final, 11.

[133] Better work is a partnership between the ILO and the International Finance Corporation, a member of the World Bank Group, which brings diverse groups together – governments, global brands, factory owners, and unions and workers – to improve working conditions in the garment industry and make the sector more competitive, see betterwork.org/.

[134] The Vision Zero Fund was launched by the G7 and endorsed by the G20. It is part of Safety & Health for All, an ILO flagship programme building a culture of safe, healthy work. By mobilising governments, employers, workers and the private sector in communities and countries around the world, the Vision Zero Fund builds sustainable, safe and healthy supply chains, see 'Vision Zero Fund' (*International Labour Organization*), www.ilo.org/vzf/.

[135] The Communication 2022 also refers to another EU funded project promoting decent work in the garment supply chain: 'Sustainable Supply Chains to Build Forward Better' (*International Labour Organization*, 2020) www.ilo.org/wcmsp5/groups/public/---ed_dialogue/---sector/documents/genericdocument/wcms_791245.pdf.

[136] European Commission, 'Communication on Decent Work Worldwide for a Global Just Transition and a Sustainable Recovery' (2022) COM(2022) 66 final, 11-12, with reference to 'Rights for Workers' (*Together for Decent Leather*), www.togetherfordecentleather.org.

[137] 'EU Strategy for Sustainable Textiles' (*European Commission*), www.ec.europa.eu/info/law/better-regulation/have-your-say/initiatives/12822-EU-strategy-for-sustainable-textiles_en.

[138] European Commission, 'Communication on Decent Work Worldwide for a Global Just Transition and a Sustainable Recovery' (2022) COM(2022) 66 final, 12.

[139] ibid.

[140] See text at notes 59 et seq.

[141] European Commission, 'Communication on Decent Work Worldwide for a Global Just Transition and a Sustainable Recovery' (2022) COM(2022) 66 final, 13, with reference to Gender Action Plan III, 'Gender Action Plan – Putting Women and Girls' Rights at the Heart of the Global Recovery for a Gender-Equal World' (*European Commission*, 25 November 2020), www.ec.europa.eu/commission/presscorner/detail/en/IP_20_2184; European Commission, 'A Union of Equality: Gender Equality Strategy 2020-2025' (2020) COM(2020) 152 final.

consumers'.[142] The Communication refers to EU initiatives in the area,[143] including the proposal for a Corporate Sustainability Due Diligence Directive,[144] which was adopted together with this Communication, and the 'ongoing review of the 15-point Action Plan on Trade and Sustainable Development in the EU's trade policy'.[145]

The Commission's Due Diligence Proposal of 2022 recognises that '[t]he connection of the EU economy to millions of workers around the world through global value chains comes with a responsibility to address adverse impacts on the rights of these workers'; pursuing human rights- and environment-related objectives, there is need of

> implementing comprehensive mitigation processes for adverse human rights and environmental impacts in their value chains, integrating sustainability into corporate governance and management systems, and framing business decisions in terms of human rights, climate and environmental impact, as well as in terms of the company's resilience in the longer term.[146]

The Proposal recognises that voluntary action of companies, based on international standards of business conduct,[147] have not resulted in significant improvements across sector.[148] Moreover, EU companies 'have been associated with adverse human rights and environmental impacts, including in their value chains'.[149]

[142] European Commission, 'Communication on Decent Work Worldwide for a Global Just Transition and a Sustainable Recovery' (2022) COM(2022) 66 final, 13.

[143] See section 3 of European Commission, 'Communication on Decent Work Worldwide for a Global Just Transition and a Sustainable Recovery' (2022) COM(2022) 66 final and also European Commission, 'Commission Staff Working Document: Promote Decent Work Worldwide Responsible Global Value Chains for a Fair, Sustainable and Resilient Recovery from the COVID-19 Crises' (2020) SWD(2020) 235 final.

[144] European Commission, 'Proposal for a Directive of the European Parliament and of the Council on Corporate Sustainability Due Diligence and Amending Directive (EU) 2019/1937' (2022) COM(2022) 71 final.

[145] 'EU Trade Meetings with Civil Society' (*European Commission*), trade.ec.europa.eu/dialogue/meetdetails.cfm?meet=11601.

[146] European Commission, 'Proposal for a Directive of the European Parliament and of the Council on Corporate Sustainability Due Diligence and Amending Directive (EU) 2019/1937' (2022) COM(2022) 71 final, 2022/0051 (COD), 1.

[147] Office of the High Commissioner for Human Rights, 'Guiding Principles on Business and Human Rights: Implementing the United Nations "Protect, Respect and Remedy" Framework' (*United Nations*, 2011) HR/PUB/11/04; 'OECD Guidelines for Multinational Enterprises: 2011 Edition' (*Organisation for Economic Co-operation and Development*, 29 September 2011), www.oecd-ilibrary.org/governance/oecd-guidelines-for-multinational-enterprises_9789264115415-en, with set of recommendations on responsible business conduct, as well as specific OECD Due Diligence Guidance for Responsible Business Conduct (2018) and OECD sectoral guidance, available at: 'OECD Responsible Business Conduct – OECD Guidelines for Multinational Enterprises' (*Organisation for Economic Co-operation and Development*), mneguidelines.oecd.org/mneguidelines/.

[148] European Commission, 'Proposal for a Directive of the European Parliament and of the Council on Corporate Sustainability Due Diligence and Amending Directive (EU) 2019/1937' (2022) COM(2022) 71 final, 2022/0051 (COD), 2.

[149] European Commission, 'Proposal for a Directive of the European Parliament and of the Council on Corporate Sustainability Due Diligence and Amending Directive (EU) 2019/1937' (2022) COM(2022) 71 final, 2022/0051 (COD), 2, with reference to L Smit et al, 'Study on Due Diligence Requirements through the Supply Chain: Final Report' (*European Commission*, January 2020), op.europa.eu/en/publication-detail/-/publication/8ba0a8fd-4c83-11ea-b8b7-01aa75ed71a1/language-en, 221, which indicates that corporate risk assessment processes continue to focus on the materiality of the risks to the company, despite international guidance (UNGPs, OECD) which clarifies that the relevant risks for due diligence must extend beyond the risks of the company to those who are affected (the rights-holders). Negative

In spite of the global effect envisaged by the Due Diligence Directive, the EU Commission based the proposal on Articles 50 and 114 of the Treaty on the Functioning of the European Union (TFEU). The proposal affirms the scope of application of the freedom of establishment where measures aim to prevent obstacles 'resulting from the divergent development of national law'.[150] The directive is aimed at creating an even playing field for companies within the EU internal market, avoiding distortions of competition and creating one legal framework on sustainable corporate governance for all, and creating legal certainty.[151] It is thus the approximation of law in the field of establishment and the interest in the functioning of the internal market that lies at the heart of the directive, rather than external policy interests.

The Due Diligence Proposal does not mention explicitly gender equality. However, the promotion of gender equality is to be covered by the directive, which aims 'to foster sustainable and responsible corporate behaviour and to anchor human rights and environmental considerations in companies' operations and corporate governance'.[152] Companies need to 'take due account of the impact their activities have on human rights included in international conventions', including CEDAW, the ILO's 1951 Equal Remuneration Convention (No. 100) and its 1958 Discrimination (Employment and Occupation) Convention (No. 111).[153] According to the Commission, '[t]his will help prevent and address impacts that EU companies' activities may have on women's rights in their value chains inside and outside Europe'.[154]

The European Parliament recently suggested amendments to the wording of the proposal, including commitment to gender equality in various places.[155] Accordingly, companies should take a gender-responsive approach to their engagement with affected

corporate impacts as a consequence of globalisation and failure to undertake due diligence, ranging from environmental disasters (see at J Mello Neiva, 'Brumadinho Dam Collapse: Lessons in Corporate Due Diligence and Remedy for Harm Done' (*Business & Human Rights Resource Centre*, 28 January 2019), www.business-humanrights.org/en/blog/brumadinho-dam-collapse-lessons-in-corporate-due-diligence-and-remedy-for-harm-done/) and land grabbing (see SM Borras Jr et al, 'Land Grabbing and Human Rights: The Involvement of European Corporate and Financial Entities in Land Grabbing outside the European Union' (*European Parliament*, 10 May 2016), www.europarl.europa.eu/RegData/etudes/STUD/2016/578007/EXPO_STU(2016)578007_EN.pdf) to serious violations of labour and human rights, (see at E D'Ambrogio, 'Worker's Conditions in the Textile and Clothing Sector: Just an Asian Affair? Issues at stake after the Rana Plaza Tragedy' (*European Parliamentary Research Service*, 15 August 2014), www.europarl.europa.eu/RegData/etudes/BRIE/2014/538222/EPRS_BRI(2014)538222_REV1_EN.pdf) are well documented.

[150] European Commission, 'Proposal for a Directive of the European Parliament and of the Council on Corporate Sustainability Due Diligence and Amending Directive (EU) 2019/1937' (2022) COM(2022) 71 final, 10.

[151] ibid 10.

[152] '2023 Report on Gender Equality in the EU' (*European Commission*, April 2023), commission.europa.eu/system/files/2023-04/annual_report_GE_2023_web_EN.pdf, 55.

[153] As mentioned before, the ILO Violence and Harassment Convention, No. 190 (2019) is currently missing in the Commission's proposal, possibly due to the currently mixed ratification record of EU Member States, see 'Ratifications of C190 – Violence and Harassment Convention, 2019 (No. 190): Countries that Have Not Ratified this Convention' (*International Labour Organization*) www.ilo.org/dyn/normlex/en/f?p=NORMLEXPUB:11310:0::NO:11310:P11310_INSTRUMENT_ID:3999810:NO.

[154] '2023 Report on Gender Equality in the EU' (*European Commission*, April 2023), commission.europa.eu/system/files/2023-04/annual_report_GE_2023_web_EN.pdf, 55.

[155] European Parliament, 'Amendments Adopted on the Proposal for a Directive of the European Parliament and of the Council on Corporate Sustainability Due Diligence and Amending Directive (EU) 2019/1937 (COM(2022)0071 – C9-0050/2022 – 2022/0051(COD))' (2023) P9_TA(2023)0209, 2022/0051 (COD).

stakeholders (Amendment 60, Recital 44 c (new)), Member States should be obliged to ensure an effective remedy, recognising also gender disparity as obstacle for the persons concerned (Amendment 79, Recital 59 a (new)), include intersectional factors, such as sex and gender as defining factors of 'vulnerable stakeholders' (Amendment 122, Article 3 – paragraph 1 – point n a (new)), carry out gender-sensitive engagement with stakeholders and companies to 'pay particular attention to the needs of vulnerable stakeholders, and overlapping vulnerabilities and intersecting factors' and 'ensure a gender-responsive approach' (Amendment 206, Article 8 d (new)), ensure that notification and grievance mechanisms set up by companies are gender responsive (Amendment 214, Art 9 para 3 a (new)), and provide guidelines on how companies should fulfil their due diligence obligations that includes gender-responsive due diligence (Amendment 231, Article 13 – paragraph 1 a (new)).

The challenge of operationalising such a system of due diligence should be no reason to refrain from it. The system builds on national practice.[156] With regard to gender equality in particular, it has been suggested to strengthen and refine existing practices of existing Domestic Advisory Groups established on the basis of EU trade agreements.[157] Moreover, there is EU practice in supporting private stakeholders in undertaking due diligence, which the EU established in other areas. For instance, the EU has funded the initiative 'Due Diligence Help Desk on EU Sanctions' to support EU businesses, in particular small and medium-sized enterprises (SMEs) to enable them to engage with Iran 'legitimately, in compliance with EU legislation and within the framework of the Joint Comprehensive Plan of Action (JCPoA)'.[158] Regarding due diligence in light of gender-responsive standards, the EU should continue to support international initiatives,[159] equipping itself to provide the best possible support to traders.

5.3. Public Procurement

Gender mainstreaming efforts have been made also in the field of public procurement. In 2022, the European Institute for Gender Equality (EIGE) carried out a study on 'supporting gender equality in the EU economy through public procurement'.[160] With

[156] According to European Commission, 'Proposal for a Directive of the European Parliament and of the Council on Corporate Sustainability Due Diligence and Amending Directive (EU) 2019/1937' (2022) COM(2022) 71 final, 2022/0051 (COD), 1 (footnote 3): 'So far France (*Loi relative au devoir de vigilance, 2017*) and Germany (*Sorgfaltspflichtengesetz, 2021*) have introduced a horizontal due diligence law, other Member States (Belgium, the Netherlands, Luxembourg and Sweden) are planning to do so in the near future, and the Netherlands has introduced a more targeted law on child labour (*Wet zorgplicht kinderarbeidm 2019*)'.

[157] Gammage (n 17) 173.

[158] 'About the Due Diligence Helpdesk on EU Sanctions' (*Due Diligence Helpdesk on EU Sanctions*), www.sanctions-helpdesk.eu/about-us.

[159] Gammage (n 17) 173, with reference to 'Guidelines on Developing Gender-Responsive Standards: Advanced Copy' (*United Nations Economic Commission for Europe*, January 2022), www.unece.org/sites/default/files/2022-01/Guidelines%20on%20developing%20gender%20responsive%20standards%20Advanced%20Copy%20v0_1%20220119.pdf. See also above, notes 134 et seq.

[160] European Institute for Gender Equality, *Gender-Responsive Public Procurement in the EU: Report* (Luxembourg, Publications Office of the European Union, 2022).

the objective of contributing to a gender-equal distribution of economic resources in the EU, the EIGE developed a step-by-step toolkit.[161] It recommends EU institutions to 'recognise the role of gender-responsive public procurement (GRPP) in the EU legal and policy frameworks and that national, regional and local procurement policies, strategies and guidance clearly identify gender equality as an essential aim of procurement'.[162]

According to the EIGE, 'the EU public procurement legal framework provides for the possibility of implementing GRPP, although gender equality is not mentioned as a specific objective'; while there are variations in the implementation of Directive 2014/24/EU, this is also true for the Member States' legal frameworks, even though there is currently little reference to public procurement as a tool to advance gender equality.[163] In order to make legislation on the matter efficient, it needs to be combined with adequate policy frameworks, strategies and capacity-building programmes.[164]

According to the Commission's 2023 Report on Gender Equality, it has continued to promote its 2021 'Buying Social' guide on gender-responsive public procurement; moreover, a webinar on gender equality and public procurement in February 2022 presented the Toolbox on Gender-responsive public procurement developed by EIGE, and showcased a good practice in the field in the Basque Country.[165]

What are the potential implications of such efforts then for EU based procurement dealing with non-EU markets and traders? The EU's 'International Procurement Instrument' (IPI) concerns access to the EU Procurement market. However, the Commission constrains such access, by excluding bids, where EU companies 'are facing serious and recurring obstacles to access third-country procurement markets',[166] not on the basis of eg human rights grounds related to the procurement itself. The EIGE toolkit does not make any explicit reference to the approach to be taken vis-à-vis traders based outside the EU, and the support needed by EU or Member State authorities in that context. However, given the international context of the EU's procurement legislation, it is difficult to imagine that authorities within the EU would not need to require the same standards when dealing with non-EU bidders as they do when dealing with EU internal bidders.

[161] See 'Gender-Responsive Public Procurement' (*European Institute for Gender Equality*), www.eige.europa.eu/gender-mainstreaming/toolkits/grpp.

[162] '2023 Report on Gender Equality in the EU' (*European Commission*, April 2023), commission.europa.eu/system/files/2023-04/annual_report_GE_2023_web_EN.pdf, 55.

[163] 'Gender-Responsive Public Procurement in Practice: Importance of Legal, Regulatory and Policy Framework' (European Institute for Gender Equality), www.eige.europa.eu/gender-mainstreaming/toolkits/grpp/gender-responsive-public-procurement-practice.

[164] ibid, with reference to the UN Women's web page on gender-responsive procurement ('UN Women: Gender Responsive Procurement' (*United Nations Global Market Place*), www.ungm.org/Shared/KnowledgeCenter/Pages/PT_GRP) and European Commission – Executive Agency for Small and Medium-Sized Enterprises, 'Buying for Social Impact' (*Publications Office of the European Union*, 2020), op.europa.eu/en/publication-detail/-/publication/b09af6a5-513a-11ea-aece-01aa75ed71a1/language-en/format-PDF/source-search.

[165] '2023 Report on Gender Equality in the EU' (*European Commission*, April 2023), commission.europa.eu/system/files/2023-04/annual_report_GE_2023_web_EN.pdf, 55, with reference to *3rd #WeBuySocialEU Lunchtime Talk on Gender Equality* (Directed by EU Growth, 24 February 2022), www.youtube.com/watch?v=q_JUKdzz8nc.

[166] F Hoffmeister, 'Strategic Autonomy in the European Union's External Relations Law' (2023) 60 *CML Rev* 667, 677.

The EU – together with its 27 Member States and 20 other members of the WTO – is party to the Agreement on Government Procurement (GPA 2012), which is based on the principles of non-discrimination, transparency and procedural fairness. As a consequence of such liberalisation, access to the EU and its Member States' procurement market has been expanded. At the same time, the Agreement contains 'General and Security Exceptions' in Article III. Accordingly, nothing prevents the parties from imposing or enforcing measures 'necessary to protect public morals', as long as applied without discrimination or constituting a disguised restriction on international trade. In other words, it might well be considered justifiable to derogate from procurement obligations to advance gender equality.[167]

To conclude this section, there has to date been some engagement in internal trade-related legislation with opportunities to promote gender equality globally by imposing obligations on Member States, EU institutions and EU private actors concerning their extra-EU trade. The interplay between EU internal and external objectives, values and principles on the one hand, and the EU and its Member States' international commitments and legal obligations on the other, requires the EU to further align external and internal measures to make trade more gender-responsive. It is on this basis that the EU could strengthen its credibility as regards being a 'good global actor', coherence and impact of trade policy.

6. CONCLUSION

The making and implementation of the EU's trade policy has been framed by EU Treaty commitment to the EU's values, principles and objectives, which have established the commitment to gender equality as a cross-cutting issue.[168] The EU has complemented its Treaty commitments to the promotion of gender equality with its gender action plans and strategies adopted to promote gender equality in all its internal and external action. Its commitment to international collaboration and the development of international law should be read together with the commitment to the promotion of equality, establishing the EU's roadmap as a global actor. The EU's specific commitment to the promotion of gender equality and mainstreaming have thus been made part of the EU's external action legal framework,[169] and been recognised by the Commission as 'cross-cutting priority of the EU's international relations and partnerships'.[170] The EU has endorsed its Member States' international legal obligations (eg CEDAW, ILO Conventions) and political commitments on the global stage (eg Sustainable Development Goals, Beijing Declaration) related to gender equality. The EU has also become an active participant itself in international fora working on trade and gender. These legal and political commitments of the EU have

[167] For WTO caselaw on the interpretation of 'public morals' see eg *European Communities – Measures Prohibiting the Importation and Marketing of Seal Products*, WTO/DS400, recognising concerns on seal welfare as legitimate objective of addressing EU public moral.

[168] Arts 2, 3(5), 21 Consolidated version of the Treaty on European Union (TEU) [2016] OJ C202/13.

[169] Arts 3(5), 21 TEU; Art 8 TFEU.

[170] '2023 Report on Gender Equality in the EU' (*European Commission*, April 2023), commission.europa.eu/system/files/2023-04/annual_report_GE_2023_web_EN.pdf, 67.

shaped its external trade action. The EU has started to demonstrate commitment to gender equality not only based on its own constitutional values and principles but employs international law as a significant component of good global governance.

The EU's global commitment to the promotion of gender equality manifests itself in its external trade measures. EU trade agreements increasingly contain gender equality provisions and chapters, and the GSP(+) system includes gender equality obligations too. EU trade agreements' incorporation of international treaties arguably constitutes at least unilateral commitment to comply with relevant laws and standards, 'making pre-existing multilateral commitments applicable between the EU and the third country on the basis of the FTA itself and, hence, enforceable in accordance with the FTA dispute settlement procedures in addition to multilateral compliance mechanisms'.[171] While the EU has been criticised for lacking consistency in its interaction with third states, including the preparation, wording and implementation of trade agreements, the EU has also been praised at global level for its active engagement with how best to advance gender equality and women's economic empowerment.

The capacity of the EU to be a 'good global actor', however, is not limited to its interaction with non-EU states and international organisations/fora. One of the most powerful tools for the EU to induce change remains its capacity to foster legal integration within its own legal order. Such legal integration can unfold implications for non-EU actors too. Complementing the EU's own engagement with non-EU states and international organisations, the EU has the capacity to oblige the EU Member States, EU institutions and private actors to increase the gender-responsiveness of trade. Linking the internal market objectives and the EU's external objectives, values and principles, the EU is empowered to include gender equality commitments in its trade policy, trade agreements and internal trade-related legislation and other measures, embedded in the EU and its Member States' international legal obligations.

As the chapter has shown, recent EU Communications related to the advancement of gender equality, market access and trade and sustainable development issues demonstrate the EU's willingness to strengthen the role of private actors, Member States and other stakeholders in the monitoring of third countries' obligations under trade agreements concluded with the EU. While inviting them to bring alleged infringements of treaty obligations to the attention of the EU, it is only the EU that could enforce such obligations vis-à-vis its international treaty partners (to the extent possible according to the agreements). However, private actors, Member States and other stakeholders affected by third country non-compliance with gender equality commitments (or other matters covered by the agreements) have the capacity to trigger debate and thus exercise pressure not only on the third country but also on the EU to have consequences on the global stage – as well as increasing global visibility and awareness of incompliance.

In addition to the role of internal EU stakeholders in enforcing the obligations of third countries, the interaction of EU traders with businesses outside the EU are also being made subject to EU legislation. Given their economic and global standing,

[171] Marín Durán (n 82) 1038.

certain EU market players have the capacity to increase globally the protection of human rights, including gender equality. EU legislation that establishes obligations on EU traders participating in international trade thus has the potential of strengthening gender equality and economic empowerment of women on a larger scale. For instance, creating due diligence obligations for EU traders and public procurement rules for EU Member States and EU institutions to make trade with actors outside the EU more gender-responsive could foster the EU's standing as a 'good global actor'. Because of the nature and legal structure of the EU, the roots for such external reach thereby remain anchored in its own legal integration and constitutional order, addressing its own actors involved in international trade, rather than imposing obligations on non-EU trade actors only.

Epilogue

Epilogue

ALAN DASHWOOD

THIS VOLUME OF essays shows the affectionate admiration and gratitude felt towards Marise Cremona for her many years of intellectual leadership as a scholar and teacher of EU law, more particularly in the field of EU external relations. The contributors are a group of close colleagues and collaborators of Marise but they speak for a much wider public – academic, practitioner and judicial – among whom her work commands deep respect. Through her writings, Marise has influenced the development of almost every aspect of EU external relations law. She has also been a great intellectual entrepreneur, as the editor (alone or with others) of numerous collective works, a publishing strategy particularly suited to the exploration of a rapidly evolving and much contested branch of law. The range of topics covered in the volume represents a well-judged homage to the rich diversity of her scholarship.

Marise and I have been friends for many years and we have worked together productively on a whole variety of projects. I share her abiding concern with the subtle interplay between the concepts and principles that provide the constitutional framework of EU external relations law. My understanding of these matters owes a great deal to her thinking. She is always coming up with intriguing new ideas, expounded with a clarity and elegance that heighten their persuasive force.

I offer here an example to illustrate what I mean. It is taken from the chapter that Marise contributed to her edited volume, published in 2018, on *Structural Principles in EU External Relations Law*.[1] The main thrust of the chapter is the identification and (tentative) categorisation of the structural principles of EU external relations law that, in her words:

> establish a framework expressed in (or implied from) the Treaties, protecting an institutional space within which policy may be formed, in which the different actors understand and work within their respective roles.[2]

This is an insightful study of a theme which Marise, in typical style, develops by opening up a debate among her team of distinguished fellow contributors. My focus, however, is on an issue which she analyses, as a prelude to the main discussion in her chapter, to explain the importance she attaches to structural issues in the formation

[1] M Cremona, 'Structural Principles and their Role in EU External Relations Law' in M Cremona (ed), *Structural Principles in EU External Relations Law* (Oxford, Hart Publishing, 2018).

[2] ibid 12.

of EU external policy. It is an issue that I thought I knew from top to bottom, but on which, for me at least, she was able to shine fresh light, namely the attribution of the general competences expressly conferred by the Treaties that specifically and primarily authorise action by the EU in the international sphere. I shall refer to these, for short, as 'express EU external competences.'[3]

The key idea in Marise's analysis of this issue is encapsulated in the vivid phrase, 'the absence of a *telos* in EU external policy', which serves as the heading to section II of her chapter.[4] This conveys a truth Marise has spotted about the nature of the express EU external competences: their Treaty definitions identify broad fields of external action in which the Union is authorised to operate, but they do not prescribe specific end-goals to be attained through such action. Marise recalls that the primordial EEC Treaty contained only two such competences, the common commercial policy (CCP) and association agreements. The CCP mandated the establishment of a policy based on 'uniform principles', but it was the uniformity that mattered, not the content of the common rules; while association agreements were defined simply as involving reciprocal rights and obligations, common action and special procedures. It was, therefore, possible for those competences to be used 'for a wide variety of purposes, from establishing the World Trade Organisation (WTO) to development-oriented selective trade preferences; from pre-accession to integration without accession; from preferential status for former colonies to free trade agreements with strategic trading partners'.

Express external EU competences conferred by subsequent amending Treaties in the fields of development cooperation and the common foreign and security policy (CFSP) share the same 'open-ended character' as the two original ones. That character has not been altered by the introduction by the Lisbon Treaty of the list of external objectives in Article 21(2), since these are not linked to any specific external competence but are stated to apply 'in all fields of international relations.'[5] The analysis of the four express external EU competences summarised here is substantiated by Marise with examples drawn from the Court's case law.[6]

In contrast to those competences, Marise explains that the EU's internal competences were, and are, for the most part, 'designed to achieve specific objectives, such as the removal of obstacles to freedom of movement, the establishment of a common or internal market, undistorted competition or non-discrimination'; with the overall aim of 'the implementation of the process of integration that is the raison d'etre of the EU itself.'[7] Or, as she says later in her chapter, 'in its internal policies, the Union is generally instructed to construct *something* (an internal market, an area of freedom

[3] In an essay published in 2000, I referred to them, perhaps too grandly, as 'dedicated external relations provisions': see A Dashwood, 'The Attribution of External Relations Competence' in A Dashwood and C Hillion (eds), *The General Law of EU External Relations* (London, Sweet & Maxwell, 2000) 115, 121. As there explained, express external competences, in my sense, are to be distinguished from competences that expressly authorise the EU to engage in international cooperation in areas where the main thrust of policy is directed towards internal activity, eg Article 191(4) on the Environment.

[4] The phrase is found in the heading of section II of Cremona (n 1).

[5] As to all of this, see Cremona (n 1) 5–6.

[6] Cremona (n 1) 9–11.

[7] Opinion 2/13, EU:C:2014:2454, para 172.

security and justice, a system of undistorted competition).'[8] Importantly, the contrast with express external EU competences applies equally to implied external competences arising pursuant to the *AETR* case law, since these are tied to the internal objectives that they either protect (under the pre-emption rationale of implicit conferral) or complement (under the *effet utile* rationale).[9]

I have found what Marise says about express external EU competences illuminating in various ways. I was, of course, aware of the broad scope of the different competences, but had not identified this as being due to the absence of concrete end-goals from the definition provided by their respective legal bases, and common to all four of them. Clearly, she is right.

In the case of the CCP, Article 207(1) TFEU still provides for it to be 'based on uniform principles' in respect of the matters there listed, while saying nothing about the policy content of such principles. The traditional approach of the Court of Justice is that a measure will fall within the scope of the CCP if it 'relates specifically to international trade, in that it is essentially intended to promote, facilitate or govern trade and has direct and immediate effects on trade.'[10] CCP competence is thus seen as essentially instrumental. What counts is the existence of an effect (positive or negative) on trade. In another memorable quote, Marise has observed that the CCP 'is not likely to see a "tobacco advertising" moment.'[11]

The other express external EU competences are similar in nature. In the case of association agreements, nothing whatever is said in Article 217 TFEU about their possible content. The Article refers only to the legal machinery they should contain, 'involving reciprocal rights and obligations, common action and special procedures'. As for development cooperation, its 'primary purpose' is stated by Article 208(1), second subparagraph TFEU to be 'the reduction and, in the long term, the eradication of poverty.' An aim so worthy but so vague, which moreover can certainly not be achieved by the Union on its own, amounts to scarcely more than an aspiration. The Court of Justice, as Marise points out, has contextualised that aim by drawing on references in the European Consensus on Development to sustainable development and the pursuit of the Millenium Development Goals.[12] Lastly, the scope of the CFSP is defined by Article 24(1) TEU in the broadest terms conceivable, as covering '*all* areas of foreign policy and *all* questions relating to the Union's security, including the progressive framing of a common defence policy that might lead to a common defence.'[13] As Marise puts it, the CFSP 'relies on the general external objectives turned into more specific policy objectives by the political institutions.'[14]

[8] Cremona (n 1) 11.

[9] As explained in M Cremona, 'EU External Competence – Rationales for Exclusivity' in I Govaere and S Garben (eds), *The Division of Competences between the European Union and its Member States: Reflections on the Past, Present and Future* (Oxford, Hart Publishing, 2017).

[10] See, *ex abundantia*, Case C-137/12 *Commission v Council* ECLI:EU:C:2013:675, para 57.

[11] Cremona (n 1) 9.

[12] ibid 10.

[13] Emphasis added.

[14] M Cremona, 'The Principle of Conferral and Express and Implied External Competences' in E Nefrani and M Gatti (eds), *Constitutional Issues of EU External Relations Law* (Baden-Baden, Nomos, 2018) 33.

The freedom those competences enjoy, from the constraints that a Treaty requirement to pursue prescribed substantive aims would necessarily entail, provides a convincing explanation of their ability to serve as the legal basis for international agreements encompassing a wide range of matters, some of which may be the subject of specific internal competences. This accounts, in turn, for the familiar problem of disputes regarding the correct legal basis for such agreements, where a plausible case can be made for the choice of one or more implied external competences linked to the internal competences in question.

The fact that Marise included the CFSP in her analysis of express external EU competences, alongside the CCP, association agreements and development cooperation, made me re-visit an issue on which I thought my position was settled. I have written in the past about the continuing bipolarity of EU external relations in the post-Lisbon era.[15] While it is clearly the case that the legal organisation of the CFSP remans significantly different from other fields of EU competence, I have been persuaded by Marise that the Lisbon Treaty has integrated the CFSP 'into the general framework of EU external action, including its general objectives and procedures for Treaty-making.'[16] As she says, 'there is no CFSP carve-out'. Article 24(1) TEU does not completely exempt the CFSP from the general rules but means rather 'that the general rules and principles will apply by default, subject to exceptions and specific conditions'.[17] This is tellingly illustrated by the fact that the Court of Justice employs its usual reasoning, based on the aim and content of the measure in question,[18] in choosing between a CFSP or non-CFSP legal basis for the adoption of a measure. Where an international agreement falls predominantly within the scope of the CFSP, while including elements relating to, say, judicial cooperation in criminal matters or police cooperation, which are judged to be purely incidental, the choice of a CFSP legal basis alone, without the addition of implied legal bases relating to those elements, has been found appropriate.[19]

A final insight concerns the connection that Marise makes between the Treaty definition of express external EU competences and the significance of structural principles in the framing of external policy by the institutions. This is another consequence of the freedom from substantive constraints, noticed above, that the open-endedness of the competences gives. It means that 'the direction and goals of EU external policy must be set by the institutions themselves.'[20] Article 22 TEU spells out that it falls to the European Council, on the basis of the principles and objectives in Article 21, to 'identify the strategic interests and objectives of the Union'. There is very little

[15] A Dashwood, 'The Continuing Bipolarity of EU External Action' in I Govaere, E Lannon, P Van Elsuwege and S Adam, *The European Union in the World – Essays in Honour of Marc Maresceau* (Leiden/Boston, Martinus Nijhoff, 2014) 3.

[16] Cremona (n 14) 39.

[17] See M Cremona, 'The Position of CFSP/CSDP in the EU's Constitutional Architecture' in S Blockmans and P Koutrakos, *Research Handbook on the EU's Common Foreign and Security Policy* (Cheltenham, Edward Elgar, 2018) 8.

[18] Case C-377/12 *Ex abundantia, Commission v Council* EU:C:2014:1903, para 34.

[19] Case C-263/14 *European Parliament v Council* EU:C:2016:435. See the discussion in Cremona (n 14) 39–47; Cremona (n 17) 12–13.

[20] Cremona (n 1) 4.

substantive content in the respective legal bases of the four competences that could inhibit policy choices, dictate priorities or provide grounds for judicial review leading to a finding that the competences have been misused.[21] As Marise observes: 'a Union which is granted broad policy fields in which to exercise its external capacity, with little by way of clear guidance in the constituent Treaties as to the ends for which those powers have been given, may seem to have much in common with a sovereign state', which would be incompatible with the character of the EU as a rule-based international actor that operates through law, with powers derived from law.[22] The structural principles show the impression of a sovereign competence to be false. The principles do not interfere with policy agenda-setting but "structure the system, functioning and exercise of EU external competences".[23] In other words, structural principles are 'not concerned with the *substantive content* of policy but rather with *process* and the *relationship* between the actors in those processes, and their normative content reflects this.'[24] Their role in EU external policy is thus to make up for the 'absence of a *telos*' in that policy, by orienting policy choices towards the furtherance of the Union's fundamental aims and values.

This Epilogue is my personal homage to Marise. To have attempted a summation of a scholarly *oeuvre* as extensive and varied as hers seemed too daunting. I hope, though, that I may at least have succeeded in capturing its unique flavour.

[21] ibid. Marise notes, in fn 9, that there have been only two cases where the Court of Justice has held that the EU lacked external competence: Opinion 2/94, ECLI:EU:C:1996:140, where the Court held that, as European Community law stood at the time, the Community had no competence to accede to the European Human Rights Convention; and Joined Cases C-317/04 and 318/04 *European Parliament v Commission* ECLI:EU:C:2006:346, where it was held that internal powers could not be used as a legal basis for external action the purposes of which were expressly excluded by the internal legislation.

[22] Cremona (n 1) 12.

[23] ibid 12.

[24] ibid.

A Thematic Bibliography of the Scholarship of Marise Cremona

TINE DESCHUYTERE

SUBSTANTIVE ISSUES OF EU EXTERNAL RELATIONS LAW

Common Commercial Policy

Cremona M, 'The "Dynamic and Homogeneous" EEA: Byzantine Structures and Various Geometry' (1994) 19 *European Law Review* 508

——, 'Human Rights and Democracy Clauses in the EC's Trade Agreements' (1995) 126/127 *Law & Justice – The Christian Law Review* 105

——, 'Human Rights and Democracy Clauses in the EC's Trade Agreements' in N Emiliou and D O'Keeffe (eds), *The European Union and world trade law : after the GATT Uruguay Round* (Wiley, 1996)

——, 'Case C-432/92, *R. v. Minister of Agriculture, Fisheries and Food, Ex Parte S.P. Anastasiou (Pissouri) Ltd. and Others*, Judgment of 5 July 1994' (1996) 33 *Common Market Law Review* 125

——, 'Flexible Models: External Policy and the European Economic Constitution' in G de Búrca and J Scott (eds), *Constitutional Change in the EU: From Uniformity to Flexibility* (Bloomsbury Publishing, 2000)

——, 'Multilateral and Bilateral Approaches to the Internationalisation of Competition Law: An EU Perspective' in IF Fletcher, LA Mistelis and M Cremona (eds), *Foundations and Perspectives of International Trade Law* (Sweet & Maxwell, 2001)

——, 'Variable Geometry and Setting Membership Conditionalities: A Viable Strategy?' in C Clapham and others (eds), *Regional integration in Southern Africa: comparative international perspectives* (South African Institute of International Affairs, 2001)

——, 'Rhetoric and Reticence: EU External Commercial Policy in a Multilateral Context' (2001) 38 *Common Market Law Review* 359

——, 'Neutrality or Discrimination? The WTO, the EU and External Trade' in G de Búrca and J Scott (eds), *The EU and the WTO: Legal and Constitutional Issues* (Bloomsbury Publishing, 2003)

——, 'Regional Integration and the Rule of Law: Some Issues and Options' in R Devlin and A Estevadeordal (eds), *Bridges for Development: Policies and Institutions for Trade and Integration* (Inter-American Development Bank, 2003)

——, 'The European Union and Regional Trade Agreements' in C Herrmann and J Philipp Terhechte (eds), *European yearbook of international economic law 2010* (Springer, 2010)

——, 'The Single Market as a Global Export Brand: Exporting the Single Market' (2010) 21 *European Business Law Review* 663

——, 'The EU's International Regulatory Policy, Democratic Accountability and the ACTA: A Cautionary Tale' in M Cremona and T Takács (eds), *Trade liberalisation and standardisation: new directions in the 'low politics' of EU foreign policy* (Centre for the Law of EU External Relations, 2013)

Cremona M and Takács T (eds), *Trade Liberalisation and Standardisation: New Directions in the 'low Politics' of EU Foreign Policy* (Centre for the Law of EU External Relations, 2013)

Cremona M, 'Expanding the Internal Market: An External Regulatory Policy for the EU?' in B Van Vooren, S Blockmans and J Wouters (eds), *The EU's Role in Global Governance* (Oxford University Press, 2013)
Cremona M and Marín Durán G, 'The International Fair Trade Movement: Actors and Regulatory Approaches' in B Granville and J Dine (eds), *The processes and practices of fair trade: trust, ethics and governance* (Routledge, 2013)
——, 'Fair Trade in the European Union: Regulatory and Institutional Aspects' in B Granville and J Dine (eds), *The processes and practices of fair trade: trust, ethics and governance* (Routledge, 2013)
Cremona M, 'International Regulatory Policy and Democratic Accountability: The EU and the ACTA' in M Cremona and others (eds), *Reflections on the constitutionalisation of international economic law: liber amicorum for Ernst-Ulrich Petersmann* (Martinus Nijhoff Publishers, 2014)
Cremona M and others (eds), *Reflections on the Constitutionalisation of International Economic Law: Liber Amicorum for Ernst-Ulrich Petersmann* (Martinus Nijhoff Publishers, 2014)
Cremona M, 'Guest Editorial: Negotiating the Transatlantic Trade and Investment Partnership (TTIP)' (2015) 52 *Common Market Law Review* 351
——, 'The Transatlantic Trade and Investment Partnership Negotiations and Their Consequences for the European Union' in G Bándi, P Darák and K Debisso (eds), *Speeches and presentations from the XXVII FIDE congress: congress proceedings vol. 4* (Wolters Kluwer, 2016)
——, 'Regulating FDI in the EU Legal Framework' in JHJ Bourgeois (ed), *EU framework for foreign direct investment control* (Wolters Kluwer, 2020)
——, 'Human Rights as a Value of EU Trade Policy' in M Balboni and C Danisi (eds), *Human rights as a horizontal issue in EU external policy/Les droits de l'homme comme domaine horizontal de la politique extérieure de l'Union européenne* (Editoriale scientifica, 2021)

EU Enlargement Policies

Cremona M, 'Community Relations with the Visegrad Group' (1993) 18 *European Law Review* 345
——, 'Migrant Workers under the Europe Agreements' [1994] The European Advocate
——, 'The New Associations: Substantive Issues of the Europe Agreements with the Central and Eastern European States' in SV Konstadinidis (ed), *The legal regulation of the European Community's external relations after the completion of the internal market* (Dartmouth, 1996)
——, 'Movement of Persons, Establishment and Services' in M Maresceau (ed), *Enlarging the European Union: relations between the EU and Central and Eastern Europe* (Longman, 1997)
——, 'Free Movement of Goods in the Wider Europe' in P Xuereb (ed), *Proceedings of the State of the European Union Conference 1998* (EDRC, 1998)
——, 'Free Movement of Persons, Firms and Services in the Wider Europe' in P Xuereb (ed), *Proceedings of the State of the European Union Conference 1998* (EDRC, 1998)
——, 'Creating the New Europe: The Stability Pact for South-Eastern Europe in the Context of EU-SEE Relations' (1999) 2 *Cambridge Yearbook of European Legal Studies* 463
——, 'Accession to the European Union: Membership Conditionality and Accession Criteria' (2001) 25 *Polish Yearbook of International Law* 219
——, 'Services' in A Ott and K Inglis (eds), *Handbook on European enlargement: a commentary on the enlargement process* (TMC Asser Press, 2002)
——, 'State Aid Control: Substance and Procedure in the Europe Agreements and the Stabilisation and Association Agreements' (2003) 9 *European Law Journal* 265
—— (ed), *The Enlargement of the European Union* (Oxford University Press, 2003)
——, 'The Impact of Enlargement: External Policy and External Relations' in M Cremona (ed), *The Enlargement of the European Union* (Oxford University Press, 2003)
——, 'Enlargement: A Successful Instrument of Foreign Policy?' in T Tridimas, P Nebbia and P Matthews (eds), *European Union Law for the Twenty-First Century: Volume 1: Rethinking the New Legal Order* (Bloomsbury Publishing, 2004)
——, 'EU Enlargement: Solidarity and Conditionality' (2005) 30 *European Law Review* 3
Cremona M and Skoutaris N, 'Speaking of the de … rogations: Accommodating a Solution of the Cyprus Issue within the Union Legal Order' (2009) 11 *Journal of Balkan and Near Eastern Studies* 381

——, 'Taking Cyprus' EU Membership into Account: Strict Compliance or Accommodation?' in A Auer and V Triga (eds), *A constitutional convention for Cyprus* (WVB, Wissenschaftlicher Verlag Berlin, 2009)

Cremona M, 'Editorial Note' (2011) 7 *Croatian Yearbook of European Law and Policy* vii

——, 'Enlargement as Foreign Policy: A Research Agenda', *European Enlargement across Rounds and Beyond Borders* (Routledge, 2017)

European Neighbourhood Policy and Related action

Cremona M, 'The Euro-Mediterranean Partnership: A Regional Strategy for the EU', *The European Union, the IGC and the Mediterranean, proceedings of the State of the European Union Conference 1996 EDRC* (1996)

——, 'European Neighbourhood Policy: Legal and Institutional Issues' (Center on Democracy, Development and the Rule of Law – Stanford Institute for International Studies 2004) CDDRL Working Papers 25

——, 'The European Neighbourhood Policy: Partnership, Security and the Rule of Law' in AlMayhew and N Copsey (eds), *European Neighbourhood Policy and Ukraine* (Sussex European Institute, 2005)

Cremona M and Hillion C, 'L'Union Fait La Force? Potential and Limitations of the European Neighbourhood Policy as an Integrated EU Foreign and Security Policy' (European University Institute, 2006) EUI Working Papers LAW No. 2006/39

——, 'L'Union Fait La Force? Potential and Limitations of the European Neighbourhood Policy as an Integrated EU Foreign and Security Policy' in N Copsey and A Mayhew (eds), *European Neighbourhood Policy: the Case of Ukraine* (Sussex European Institute, 2007)

Cremona M and Meloni G (eds), 'The European Neighbourhood Policy: A Framework for Modernisation?' (European University Institute, 2007) EUI Working Papers LAW 2007/21

Cremona M, 'Circular Migration: A Legal Perspective' (CARIM Euro-Mediterranean Consortium for Applied Research on International Migration, 2008) Analytic and Synthetic Notes – Circular Migration Series Legal Module CARIM-AS 2008/30

——, 'The European Neighbourhood Policy: More than a Partnership?' in M Cremona (ed), *Developments in EU External Relations Law* (Oxford University Press, 2008)

——, 'The European Neighbourhood Policy' in A Ott and E Vos (eds), *Fifty years of European integration: foundations and perspectives* (Asser Press, 2009)

——, 'The European Neighbourhood Policy as a Framework for Modernization' (2009) EUI Working Paper MWP 2009/10

——, 'The ENP and Multilateralism' in S Poli (ed), *The European Neighbourhood Policy – Values and Principles* (Routledge, 2016)

Cremona M and Nic Shuibhne N, 'Integration, Membership, and the EU Neighbourhood' (2022) 59 *Common Market Law Review* 155

Human Rights, Democracy and Rule of Law in EU External Relations

Cremona M, 'Human Rights and Democracy Clauses in the EC's Trade Agreements' (1995) 126/127 *Law & Justice – The Christian Law Review* 105

——, 'Human Rights and Democracy Clauses in the EC's Trade Agreements' in N Emiliou and D O'Keeffe (eds), *The European Union and world trade law: after the GATT Uruguay Round* (Wiley, 1996)

——, 'The EU and the External Dimension of Human Rights Policy' in SV Konstadinidis (ed), *A people's Europe: a concept into content* (Ashgate, 1999)

——, 'Regional Integration and the Rule of Law: Some Issues and Options' in R Devlin and A Estevadeordal (eds), *Bridges for Development: Policies and Institutions for Trade and Integration* (Inter-American Development Bank, 2003)

——, 'The European Neighbourhood Policy: Partnership, Security and the Rule of Law' in A Mayhew and N Copsey (eds), *European Neighbourhood Policy and Ukraine* (Sussex European Institute, 2005)
——, 'The Promotion of Democracy in the EU's External Relations' (2007) 4 *EUI Review* 9
Rijpma JJ and Cremona M, 'The Extra-Territorialisation of EU Migration Policies and the Rule of Law' (European University Institute, 2007) EUI Working Papers LAW 2007/01
Cremona M, 'Economic and Social Rights in EU External Policy' [2008] Jus: rivista di scienze giuridiche: 2/3, 2008 437
——, 'Human Rights as a Value of EU Trade Policy' in M Balboni and C Danisi (eds), *Human rights as a horizontal issue in EU external policy/Les droits de l'homme comme domaine horizontal de la politique extérieure de l'Union européenne* (Editoriale scientifica, 2021)

Miscellaneous

Cremona M, 'The Role of the EEC in the Control of Oil Pollution' (1980) 17 *Common Market Law Review* 171
——, 'Values in the EU Constitution: The External Dimension' (Center on Democracy, Development and the Rule of Law – Stanford Institute for International Studies 2004) CDDRL Working Papers 26
Rijpma JJ and Cremona M, 'The Extra-Territorialisation of EU Migration Policies and the Rule of Law' (European University Institute, 2007) EUI Working Papers LAW 2007/01
—— (ed), *Developments in EU External Relations Law* (Oxford University Press, 2008)
Cremona M, Francioni F and Poli S (eds), 'Challenging the EU Counter-Terrorism Measures through the Courts' (2009) EUI Working Papers AEL 2009/10
Cremona M, 'Disconnection Clauses in EU Law and Practice' in C Hillion and P Koutrakos (eds), *Mixed agreements revisited: the EU and its member states in the world* (Hart Publishing, 2010)
Cafaggi F and others, 'Europeanization of Private Law in Central and Eastern Europe Countries (CEECs): Preliminary Findings and Research Agenda' (2010) EUI Working Papers LAW 2010/15
Cremona M, 'Justice and Home Affairs in a Globalised World: Ambitions and Reality in the Tale of the EU-US SWIFT Agreement' (Austrian Academy of Sciences Institute for European Integration Research, 2011) Working Paper No. 04/2011
——, 'The EU and Global Emergencies: Competence and Instruments' in A Antoniadis, R Schütze and E Spaventa (eds), *The European Union and global emergencies: a law and policy analysis* (Hart Publishing, 2011)
Cremona M, Monar J and Poli S (eds), *The External Dimension of the European Union's Area of Freedom, Security and Justice* (Peter Lang, 2011)
Cremona M, 'The Internal Market and Private International Law Regimes: A Comment on Case C-533/08 TNT Express Nederland BV v AXA Versicherung AG, Judgment of the Court (Grand Chamber) of 4 May 2010' (2014) EUI Working Papers LAW 2014/08
——, 'Risk in Three Dimensions: The EU–US Agreement on the Processing and Transfer of Financial Messaging Data' in H-W Micklitz and T Tridimas (eds), *Risk and EU Law* (Edward Elgar, 2015)
Cremona M and Micklitz H-W (eds), *Private Law in the External Relations of the EU*, 1st edn (Oxford University Press, 2016)
Cremona M, Thies A and Wessel RA (eds), *The European Union and International Dispute Settlement* (Hart Publishing, 2017)
Cremona M and Dimopoulos A, 'The Impact of Brexit on the Careers of EUI Law Graduates' (2019) 53 *The Law Teacher* 189
Cremona M and Scott J (eds), *EU Law beyond EU Borders: The Extraterritorial Reach of EU Law* (Oxford University Press, 2019)
Cremona M, 'The Withdrawal Agreement and the EU's International Agreements' (2020) 45 *European Law Review* 237
Cremona M and Leino-Sandberg P, 'International Agreements of The EU in The Field of EMU' in F Amtenbrink, C Herrmann and R Repasi (eds), *The EU Law of Economic and Monetary Union* (Oxford University Press, 2020)

CONCEPTUAL AND FOUNDATIONAL ISSUES OF EU EXTERNAL RELATIONS LAW

Structural Principles and the Operation of EU External Relations

Cremona M, 'The Doctrine of Exclusivity and the Position of Mixed Agreements in the External Relations of the European Community' (1982) 2 *Oxford Journal of Legal Studies* 393

——, 'The Common Foreign and Security Policy of the European Union and the External Relations Powers of the European Community' in D O'Keeffe and PM Twomey (eds), *Legal issues of the Maastricht Treaty* (Chancery Law Pub, 1994)

——, 'External Relations and External Competence: The Emergence of an Integrated Policy' in P Craig and G de Búrca (eds), *The evolution of EU law* (Oxford University Press, 1999)

——, 'External Relations of the EU and the Member States: Competence, Mixed Agreements, International Responsibility, and Effects of International Law' (European University Institute, 2006) EUI Working Papers LAW No. 2006/22

——, 'A Constitutional Basis for Effective External Action? An Assessment of the Provisions on EU External Action in the Constitutional Treaty' (European University Institute, 2006) EUI Working Papers LAW No. 2006/30

——, 'The Union's External Action: Constitutional Perspectives' in G Amato, H Bribosia and B de Witte (eds), *Genèse et destinée de la Constitution européenne : commentaire du Traité établissant une Constitution pour l'Europe à la lumière des travaux préparatoires et perspectives d'avenir/Genesis and destiny of the European Constitution : commentary on the Treaty establishing a constitution for Europe in the light of the 'travaux préparatoires' and future prospects* (Bruylant, 2007)

——, 'Coherence through Law: What Difference Will the Treaty of Lisbon Make?' (2008) 3 *Hamburg Review of Social Sciences: Special Issue on Revisiting Coherence in EU Foreign Policy* 11

——, 'Defending the Community Interest: The Duties of Cooperation and Compliance' in M Cremona and B de Witte (eds), *EU Foreign Relations Law: Constitutional Fundamentals* (Bloomsbury Publishing, 2008)

——, 'Defining Competence in EU External Relations: Lessons from the Treaty Reform Process' in A Dashwood and M Maresceau (eds), *Law and Practice of EU External Relations: Salient Features of a Changing Landscape* (Cambridge University Press, 2008)

——, 'EC Competence, "Smart Sanctions", and the *Kadi* Case' (2009) 28 *Yearbook of European Law* 559

——, 'Extending the Reach of the AETR Principle: Comment on Commission v Greece (C-45/07)' (2009) 34 *European Law Review* 754

——, 'Member States as Trustees of the Community Interest: Participating in International Agreements on Behalf of the European Community' (2009) EUI Working Papers LAW 2009/17

——, 'Disconnection Clauses in EU Law and Practice' in C Hillion and P Koutrakos (eds), *Mixed agreements revisited: the EU and its member states in the world* (Hart Publishing, 2010)

——, 'Case C-246/07, Commission v. Sweden (PFOS), Judgment of the Court of Justice (Grand Chamber) of 20 April 2010, Nyr.' (2011) 48 *Common Market Law Review* 1639

——, 'Coherence in European Union Foreign Relations Law' in P Koutrakos (ed), *European Foreign Policy: Legal and Political Perspectives* (Edward Elgar, 2011)

——, 'External Relations and External Competence of the European Union: The Emergence of an Integrated Policy' in P Craig and G de Búrca (eds), *The evolution of EU law*, 2nd edn (Oxford University Press, 2011)

——, 'Member States as Trustees of the Union Interest: Participating in International Agreements on Behalf of the European Union' in A Arnull and others (eds), *A constitutional order of states?: Essays in EU law in honour of Alan Dashwood* (Bloomsbury Publishing, 2011)

——, 'Who Can Make Treaties? The European Union' in DB Hollis (ed), *The Oxford guide to treaties* (1. published in paperback, Oxford University Press, 2012)

——, 'The Two (or Three) Treaty Solution: The New Treaty Structure of the EU' in A Biondi, P Eeckhout and S Ripley (eds), *EU Law after Lisbon* (Oxford University Press, 2012)

——, 'EU External Relations: Unity and Conferral of Powers' in L Azoulai (ed), *The Question of Competence in the European Union* (Oxford University Press, 2014)

——, 'EU External Relations and the Law', *A Companion to European Union Law and International Law* (John Wiley & Sons, Ltd, 2016)
——, 'Implementation of the Lisbon Treaty – Improving Functioning of the EU: Foreign Affairs' (Directorate General for Internal Policies – Policy Department C: Citizen's Rights and Constitutional Affairs, 2016)
——, 'Structural Principles and Their Role in EU External Relations Law' (2016) 69 *Current Legal Problems* 35
——, 'EU External Competence – Rationales for Exclusivity' in S Garben and I Govaere (eds), *The Division of Competences between the EU and the Member States: Reflections on the Past, the Present and the Future* (Hart Publishing, 2017)
——, 'EU Treaty-Making after the Lisbon Treaty – A Test Case for Mutual Sincere Cooperation?', *The EU as a Global Actor – Bridging Legal Theory and Practice* (Brill Nijhoff, 2017)
——, 'Structural Principles and Their Role in EU External Relations Law' in M Cremona (ed), *Structural Principles in EU External Relations Law* (Hart Publishing, 2018)
—— (ed), *Structural Principles in EU External Relations Law* (Hart Publishing, 2018)
——, 'The Principle of Conferral and Express and Implied External Competences' in E Neframi and M Gatti (eds), *Constitutional issues of EU external relations law* (Nomos, 2018)
——, 'External Competences and The Principle Of Conferral' in R Schütze and T Tridimas (eds), *Oxford Principles Of European Union Law: The European Union Legal Order: Volume I* (Oxford University Press, 2018)
——, 'Internal Differentiation and External Unity' in D Kochenov and others (eds), *The Internal Market and the Future of European Integration: Essays in Honour of Laurence W. Gormley* (Cambridge University Press, 2019)
——, 'Making Treaties and Other International Agreements: The European Union' in CA Bradley (ed), *The Oxford Handbook of Comparative Foreign Relations Law* (Oxford University Press, 2019)
Bosse-Platière I and Cremona M, 'Facultative Mixity in the Light of the Principle of Subsidiarity', *EU External Relations Post-Lisbon* (Brill Nijhoff, 2020)
Cremona M, 'External Relations of the European Union: The Constitutional Framework for International Action' in P Craig and G de Búrca (eds), *The Evolution of EU Law* (Oxford University Press, 2021)
——, 'Mixed Agreements and Constitutional Gaps' in M Claes and E Vos (eds), *Making sense of European Union law* (Hart Publishing, 2022)
Chamon M and Cremona M, 'The Representation of the EU and Its Member States in Multilateral For a: The AMP Antarctique Effect' in N Levrat and others (eds), *The EU and its Member States' Joint Participation in International Agreements* (Hart Publishing, 2022)

Interactions Between EU and Other Legal Orders

Cremona M, 'The Effect in Community Law of Treaty Obligations between Member and Non-Member States of the European Community' (1983) 1983 *City of London Law Review* 65
——, 'External Relations of the EU and the Member States: Competence, Mixed Agreements, International Responsibility, and Effects of International Law' (European University Institute 2006) EUI Working Papers LAW No. 2006/22
——, 'Disconnection Clauses in EU Law and Practice' in C Hillion and P Koutrakos (eds), *Mixed agreements revisited: the EU and its member states in the world* (Hart Publishing, 2010)
——, 'Member States Agreements as Union Law', *International Law as Law of the European Union* (Brill Nijhoff, 2012)
——, 'A Triple Braid: Interactions between International Law, EU Law, and Private Law' in M Cremona and H-W Micklitz (eds), *Private Law in the External Relations of the EU* (Oxford University Press, 2016)
Cremona M and Micklitz H-W (eds), *Private Law in the External Relations of the EU*, 1st edn (Oxford University Press, 2016)
Cremona M, 'Opinions 1/13 and 2/13 and EU External Relations Law' in P Franzina (ed), *The External Dimension of EU Private International Law after Opinion 1/13* (Intersentia, 2016)
——, 'External Relations of the European Union: The Constitutional Framework for International Action' in P Craig and G de Búrca (eds), *The Evolution of EU Law* (Oxford University Press, 2021)

EU as a Legal International Actor

Cremona M, 'The European Union as an International Actor: The Issues of Flexibility and Linkage' (1998) 3 *European Foreign Affairs Review* 67

——, 'External Relations and External Competence: The Emergence of an Integrated Policy' in P Craig and G De Búrca (eds), *The evolution of EU law* (Oxford University Press, 1999)

——, 'The Question of Legal Personality' in A Ott and K Inglis (eds), *Handbook on European enlargement: a commentary on the enlargement process* (TMC Asser Press, 2002)

——, 'The Union as a Global Actor: Roles, Models and Identity' (2004) 41 *Common Market Law Review* 553 (also published as: Cremona M, 'The Union as a Global Actor: Roles, Models and Identity' in A McDonnell (ed), *A review of forty years of Community law: legal developments in the European Communities and the European Union* (Kluwer Law International, 2005))

——, 'The European Union as an International Actor: The Issues of Flexibility and Linkage' in W Rees and M Smith (eds), *International Relations of the European Union* (Sage, 2008)

——, 'External Relations and External Competence of the European Union: The Emergence of an Integrated Policy' in P Craig and G de Búrca (eds), *The evolution of EU law*, 2nd edn (Oxford University Press, 2011)

——, 'Extending the Reach of EU Law: The EU as an International Legal Actor' in M Cremona and J Scott (eds), *EU Law Beyond EU Borders: The Extraterritorial Reach of EU Law* (Oxford University Press, 2019)

——, 'External Relations of the European Union: The Constitutional Framework for International Action' in P Craig and G de Búrca (eds), *The Evolution of EU Law* (Oxford University Press, 2021)

Values, Principles and Objectives of EU External Action

Cremona M, 'The Union as a Global Actor: Roles, Models and Identity' (2004) 41 *Common Market Law Review* 553 (also published as: Cremona M, 'The Union as a Global Actor: Roles, Models and Identity' in A McDonnell (ed), *A review of forty years of Community law: legal developments in the European Communities and the European Union* (Kluwer Law International, 2005))

——, 'Values in the EU Constitution: The External Dimension' (Center on Democracy, Development and the Rule of Law – Stanford Institute for International Studies 2004) CDDRL Working Papers 26

——, 'Values in EU Foreign Policy' in M Evans and P Koutrakos (eds), *Beyond the established legal orders: policy interconnections between the EU and the rest of the world* (Hart Publishing, 2011)

——, 'A Reticent Court? Policy Objectives and the Court of Justice' in M Cremona and A Thies (eds), *European Court of Justice and external relations law: constitutional challenges* (Hart Publishing, 2014)

——, 'Values in EU Foreign Policy' in E Sciso, R Baratta and C Morviducci (eds), *I valori dell'Unione Europea e l'azione esterna* (G Giappichelli Editore, 2016)

Application to Specific Policies

Cremona M, 'The Completion of the Internal Market and the Incomplete Commercial Policy of the European Community' (1990) 15 *European Law Review* 283

——, 'The Common Foreign and Security Policy of the European Union and the External Relations Powers of the European Community' in D O'Keeffe and PM Twomey (eds), *Legal issues of the Maastricht Treaty* (Chancery Law Pub, 1994)

——, 'Case C-360/93, European Parliament v. Council of the European Union, Judgment of 7 March 1996, [1996] ECR I-1195' (1997) 34 *Common Market Law Review* 389

——, 'External Economic Relations and the Amsterdam Treaty' in P Twomey, D O'Keeffe, and Lord Slynn of Hadley (eds), *Legal Issues of the Amsterdam Treaty* (Bloomsbury Publishing, 1999)

——, 'A Policy of Bits and Pieces? The Common Commercial Policy after Nice' (2001) 4 *Cambridge Yearbook of European Legal Studies* 61

——, 'EC External Commercial Policy after Amsterdam: Authority and Interpretation within Interconnected Legal Orders' in JHH Weiler (ed), *The EU, the WTO, and the NAFTA: Towards a Common Law of International Trade?* (Oxford University Press, 2001)
——, 'The External Dimension of the Single Market: Building (on) the Foundations' in C Barnard and J Scott (eds), *The law of the single European market : unpacking the premises* (Hart Publishing, 2002)
——, 'The Common Commercial Policy' in C Saunders and GD Triggs (eds), *Trade and Cooperation with the European Union in the New Millenium* (Brill Nijhoff, 2002)
——, 'The Draft Constitutional Treaty: External Relations and External Action' (2003) 40 *Common Market Law Review* 1347
Cremona M and Hillion C, 'L'Union Fait La Force? Potential and Limitations of the European Neighbourhood Policy as an Integrated EU Foreign and Security Policy' (European University Institute 2006) EUI Working Papers LAW No. 2006/39
——, 'L'Union Fait La Force? Potential and Limitations of the European Neighbourhood Policy as an Integrated EU Foreign and Security Policy' in N Copsey and A Mayhew (eds), *European Neighbourhood Policy: the Case of Ukraine* (Sussex European Institute, 2007)
Rijpma JJ and Cremona M, 'The Extra-Territorialisation of EU Migration Policies and the Rule of Law' (European University Institute 2007) EUI Working Papers LAW 2007/01
Cremona M, 'EU External Action in the JHA Domain: A Legal Perspective' (European University Institute, 2008) EUI Working Papers LAW 2008/24
——, 'Case C403/05, European Parliament v. Commission (Philippines Border Management Project), Judgment of the Grand Chamber of 23 October 2007, [2007] ECR I–9045' (2008) 45 *Common Market Law Review* 1727
——, 'Enhanced Cooperation and the Common Foreign and Security and Defence Policies of the EU' (2009) EUI Working Papers LAW 2009/21
——, 'Enhanced Cooperation and the European Foreign and Security and Defence Policy', *Unity and Flexibility in the future of the European Union: the challenge of enhanced cooperation* (CEU Ediciones, 2009)
——, 'Extending the Reach of the AETR Principle: Comment on Commission v Greece (C-45/07)' (2009) 34 *European Law Review* 754
——, 'EC Competence, "Smart Sanctions", and the *Kadi* Case' (2009) 28 *Yearbook of European Law* 559
——, 'Balancing Union and Member State Interests: Opinion 1/2008, Choice of Legal Base and the Common Commercial Policy under the Treaty of Lisbon' (2010) 35 *European Law Review* 678
——, 'EU External Action in the JHA Domain: A Legal Perspective' in M Cremona, J Monar and S Poli (eds), *The external dimension of the European Union's area of freedom, security and justice* (Peter Lang, 2011)
Cremona M, Monar J and Poli S (eds), *The External Dimension of the European Union's Area of Freedom, Security and Justice* (Peter Lang, 2011)
——, 'The EU and Global Emergencies: Competence and Instruments' in A Antoniadis, R Schütze and E Spaventa (eds), *The European Union and global emergencies: a law and policy analysis* (Hart Publishing, 2011)
——, 'Coherence and EU External Environmental Policy' in Elisa Morgera (ed), *The External Environmental Policy of the European Union: EU and International Law Perspectives* (Cambridge University Press, 2012)
——, 'Expanding the Internal Market: An External Regulatory Policy for the EU?' in B Van Vooren, S Blockmans and J Wouters (eds), *The EU's Role in Global Governance* (Oxford University Press, 2013)
Kulovesi K and Cremona M, 'The Evolution of EU Competences in the Field of External Relations and Its Impact on Environmental Governance Policies' (2013) Transworld Working Papers No. 17
Cremona M and Kulovesi K, 'The Evolution of EU Competences in the Field of External Relations and Its Impact on Environmental Governance Policies' in C Bakker and F Francioni (eds), *The EU, the US and global climate governance* (Ashgate, 2014)
Cremona M, 'A Quiet Revolution: The Common Commercial Policy Six Years after the Treaty of Lisbon' (Swedish Institute for European Policy Studies, 2017) Working Paper 2017/02
——, 'Distinguished Essay: A Quiet Revolution – The Changing Nature of the EU's Common Commercial Policy' in M Bungenberg and others (eds), *European Yearbook of International Economic Law 2017* (Springer International Publishing, 2017)

——, 'The Internal Market and External Economic Relations' in P Koutrakos and J Snell (eds), *Research handbook on the law of the EU's internal market* (Edward Elgar, 2017)

Cremona M and Leino P, 'Introduction: The New Frontiers of EU Administrative Law and the Scope of Our Inquiry' (2017) 2017 2 *European Papers – A Journal on Law and Integration* 467

Cremona M, '"Effective Judicial Review Is of the Essence of the Rule of Law": Challenging Common Foreign and Security Policy Measures Before the Court of Justice' (2017) 2017 2 *European Papers – A Journal on Law and Integration* 671

Cremona M and Leino P, 'Is There an Accountability Gap in EU External Relations? Some Initial Conclusions' (2017) 2017 2 *European Papers – A Journal on Law and Integration* 699

Cremona M, 'Shaping EU Trade Policy Post-Lisbon: Opinion 2/15 of 16 May 2017: ECJ, 16 May 2017, Opinion 2/15 Free Trade Agreement with Singapore' (2018) 14 *European Constitutional Law Review* 231

——, 'The Position of CFSP/CSDP in the EU's Constitutional Architecture', *Research Handbook on the EU's Common Foreign and Security Policy* (Edward Elgar, 2018)

——, 'Internal Differentiation and External Unity' in D Kochenov and others (eds), *The Internal Market and the Future of European Integration: Essays in Honour of Laurence W. Gormley* (Cambridge University Press, 2019)

——, 'Defining the Scope of the Common Commercial Policy' in M Hahn and G Van der Loo (eds), *Law and Practice of the Common Commercial Policy: The First 10 years after the Treaty of Lisbon* (Brill Nijhoff, 2020)

——, 'External Unity, Institutional Complexity and Structural Fragmentation: The Evolution of EU External Competence in the AFSJ' in M Telò and A Weyembergh (eds), *Supranational Governance at Stake* (Routledge, 2020)

Cremona M and Leino-Sandberg P, 'External Relations of the EU and Euro Area in the Field of EMU' in F Amtenbrink, C Herrmann and RRepasi (eds), *The EU Law of Economic and Monetary Union* (Oxford University Press, 2020)

——, 'International Agreements of The EU in The Field of EMU' in F Amtenbrink, C Herrmann and R Repasi (eds), *The EU Law of Economic and Monetary Union* (Oxford University Press, 2020)

Cremona M, 'Managing EU Cooperation Agreements, Council Discretion and Legal Basis: European Commission v Council of the European Union (C-180/20)' (2022) 47 *European Law Review* 273

Cremona M and Kukavica J, 'Common Commercial Policy and the Determination of Exclusivity: Opinion 1/75 (Local Cost Standard)' in G Butler and RA Wessel (eds), *EU External Relations Law: The Cases in Context* (Hart Publishing, 2022)

Cremona M and Nic Shuibhne N, 'Integration, Membership, and the EU Neighbourhood' (2022) 59 *Common Market Law Review* 155

Miscellaneous

Boss S and others, 'Comment: Sixteen Lay People on the Laity' (1986) 67 *New Blackfriars* 150

Cremona M, *Criminal Law* (Palgrave Macmillan UK, 1989)

Cremona M and Hodgkin A, 'Electronic Publishing in Law: A Text-Base Approach' (1989) 9 *Oxford Journal of Legal Studies* 323

Herring J and Cremona M, *Criminal Law* (Macmillan Education UK, 1998)

Fletcher IF, Mistelis LA and Cremona M (eds), *Foundations and Perspectives of International Trade Law* (Sweet & Maxwell, 2001)

Cremona M and others (eds), *Reflections on the Constitutionalisation of International Economic Law : Liber Amicorum for Ernst-Ulrich Petersmann* (Martinus Nijhoff Publishers, 2014)

Cremona M and others, *ASEAN's External Agreements: Law, Practice and the Quest for Collective Action* (Cambridge University Press, 2015)

Cremona M, 'Negotiating Trade Deals Before Brexit?' (Social Europe, 25 July 2016) www.socialeurope.eu/negotiating-trade-deals-brexit

——, 'UK Trade Policy' in M Dougan (ed), *The UK after Brexit: Legal and Policy Challenges* (Intersentia, 2017)

Cremona M and Dimopoulos A, 'The Impact of Brexit on the Careers of EUI Law Graduates' (2019) 53 *The Law Teacher* 189

Monti G and others, 'Editorial: A Special Issue in Honour of Alison McDonnell: Basso Continuo of the Common Market Law Review' (2022) 59 *Common Market Law Review* 5

GENERAL EU LAW

Cremona M, 'A European Passport for Investment Services' [1994] *Journal of Business Law* 195

——, 'Citizens of Third Countries: Movement and Employment of Migrant Workers within the European Union' (1995) 22 *Legal Issues of Economic Integration* 87

——, 'EC Financial Services Law' in Caiger and Demetriou (eds), *Towards 1996: Overcoming the barriers* (Wiley, 1997)

——, 'The Distance Selling Directive' [1998] *Journal of Business Law* 613

——, 'EC Law – Commentary and Materials' in R Miles Goode (ed), *Consumer credit law and practice* (Butterworths, 1999)

—— (ed), *Market Integration and Public Services in the European Union* (Oxford University Press, 2011)

—— (ed), *Compliance and the Enforcement of EU Law* (Oxford University Press 2012)

Azoulai L and others, 'Another Legal Monster? An EUI Debate on the Fiscal Compact Treaty' (2012) EUI Working Papers LAW 2012/09

Cremona M, 'The Judgment – Framing the Argument' in A Tizzano, J Kokott and S Prechal (eds), *50th anniversaire de l'arrêt Van Gend en Loos, 1963–2013: Actes du colloque, Luxembourg, 13 Mai 2013 = 50th anniversary of the judgment in Van Gend en Loos, 1963–2013: Conference proceedings, Luxembourg, 13 May 2013* (Publications Office of the European Union, 2013)

—— (ed), *New Technologies and EU Law* (Oxford University Press, 2017)

Cremona M and Kilpatrick C (eds), *EU Legal Acts Challenges and Transformations* (Oxford University Press, 2018)

Cremona M, Kilpatrick C and Scott J (eds), 'Using the Historical Archives of the EU to Study Cases of the CJEU – First Part' (2021) 6 *European Papers – A Journal on Law and Integration* 527

——, 'The Court of Justice in the Archives: Introduction' (2021) 6 *European Papers – A Journal on Law and Integration* 527

—— (eds), 'Using the Historical Archives of the EU to Study Cases of CJEU – Second Part' (2021) 6 *European Papers – A Journal on Law and Integration* 869

Monti G and others, 'Editorial: A Special Issue in Honour of Alison McDonnell: Basso Continuo of the Common Market Law Review' (2022) 59 *Common Market Law Review* 5

Index

Introductory Note

References such as '178–79' indicate (not necessarily continuous) discussion of a topic across a range of pages. Wherever possible in the case of topics with many references, these have either been divided into sub-topics or only the most significant discussions of the topic are listed. Because the entire work is about 'EU external relations' and the 'power of law', the use of these terms (and certain others which occur constantly throughout the book) as an entry point has been restricted. Information will be found under the corresponding detailed topics. Cross-references in a form such as 'institutions, *see also individual institutions*' direct the reader to headings in a particular class (e.g. in this case 'Court of Justice') rather than a specific '*individual institutions*' entry.

www.ingramcontent.com/pod-product-compliance
Ingram Content Group UK Ltd.
Pitfield, Milton Keynes, MK11 3LW, UK
UKHW020239290926
15470UKWH00002B/621

9 781509 940950